BEATBOXING

BEAT
BOXING
HOW HIP-HOP CHANGED THE FIGHT GAME
TODD D. SNYDER

HAMILCAR
PUBLICATIONS
BOSTON

ISBN: 978-1-949590-39-5

Publisher's Cataloging-in-Publication Data
Names: Snyder, Todd D, 1981–, author.
Title: Beatboxing : how hip-hop changed the fight game / Todd D. Snyder.
Description: Boston, MA: Hamilcar Publications, 2021
Identifiers: LCCN: 2021942274 | ISBN: 9781949590395
Subjects: LCSH Rap (Music)—History and criticism. | Boxing. | Music and sports. | Popular music—Social aspects. | Popular music—History and criticism. | Sports in popular culture. | BISAC MUSIC / Genres & Styles / Rap & Hip Hop | SPORTS & RECREATION / Boxing | BIOGRAPHY & AUTOBIOGRAPHY / Cultural, Ethnic & Regional / African American & Black
Classification: LCC ML3531 .S69 2021 | DDC 782.42164—dc23

Hamilcar Publications
An imprint of Hannibal Boxing Media
Ten Post Office Square, 8th Floor South
Boston, MA 02109
www.hamilcarpubs.com

On the cover: Iron Mike and Tupac

To Stephanie Nicole and Huntington Jay,
my heartbeat.

CONTENTS

PRELUDE

TALE OF THE (CASSETTE) TAPE

A-SIDE

I found it on the dusty screen of a hand-me-down down television set, flickering images casting late-night shadows on the paneling of my bedroom walls. It found me in the passenger seat of my Aunt Michele's two-door Ford Escort, windows down, curvy mountain roads leading nowhere. *The Message. Planet Rock. Tougher Than Leather. The Great Adventures of Slick Rick. Paid in Full.*[1] Yellow number-two pencils carefully rewinding 120-minute Maxwell cassette tapes, scenes from my trailer-park childhood.

I found it in wrinkled pages of *The Source* hidden underneath hardback textbooks, foam-covered ear buds, Dollar Store brand, transmitting the Eden story of a displaced people, a culture born of breakbeat poets. *Cross Bronx Expressway. Overcrowded project buildings. Block parties. Graf writers. B-boys. B-girls. DJs. Crate diggers. Masters of ceremony.* The spirit traveled from the Boogie Down Bronx, 1520 Sedgwick Avenue, made its way from one borough to the next, migrated west to California, showed itself in Miami, Houston, New Orleans, and Atlanta, all while snaking its way down those twisting and turning back roads of the *Dirty South.*[2]

I found it on two-hour pilgrimages to Crossroads Mall, captured it on handheld cassette recorders, carefully positioned inches away from television speakers during episodes of *Yo! MTV Raps*. It found me tucked away in the Appalachian Mountains—Cowen, West Virginia, to be exact. Ours is the story of coal camps, company scrip, and absentee owners. We are the descendants of blood feuds and bearded hillbillies, they say. *Backwoods yokels. Rugged mountaineers. Moonshine distilleries. Outhouses. Welfare queens. Opioid epidemics. Eden stories of a different variety, stereotypical notions of life in the mountains that shape and exaggerate our isolation.*[3] And yet the spirit of hip-hop culture found us just the same.

It was baggy Levi's jeans, crooked baseball caps, and oversized flannel shirts. It was that hip, spicy lingo, colorful urban vernacular, mixed with a slow southern drawl. It was an identity performance that, more often than not, received poor reviews. It was poor old Ray Brown, peering out of the school bus window, elbows spilling over the metal railing, hollering, "Hey Todd, where'd ya get those *nigger* clothes?" It was a series of parent-teacher conferences, well-meaning concerns mixed with a few racist comments. It was long and often-painful conversations at the supper table, both supportive and cautionary. It was a topic of debate among a rowdy group of snuff-dipping vo-tech boys lurking the hallways of Webster County High School. It wasn't easy.

It was a foreign language, coded, rich with metaphor and double entendre. It was Malcolm X peering out the window with an assault rifle. It was John Carlos and Tommie Smith and their defiant Black fists. It was the greatest of all time, Muhammad Ali. It was his sidekick and poet laureate Drew Bundini Brown. *Float like a butterfly, sting like a bee. Your hands can't hit what your eyes can't see.* It was the Nation of Islam. It was the Honorable Elijah Muhammad. It was Afros. It was braids. It was *style. Flavor.* It was a different way of seeing and understanding the world, conversations that *wasn't nobody* having in my neck of the woods. It was a window, an education.

We are children of coal miners and loggers, blue-collar workers. We were born and raised in the sticks, way up the holler. We are the generation of Appalachian kids raised on bluegrass fiddles and breakbeats, Yonder Mountain String Band and Tupac Shakur. We are contradictions, walking juxtapositions. Appalachian rap didn't exist back when we were *youngins'*. There were no country rappers, no hip-hop producers sampling bluegrass fiddles and washboard rhythms. Hip-hop didn't belong to us and we were only spectators and yet we loved it just the same. We are the first wave of Appalachian kids who fell head over heels. *It's just a fad. It'll die out. It's just a phase.* Anyone who knew kids like us, anyone who was paying any measure of attention, should have seen it coming. The spirit of hip-hop culture turned us into scavengers of language, fashion, sports, art, and politics; led us to those black-and-white composition notebooks, 25 cents apiece down at the Foodland; and we wrote our way out of the hollers.

B-SIDE

The crudely welded apparatus, constructed by a few of my father's cronies down at the coal mine, shook with each thudding blow, briefly lifting itself off the dirt, giving birth to small clouds of dust. After my father transported the gangly structure home from the mines, he spray-painted it yellow and hung a sand-filled heavy bag wrapped in duct tape. His evening workouts were legendary, at least to the kids in Willoughby Trailer Park. The rattling chains gave way to a violent and beautiful soundtrack. Most days, it was Dustin Sears, Mitchell Williams, Big Dave, and a few of his scraggly cousins. We'd scuttle around to watch as if my father were giving lessons on manhood.

"I got a call. They want me to spar Tyson. I'm seriously thinking about doing it," he'd tell the shirtless, dirty-faced boys.

They believed it.

Or at least no one had the courage to challenge the ruse.

I knew better but found magic in the fantasy just the same. At ten years old, on warm West Virginia summer evenings, sunlight reflecting from the tin underpinning of our trailer, my father digging southpaw left hooks into Mike Tyson's imaginary ribs, I fell in love with the *idea* of boxing.

In those days, my father looked the part of a pug-nosed club fighter. If he'd told you he was Mike Tyson's chief sparring partner, you might have believed it too. For much of my childhood, he maintained a stocky, powerfully built physique, big shoulders, and thick, veiny biceps. The cyst on his larynx, never surgically repaired, gave way to the raspy voice one might expect from a slugger or mauler. My father wasn't a prizefighter, however. He'd competed in only a handful of amateur bouts. Mike "Lo" Snyder was fifth-generation West Virginia coal miner, born in a middle-of-nowhere mountain town that was originally founded as a coal camp. He was a young father, energetic and imaginative, not too far removed from his brief stint as local tough man. My budding concept of masculinity was undoubtedly shaped by the homespun hyperbole of his fight stories, some of which were occasionally verified by the local Webster County sages.

"Your daddy fought low to the ground, in a ducking, peekaboo style just like Smokin' Joe Frazier. We used to call him Smokin' Lo," they'd say.

Despite the stylistic comparisons to Smokin' Joe, it was Muhammad Ali who had served as my father's boyhood hero. Ali was the singular figure who'd cast the spell, turning him into a lifelong fan of the sweet science. My father took great pride in Muhammad Ali being a Kentucky boy, a fellow Appalachian. He also loved that Tunney Hunsaker, a police chief from Fayetteville, West Virginia, served as Ali's first professional opponent, lasting the six-round distance. This Appalachian proximity fueled my father's belief in the magic of the sport, one specifically suited for folks like us, those from the lower rungs of society. The Muhammad Ali of my father's fantastic imagination was evidence of a pathway out of the mountains.

Growing up in Cowen, it wasn't easy for my father to be a fan of Muhammad Ali.[4] The Cowen of my father's youth was an all-white community that prided itself on a working-class brand of humility. "Getting too big for your britches" was a cardinal sin. Thus, to many Cowen residents, Ali's boasting was unforgivable. And there was Ali's stance on the Vietnam War. My father's uncle, Denny, fought and was wounded in Vietnam. For many folks in town, Ali's refusal to accept induction into the United States military was the main reason to cheer against the so-called "Louisville Lip." Ali's religion didn't do him any favors in Cowen, West Virginia, either. In a community with deep Christian roots, overwhelmingly Protestant, cheering for a Black Muslim was hardly a popular move. Yet my father persisted. Ali's bravery and bravado spoke to him in a deeply spiritual way. For my father, Ali was the champion of the underdogs, the little guys—those who had been victimized by the establishment. His admiration for The Greatest got him into more than a few playground scuffles.

Had my white, working-class, coal mining father not been so passionately enamored with Muhammad Ali, I probably would not have been allowed to listen to hip-hop music, the cultural medium that still, to this day, functions as my artistic muse. Most of my friends had parents who strictly forbade rap music in their homes. I know this because my friends would often sneak hip-hop cassettes into their bedrooms as if they were contraband. My father, on the other hand, wasn't at all critical of rap music. He felt a measure of familiarity with Ali's stance on social justice issues in the Black community, didn't mind the cursing, and liked the swagger Ali and Bundini brought to the fight game. Ali was hip-hop before there ever was such a thing, my father would often say.

Of my two lifelong passions, it was boxing, at first, that held a more tangible presence in my life. Thanks to a hacked cable box, my father and I didn't miss a single televised fight. Regardless of the quality of matchup, I recorded the fights on our Magnavox VCR. As I grew older, I lined multiple bookshelves with those tapes, a fight collection that might even have impressed Jim Jacobs. To this day, I can close my eyes and see the light blue packaging of the four-packs my mother bought down at the Dollar Store. There wasn't a birthday or Christmas that I didn't receive a new crop of Maxwell Standard Grade T-120 videocassette tapes.

As hip-hop culture became an increasingly visible presence in boxing, the blinking red light of our Magnavox VCR captured the transitional era detailed in this book, one in which the sport gradually slipped away from my father's generation.

"Dad, that's Tupac and Suge celebrating with Tyson . . ."
"That's Big Pun and Fat Joe rapping Tito Trinidad to the ring."
"J Prince isn't just a boxing manager, he's a hip-hop mogul, Dad."

While hip-hop culture clearly shaped my ambitions as a writer, boxing, in a more physical sense, took me out of the mountains. There were always local roughnecks coming around the trailer park, asking my father to show them how to fight. By the late 1990s, he was a known commodity in the West Virginia Tough Man circuit, working as a cornerman, referee, and even a judge. When I entered high school, my father opened a series of makeshift gyms and began mentoring area youth. I boxed as an amateur for a few years before shipping off to college. (I'm a far better writer than pugilist, I will humbly admit.) After enrolling in college, I continued training boxers with my father during winter and summer breaks. When I traveled with my father's club, as both a boxer and trainer, I made friends from a variety of races, religions, and ethnic backgrounds. During those pivotal years in my life, hip-hop music served as a conversational bridge, a shared language. Back at "Lo's Gym Boxing Club," my father's gym, hip-hop music served as the soundtrack to our nightly training sessions. Boxing was my father's first love; hip-hop was mine. In the gym, amid the ricochet of speed bags and the sound of gloves pounding heavy bags and jump ropes skimming a hard wood floor, the two passions that transformed our lives combined into one.

Today, hip-hop, more so than boxing, is how I help put food on the table for my family. I am a professor of rhetoric and writing at Siena College in Albany, New York, where I regularly teach courses on hip-hop culture. As part of my college's cross-cultural solidarity initiative, I have worked with hip-hop icons such as Grandmaster Flash, Chuck D, Sha Rock, and Biz Markie, just to name a few. Students in my courses come to see hip-hop as a full-blown culture, one with its own set of early pioneers and practitioners. On the first day of class each semester, I begin with a discussion of the social, political, and artistic movements that serve as the foundational backdrop to the rise of hip-hop. For members of the millennial generation, who have never known a world without rap music, exploring this history can be enlightening. "Where does hip-hop come from?" my incoming students often ask. My goal is to tell that story.

On a diasporic flowchart, one could certainly trace hip-hop's origins from Africa to the Caribbean and on to the United States. Aside from its larger global influences, hip-hop, as a musical genre, has its roots in gospel, blues, ragtime, jazz, rock 'n' roll, funk, reggae, R&B, and disco. More important to our classroom discussion, however, is paying close attention to the sociopolitical influences that affected hip-hop's ideological and stylistic formation. One cannot outline this history without first discussing the Harlem Renaissance, urban folk poetry of the late 1960s, or the key orators of the American Civil Rights Movement. Hip-hop, I tell my students, was not born in a vacuum. It's a cultural movement whose origin story is directly tied to boxing history.

Each semester, I end my initial classroom lecture with a clip from ESPN's 2006 documentary *Ali Rap*. Hosted by hip-hop icon Chuck D (of Public Enemy), the film aims to position three-time heavyweight champion Muhammad Ali as the first *rapper*. Throughout the documentary, hip-hop artists such as Jermaine Dupri, MC Lyte, Ludacris, Doug E. Fresh, and Rakim recite some of Ali's most famous poetic lines, discussing and demonstrating how the Ali formula served as a template for early emcees. Hip-hop is something you live, rap is something you do, the great KRS-One famously states. And you can't talk *rap* without first talking Ali. There isn't a reputable hip-hop history book that doesn't, in some form or fashion, pay homage to Ali's influence.

Looking back, boxing and hip-hop have long served as the compass points of my identity, the A side and B side of my personality. Because of my unique background, I see the connective forces at play. The first cassette tape that I ever purchased with my *own money* was DJ Jazzy Jeff & the Fresh Prince's [Will Smith] *And in This Corner* (1987), an album that featured the hit single "I Think I Can Beat Mike Tyson." The first book I attempted to read cover to cover was my father's tattered copy of Muhammad Ali's 1975 biography, *The Greatest: My Own Story.* It is no coincidence the Fresh Prince eventually went on to play The Greatest in a Hollywood film. What has always been intuitive for me, personally, often comes as a surprise to my students, many of whom weren't alive for the theatrical release of Michael Mann's 2001 biopic *Ali,* starring rapper-turned-actor Will Smith.

As a writer and educator, I am guided by my passions. You could say that *recording* culture is what I do best. In writing this book, which aims to tether boxing history to that of hip-hop, I find myself back at Willoughby Trailer Park, face-to-face with that inquisitive Appalachian boy and his bedroom full of blank cassette tapes. *BeatBoxing* is written for people like me, who have long kept a foot in both worlds. It is a collection of histories centered on the concept of community, collectives of people from shared social spaces, as well as those who think of themselves as part of an extended family of shared interests, values, and attitudes. This feels like the book I was born to write, one I have been researching my entire life, a karmic debt to forces that have guided my life, both personally and professionally.

—*Todd D. Snyder*

INTRODUCTION

CHECK THE RHIME

The stories I'm telling in this book are largely focused on hip-hop culture's impact on professional boxing. I say *largely* because it would be remiss to assume the influence is not reciprocal. No genre of music comes close to covering the sport of boxing like hip-hop. For over forty years, rappers have regularly integrated the names of legendary fighters into their lyrics, along with allusions to some of boxing's most iconic bouts. It has been this way since the beginning. "Rapper's Delight" (1979) by Sugarhill Gang, often credited as *the* song that introduced hip-hop to the masses, contains a reference to Muhammad Ali. "The Message" (1982) by Grandmaster Flash and the Furious Five, the first rap song to overtly employ social commentary, features a reference to Sugar Ray Leonard. If you were to compile a list of hip-hop's most important and influential albums, most, if not all, of the top selections would contain at least one boxing reference (see Appendix). As a hip-hop scholar and the son of a boxing trainer, these cross-cultural occurrences always resonate with me.

Despite the sport's diminished popularity in the United States, professional boxing remains a prevalent topic in rap music. Aside from references to classic fights, several rap songs are titled with the names of world champion boxers. "Floyd 'Money' Mayweather" by Dizzy Wright (2015), "Cassius (Excellence)" by Wale (2018), and "Roy Jones" by D Von (2018) serve as contemporary examples. Rap artists Roc Marciano (formerly of the Flipmode Squad) and Vinnie Paz (formerly of Jedi Mind Tricks), of course, borrow their rap monikers from pugilists. You could easily argue that understanding the language of hip-hop requires a certain amount of boxing literacy. Boxing references make up a sizeable portion of hip-hop's lyrical pie chart.

The degree to which rap artists draw inspiration from boxing has been largely overlooked in hip-hop scholarship. Rap's most prolific journalists often miss the boxing gems. The reverse can be argued for boxing's literary crowd. *BeatBoxing* attempts to readjust the research scope in both arenas, panning outward to reveal a more complete picture of this symbiotic relationship. That said, aficionados in either arena are likely to approach this book with some understanding that such a connection exists. My magic trick, so to speak, will be to reveal the depth of this relationship. Boxing shaped hip-hop's attitude long before there ever was such a thing as rap music. Hip-hop, in return, has altered the sport of boxing in a variety of ways, both in and out of the ring. This book serves as a testament to those transformations.

To demonstrate the depths of hip-hop's boxing fixation, for those less familiar with the culture, I compiled a list of approximately five hundred rap songs that contain direct references to boxing personalities (e.g., champions, trainers, managers, promoters, and ring announcers). In compiling this list, I didn't include songs written by world champions who moonlight as rappers.[5] Roy Jones Jr. and Adrien Broner, for example, have put out a bunch of original rap records.[6] I also didn't include songs that reference characters from Sylvester Stallone's *Rocky* movie franchise (e.g., Rocky Balboa, Apollo Creed, and Ivan Drago). If I had, the list might have doubled. To preserve the integrity of my research sample, I avoided all songs composed for boxing-themed Hollywood movies. The soundtracks for both films in the *Rocky* spin-off franchise, *Creed*, are, for example, mostly composed of hip-hop songs. The soundtrack to Jake Gyllenhaal's gritty boxing flick *Southpaw* was executive produced by Eminem.

In the same vein, boxing documentaries frequently tap rap artists for their musical backdrops. The lead single for the soundtrack to Leon Gast's iconic documentary *When We Were Kings* was supplied by The

Fugees, a song titled "Rumble in the Jungle." For James Toback's 2005 Mike Tyson documentary *Tyson*, Queensbridge rap giant Nas composed "Legendary (Iron Mike)." Chuck D, of Public Enemy, has on separate occasions recorded original rap songs for ESPN boxing documentaries (e.g., *Ali Rap* and *Hit Em Mike Get Em*). To maintain the integrity of my data, I steered clear of scenarios where rappers were paid to write rhymes about the sweet science.

The five hundred titles listed in Appendix A are meant to show how much boxing appears in hip-hop lyrics. To avoid skewing my data, R.A. the Rugged Man's underground classic, "Boxing Freestyle," which contains references to forty-seven individual boxers, was left off my list. I also chose to exclude songs that contain guest vocals from professional boxers, such as Canibus's "Second Round K.O.," featuring Mike Tyson, Lil' Jon's "Put Yo Hood Up (Remix)," featuring Roy Jones Jr., and Ludacris's "Undisputed," where Floyd Mayweather Jr. shows up as a lyrical chief second. The fact that these options exist does, to a certain extent, prove my underlying point. My goal wasn't to put together a comprehensive list of boxing-themed rap songs but, rather, to show a consistent pattern, one that illuminates the myriad ways that boxing seeps into hip-hop's narrative tradition.

Of the five hundred rap songs analyzed in Appendix A, sixty-nine different boxers or boxing personalities are referenced by name. As one might suspect, Muhammad Ali and Mike Tyson led the way. Ali is referenced in eighty-five of the five hundred songs. Tyson's name shows up in seventy-three songs. At a distant third, promoter Don King is referenced in thirty-seven individual songs, edging out Floyd Mayweather Jr., who appears on my list thirty-four times. Rounding out the top-ten most referenced names are (fifth) Evander Holyfield, with eighteen references; (sixth and seventh) George Foreman and Zab Judah, who both come in with fifteen references; (eighth) Riddick Bowe, with fourteen references; (ninth) Manny Pacquiao, with twelve references; and (tenth) "Sugar" Shane Mosley and Joe Frazier, who are each referenced in eleven tracks. To understand these lyrical punch lines, listeners need to be at least somewhat familiar with the sport. Because the songs included in my list span over forty years of hip-hop history, from 1979 to 2021, it's difficult to argue that such a pattern is coincidental. Hip-hop artists, operating in a cultural medium full of metaphor, simile, personification, and double entendre, are keenly aware of how audiences are likely to react to these names.

To all of this, you might ask: why is the hip-hop community so literate when it comes to boxing? Several competing factors are, of course, at play. I start with race and gender because these factors are perhaps the most obvious sociocultural influences.

To begin, when I use the term *hip-hop*, I am not just referring to a musical genre, a cultural commodity sold to consumers by the record industry. Hip-hop is rather a full-blown cultural movement. The core elements of hip-hop (graffiti, break dancing, deejaying, and emceeing/rapping) were born amid the hard socioeconomic conditions of the South Bronx during the 1970s. These elements were created, and later elevated, by primarily Black and Latino practitioners, most of whom were men. Professional boxing, during this same time period, particularly in the United States, was, as you might suspect, made up of a similar demographic (urban males from minority groups). It should be pointed out, however, that rap music is only one element of hip-hop culture—no more important, or representative, than the shifting vernacular or fashion trends found in the communities that birthed the culture. That said, you can't deny that hip-hop began as a Black, male-dominated art form. Rap music's hypermasculine rhetoric has long been documented.

Bill Adler, the former head of publicity for Def Jam Records: "It is not unusual for young men to idolize great athletes and, maybe, the physical prowess of boxers in particular. This tendency might be at least slightly more pronounced in the Black community because of the enduring effects of racism. Sports, including boxing, are one of the few arenas in which Black men are allowed and encouraged to shine. Jack Johnson, during his time period, is an example. Muhammad Ali's individual talents aside, one of the reasons he was such a monumental figure in hip-hop is because his career spanned the Civil Rights era and his personal journey embodied the evolution of the struggle from MLK to Malcolm X and Black Power."

While most of the boxers referenced on my list are indeed Black men, it would be wrong to suggest such a narrow focus. A long list of formidable female emcees can be found in Appendix A (e.g., Salt-N-Pepa, Lil' Kim, Foxy Brown, Missy Elliott, Da Brat, Lauryn Hill, Nicki Minaj), proving that the ladies know boxing too. A number of white emcees are also represented (e.g., House of Pain, Beastie Boys, Vanilla Ice, Eminem, Paul

Wall, Mac Miller, Asher Roth, Hoodie Allen, Machine Gun Kelly). The connection between hip-hop and boxing, therefore, goes deeper than gender and race. Latino fighters such as Julio César Chávez, Hector "Macho" Camacho, Oscar De La Hoya, Félix Trinidad, and Miguel Cotto are frequently referenced in hip-hop. The names of white fighters, such as Willie Pep, Rocky Marciano, Ray "Boom Boom" Mancini, Gerry Cooney, Arturo Gatti, Micky Ward, and even the Klitschko brothers, Vitali and Wladimir, show up in rap lyrics as well. Jack Dempsey's name, for example, appears in ten rap songs listed in Appendix A, each written by Black artists.

It would also be wrong to assume that rappers reference only contemporary prizefighters. Jack Johnson, Jake LaMotta, and Sugar Ray Robinson, who, of course, predate hip-hop, each show up on my list, cited in multiple songs. References to legendary trainers Cus D'Amato, Angelo Dundee, Lou Duva, and Freddie Roach; along with lyrical nods to promoter Don King and Al Haymon; referees Richard Steele and Mills Lane; and ring announcer Michael Buffer, demonstrate the degree to which rap artists follow the sport.

You could easily argue that hip-hop preserves boxing history. Analyzing this particular component of hip-hop's tradition can teach us plenty about the backgrounds and world views of the rappers spitting these lyrics, possibly serving as a window into the underlying nature of hip-hop's complex, and often shifting, discourse patterns. Doing so also opens the door for new opportunities to see the cultural evolution of professional boxing in the twenty-first century.

✳ ✳ ✳

To better understand hip-hop's love affair with boxing, one that's stood the test of time in a rapidly changing genre, I first sought the perspectives of two of hip-hop's biggest boxing aficionados, Philadelphia's underground kingpin, Vinnie Paz, and New York's self-proclaimed lyrical derelict, R.A. the Rugged Man. Serious fans of boxing, Paz and the Rugged Man have contributed guest columns to mainstream boxing media outlets such as MaxBoxing and *The Ring*.

"When I reference a fighter like John 'The Beast' Mugabi in a song, that's an Easter egg. Most listeners won't catch that, or understand it,"

Vinnie Paz said. "Only real boxing fans are gonna know that great champion from Uganda. When I rhyme, 'I'm a beast, like John Mugabi,' I do that specifically for fans, like us, people from both worlds."

R.A. the Rugged Man: "We do that for the kind of people who can catch it. It makes them feel good. It's also to give new life to a great champion or a certain part of the fight game that had an impact on me personally. It's just something hip-hop does, reaching back. It's no different than me referencing a rapper who influenced me, maybe someone lesser-known to my mainstream fans. I like to drop the names of people I wish the world would talk about. You hear the kids singing the lyrics and those names stay implanted in their heads. For me, it's about giving new light to someone you admire."

For both rappers, a genuine love and respect for the sport of boxing was passed down from their fathers, deeply rooted cultural—and familial—connections that underscore boxing's place in hip-hop.

Vinnie Paz's boxing roots run deep. "My uncle, Willy, trained bantamweight champion Joltin' Jeff Chandler," said Paz. "I was like two years old when Jeff had the belt so I missed that. Some of my earliest memories, though, are sitting on my dad's lap, watching *ABC's Wide World of Sports*. If I recall correctly, that was the first time I saw Vinny Paz. Because Vinnie is my first name, my father started calling me that. My rap name is paying homage to Vinny Paz, the fighter, and my father, who loved his toughness and fighting style. My father died when I was ten years old, so I didn't get to have deep conversations with him. But boxing brought us together."

Vinnie Paz's story reminded me of my relationship with my own father, the countless hours we spent together in front of the television watching boxing. Yet I was curious to discover whether or not *the real* Vinny Paz was aware of his hip-hop namesake. Had the "Pazmanian Devil" approved the rap moniker, I wondered?

"Absolutely! I met Vinny Paz at the first Ward–Gatti fight in Atlantic City. We talked and I got his blessing [to use the rap name]," Vinnie continued. "Then I saw Vinny again at the Ward–Gatti rematch. We started talking and I shared my music. He did this little DVD, a mini-documentary. He was trying to use the documentary to get the film made. On the DVD, Vinny used one of my solo joints during the knockout scenes. When *Bleed for This* finally did happen, he flew me out for the premiere. I got to see it with him and Miles Teller, Rey Mysterio [of the WWE], and all these Hollywood people. It was such an honor. Everything came full circle."

Although he did not base his stage name after a famous boxer, R.A. the Rugged Man, a native of Long Island, New York, also shares a family connection to the sport of boxing. R.A.'s introduction to the sweet science, much like that of Vinnie Paz, began with his father.

"I grew up on Larry Holmes. My dad loved Holmes. He was my idol. I used to box as a little kid. I was nine when I started sparring. Because my father liked boxing, I started boxing at this gym up in Port Jeff in Long Island," R.A. said. "At ten, I developed a bleeding ulcer. It didn't have anything to do with boxing. By the time I was eleven, my mother didn't want me to box anymore because of the ulcer. She was a single mother at the time, my father was in another place, so she stopped giving me the cab fare to go to the gym. I had no way to get there. And around that same age, I became introduced to rapping. My mother not giving me the cab fare might be the reason I'm a rapper, not a boxer. Rapping was free."

Because I was familiar with both artists' catalogs, aware of each rapper's tendency to work boxing metaphors into their art, I wasn't surprised to discover both men had initially wanted to be fighters. For Vinnie Paz in particular, factors such as class, geography, and accessibility play a major role in shaping and maintaining hip-hop's connection to boxing. Rappers and boxers often walk the same cracked pavement streets, I was reminded.

"Historically, most boxers come from impoverished circumstances. The same can be said for hip-hop when it was finding its footing. The options were to sell drugs, be a stick-up kid, try to go to the NBA. Or I can box, or I can rap," Vinnie Paz said. "If you don't want to go the route of being a criminal, and you aren't six-foot-eight, boxing and rap are options."

Paz continued: "Both are for *everybody*. You can be five-foot-two and 115 pounds and do boxing or hip-hop. Boxing is a very different community than sports like football and basketball. It's an underground family. Being from Philly, you had Joe Frazier, Joey Giardiello, Matthew Saad Muhammad, Dwight Qawi, and Bernard Hopkins. These were people you would see around. Philly doesn't have five boroughs like New York. You could actually see those people. When my father died, and Willy died, I somewhat lost that connection. I'd started out wanting to fight, but, in my teenage years, that age when everybody was having fun, smoking blunts and drinking 40s, I had to make that decision, was I gonna rhyme or get punched in the face."

For R.A. the Rugged Man, hip-hop's connection to boxing, in the beginning, occurred largely because of timing. Hip-hop's golden era, the underground legend reminded me, coincided with an equally transformative time in boxing history. Had hip-hop been invented in 2021, this lyrical tradition might never have formed.

R.A. the Rugged Man: "Think of Wu-Tang. 'Smoke on the mic like Smokin' Joe Frazier.' That was the first line anyone heard from Wu-Tang. What boxer, today, does a ten-year-old boy in America want to be right now? Nobody. Back in the day, all of us kids wanted to be Sugar Ray Leonard, Joe Frazier, Muhammad Ali. So, that's why so many boxing references showed up in those early rhymes. That's also why nobody in America is really boxing these days."

Aside from Vinnie Paz and R.A. the Rugged Man, two of the sharpest boxing minds in the game, hip-hop superpower Wu-Tang Clan is the mainstream rap group that most noticeably integrates boxing into their music. As R.A. the Rugged Man correctly pointed out, when the Staten Island rap conglomerate emerged on the scene in 1993, with the classic album *Enter the Wu-Tang (36 Chambers),* the first line on the group's first song, delivered by emcee Inspectah Deck, began with a boxing simile. To tap into Wu-Tang's role in advancing hip-hop's boxing tradition, I spoke with the Wu-Tang swordsman who wrote that famous line.

Inspectah Deck: "I could reference boxing all day in my rhymes. I probably have a million of them. Boxing is my favorite sport. I was born in the 1970s, so I grew up watching Tommy 'The Hitman' Hearns, Marvelous Marvin Hagler, the 'Hands of Stone,' Roberto Duran. When I rhymed, 'Smoke on the mic, like Smokin' Joe Frazier,' on *Protect Ya Neck*, that's me saying, just like Frazier in those first couple of rounds, Wu-Tang ain't no joke. If you hear that lyric, and you know who that is, you known Wu-Tang is coming pretty tough."

Fellow Wu-Tang member, Masta Killa: "I'm a die-hard boxing fan and most of Wu-Tang is. My love [for boxing] goes all the way back. I remember I got a pair of boxing gloves for my birthday when I was a kid. I even had the Muhammad Ali boxing doll. I've always been a fan. Even now, I won't miss a Terence Crawford fight. I won't miss an Errol Spence fight. I won't miss that that young kid, the former Olympian, Shakur Stevenson."

Many of hip-hop's first two waves of superstars came of age during an era when boxers were major U.S. sports celebrities. These emcees were just old enough to catch the tail end of Muhammad Ali's career. Hip-hop's golden era, as I will discuss in Chapter 4, coincides directly with Mike Tyson's reign as the *baddest man on the planet*. Accordingly, hip-hop culture's historical timeline helps explain, to a certain degree, rap music's propensity for boxing references.

✳ ✳ ✳

In talking with Inspectah Deck and Masta Killa, I was reminded that hip-hop doesn't just preserve boxing history. Hip-hop also reimagines it. Wu-Tang's 1997 song "MGM," for example, seats listeners next to rappers Ghostface Killah and Raekwon as they attend the fictitious rematch to Pernell Whitaker and Julio César Chávez's hotly disputed 1993 draw, held at the MGM Grand in Las Vegas, as the song's title suggests. Complete with a timekeeper's bell and crowd noise, the song follows Ghost and Rae as they make their way to their expensive ringside seats.

"They wound up stopping the fight / [Richard] Steele took a point from Chávez, rematch scheduled on October 9th," the duo rhymes in the track's crescendo bar.[7]

The ringside seats occupied by Ghost and Rae in "MGM" have, over the years, become status symbols in hip-hop culture. While rappers often compare their lyrical greatness to Muhammad Ali's or their tenacity in the streets to Mike Tyson's, the lyrical device found in Wu-Tang's "MGM" serves an entirely different function. Many of the boxing references cataloged in Appendix A use this particular type of narrative technique as a status marker, placing rappers in the so-called best seats in the house. This boastful tradition is still found in contemporary hip-hop.

"My bitch looking like a young Saana Lathan / Sitting ringside watching Tank Davis, Johnny Chang bracelet," Conway rhymes on his 2020 track "Sicarios," using a range of cultural signifiers (a beautiful actress, a world champion boxer, and a high-end jeweler) to mark his status.

Conway's line reminds us that hip-hop's love affair with boxing is also tied to a particular notion of upward mobility. The romantic arc of a boxer's life—from rags to riches—is also a part of the allure. High-profile boxing venues, such as Madison Square Garden and the MGM Grand, often serve as the setting of hip-hop narratives because, as many cultural critics have argued, these places represent a unique brand of class ascension.

"A [Mike] Tyson fight is an unofficial gangsta party. It's where the ghetto elite meet: rich niggas with nothing to lose, indulging their contradictions," *Vibe* magazine journalist Rob Marriott once wrote.

In Jay-Z's autobiography, *Decoded*, the rap mogul reflects on the similarities between boxing and his days hustling in the streets of Brooklyn.

"I was making money, but winning in the streets, really winning, is nearly impossible. Maybe that's why boxing is almost a religion to hustlers and the big title fights in Vegas are like pilgrimages," Jay-Z writes.

This philosophy, of course, also shows up in Jay-Z's catalog. Perhaps more so than any of his contemporaries, the Roc-A-Fella mogul often places himself, both lyrically and literally, ringside at boxing's biggest events.

"Name keep poppin' up, face keep poppin' up / On the tube, I'm just watching Pacquiao box 'em up / How should I know, HBO would get a shot of us / Sitting so close that we almost got snot on us," Jay-Z rhymes on "Thank You."

This expression of urban upward mobility has a dual effect on listeners. Such moves do more than simply display an artist's status and wealth. These references are also designed to pay homage to regional identity. New York emcees often rhyme about New York boxers, particularly from their home boroughs. Brooklyn's Zab Judah frequently shows up in the music videos of rappers from his neighborhood—Shyne, Lil' Kim, and Jay-Z, for example. Virginia-based rapper Fam-Lay references Norfolk legend Pernell Whitaker in a guest verse on the Clipse's 2004 debut *Lord Willin'*. In the music video for "Country Grammar," St. Louis native Terron Millett poses with his toddler son and an IBF title belt, mean-mugging in the streets of Nelly's hometown. Spatial identity is, of course, a core component of hip-hop. This cultural phenomenon, I quickly learned, is one that's understood instinctively by both rappers and boxers alike.

Bernard Hopkins: "The culture of rap and boxing go hand in hand in places like New York and my hometown of Philadelphia. The struggle is the same. We escape the same traps. I came out of prison, with nine years of strict parole. Everybody was hustling crack cocaine, making fast money. And, at the time, I was very respected in every neighborhood in

Philadelphia. I could have easily got fronted a kilo of cocaine. Coming out of prison, living at my mom's house, where I got in trouble at, I had to navigate the big drug dealers, who I used to take they stuff, now they big shit. That's what it was back then. I didn't have plan B. This [boxing] had to work. It's the same thing in the rap. Hip-hop understands boxing and vice versa. Still today, Meek Mill comes out and supports Philly fighters like Danny Garcia. Just like the State Property guys supported me during my reign."

Rap star Peter Gunz: "There is something about a boxer being from your city, especially your borough. Iran Barkley is from the Bronx. I would always cheer for him, even if I didn't think he was going to win. You know the struggles of where you come from. You can't help but feel pride. I was from the Bronx and this is all we had. I would even bag on guys from Brooklyn who would wear that New York Yankees hat. I would remind them they was repping the Bronx Bombers."

Hall-of-fame boxing promoter Lou DiBella: "At my Broadway Boxing shows, you could make a pretty impressive list of the hip-hop icons who attended. From 50 Cent to Raekwon to Fat Joe to Cam'Ron, the list is endless. That wasn't because of me. It was because I concentrated on New York fights. These guys knew each other. When Fat Joe came to my fights, he was supporting this Puerto Rican kid from his neighborhood."

Aside from hometown rooting interests, many hip-hop stars are drawn to the sport because they're connected to it through their family. Grandmaster Flash, Joseph Saddler, is the nephew of featherweight champion Sandy Saddler. LL Cool J's grandfather, Nathaniel Christy Lewis, was a professional boxer. LL Cool J's uncle, John Henry Lewis, was the first Black light heavyweight champion in the United States. Geto Boys rapper Willie D is the nephew of Melvin Dennis, who fought Wilfred Benitez, Vito Antuofermo, and once knocked out Roy Jones Jr.'s father in a middleweight fight. As a teenager, Willie D himself won a Golden Gloves championship in his home state of Texas. Rapper Noreaga (N.O.R.E.) is the son of Victor Santiago, a New York Golden Gloves champion. A photograph of Noreaga's father wearing boxing gear and bag gloves is proudly displayed in the artwork of his second solo album.

Rap music's boxing fixation can also be explained in terms of the uniquely competitive spirit found in hip-hop culture. Battling, so to speak, has always been one of hip-hop's core elements.

"Aside from the direct family connections, I think competition is a big part of it," said Bill Adler. "In our Def Jam offices, the rappers would just start snapping on each other. I remember Run [of Run-DMC] and LL [Cool J] snapping on each other all of the time. Then a battle would break out. Hip-hop is hypercompetitive. Part of the connection between hip-hop and boxing is that competitive spirit."

There are, of course, several high-profile rap artists who have firsthand experience in the ring. 50 Cent's amateur boxing career, which featured appearances in the Junior Olympics and the New York State Golden Gloves, has been the subject of numerous articles and photo shoots in hip-hop publications such as *The Source*. In 1992, the aforementioned Willie D, who competed in a handful of professional bouts, knocked out rap legend Melle Mel in a celebrity boxing match. In 1998, Onyx rapper Sticky Fingaz performed poorly in his MTV celebrity match against X-Games athlete Simon Woodstock. In 2008 Roy Jones Jr. trained Snoop Dogg for a reality-television show and sparred with the rapper in one episode. The spirit of hip-hop, at its core, is, as Bill Adler pointed out, driven by competition. From neighborhood ciphers in which emcees challenge the skills of their opponents, to the famous break-dancing battles of the 1980s, to the back and forth verbal digs found in contemporary diss tracks, hip-hop culture has always been uniquely competitive.

When you consider this long list of sociocultural similarities, looking at hip-hop and boxing as two separate worlds seems misguided. Even Max Kellerman, the hip-hop generation's Bert Sugar, began as a rapper, releasing the 1994 music video titled "Rumble, Young Man Rumble."[8] You could argue that, thanks to the enduring influence of Muhammad Ali, the two cultures have always been, and perhaps will forever be, tied to each other. Before compiling the list of songs found in the index of this book, I could have easily predicted Ali as the most referenced boxer in hip-hop history. Even the Champ's daughter, Maryum "May May" Ali, released a rap album, "The Introduction," in 1992.

"[My father] didn't think rap was gonna last," Maryum Ali said in a 1992 interview with Charlie Gibson. "Now he sees rap is lasting. He heard my lyrics and saw they were positive and strong; he saw that I was dedicated. He's very supportive now. At first, he was skeptical."[9]

"When I first heard you were doing this I thought, 'Well, that's pretty natural, her dad was a rapper in a way,'" Gibson replied.

Hip-hop scholars, in particular, are keenly aware of Muhammad Ali's role in shaping the culture's artistic, political, and competitive sensibilities.

"Muhammad Ali was the ultimate battle rapper. He rapped to you and then he went to battle," Dr. Khalid el-Hakim, author, activist, and professor of African American Studies at Western Michigan University, told me.

Aside from Muhammad Ali's obvious sociopolitical impact on American culture, Dr. el-Hakim reminded me of the three-time heavyweight champion's pivotal role in shaping the Black poetic tradition. The 1963 release of *I Am the Greatest,* Muhammad Ali's spoken word album for Columbia Records, which earned the boxer a Grammy nomination and sold over 500,000 copies, created a market for acts such as The Last Poets (1968), Gil Scott-Heron (1970), and others that would follow, and paved the way for the emergence of hip-hop. From his proud Afrocentricity, to the hyperbolic boasting, to the comical trash talk, Ali's rhymes, flow, and braggadocio provided a template for early hip-hop stars such as Run-DMC and LL Cool J.

Dr. Khalid el-Hakim: "To put this into historical context, before Ali started rhymin' with Bundini, you had the Last Poets and the Last Poets inspired Gil Scott-Heron, and out on the West Coast you had the Watts Prophets, who were doing a similar thing. In Chicago you had Oscar Brown. In the Bay Area, you had Marvin X. In terms of poetry, Black expression, Muhammad Ali just took it to a new level. Ali is hip-hop."

He continued: "But the connection between Ali and hip-hop starts with Ali's activism, in my opinion, his ability to speak to the social conditions of our people, using his platform to uplift a people who were socially and economically oppressed because of the color of their skin. It was Ali's connections to that grassroots tradition. He was among the people, accessible. Hip-hop, as a culture, is on that same level. Think of the work done by Afrika Bambaataa, his connections to Islam and the Universal Zulu Nation. Hip-hop, early on, was about understanding the power of your voice and using it to change people. Ali comes from that tradition and [he] made a huge imprint on the type of Black manhood that shows up in early hip-hop. This is an identity performance that goes all the way back to Jack Johnson."

Dr. Akil Houston, a professor of African American Studies at Ohio University, had a similar perspective in a separate interview, reminding me that before Muhammad Ali it was Jack Johnson who served as a prototype for the unique brand of Black manhood adopted by the hip-hop generation.

"Even before we had this thing called hip-hop, there were these moments in Black history where you see peaks of certain performances of Black masculinity. Muhammad Ali is a pivotal template for a new kind of Black masculinity, wrapped up in the political context of the time. He thumbed his nose at the mold set by guys like Joe Louis. Hip-hop does everything you are not supposed to do," said Dr. Houston. "If you go all the way back to Jack Johnson, he is the champion creating the path Ali is walking on. Johnson wasn't a political revolutionary trying to change the social structure, Jack Johnson was a person who was just trying to be what he wanted to be, regardless of what societal expectations for Black men were. Hip-hop as always exhibited those two strands of thinking. There is a cultural link between Jack Johnson, Muhammad Ali, and even Drew Bundini Brown, and the hip-hop attitude. Sometimes I think these connections are not evident to both sides of the aisle when it comes to those who write about the boxing world and those who write about the hip-hop community."

The dynamic of Muhammad Ali's relationship with Drew Bundini Brown, in particular, surfaced often in my conversations with rap legends. Many of these artists were quick to label Bundini as the archetype for the role of hype man.

Legendary producer Eric B: "It's this simple: Ali and Bundini were our iconic guys that we [in the hip-hop generation] looked up to. Ali and Bundini were our iconic figures. Bundini was the original hype man. To me, he was the original. Those rhymes were iconic. Ali had Bundini and years later Tyson had Crocodile. The concept of a hype man comes from hip-hop but you see it in boxing first."

Peter Gunz: "If you aren't an artist or a boxer, you wouldn't understand the importance of a guy like Bundini. He wasn't even a trainer. He wasn't doing technical work. His job was to remind Ali of who he is. He was like Flavor Flav, he was the hype man. The greatest hype men, guys like Flavor Flav, Fatman Scoop, Rampage, they were stars too. Jim Jones was Cam'Ron's hype man but he went on to become a star in his own right. Some headliners didn't even want to go out on stage before the hype man set the tempo. A hype man isn't a yes man or a non-talent. Without Flavor Flav, what would Public Enemy's stage show be? Ali needed that too."

Rap legend Big Daddy Kane, more than any rapper I interviewed, identified Muhammad Ali as his hip-hop muse.

"I started out as a battle emcee. And I got all my techniques from Muhammad Ali. I didn't get that persona from a rapper. I learned that from Ali. He taught me how to get inside my opponent's head before I ever spit my rhymes," Kane said. "Look back to the origins of hip-hop, Cold Crush versus Fantastic Five, Kool Moe Dee versus Busy Bee, that whole competitive nature has always been a part of the game. And Ali was the primary inspiration for a lot of us."

Connecting boxing's history to hip-hop's does, of course, require several careful qualifications. One is to make clear that boxing isn't the only sport that appears in rap music. Rappers have long paid homage to professional basketball players, incorporating figures such as Julius Irving, Magic Johnson, and Michael Jordan into their lyrics. And a number of NBA stars, such as Shaquille O'Neal, Kobe Bryant, Allen Iverson, and, more recently, Damian Lillard, have tried their hand at rapping. NBA players such as Chris Webber, Rasheed Wallace, and Ron Artest (now known as Metta Sandiford-Artest) have also ventured into hip-hop entrepreneurship. So hip-hop has, without question, left an indelible imprint on the National Basketball Association. But with all that said, you can still argue that hip-hop's boxing roots run much deeper than its ties to the NBA, a point made to me by West Coast rapper D Smoke.

"You gotta think about what boxing gyms are to the hood. It's that outlet. Boxing is made up of everybody who would make worse decisions, like gangbanging, if they weren't boxing. Boxing is the outlet that keeps them off that," D Smoke argued. "Even a sport like basketball, and Inglewood [D Smoke's hometown] is a basketball city, doesn't quite draw the same type of crowd. Basketball is more socially acceptable and more palatable than a sport like boxing where, if those guys weren't boxing, [they] would definitely be in the streets. With boxing and hip-hop, it's a more direct cultural connection."

It would also be wrong to suggest hip-hop is the only style of music that draws inspiration from boxing. Following the passing of featherweight champion Davey Moore, who died as a result of head trauma suffered in his tenth-round knockout loss to Cuban Sugar Ramos in 1963, folk singer Phil Ochs recorded an ode to the boxer, "Davey Moore," that called into question the morality of the sport. The following year, Bob

Dylan delivered his own take on the controversy in "Who Killed Davey Moore?" In the 1970 folk ballad "The Boxer," Simon and Garfunkel famously use a third-person sketch of a fighter as a poetic device. In 1974, British reggae-rocker Johnny Wakelin released "Black Superman (Muhammad Ali)," a song that, for a brief period, served as Ali's unofficial theme song. One year later, in 1975, Bob Dylan and Jacques Levy co-wrote "Hurricane," a protest song that spoke out against the injustices endured by Rubin "Hurricane" Carter, who was wrongfully convicted of murder. The bravery of prize fighters, as well as the underlying tragedy of their social circumstances, has long inspired poets and musicians alike.

Compiling a comprehensive list of songs about boxers, as Michael Rosenthal once said in *The Ring*, is an impossible task. "There are too many to count," Rosenthal argues. Boxing has impacted a variety of musical traditions. In 1987, rocker Warren Zevon released a song dedicated to the pride of Youngstown, Ohio—"Ray 'Boom Boom' Mancini." In 2003, rock band Sun Kil Moon released "Duk Koo Kim," a song that pays homage to Mancini's fallen opponent. English rocker Morrissey recorded a popular song titled "Boxers" in 1995. That same year, Ben Folds Five closed their debut album with a song titled "Boxing," a melodic tune that features a haunting chorus: "Has boxing been good to you?" One year later, Bruce Springsteen released "The Hitter." In 2005, the Irish-American punk band Dropkick Murphys recorded an ode to Micky Ward, "The Warrior's Code." An image of Ward is also featured on the cover of the band's album. More recently, in 2017, Las Vegas indie rock group The Killers released "Tyson vs. Douglas," a song more about disillusionment than the actual fight. Even Nashville star Waylon Jennings recorded a song, "Muhammad Ali," released posthumously in 2017. Ali's rival, Sonny Liston, also shows up in songs by Tom Petty and Billy Joel. I graciously concede that boxing inspires musicians of all genres and backgrounds. Hip-hop, however, as Appendixes A, B, and C can attest, is more intimately tethered to the sport than any other genre.

The stories in this book are loosely chronological and focus more on topics and trendsetters than historical timelines. These stories have been written to acknowledge the fighters and emcees who transformed boxing and hip-hop. Note that I keep using the word *story*. This is intentional. Throughout the book, I tell the stories of rappers and rhymes, fights and friendships, both in the ring and in the streets, because *stories*, as hip-hop scholar Mark Katz eloquently writes, "are powerful conveyers of knowledge; they preserve traditions and reveal the values of a community, they connect us to the past and keep the dead in living memory; they illuminate the present and suggest possible futures."

My goal here is to tell stories. I want to tell stories that connect the dots, that outline the contributions of those who have strengthened the bond between hip-hop and boxing. I want to highlight stories of rap moguls turned fight promoters, boxers turned rappers, and rappers turned boxers. I aim to bring overdue attention to a complex cultural bond that fundamentally altered the dynamics between popular music, race, sports, and national politics. In telling these stories, I invite you to reassess how the sport of boxing was shaped by the voice of hip-hop and, conversely, how boxing continues to inspire hip-hop artists in the United States and around the world.

STREETS
IS
WATCHING

T he extravagant homes decorating the curving and secluded streets of the 2000 block of Hercules Drive stand proudly above the legendary Sunset Strip, giving residents unobstructed, panoramic canyon and city views. Open balconies and infinity pools achieve the desired effect. Totems of privilege and exclusivity, beacons of success perched atop Los Angeles, the lavish neighborhoods of Hollywood Hills are as symbolic as they are material.

The $2.5 million home located on 2033 Hercules Drive was no different. The architectural design capitalized on a breathtaking backyard view, the visual embodiment of *elevation* in all of its competing definitions. Owned by reality-television star Teddi Mellencamp and her husband Edwin Arroyave, the property functioned as a rental for high-profile celebrities.[10] For twenty-year-old Brooklyn-born rapper Bashar Barakah Jackson, better known in the hip-hop world as Pop Smoke, renting the posh Hollywood Hills abode must have felt like the start of a new chapter. Occupying such a space, for a young Black man from the gang-ridden neighborhood of Canarsie, was cause to celebrate all he had escaped back in New York City.

But much like the visual effects created by the razor-edge pool in the backyard, this privileged vantage point would prove to be an optical illusion.

On Wednesday, February 19, 2020, just after 4 a.m., four men dressed in hoodies, one wearing a mask and brandishing a firearm, invaded the posh home. One suspect made his way into the property from a rear entrance; the other three assailants entered through the front door shortly thereafter. The alarm system had not been activated.

When authorities arrived on the scene at around 4:30 a.m., they found Pop Smoke with multiple gunshot wounds to his abdomen. Soon after, the promising young entertainer was transported to Cedars-Sinai Medical Center where he was pronounced dead at the age of twenty.

At the time of his passing, Pop Smoke was in the process of becoming the leading voice of Brooklyn's so-called drill movement, an emerging sound marked by trap beats and gritty lyrics, a subgenre whose influence spans from the South Side of Chicago to the Brixton district of South London.

He'd had a swift rise to mainstream visibility. Less than eighteen months into his deal with Republic Records, Pop Smoke found himself working side by side with industry heavyweights such as Travis Scott and Nicki Minaj. Pop Smoke's second mixtape, *Meet the Woo 2,* was released on February 7, 2020, less than two weeks before his life was cut short by gunfire.

On Wednesday, February 19, 2020, I discovered the news of Pop Smoke's death just like most of the social media world. Scrolling through my Twitter feed, moments before a scheduled phone interview with former world champion, Zab "Super" Judah, I read the Associated Press headline.

My initial reaction to the news, for reasons I can't fully articulate, was to visit Pop Smoke's social media accounts. Hours before Pop Smoke's murder, he had posted photos on Facebook and Instagram that flaunted stacks of money, images of him and his friend Mike Dee posing in a luxury car.

I dialed Zab Judah's number, unsure if moving forward with the call was now in bad taste. Aside from Mike Tyson, no professional boxer has personified Brooklyn's hip-hop ethos more than Judah.

"The whole town is trippin' right now. There has never been a prominent rapper or athlete from LA to ever get gunned down in Brooklyn. But, on the Brooklyn side of things, LA has taken a lot of us," Judah told me, his voice somber.

Judah was, of course, referring to the tragic murder of Brooklyn's most celebrated hip-hop icon, Christopher Wallace, better known in rap game, of course, as the Notorious B.I.G. On March 9, 1997, Wallace was killed in a drive-by shooting in Los Angeles, following his appearance at an after-party held in conjunction with the Soul Train Awards. Wallace's second studio album, ironically titled *Life After Death*, was released on March 25, 1997, sixteen days after his murder.

"This definitely brings back those memories. It makes you think back to where you were when you heard the news. B.I.G.'s death touched everybody in Brooklyn. I was actually in the Biggie tribute video," Judah continued.

At the time of Christopher Wallace's death, Zab Judah was a 5-0 junior welterweight prospect, determined to erase the memories of a disappointing loss to David Díaz in the finals of the 1996 U.S. Olympic trials. Wallace, the self-proclaimed "King of New York," had successfully brought a second wave of stardom to the city that gave birth to hip-hop culture. Along with Nas, the Wu-Tang Clan, and fellow Brooklynite Jay-Z, Wallace provided a needed boost for New York hip-hop during a time when the West Coast sound dominated the charts.

In his own craft, Judah aimed for this same level of recognition. His goal was to climb to the top of the boxing world, reppin' BK every step of the way, as he advanced his home borough's boxing tradition. His identity, much like B.I.G.'s, was tied to the streets of Brooklyn.

"Today is just another sad day for hip-hop. We lost one of our guys. He was young, trying to make his mark in the world. I know that feeling. I understand his hustle. But his life was cut short tragically. I can't even pretend that it's all good right now," Judah said, returning to the present moment.

As our conversation continued, Judah often talked about Pop Smoke as if the two had grown up together in the same project building. It was clear that the former welterweight champion saw some of himself in the cautionary story of the Brooklyn rapper. The two were connected by more than a borough. When reflecting on his own career, Judah spoke of his intrinsic drive to escape poverty and the projects, his quest to create his own legacy. At forty-one years old, this was a different Zab Judah.

"I was blessed to have the career that I did have. Twenty some years in the game at an elite level. Anything could happen in the streets. [It] could have been me," Judah said.

Early headlines positioned Pop Smoke's murder as a robbery, a result of the New York rapper flaunting expensive jewelry and stacks of money on social media earlier in the day. Yet security cameras revealed images of the four suspects fleeing the Hollywood Hills residence empty-handed. Other media outlets framed Pop Smoke's death as a targeted hit connected to the Brooklyn rapper's known gang affiliation with the Crips. Pop Smoke's social media accounts, like Judah's, are filled with blue rags and Crip references.

As we talked more, I could sense the emotion behind Judah's words. I didn't ask questions about his ties to gang life in Brownsville. In the wake of everything we'd learned just moments before our conversation, there was nothing left to say. The question remained on the notepad resting on my kitchen table. Two weeks later, I'd have my answer.

In an interview with hip-hop media icon DJ Vlad, released shortly after my conversation with Judah, the Brooklyn boxer publicly addressed his alleged ties to the Crips for the first time. When asked about Crip references on his social media accounts, Judah responded with the following statement:

Affiliation. Always been. I was born and raised in Brownsville. My whole neighborhood. It's a community walk for me. It's my community. It's my peoples. I'm just helping my people get by to the next level. That's it. We not doing no wrong. I don't gangbang out in the streets. It's a difference. Out there putting in work and hurting people? Nah. We not doing that. If anything, I am trying to help my people mentally. Showing them there is a different way we can achieve and obtain wealth without hurting each other.[11]

While Judah's ties to the streets of Brooklyn played a significant role in shaping his place in hip-hop culture, those connections have been largely unexplored by the boxing media. At several points in his career, for example, Judah and members of his entourage wore Black Mafia Family (BMF) T-shirts before fights. This coded message went unnoticed, or at least was unaddressed, by HBO and Showtime commentators.

Judah: "I wore BMF a lot of times. When I was wearing BMF in the ring, people didn't even know what it was. Now they look back and go to my fights and be like, 'Oh, you was defending the championship of the world and that's the T-shirts y'all have on?'"[12]

The story of Black Mafia Family is the hip-hop equivalent of Oliver Stone's film *Scarface* come to life. What began with two brothers, Demetrius "Big Meech" Flenory and Terry "Southwest T" Flenory, selling fifty-dollar bags of cocaine in the streets of Detroit grew into an organized crime empire; you could easily argue that BMF was the most powerful and influential drug-trafficking and money-laundering organization in recent history. The organization's improbable rise and fall, making cocaine sales in the United States through a Los Angeles–based distribution source with links to Mexican drug cartels, has been profiled in several books and documentaries.

At the height of BMF's success, Big Meech and other key members of the organization became celebrated figures in the hip-hop community because of their lavish lifestyles. Big Meech and Southwest T were known to associate with artists such as Jay-Z, Fabolous, E-40, T.I., and Trina. By the early 2000s, Big Meech had entered the rap game, branding his enterprise BMF Entertainment, a promotional agency and record company that, according to authorities, served as a front organization to launder money made from cocaine sales. During the company's brief life, BMF promoted several high-profile hip-hop acts and launched the career of Los Angeles–based rapper Bleu DaVinci. It was during this time period that Big Meech also became a fixture at Judah's championship fights.

"We don't talk about the Mafia business. It just go like this: Big Meech was a great person. From day one, he always supported me. He taught me a lot," Judah told VladTV. "We had a lot of conversations. He tried to support people. He tried to help people live out their dreams. No matter how he was doing it, he was very supportive. I don't know the Big Meech from TV. I know Big Meech from face-to-face, one-on-one."

Thanks to a joint project code-named "Operation Motor City Mafia," a two-year Organized Crime Drug Enforcement Task Force investigation, the BMF empire came crashing down. Drug raids gave way to a snowball effect of informant testimonies. In 2005, the DEA indicted and secured convictions for both Flenory brothers, who are currently serving thirty-year prison sentences. Subsequent indictments targeted over 150 members of the organization, and over 25,000 people were estimated to be members or associates.[13]

"It was shocking. You wake up, hear the news. When you knew Big Meech, you were like dude can't get caught. He was cool. He never did nothing. It was all word-of-mouth. Snitches. He tried to help people live out their dreams," said Judah.[14]

During his younger days, many boxing insiders feared that Judah's connections to the streets would eventually result in a fate similar to that of Pop Smoke or Big Meech. In 2001, Zab and his brother, Katon, got robbed at gunpoint in Brooklyn.[15] In 2003, Judah was involved in an infamous dice-game fight in Miami that was caught on video and subsequently went viral.[16] When Judah and his crew allegedly discovered they were being scammed, a scuffle ensued. In 2006, the boxer was arrested at a celebrity basketball game at Madison Square Garden because of a family court warrant. One month later, three men attempted to rob Judah on West 27th Street at 10th Avenue in New York City, a well-documented story that plays out like a scene from a gangster movie.

According to police reports, when the Brooklyn boxer left a Manhattan night club at around 5 a.m., a minivan pulled up next to his yellow Lamborghini. As the rear doors of the minivan swung open violently, two gang members instructed Judah to place his jewelry on the hood of his car, while a third man, brandishing a handgun, approached the boxer from behind. When Judah swiftly knocked the gun out of the assailant's hands, the van sped off. After beating up his attacker, Judah grabbed the gun, jumped into his Lamborghini, and chased down the minivan, swerving down one-way streets in the early daylight. After the minivan crashed into a tree, one block from the night club, Judah held the men at gunpoint until a Homeland Security officer arrived on the scene.

"[The police] were mad because I didn't want to press charges and go through with a full investigation about what happened. I was like, 'Nah, just give me their names and addresses of where they at and I'll handle the shit myself.'. . . At these times, we held court in the streets," Judah insisted.[17]

Less than a year after the bizarre incident, Judah was once again involved in a fight, at Stereo nightclub in New York City. After reviewing surveillance footage, authorities determined that Judah had, once again, been the target of a robbery. Judah's growing string of controversial incidents, coupled with increasingly inconsistent performances in the boxing ring, led some to speculate that the young champion's life was going out of control. Death or jail awaited the enigmatic boxing star, some said.

The irony of Zab Judah's story is that his closest brush with death would come not in the streets of Brooklyn but in the boxing ring. The news of Pop Smoke's death, I suspected, was not the only reason for Judah's reflective mood. Just eight months before our conversation, the Brooklyn boxer had faced his own mortality.

✳ ✳ ✳

On Friday, June 7, 2019, at the Turning Stone Resort & Casino in Verona, New York, Judah squared off against fellow Brooklynite Cletus "The Hebrew Hammer" Seldin in a junior welterweight main event held in conjunction with the thirtieth annual International Boxing Hall of Fame induction festivities. In Judah's prime, Seldin, an unorthodox brawler who sprints to the ring and never stops punching, would have been considered a tune-up opponent. At forty years old, however, some questioned Judah's motives for taking the fight. Judah's ring inactivity, along with his decision to film a reality series titled *Boxer Wives* during training camp, did little to temper the underlying criticism surrounding the bout.

I attended the Judah–Seldin fight and sat only a few rows away from ringside. Earlier that day, Judah made a surprise visit to the Hall of Fame museum grounds. Despite being swarmed by boxing fans, Judah had been kind enough to stop and take a picture with me. Before Judah departed, I was able to wish him luck, briefly thanking him for the memories he'd provided me as a boxing fan. I had been to Judah fights before—his pay-per-view showdown with Miguel Cotto, for example—but this one felt different. The recent years of Judah's career had been marked by disappointing losses to Amir Khan, Danny Garcia, and Paul Malignaggi, losses that suggested that the Brooklynite was no longer a premier player in the welterweight division. Yet when the Seldin bout was announced, I selfishly welcomed the opportunity to see hip-hop's welterweight champion fight one last time. With Judah, his appeal never depended entirely on wins and losses.

Just as fighters like Ray "Boom Boom" Mancini resonated with certain working-class fight fans, Zab Judah spoke to the hip-hop generation. Maybe it was the gold fronts and tattoos? Maybe it was the fashion, the bling, and the bravado? Maybe it was the fact that Judah's name showed up so much in hip-hop music; no boxer of his generation made more cameos in rap music videos. Even in defeat, Judah's street ethos was on full display. You might beat "Super Judah" in the ring, but you couldn't break his spirit.

For over two decades, Judah was the closest thing to a Brooklyn rapper in boxing gloves. *KO* magazine, in a 2009 cover story, dubbed the welterweight "Boxing's King of Bling." Hip-hop loved Judah for the way he fought, the style and bravado he brought to the sport, just as much as we loved him for his accomplishments in the ring. You didn't need to be from Brownsville to admire Judah's tenaciousness, even if it was, at times, misguided.

The final fight of Zab Judah's twenty-three-year career was waged at a furious pace. Charging headfirst into harm's way, Cletus Seldin waded through Judah's punches, cutting off the ring and pinning the former world champion in the corner and against the ropes. Seldin's unorthodox attack was as aesthetically displeasing as it was relentless, an onslaught of body punches followed each Judah counterpunch.

The first signs of damage came in the third. With less than ten seconds left in the round, a wild overhand right landed squarely on Judah's jaw, wobbling the former champion. On unsteady legs, Judah staggered into the neutral corner. Seldin rushed in for the finish. The bell rang, saving Judah from a series of clubbing power punches.

As the fight progressed, Seldin continued to overwhelm the former champion with thudding shots to the arms, ribs, and head. In the eleventh round, Seldin landed a sweeping hook—his best punch of the fight—once again causing Judah to stumble awkwardly. Seldin then pinned Judah against the ropes and unleashed an assortment of unanswered punches. Referee Charlie Fitch, who might have saved Judah's life, stopped the bout at 1:40 of the eleventh round. In protest of the stoppage, Judah stormed angrily out of the ring, ignoring his father's repeated attempts to calm him down.

Some fans booed the stoppage. There had been no knockdowns, no visits from the ringside physician, no Arturo Gatti–style cuts. Others voiced their displeasure with Judah's post-fight antics.

"That right there. . . . That's the problem with this guy," an older white man seated next to me barked in disgust, his finger wagging at Judah.

As Judah went to the locker room, his cornermen still in the ring, much of the crowd looked bewildered. None of us understood what we had just witnessed.

When I arrived on the Hall of Fame museum grounds the following morning, I was greeted by a steady hum of gossip. The news of Judah's condition spread quickly among those in attendance.

"Did you hear, Zab Judah was hospitalized last night?"
"I've heard they called in the family."
"I read they flew him to Syracuse by helicopter."
"I read that he is in a coma."
"They say it's a hematoma."
"I heard that it doesn't look good."

Following the stoppage, Judah had indeed been taken to a local hospital. After being examined, he was released and returned to his hotel room. In the early hours of the following morning, however, Judah's condition worsened and he was sent back to the hospital, where doctors discovered a brain bleed. The following evening, promoter Joe DeGuardia issued a statement on Judah's condition.

"[He] is awake, communicating with his family and doctors and making progress. Beyond that his family is requesting privacy at this time about his medical condition," DeGuardia told ESPN.[18]

When news broke that Judah had been released from the hospital on Tuesday, June 10, it appeared that Judah had cheated death once again. His fight was just beginning. On *Smoke Box*, an online television show produced and hosted by B-Real, the lead emcee from the rap group Cypress Hill, Judah spoke about what happened that night for the first time.

"From June 8th to July 11th, I had a big explosion going on in my head. I was having a lot of headaches and all that would make it go away was the weed. So I kept smoking, smoking, and smoking. Long story short, one day, me and my girl, we out shopping, we're downtown, and my head is killing me, it feels like somebody is trying to bust out this motherfucker. We are downtown, where my doctor is at, he is a neuro doctor. I go to him and ask for some pain medicine. He said, 'on a scale of one to ten, how bad is it?' I said, 'it's bad.' We go downstairs, we take an X-ray, and he seen it. He was like, 'we have to have emergency brain surgery right now," Judah recalled.[19]

On March 12, 2020, a few weeks after my conversation with Judah, the former champion posted a photo to his Instagram account. Taken after his brain surgery, the photo shows Judah relaxing in his hospital bed, wearing a hospital gown, a large medical tube attached to his skull.

"July 2019 when I was recovering from my brain surgery. I thought about and planned all of my next steps so just know every move is calculated," Judah wrote in his post.

In hindsight, Judah's boxing career, not unlike Pop Smoke's fast rise to hip-hop stardom, represents an inexplicable achievement.

To understand Judah fully, you would need to endure a lifetime of experiences in the streets of Brooklyn, walking past the red caps scattered along the pavement, blue flags tied around tattooed wrists, by-products of cyclical poverty and institutional racism.

Zab Judah's boxing career was a hip-hop track set to the tune of a bell, the story of an entrepreneurial spirit propelled by hopeless circumstances. The lyrics weren't always clean, the message wasn't always politically correct, but it was a rhythm that inspired those left behind. To understand Judah fully, one must rewind the soundtrack to his controversial and contradictory life, taking note of the uniquely Brooklyn refrain that best exemplifies his contribution to the sport:

Brownsville.
Never Ran.
Never Will.

BROOKLYN GO HARD

The story of Zab Judah begins with his father, Yoel "The Lion" Judah, a three-time featherweight kickboxing world champion and ninth-degree black belt in karate who was born and bred in the streets of Brooklyn. From the cornrows in his hair, to his groomed goatee, to his hawking eyebrows, Yoel was as intimidating figure as a five-foot-seven man can possibly be. His aura exceeded his small frame. Yoel's father, James, a veteran of the Korean War, had been a low-level professional boxer. His uncle, Johnny Saxton, was a former welterweight champion who once defeated Kid Gavilan. For the men in Yoel's family, fighting was a way of life.

Unlike his father and grandfather, Yoel Judah made his mark in the world of professional kickboxing, making eleven successful title defenses while pulling off several notable upsets along the way. While Yoel fought in historic venues such as Madison Square Garden, he never made any real money from the Japanese-born sport. At the height of his popularity, Yoel and his growing family lived in the projects of Brownsville, surrounded by the wreckage of the borough's growing crack epidemic. To earn larger purses, the aging kickboxer followed in his father's footsteps for a brief period, attempting to make a late transition to professional boxing. When his boxing career ended, Yoel became a trainer and shifted his focus to his sons.

The story of the fighting Judah boys—Zab and his brothers—first profiled in Kelly Crow's *New York Times* piece, "The Patriarch and the Fighting Sons," is as tragic as it is inspiring. According to Crow, Yoel was a distant presence in the lives of his children for a time during his fighting days. This changed after Yoel returned home from a kickboxing match in the early 1980s to discover that Yamima, the mother of his children, whom he was living with but never married, was addicted to drugs.

"I was fighting then, and I went away to Florida to a fight, and she was messing with the drugs here," Yoel told Crow. "She got messed up, and basically, she left them [his children] for two days in the house. So the authorities came in and snatched them. I came home, and my whole family is just gone."

As a result of the incident, the Judah children were placed in foster care for the next year and a half. Yoel was given weekly visitation rights and, by all accounts, fought long and hard to regain custody. When the family was eventually reunited, the children, particularly the boys, were raised in boxing gyms. Like most fathers who train their kids, Yoel ruled as an autocrat.

Part of Yoel Judah's mystique stems from his unique spiritual sensibility. As a teenager, Yoel became an avowed Black Hebrew Israelite, a hybrid system that mixes Judaism and Christianity with Black Nationalism. As a result of this conversion, Yoel gave each of his sons a biblical namesake: Ariel, Daniel, Zabdiel, Joseph, Josiah, Michael, and Yoel Jr. His most famous son's name can be found in 1 Chronicles 27 of the *Old Testament*, an obscure reference to a solider in charge of David's army. For much of their adolescence, the boys were raised with militaristic discipline. They had to be more than boxers: They were soldiers. The Judah children referred to themselves as Israelites, or Black Jews, but belonged to no formal congregation. Of the Brooklyn boxing trainer's ten sons, five competed as amateur boxers and four competed at the professional level.

From a young age, the Judah boys had access to some of their father's high-profile connections. Olympic gold medalist Mark Breland, for example, was a close friend of the family. For Yoel's third son, Zabdiel, the dream of becoming a world champion boxer was, ironically, inspired by a male figure from outside his household.

"I met Mike Tyson when I was six or seven years old. Mike is from Brownsville. He and my dad knew each other from their time in the streets and in the fight game. My dad was the kickboxing champ at the same time Mike was the biggest thing in the world. As a kid, I was inspired to be a boxer, knowing that Mike Tyson is from right down the street from me. Mike is why I gravitated toward boxing," Zab told me, setting up the scene of his original meeting with Tyson.

Zab continued: "One night, it was the wee hours of the morning, maybe two o'clock in the morning, and my father came into the house and he was like, 'Wake up, wake up, I got a surprise for y'all.' I came into the living room and it was Mike Tyson. I was like seven years old. I was shocked. Mike looked at us and said, 'I hear y'all wanna be fighters.' I remember him telling us to work hard and stay focused. It kind of jump-started my life and career. Years later, as I'm working my way up through the ranks, Mike is sitting high up on the throne, we reconnected."

While many of the Judah boys showed promise in the ring, Zab quickly earned his place as the prodigy. As an amateur, Zab won 110 of his 115 bouts, including a National Golden Gloves title. Despite failing to make the U.S. Olympic boxing team—instead earning a spot as an alternate— there was no question the speedy southpaw was a blue-chip prospect.

"[Hall-of-Fame trainer] Lou Duva was the one that found me," Zab told me. "He came to the New York Golden Gloves in 1993. Duva seen me win it. He came to my locker room and said, 'Hey kid, how would you like to go to training camp with Pernell Whitaker? Come down to Virginia, Sweet Pea will teach you some things.' I'm thinking, Pernell Whitaker, he's the king of the world, the greatest fighter in boxing. I was like, Oh hell yeah."

At the time of their first meeting, Pernell Whitaker, the 1984 Olympic gold medalist at lightweight, and reigning WBC welterweight world champion, was indeed among the top boxers in the sport. With his rapid-fire hand speed and slick southpaw style, Zab had already earned comparisons to the defensive wizard from Norfolk, Virginia.

"I never liked the comparisons. When people called me 'Sweet Pea with a punch,' I didn't like that. I found out, firsthand, that wasn't the case," Zab said, laughing at his youthful exuberance.

He remembered: "I was sixteen years old, sparring Pernell Whitaker in his training camp in Virginia Beach, Virginia. Right from the start, I was like, that man hits way harder than it looks. The second time we sparred, I could tell Pernell was trying to figure out who this kid was. And I ain't gonna front, that day he came at me with something I had never seen before. I was just a kid. I'm talking big shots. *Boom. Boom. Boom.* I'm trying to slip and move. And, for a minute, I'm thinking, man I'm in trouble. We spar the three rounds, we get out of the ring, and I'm looking at him in the mirror like, 'Damn, this dude don't like me. I came all the way down to Virginia to his camp and dude don't like me. He was trying to knock me out.' In my head, I'm feeling down."

Moments after their second sparring session, Whitaker approached the visibly dejected prospect whom he had just pummeled in the ring.

"Where you learn that from?" Whitaker asked Zab, giving the young amateur a slight smirk.

"What do you mean?" Zab replied, still attempting to catch his breath.

"Where you learn my style? Where you learn to fight like me? Your daddy teach you that?" Whitaker continued.

"I don't know Mr. Whitaker, nobody taught me that. It's just my style," the sixteen-year-old replied.

To this, the welterweight champion's face contorted.

"Man, don't call me no Mr. Whitaker. My name is Pernell," the champion responded.

As Zab attempted to apologize, Whitaker put his arm around the young fighter, the pound-for-pound king's first act of humility.

"I like you. You got ability. If you keep your head on your shoulders, you got a chance to go places and see things you would never dream of," Whitaker said, a moment just as inspirational and prophetic as Zab's living room encounter with Tyson.

"Having Mike and Pernell in my life was amazing. Now that I look back at all the wonderful times we had together, and everything I learned from them, it was just amazing," Judah reflected.

Being around two of hip-hop's most beloved pugilists did, of course, come with its promotional advantages.

Lou DiBella: "The number-one boxer showing up in hip-hop songs in the early 1990s was, of course, Tyson. But when I think of hip-hop and boxing I think of Pernell Whitaker walking to the ring with Naughty by Nature. He was close friends with those guys. They loved him. Salt-N-Pepa. Naughty by Nature. There were a lot of hip-hop acts following Pernell, just as they were following the career of Mike Tyson."

Zab Judah's blinding speed and ferocious aggressiveness also appealed to fans of Tyson and Whitaker. With Lou Duva (Whitaker's longtime trainer) and his father, Yoel, guiding the way, Zab quickly shot up the professional rankings.

✳ ✳ ✳

At twenty years old, with a professional record of 15-0 (11 KOs), Zab Judah passed his first test as a professional by beating "Irish" Micky Ward, headlining a 1998 card televised by ESPN2. Two fights after his hard-fought victory over Ward, Judah knocked out Wilfredo Negron for the interim IBF junior welterweight title, a bout that took place on the undercard of Mike Tyson's comeback bout against South African heavyweight Frans Botha (Tyson's first bout since returning from his suspension from the Evander Holyfield ear-biting incident).

While Zab Judah won his interim title in front of a half-empty MGM Grand Garden Arena, the Judah–Tyson pairing clearly raised the young champion's profile. In the coming years, the two appeared to be inseparable. After knocking out undefeated Jan Piet Bergman for the vacant IBF world championship, Judah outpointed undefeated British challenger Junior Witter on the undercard of Mike Tyson's one-round destruction of Lou Savarese in Glasgow, Scotland. After his undercard bout was complete, Judah quickly showered, got dressed, and accompanied Tyson to the ring.

Two fights later, Judah defeated Hector Quiroz on the undercard of Mike Tyson's bout with Andrew Golota. For better or worse, Judah was also a member of Tyson's entourage during the infamous press conference brawl with Lennox Lewis in New York City. "Sweet Pea with a punch," as some critics called the Brooklyn star, soon became known as the junior welterweight division's "Mini Mike Tyson."

Aside from Tyson and Whitaker, there was another prominent influence in Zab Judah's life. Born in Brownsville, Brooklyn, on October 27, 1977, Judah came into his own during hip-hop music's so-called golden era, a time when rap music had unprecedented crossover success in popular culture. While boxing had always been Judah's destiny, hip-hop was his passion, a cultural presence that filled the neighborhood around him. More so than any boxer from his generation, Judah would carry this swagger into the ring.

"Growing up in Flatbush, Brooklyn, during that particular time, hip-hop was everything. I listened to Jay-Z. Kool G Rap. Big Daddy Kane. Special Ed. Boot Camp Clik. Buckshot. Biggie. Those are the guys I came up on. Hip-hop and boxing were everything to me back then," Judah said, recounting the artists who influenced his life and training.

Judah's bravado did not go unnoticed by boxing pundits. In prefight featurettes for HBO and Showtime, the subject of hip-hop always found its way into the segments.

"[Zab Judah] basically appeals to the hip-hop generation. The bling, the jewelry, the teeth, the whole thing," manager Shelly Finkel said to HBO Sports.[20]

"All of the sudden [Zab] is showing up on mixtapes, he's showing up in hip-hop videos," boxing analyst Max Kellerman added.

Zab Judah wasn't the first fighter to play rap music during ring walks, or wear hip-hop fashion when meeting with the press, or talk in the hip slang of the culture. His affinity for the culture didn't matter. Rather, Judah's appeal, as Kellerman pointed out, was built by his proximity to hip-hop royalty. Judah was connected. He didn't admire the hip-hop world from afar; he was a part of it.

In his bout with Terron Millet at Mohegan Sun Arena, August 5, 2000, Judah's connection to hip-hop was, once again, on full display. Moments before Judah made his way to the ring, Bad Boy recording artist Shyne emerged from behind a black curtain to perform his latest single, aptly titled "Bad Boyz." The Belize-born Brooklynite was, at the time, one of rap's hottest and most controversial prospects.

Just six months before the Judah–Millett bout, Shyne, Bad Boy Records CEO Sean "P. Diddy" Combs, and Combs's then-girlfriend Jennifer Lopez were involved in a nightclub shooting in New York City. While no charges were filed against Diddy and Lopez, Shyne was subsequently charged with attempted murder, assault, and reckless endangerment and eventually served ten years in prison before being deported back to his native Belize.

For rap fans like me, those who loved the pugilistic jazz of Pernell Whitaker and the raw power of Mike Tyson, Judah offered a cultural remix, something boxing had never seen before. When Shyne delivered the opening bars to his debut single, the sport changed forever. Until this point in boxing history, only Felix "Tito" Trinidad, who tapped the Puerto-Rican-American duo of Big Pun and Fat Joe for his pay-per-view showdown with Oscar De La Hoya, on September 18, 1999, had pulled such a move. Delivered in the ring before Trinidad's exit from the locker room, Pun and Joe's prefight performance was not, however, a resounding success. Jim Lampley, who called the Trinidad–De La Hoya fight for HBO, seemed, at the time, confused by the theatrics.

"So [Trinidad] comes to the ring first now, to the accompaniment of the music of a couple of fellas named Fat Joe and Big Pun," Lampley said flatly.[21]

Dressed in blinged-out cornerman jackets, Big Pun performed one verse of his song "Twinz (Deep Cover 98)" before Trinidad's customary salsa music kicked in. Unfortunately, Fat Joe's microphone malfunctioned, relegating the Terror Squad captain to the role of hype man.

For Judah–Millett, the presentation was much cleaner and far more dramatic. Shyne performed his hit song solo, rapping the lyrics as he made his way to the ring. The thumping bass and gritty rhymes set the tone perfectly for the work Judah was about to put in. At the end of the song, standing at center ring, Shyne announced, "Live from Brooklyn, Vietnam, Super Zab Judah." The ring walk, a mini-concert of sorts, was the first of its kind.

Recalled Judah: "It was Brooklyn. We both from Brooklyn. Mike Tyson's sister, Jackie, was really close to Shyne and myself. She would hang out with us on different occasions. She would always be like, 'Yo, Zab, I hung out with Shyne last night. You guys need to meet. You act so much alike.' Then vice versa she would hang out with Shyne and tell him the same thing. When we finally kicked it, we talked, and everything was smooth."

Judah continued: "I told Shyne, 'I'm champ of the world. Nobody has done this. Why don't you walk to the ring with me? Instead of playing the music, come out live with it. It will do good for me and will do good for you. You will be shown in a platform that is different than what you are used to.' He was with it and it came out dope."

After Judah's fourth-round knockout victory over Terron Millett, the champion's hip-hop reputation grew. First, Judah returned the favor and appeared in Shyne's music video for the track "That's Gangsta," much of which took place in Judah's Brooklyn boxing gym. Next, Judah made a cameo in Lil' Kim's video for "Lighters Up."

As Judah ran his record to 27-0 (21 KOs), hip-hop royalty consistently appeared at his fights. Soon, Judah's name began to show up in rap lyrics as well. Jay-Z, Wu-Tang Clan, Juelz Santana, G. Dep, Ludacris, Lil Wayne, Talib Kweli, Lil' Flip, N.O.R.E., and Busta Rhymes all mentioned Judah in their songs.

Inspectah Deck: "Zab came from where we came from. He was our champ. We watched him come up and earn his name. He was validated in the game. That's why we always threw his name in the music."

Masta Killa: "I've met Zab on several occasions. It's a mutual respect thing. It's not easy to make it when you come from the streets where we come from. To see any level of success, to see someone from Brooklyn take it to that next level, that gives me energy. It gives me a spark. It lets me know that whatever I want to apply my energy to, I can make that happen. When I see any Brooklyn representation, in music or sports, it gives me a good feeling."

Wu-Tang producer Mathematics: "Zab was one of the first to set off the hip-hop ring walk but you can go back way before that fight. If you ask me, Wu-Tang was the first to bring that to the table. That didn't happen until after that movie *The Great White Hype* where Method Man brings Damon Wayans's character into the ring, performing 'Bring the Pain.' Nobody had done that in real life. Wu-Tang kind of sparked that idea. That was [1996], way before the Zab fight. It's a case of life imitating art."

Not only did Zab Judah walk to the ring to the sounds of the rap game's hottest emcees, he did so in custom-designed garments by Rocawear, the hip-hop brand co-founded by Brooklyn icon Jay-Z. The boxer-turned-urban-fashion-model also showed up in many of the Rocawear ads that appeared in hip-hop magazines such as *Vibe* and *The Source*.

"I was the first boxer Roc-A-Fella had signed. I was the first spokes-model to wear Rocawear in the ring or anywhere, outside the Roc [the record label]. To me, Jay-Z was my favorite artist so it was a no brainer," Judah said.

Kareem "Biggs" Burke, co-founder of Roc-A-Fella Records and Rocawear: "For me and Jay and Dame [Dash], when we were young, we were like 'we want to take over the world.' We didn't know what that meant, or what that would entail. But, when it came to boxing, we were deep in that anyway. We were one of the first urban brands to start dressing boxers. We went from that to starting to manage fighters. We had Roc Sports. I created that back in 1997, which is basically the model Roc Nation uses today. It was about creating a lifestyle around it. Boxing was just one of the things we gravitated to."

The respect, between Judah and the Roc-A-Fella clique, was mutual. Soon after the partnership, Judah's name showed up on Jay-Z's classic album *The Blueprint*. "The jab is stiff and it's Zab quick," Jay-Z rhymes on the track "All I Need."

Judah added: "It was always surprising to hear my name on a rap record. Nobody ever said to me, 'Yo, Zab I'm about to go to the studio and put your name in a record.' It would come out, they would drop a record, and I would hear it like everyone else. But I'm gonna keep it real. I got stupid excited when I heard Hov [Jay-Z] spit his joint."

Judah's friendship with Jay-Z catapulted the young star into a different level of fame in Black popular culture. In Jay-Z's mafioso-inspired video for "Roc Boys," for example, Judah can be seen with industry greats such as Mariah Carey, Sean Combs, and Nas. For a few years, Judah was second only to his Brooklyn mentor, Mike Tyson, when it came to hip-hop respectability.

As Judah entered his unification showdown with WBA and WBC champion Kostya Tsyzu, it was Tyson who served as a member of his entourage, a role-reversal that signaled the undefeated welterweight's coming of age.

In the first round, Judah's coronation appeared to be a forgone conclusion. The Brooklyn native overwhelmed the power-punching Australian multiple times, hitting Tsyzu with perfectly timed uppercuts and pinpoint left hands.

With three seconds left in the second round, it all came crashing down. Tsyzu landed a brilliant right hand that planted Judah flat on his back. Before the count of two, Judah scrambled to his feet, attempting to show referee Jay Nady that he was not hurt.

Unsteady on his legs, Judah wobbled forward awkwardly and fell back down to the canvas. Although the round was finished, Nady waved off the fight, forgoing the traditional eight count. In a scene not unlike

Tyson's post-Holyfield rebellion, a near-scuffle ensued, the consequences of which would prove to be far more detrimental to Judah's career than the loss itself.

In a fit of rage, Judah approached Nady to protest the stoppage. Seconds into the altercation, Judah forcefully positioned his right glove underneath Nady's chin, forcing the referee's head backward. As Judah cocked back his left hand, he was restrained by his father and members of security. The chaos would ebb and flow for over ten minutes.

As Tszyu celebrated his victory, Judah, still gloved, picked up his stool and tossed it to center ring. On repeated occasions, Judah broke loose from his father's restraint and tried to incite violence. As a result of Judah's wild behavior, he was fined $100,000 by the Nevada State Athletic Commission and suspended for one year.

With the incident hanging over his career, Judah returned to the sport in 2002, racking up wins over Omar Weis, DeMarcus "Chop Chop" Corley, and Jaime Rangel, victories that set up a high-profile matchup with undisputed welterweight champion Cory Spinks, the son of former heavyweight champion Leon Spinks.

In his initial fight at the welterweight division, Judah at first boxed cautiously, falling behind on the scorecards. Spinks won the first three rounds. As the fight progressed, Judah started to land power shots, imposed his will, and occasionally gained momentum. In the eleventh round, however, Judah pulled straight back from an exchange and was dropped by a quick left hand. While Judah wasn't visibly shaken by the blow, the knockdown all but assured he would need a knockout to win the fight.

The miracle comeback, shades of Julio César Chávez versus Meldrick Taylor, almost happened in the final round. With only twenty-nine seconds left in the bout, Judah landed a powerful left hand that sent Spinks to the canvas. The champion survived the devastating punch, rising to his feet at the count of eight. After being saved by the final bell, Spinks was awarded a close but heavily disputed unanimous decision, setting up an anticipated rematch.

In my conversation with Judah, it was clear to me that he viewed the Cory Spinks rematch in a special light. For Judah, it was a do-or-die moment in his rollercoaster career.

"That was one of the biggest nights for me. You had Big Meech [Black Mafia Family] sitting there. Nelly was there, he brought Spinks out.

Jermaine Dupri was there. All these hip-hop artists were there," Judah said. "My back was against the wall. I had to dig deep to go pull that out. It was a hostile environment. I was in his backyard. I didn't go into the fight to win; I went into the fight to knock him out."

Just as had been the case for much of his life, the odds were indeed stacked against Judah. After suffering his second professional loss, Judah was now the B-side to the Spinks promotion. Not only was the rematch held in Spinks's home city of St. Louis, Missouri, promoter Don King exploited Judah's desperation and refused to offer the former champion headliner money.

Recalled Judah: "Don King did me dirty in that fight. The first fight I made $1.2 million, the second fight I made like $100,000. I had to go in there and go hard with it. It was nothing personal against Cory. It was the situation. People don't understand the adversity that I was up against. I got death threats and everything in St. Louis. We had people calling and saying they was gonna kill me and all this crazy shit."

In what many pundits consider his greatest, and perhaps most disciplined, performance, Judah knocked out Spinks in the ninth round of a mostly one-sided fight, capturing all three major title belts at welterweight. For a brief moment, Judah, now a two-division champion, silenced critics who said he was one of boxing's most talented underachievers.

✳ ✳ ✳

Now that Judah was back atop the boxing world, the fight everyone in the hip-hop community wanted to see was a matchup with Floyd Mayweather Jr., who competed at junior welterweight. At 35-0 (24 KOs), Mayweather had already secured his place as one of boxing's best fighters by winning world titles in three different weight classes.

Despite all of his accomplishments in the ring, however, what Mayweather wanted most in his career had eluded him.

With only one pay-per-view bout on his résumé, a dismantling of fan-favorite Arturo "Thunder" Gatti, some questioned whether Mayweather could be a box-office star. Aside from Oscar De La Hoya, who was truly boxing's nonheavyweight cash cow, pound-for-pound greats Roy Jones Jr., "Sugar" Shane Mosley, and Bernard Hopkins had largely failed at becoming pay-per-view stars at the time. Because of his hip-hop celebrity, Judah, it appeared, provided the perfect foe for Mayweather. When rumors emerged that "Pretty Boy Floyd" was looking to move up in weight, a Judah–Mayweather blockbuster event seemed inevitable. The two champions mirrored each other. Both were brought into the fight game by their fathers, born into boxing families. Both were also heavily connected in the hip-hop world. Mayweather was attempting to launch Philthy Rich Records. Judah, at the same time, was attempting to start his own label, Super Cartel.

"That was a wave. I was a young guy. I was out front. I had some influence," Judah reminisced. "There were guys from my hood who could rap so I said, 'let's start a record label.' I had a bunch of artists. We were the first guys on the Smack DVD. We acting up and all that, underneath the Brooklyn Bridge. It was family. It was their dreams and I had a lane. I tried to use that lane to help people."

Leading up to the Judah fight, Mayweather made a cameo in Raekwon's music video for the song "100 Rounds." Raekwon later escorted Mayweather to the ring with a live performance similar to that of Shyne and Judah. As comparisons between Judah and Mayweather began to mount, a nasty war of words erupted.

Mayweather told *All Hip-Hop*: "I love hip-hop, and I love R&B, and I love rap artists, but I'm a little different from Zab Judah. I got my fame from putting fighters on their back pocket, and putting them on their face, and racking up [victories]—that's how I got my fame. He got his fame from being a video groupie. I like rap artists and they're good; some of them even come over to my house and hang out. But I ain't into being in everybody's video and all that."[22]

When pressed on his cameo in Raekwon's video, Mayweather doubled down on the insults, further building the hype for a potential showdown: "I did a little clip for Raekwon because he brought me out into the ring one time, and I gave him a little exposure, a favor for a favor, two times in ten years. Every time you see me, I ain't tryin' to light no lighter and dance behind Lil' Kim or chase Jay-Z, that ain't my style! I got my own fame, I'm my own man."[23]

In typical hip-hop fashion, Judah fired back, calling into question Mayweather's credibility in the streets. "He's a good fighter, but as far as him having notoriety in the hood, outside of boxing, he really can't get it," Judah said. "When they hear him shout my name out, people say,

'Oh, this guy is fighting Zab.' But he doesn't even have to take it to that extreme. If he gives me a couple of hours, I'll market him right. I'll let the world know who he is. It's going to be bad. He pops a lot of shit, but I'm going to knock him the fuck out, man."[24]

To the dismay of fans and promoters alike, the Mayweather–Judah megafight would lose much of its appeal before it could actually take place. In a mandatory title defense against little-known Argentinian challenger Carlos Baldomir, held in The Theater at Madison Square Garden, Judah struggled to make weight and then struggled to win rounds. Rumors surrounding the fight suggested that Judah celebrated his upset victory over Cory Spinks long and hard. Looking toward his pay-per-view showdown with Mayweather, Judah clearly overlooked the unheralded fighter standing in his way. At the end of the night, the scorecards read 115-113, 115-112 and 114-113, all in favor of Baldomir.

Despite the embarrassing upset loss, Mayweather–Judah proceeded as planned. Because Baldomir had refused to pay the belt fee for the IBF portion of Judah's unified title, only two belts had officially been on the line. Because of the odd circumstances, the WBC and WBA titles went to Baldomir, while Judah remained IBF champion.

On April 8, 2006, at the Thomas & Mack Center in Las Vegas, Floyd Mayweather Jr. moved up in weight to challenge Zab Judah for a title he held as the result of the financial technicality. Boxing insiders rolled their eyes at the so-called championship fight.

While the loss to Baldomir didn't prevent Judah from getting a fight with Mayweather, it did affect the percentage of the purse he got. Judah was originally set to earn $3 million plus a percentage of the profits. That figure dropped to $1 million.

In one of the few events to be co-promoted by rivals Don King and Bob Arum, Mayweather–Judah generated much interest from the public. Despite Judah's loss to Baldomir, HBO didn't abandon its plans to host the event on pay-per-view. Hip-hop luminaries picked sides as the war of words between the two fighters escalated.

"I can't wait to knock him out in front of Jay-Z. This is flawless versus jawless,"[25] Mayweather bragged.

Judah fired back with his own insults. The constant volleys between the camps led some in the media to label the fight "the biggest beef between hip-hop entrepreneurs since Jay-Z and Nas."[26]

"It was built up big because we had a friendship at first. We were young. We fell into the stupidity of the media and just being young and fly and flashy. We let that shit get the best of us. We were young million-aires. We had the jewelry and the homes and the cars. But I truly didn't believe that Floyd could beat me," Judah said, recounting the prefight trash talk.

Against Mayweather, Judah, for the first time in his career, came into the ring a 5-1 underdog. During the first half of his fight, however, those odds appeared to be inflated. Judah carried the first round, which was highlighted by two cracking lead left hands that landed straight on Mayweather's chin.

In the second round, Judah landed a flashy right hook that caused Mayweather to stagger backward, his right glove brushing the canvas. Referee Richard Steele incorrectly called the knockdown a slip. Had it been ruled correctly the punch would have served as the answer to an excellent boxing trivia question: Who was the only fighter to knock down Floyd Mayweather Jr.?

"Go watch the replay. I landed a hook. His glove touched the canvas. 100 percent. It was a knockdown." Judah told me, his voice trembling with frustration.

As the bout proceeded, Judah connected consistently with straight lefts. To the surprise of many, Mayweather struggled to return fire. As Judah became the aggressor, Mayweather uncharacteristically lunged forward, missing wildly.

"He's scared. He don't wanna fight. Let your hands go. Get into fight mode. He can't hurt you. The more you hit him, the more he's gonna run,"[27] an ecstatic Yoel Judah barked at his son between rounds.

Early in round four, Judah landed a powerful overhand left that stag-gered Mayweather, knocking him against the ropes. The pro-Judah crowd came to life, chanting his name. After four rounds, HBO's unofficial judge Herald Lederman scored the bout 3-1 in favor of Judah. At the end of the fifth, Mayweather's best round to this point, Judah countered with a vicious combination at the bell, taunting the undefeated champion as he made his way back to the corner.

"Those who suggested that Judah's southpaw style, hand speed, and athleticism could give Mayweather problems have been right so far," HBO commentator Jim Lampley said.[28]

As the bout progressed, Mayweather's legendary pedigree showed itself more and more. In the seventh round, the fight began to shift. Mayweather bloodied Judah's nose and mouth with accurate counterpunches. Thanks to a consistent body attack, Mayweather took control of the fight, slowing Judah's punch output. By round ten, Judah appeared to be fading quickly. Mayweather picked up the pace, looking for a stoppage.

"So far, Judah has, at least, redeemed his reputation. He has taken a lot of hard, crisp, shots," Herald Lederman said as Floyd moved in for the finish.[29]

Lederman's comments proved to be premature. In the closing moments of the round, Judah threw a whipping left uppercut that hit Mayweather squarely in his groin, causing the star to double over and wince in pain. Judah then seized on the chance to land an additional punch to the back of his defenseless opponent's head.

While Mayweather hobbled to the neutral corner, his uncle and head trainer, Roger Mayweather, climbed into the ring and confronted Judah, risking disqualification. As security attempted to restrain Roger, Judah's father, Yoel, and Mayweather cornerman Leonard Ellerbe entered the ring and exchanged blows.

As security forces flooded the ring, it appeared Floyd Mayweather was headed for a disqualification loss because of his uncle Roger's actions.

"When two guys are in the boxing ring boxing and someone from the corner enters the ring during a fight, it is a disqualification. Automatic DQ. I told Floyd, 'You just got your first loss, punk.' But I guess the referee didn't see that. Didn't see his glove touch the canvas either," Judah said.

Order was eventually restored. Roger was ejected from the arena and the fight continued. Two rounds later, the judges awarded Mayweather a unanimous decision victory. The chaotic incident, now a reoccurring pattern in Judah's career, largely overshadowed his gutsy performance.

Two weeks after the fiasco, the IBF ordered a rematch. This verdict was overruled by the Nevada State Athletic Commission's decision to again suspend Judah from boxing for one year.

"I didn't get the rematch because Floyd didn't want to go through with that again. At the end of the day, we are both men. He's got his family, I have mine. He's on the West Coast, I'm on the East Coast. When we see each other, when we bump into each other, it's all love," Judah said, reminding me of the fact that he would, years later, serve as Mayweather's chief sparring partner in preparation for his blockbuster showdown with Manny Pacquiao.

After the suspension, Judah returned to boxing, won more titles, but never regained his place among the sport's elite. His primary contribution, you could argue, was more stylistic than pugilistic. After the Judah bout, rappers 50 Cent and Lil Wayne became frequent contributors to Mayweather's hip-hop-inspired ring walks. The cultural baton had been passed.

As we ended our phone conversation, Judah reflected: "I can't really say what my appeal was. My tune and swag was on point, maybe that's why hip-hop fell in love with me. The hip-hop community always turned out for me, win, lose, or draw."

In Jay-Z's 2010 memoir, *Decoded*, the Brooklyn rapper compares hustling to professional boxing. This passage captures Judah's appeal to those in the culture: "Boxing is a glorious sport to watch and boxers are incredible, heroic athletes, but it's also, to be honest, a stupid game to play. Even the winners can end up with crippling brain damage. In a lot of ways, hustling is the same. But you learn something special from playing the most difficult games, the games where winning is close to impossible and losing is catastrophic: You learn how to compete as if your life depended on it."[30]

Hip-hop loved Judah because he was a son of Brooklyn, a reflection of the culture. He personified Brooklyn's fighting spirit. Hip-hop loved Judah because of his style and his cocky attitude, his unapologetic bravado.

But, most important, hip-hop loved Zab Judah because he fought like his life depended on it.

LET THE RHYTHM HIT 'EM

On October 6, 1963, heavyweight champion Sonny Liston, fresh off his second straight knockout victory over Floyd Patterson, appeared on *The Ed Sullivan Show*, skipping rope to the sounds of the "Godfather of Soul," James Brown. The rhythm and dexterity Liston showed in his routine, uncharacteristic of the plodding heavyweight banger, were in perfect sync with the song playing on the phonograph record player, a reinterpretation of Jimmy Forrest's twelve-bar instrumental blues rhythm, "Night Train," originally composed in 1951. Over the course of his career, Liston trained to both versions. According to boxing sages, it was the only song Liston trained to, a jumpy rhythm that transported the stoic champion into an almost trancelike state during workouts.

While Liston was not the first boxer to add skipping rope to his workout, he is perhaps the first fighter to become synonymous with the exercise, largely because of the accompanying soundtrack. In fact, you would be hard-pressed to find an article, book, or documentary that doesn't tie the song to his legacy. Liston's biography, written by Nick Tosches, for example, appropriately bears the same title as the fighter's unofficial theme song, *Night Train*.

For Liston, the rhythm of the music was the attraction. The song itself contains no story or inspirational references. In James Brown's version of the song, recorded with his band in 1961, the vocals consist of shout-outs to cities on the East Coast leg of his national tour. Aside from the title and roll call, Brown offers no substantive lyrics. "Night Train," in its many incarnations, is about a rhythmic state of mind.

To this day, Liston's jump-rope routine is arguably the best example of how important music is to a professional boxer's training, a notion well understood by those who came up in the hip-hop generation. A fighter's life is made up of a series of repetitive actions. Some bring their passion for music to this painstaking process; others simply use the rhythms, as did Liston, to help their performance.

In my conversation with Zab Judah, the first in my journey to better understand the relationship between hip-hop and boxing, it quickly became apparent that Judah fell into both categories.

"Hip-hop was very important to my training. Music sets the tone in training camp. It's part of your routine. Jay-Z and Fab would always be in the training playlist. Biggie and Tupac got their spots locked in too. But Tupac's "Ambitionz Az a Ridah" was my theme song. They knew when I was in the back, getting dressed in the gym, to have it ready. When I started lacing up my boots, my brother [Daniel] would put that on," Judah said to me, positioning Tupac Shakur's song as his own personal "Night Train."

More than any other current musical genre, the rhythm and tempo found in hip-hop music lends itself to the frenetic energy of a boxing gym. As the son of a boxing trainer, raised in dingy, makeshift gyms, I've long understood the role music plays in a fighter's daily routine. When I was sixteen years old, after my father taught me all that he could, he took me to "Fighting," Tommy Small's gym on the outskirts of Beckley, West Virginia. Small, who began his career in the local Toughman circuit, was one of the few area trainers to have success at the professional level, compiling thirty-five victories, along with losses to elite fighters such as Raul Marquez, Keith Holmes, Meldrick Taylor, Julio César Chávez, and Hector "Macho" Camacho. Two minutes into my shadowboxing routine, the hard-nosed West Virginia fight veteran diagnosed my condition.

"Lord Jesus, you got the *white man syndrome*—no rhythm, son," Small instructed.

Tommy Small was as white as they come, fair-skinned, clean-shaven, with a military-style haircut and thick Appalachian accent. Yet Small honed his craft in the predominantly Black gyms of Washington D.C. He was a firm believer that great champions need rhythm and that most white guys didn't have it.

"Put on that rap music. This kid needs it," Small called to Josh Rife, the reigning Golden Gloves State Champion who served as his star pupil.

Next came the dancing piano riff, the haunting singsong vocals, the stabbing drum beat, and off-kilter Michael Buffer impersonation.

I won't deny it, I'm a straight ridah . . .
You don't wanna fuck with me . . .

The song—Tupac Shakur's "Ambitionz Az a Ridah."

✳ ✳ ✳

Over the past decade, research on workout music has gained considerable momentum. Psychologists aim to better understand the degree to which music distracts athletes from pain and fatigue, elevating moods and increasing endurance. Much of this data suggests the two most important components of the recipe are *tempo* and *rhythm response*, terms used to describe music that instinctually encourages synchronized movements such as toe-tapping and head-nodding. Rap music, an ideal companion for the fluid movements boxing requires from its participants, served as a rhythm aid for the awkward and gangly version of my teenage self.

Some might argue that hip-hop's most important contribution to the fight game takes place in the gym. Hip-hop beatmakers are, of course, equally in tune with the effect their work has on professional athletes, particularly boxers. Those who slave away at turntables, drum machines, and digital samplers craft their rhythms with this desired effect in mind. To better understand the kinetic relationship between bass and boxing, turntables and training, I sought the perspectives of veteran rap producers Bronze Nazareth and Mathematics, in-house beatmakers for Wu-Tang Clan.

"Music is emotion. There have been studies that show the relationship between the tempo and intensity of music and the rate [that] people exercise, the music helps you exercise a little harder. If I was training, I would go with my boys M.O.P. or "Triumph" [Wu-Tang Clan], something live and in-effect," Bronze said. "Maybe, Mobb Deep with "Shook Ones." That song just has a grimy mentality. It would be perfect for training for a fight. Producers go into the lab looking to cook up that kind of mentality. Why do you think they mostly play hip-hop music in between rounds at big fights? We make music that keeps the energy going."

"There has always been a connection between hip-hop and boxing," said Mathematics. "When you train, you listen to music. It's that simple. My style, as a producer, can hit you hard like Thomas 'The Hitman' Hearns. But I can also dance on you like Sugar Ray Leonard or Sweet Pea [Pernell Whitaker]. We design the beat to put you in that certain mindset."

The musical disciple of Wu-affiliate Cilvaringz, the architect behind Wu-Tang's infamous *Once Upon a Time in Shaolin* project, Bronze Nazareth's style is best described as a throwback to a bygone era. Hard-edged, gritty, and haunting, his work is the antithesis of the slickly produced, radio-friendly, trap soundscape that currently dominates the Billboard charts. The same could be said for Mathematics, the longtime Wu-Tang DJ/producer known for designing the group's world-famous logo. Wu-Tang's 2017 album, *The Saga Continues*, produced by Mathematics from top to bottom, contains numerous references to professional boxers; a nod to manager Al Haymon even shows up on one track. Because Bronze Nazareth and Mathematics make the kind of music one is likely to encounter in a boxing gym, I was eager to learn the degree to which the sport influences their unique styles.

Bronze Nazareth: "First and foremost, I am a boxing fan. I don't even need to know the boxers to enjoy the fight. I respect the commitment that goes into the game. Boxing is a lot like producing, you have to train to get nice. Nobody jumps in the ring and all of a sudden they the best. Same with producing. Nobody gets behind the boards and all of a sudden they nice. To even make it to the ring or the arena, it says something about the kind of person you are and what you put into the art. Hip-hop is one of those genres where getting old is frowned upon. Same as boxing. To have longevity in both worlds is an honor. In both arenas, you rise up from the streets, out of the ashes like a phoenix, and then you got to fight [to stay]. The respect and admiration goes both ways."

Mathematics: "Boxing was a big part of the culture in my hood. Back in the day, if you wasn't on the corner rhyming, or freestyling, or deejaying, the fights would come on and we all watching the fights. [Wu-Tang] used to all get together and have fight parties. It would be like twenty of us in my man's crib, drinking 40s and watching the fights. And then a fight would break out because of the fight [laughs]."

It is no coincidence that the sonic quality of each producer's music plays out like the score to a Hollywood fight scene. Boxing, I quickly learned, held geographical and familial significance in the upbringings of both men.

Bronze Nazareth: "Growing up in Grand Rapids, Michigan, the influence of boxing was everywhere. Even before Floyd [Mayweather Jr.], you had his father and uncles Roger and Jeff. Me and my brother went to the same high school as Floyd. My brother was his age so he had classes with him. As a boxing fan, I came up having a tough Michigan bias. Tommy Hearns. Joe Louis. James Toney. Floyd [Mayweather]. And all the great fighters coming out of Detroit. The presence of boxing was heavy in Grand Rapids."

Mathematics: "I used to box as an amateur. At the time, I was small. I was 126 pounds. But I never entered the Golden Gloves. My brother, Barice Waller [known by the stage name "Infinite"], was a serious fighter. He came in second at the New York Golden Gloves in 1985. We came up in Southside Queens and everyone looked up to him. He used to train in Queens and out in Brownsville. He even sparred with Big Daddy Bowe. Mark Breland, who was an ill boxer, was out there at the time as well. Me and my brother used to always run into Mitch Green in Southside as well. But I didn't take it as serious as my brother. I was drinking a lot of 40s at the time. When I was fifteen, I was deejaying in the projects. I was out late, hanging out at the parks. My brother was up in the morning doing his jogging. I saw from my brother [that] boxing, like hip-hop, was a 24-7 commitment and I couldn't do both."

In talking with each member of the Wu inner circle, I was reminded that world-class boxers and world-class beatmakers often walked the same streets on their paths to stardom. Boxing has always drawn from the economically disadvantaged—very few champion boxers come from privileged backgrounds. The same can be said for hip-hop, whose talent pool has been mostly composed of minorities from disenfranchised communities. The rhythm of both worlds, the sensibilities required to survive the daily struggle, are the same. It shouldn't be a surprise, then, that hip-hop music eventually found its way into boxing gyms around the country.

* * *

In my conversations with rappers, beatmakers, and boxers alike, the subject of volume came up often. Hip-hop music, born in the booming block parties of the South Bronx, is designed to pound through speakers. The music is expected to be played loudly, a perfect match for the chaotic soundscape of a crowded boxing gym.

"I'm a hip-hop-influenced person. During all of my boxing endeavors, I always played the music in the gym and probably played it louder than most," Zab Judah insisted.

Former light heavyweight champion Montell Griffin, who trains fighters at Windy City Boxing Club in his hometown of Chicago, provided a similar take.

"I must be getting old because now that I train fighters I turn the music down when they spar. When I was fighting, I hated when Eddie Futch turned down the music. When I was boxing, I wanted to listen to the loudest and most vicious and nastiest and dirtiest lyrics, [ones] that got me ready to spar and fight. I wanted the volume way up," Griffin said.

In boxing gyms around the country, the battle for the volume knob is, of course, not always won by the fighter—a fact I was reminded of in my conversation with Brooklyn brawler Heather "The Heat" Hardy, who just happens to have a Wu-Tang logo tattooed prominently on her back right shoulder.

"We're not allowed to listen to music in the gym," Hardy told me. "When you're boxing, you're at school. My coaches would slap the shit out of me if I put on loud music because that means I'm not listening to them. For me, hip-hop is my companion during conditioning, running. I listen to '90s hip-hop when I'm doing roadwork. Biggie. Pac. N.W.A. Ain't nothing like the rappers from that era. Music talks me through my moods. It gets you through roadwork. It's like they say, music is the only thing that doesn't let you down."

As for the Wu-Tang tattoo, Hardy said the following: "I'm a fan of all '90s rap. Wu-Tang. Tupac. Biggie. Nas. It was such a big part of my childhood. Riding bikes, holding the boombox. But the reason behind the Wu-Tang symbol is my cousin, Thomas Olson, who died in the summer of 2016, on his thirty-fifth birthday. We grew up together. We were best friends. It really hit me hard. And a couple of months later, I heard [Wu-Tang's] "Triumph" and thought of him. It took me fifteen minutes to stop crying. That Wu-Tang symbol represents a time in my life."

How and why a particular style of music motivates a fighter varies from culture to culture and from person to person. Some fighters are energized by the pounding bass, others get inspiration from the lyrics.

"I listened to nothing but hardcore banging beats from my friends Dr. Dre, N.W.A, Ice Cube, Ice-T, Too Short, [and] the Geto Boys. That was my playlist," former middleweight and cruiserweight champion James "Lights Out" Toney told me. "It was always the beat that got me going and can't nobody top Dr. Dre. *The Chronic*, that album right there, I have literally trained to nothing but that album on repeat. Every beat on that album was a banger. You get that extra boost of energy from the beat."

Former welterweight champion Kermit Cintrón: "I always found music helpful with my rhythm. You'd be hitting the bag or the mitts and it would help you moving around. It would help with your rhythm and timing. For me, it was a little bit of Spanish music, a little bit of hip-hop. My first trainer, Marshall, was all about having the music on loud. Emanuel Steward let you put the music on but not too loud. Same with Ronnie Shields. Have it on, just not loud. But all of my trainers understood music's importance."

In talking hip-hop with Cintrón, who was born on the island of Puerto Rico but moved to northern Pennsylvania at the age of eight, I was unsurprised by the hard-punching welterweight's taste in rap music. The artists Cintrón trained to are, in every way, emblematic of his unique cultural and ethnic identity.

Cintrón: "On the hip-hop side of things. I loved Big Pun. Fat Joe. I was listening to Big Pun when I was boxing in the amateurs, and I still listen to him today. Those guys were a good group of rap artists. They were the first to represent Puerto Rican culture. For the Spanish hip-hop music, it was Daddy Yankee, Don Omar, or anything reggaeton."

This sentiment, a deep-seated love for rap music that blends hip-hop sensibilities with Puerto Rican culture, appeared equally in my conversation with Hector Camacho Jr., the son of boxing's most polarizing showman.

Camacho Jr.: "That entire movement was major. [Fat] Joe, N.O.R.E., and especially Big Pun. They broke down barriers. They were game changers. I've chilled with N.O.R.E. a couple of times. Joe as well. And I came to the ring to Big Pun's "100%" song too. Being Puerto Rican, and being from New York City, I was proud of them. I loved the way that movement crossed over. One guy who deserves more credit is DJ Tony Touch. He had his Spanglish mix tapes [and] then of course you had guys like Daddy Yankee doing remixes with Snoop."

Cultural and ethnic affiliations aside, many fighters are inspired by artists they can identify with on a personal level. These boxers find inspiration from the life experiences detailed in the music. Among these fighters, Yonkers-native Earl Simmons, better known as DMX, was a favorite. Along with his aggressive style and gruff delivery, DMX's catalog tells the story of a long and arduous journey from the streets to the limelight, peaks and valleys—all part of a boxer's rise to the top of the sport.

"Hip-hop wasn't just hype music for me. Some fighters use the music just for the beat. I was attracted to the lyrics. I always trained to DMX," former undisputed middleweight champion Bernard Hopkins told me. "I came out to DMX for a lot of fights. I felt his pain. Ninety-nine-percent of those songs I can relate to. In training camp, I wasn't moved by songs about bitches and hoes. My drive and motivation for listening to rap music wasn't about champagne and who's ballin' and all that. I was more on the side of the rough stuff, the streets."

Former junior welterweight champion Demarcus "Chop Chop" Corley: "DMX was a favorite artist of mine during training. What he was singing was coming from his heart. I could relate to what he had been through growing up in New York. He used to be on drugs, he used to rob people, but hip-hop changed his life. Growing up in D.C., my life was brought up in poverty. I was shot. I came up around drugs and violence and poverty. I had a chance to see death up close and personal, multiple times. And I had a choice, which thing I wanted to do. And I made a choice early in life. I was going to be boxer. That's why X inspired me."

Regardless of whether they are attracted to bass or biographies, the boxers I talked to agreed unanimously that music—of any rhythmic variety—enhances a fighter's performance in the gym. Chop Chop Corley, for example, cited Sonny Liston's famous jump-rope routine without being prompted.

To further make his point, Corley raised the example of boxing's original pound-for-pound king, Sugar Ray Robinson: "The fighter has to understand the rhythm of the music can be used in training. Sugar Ray Robinson understood that when he was dancing and performing. He didn't tap dance for nothing. He had a rhythm. Nobody back then knew he was doing that for footwork and rhythm. Me, I've always loved music and I've always had rhythm. You have to find your rhythm in boxing. Me training as a kid, ten or eleven years old, I would be shadowboxing in the living room and my mother would have on some James Brown or Rick James. That's where I found my rhythm. Then when I got older and became a professional fighter, it was hip-hop. For me, music is necessary to training."

Chop Chop's former opponent, Zab Judah, echoed his position: "Fighting is about rhythm. It goes hand in hand. It's a very similar situation. Fighting is music. When I would get to moving around, my coach would always say, 'There he go, playin' that music.' That's when I had everything going and started putting it all together."

✳ ✳ ✳

The story of how hip-hop music became the official soundtrack to boxing gyms around the world parallels the culture's meteoric rise to mainstream popularity. Long before rap music took over the Billboard charts, break dancing captured the imagination of the American public. In the early days of hip-hop, the emerging dance form served as the main physical expression of the culture's rhythmic sensibilities. Pioneering DJs such as DJ Kool Herc, Afrika Bambaataa, and Grandmaster Flash perfected the art of isolating the breakdown beats in the records they played at block parties. Those who danced to the rhythms came to be known as break-dancers. Hip-hop music, in its infancy, was not made for the ears of radio listeners—it was constructed with the improvisational wit and athleticism of break-dancers in mind.

The art of break dancing matches the rhythmic movements of shadowboxing, a key component of boxing training. In "Physical Graffiti: The History of Hip Hop Dance," Jorge "Popmaster Fabel" Pabon outlines the uniquely competitive, and overtly confrontational, aspects of the dance form. The most obvious connection between break dancing and shadowboxing is exemplified in the subgenre known as rocking, or uprocking, where two opponents face each other and engage in a "war dance consisting of a series of steps, jerks, and the miming of weapons drawn against each other."[31] Battles, a staple of the tradition, have always maintained both imaginative and competitive elements. You could easily describe uprocking as an improvisational kata (choreographed karate), coordinated to the beat of a musical selection. In this respect, hip-hop music is arguably the perfect soundtrack for the sharp and rhythmic cadence of shadowboxing. Even the physical act of rapping lends itself to rhythmic movement. The fit, as Chop Chop Corley reminded me, is perfect.

"I was into break dancing as a kid. But in D.C. we mostly had go-go music. It was hard to shadowbox to that music—it has too much of a up-tempo beat. Hip-hop was a better fit for shadowboxing," Corley said.

Just as boxers are drawn to hip-hop music during their workouts, many emcees are drawn to boxing as a main source of exercise. Meek Mill, Big Sean, Ludacris, and 50 Cent, who boxed as an amateur, have all posted videos and images of their boxing workouts on social media. To discuss this phenomenon, I turned to former WBO heavyweight champion Michael Bentt. After his career as a professional boxer ended abruptly in 1994 because of a brain injury, Bentt turned to acting and landed the coveted role of Sonny Liston in Michael Mann's 2000 *Muhammad Ali* biopic. In the film, Ali was played by hip-hop-star-turned-actor Will Smith. In helping Smith transform into Muhammad Ali, Bentt found a new career. Today the former champion is a high-profile personal trainer for stars, and a number of his clients are prominent hip-hop figures.

"Heavy D was my most committed client," Bentt told me. "I met Heavy when I was doing the Ali film with Michael Mann. He was such a down-to-earth, sweet guy. He was a friend of Will Smith. Heavy was a big boxing fan. At first, I don't think he felt like he belonged there. James Toney and the other boxers were on the set. He was a little timid. Heavy hadn't tapped into that side of himself yet. He saw Will doing it and he dug it so I started working with him for a few years. I was a big fan of his album *Vibes* so I said, 'let's do it.' That experience led me to training other hip-hop guys. I used to train Damon Dash, for example. I know that Jay-Z was doing boxing workouts at the time too. All of these guys are massive boxing fans. But the best hip-hop guy I ever trained was Heavy D.

He had good timing for a big guy, he could relax during pressure. For a civilian, he had nice hands."

With respect to Bentt's work with rappers Will Smith and Heavy D, the most famous example of such a pairing is likely the Detroit-based combination of Emanuel Steward and Marshall Mathers, better known as Eminem. In preparing for a role in the movie *Southpaw*, Mathers hired the legendary Kronk trainer, along with former lightweight world champion Hilmer Kenty, to help turn him into a believable boxer on the silver screen.

On Mike Tyson's popular Hotboxin' podcast, recorded in February 2020, Eminem reflected on the experience: "I've been boxing for thirteen years, sparring and messing around. I learned from Emanuel Steward. He was such a nice dude. He would come over to my house and we would spar twice a week. He would bring his boxers from the Kronk Gym. He would show me the basics. And it took a long fucking time for me to just learn the basics. They were just up-and-coming kids. I mean, I was getting my ass kicked but I could hang with them. I was getting some hits in [laughs]."[32]

While *Southpaw* was originally green-lit with Marshall Mathers as the star, production on the film was delayed by a number of personal and professional setbacks and the lead role eventually went to actor Jake Gyllenhaal. Largely because of his love for the sport of boxing, Mathers didn't disappear from the project. Instead, the Detroit rapper decided to executive produce the soundtrack, which included his boxing-themed single "Phenomenal."

"I heard the stories when I was working with Emanuel. He would go to Eminem's house and train him. I heard Emanuel tell people he had good hands," Kermit Cintrón said.

"No joke, Hilmer Kenty once told me Em was talented. He co-signed that Em actually had some skills. Em took it serious," former Steward disciple and Mike Tyson entourage member John Lepak added, outlining the rap star's commitment to training.

Long before R&B star Usher played the role of Sugar Ray Leonard in the Roberto Duran biopic *Hands of Stone*, singers and rappers alike were showing off their boxing skills in music videos. For example, in the music video for "Undisputed," Ludacris's second single from his acclaimed album *Theater of the Mind*, the Atlanta rap star receives a private boxing lesson from Floyd Mayweather. On the track and in the video, Mayweather serves as a cornerman, giving inspiration in between verses. In brief clips sprinkled in the video, Ludacris hits the mitts with Roger Mayweather, pounds a heavy bag held by Floyd, and raps his way around the Money Team boxing ring. Luda even puts in some early morning roadwork on the Las Vegas strip, as Mayweather plays hype man in a luxury convertible.

The Ludacris–Mayweather pairing was hardly new territory in hip-hop. Rapper Canibus and Mike Tyson pulled a similar move in their 1998 video for "Second Round K.O.," a diss track aimed at LL Cool J. In the video, Canibus, assisted by hype-man vocals from Tyson, hits the mitts and speed bag, skips rope, does push-ups, and raps in a boxing ring and in between swinging heavy bags. In a visual montage similar to one in a Rocky Balboa movie, Canibus and Tyson run on the beach as the rapper gradually improves his skills. Even Fugees star Wyclef Jean makes a cameo as a ring announcer, flipping Michael Buffer's famous phrase to fit the occasion: "Let's Get Ready to Battle!"

Ironically, it was LL Cool J who established the boxing gym motif in his groundbreaking 1991 video for "Mama Said Knock You Out." The minimalist video features LL Cool J rapping into a 1920s style microphone at center ring. Shot in black-and-white, the video shows off the Queens rapper's muscular physique, splicing in clips of boxing matches and LL Cool J working out.

In his 1998 biography, *I Make My Own Rules*, LL Cool J said the idea for the song was inspired by a conversation with his grandmother. Feeling frustration because of the poor critical reception of his third album, *Walking with a Panther*, LL Cool J expressed concern that he was no longer relevant in the rap game.

"Oh baby, just knock them out!" his grandmother famously replied.

"I was already energized when we went to record, but her advice was in the back of my mind," LL Cool J reflected.

The song's opening lines, "Don't call it a comeback / I been here for years," are arguably just as iconic as the video itself, which juxtaposed the worlds of boxing and hip-hop for the first time. It's no coincidence, then, that the music video most noted for fusing hip-hop and boxing came when the rapper's back was up against the metaphorical ropes. At the time LL recorded the track, he was also transforming physically, adding a strict weightlifting and boxing-training regimen to his daily life.

"I noticed that [LL Cool J] started to physically build himself up before that song. When we started working with him, he was sixteen years old. He was long and lean. He wasn't a thick guy at all," remembered Bill Adler, director of publicity for Def Jam Records. "When he started with us [Def Jam], his DJ was Cut Creator, who was not as tall as he was thick, a former football player. He was a nice, calm guy but if you riled him you would be in trouble. I'm pretty sure, his musical chores aside, Cut Creator's job was to roll with [LL Cool J] because he would run his mouth and couldn't back it up. That's what used to happen. He was not notably built in 1984, when he started recording. He spent a lot of time building his body up, leading into that video."

Adler continued: "[LL Cool J] was coming off some negative reactions to his previous album. Before *Mama Said Knock You Out*, he also had beefs with Ice T and Kool Moe Dee. Rap is competitive. I think he felt that he had to sharpen up his rap game but also wanted to be physically stronger as well. So, that's where the boxing training came in."

"I definitely had a chip on my shoulder," LL Cool J remembered. "The video was about the microphone, about the performance, and about getting busy. So we had boxers getting hit, and me knocking out the mic. And that felt right to me. And then a lot of angles. I asked Paris [Barclay] to take it to another level when we were inspired by that *Raging Bull* motif."[33]

The end product was one of LL Cool J's most successful records, a song that solidified his place in the rap game, propelling a recording career that would span four decades.

"A fighter's DNA can be found in every facet of hip-hop," Bill Adler told me. "It is fighting in the arts, instead of the ring, but the mentality is the same. The key thing to understand is that hip-hop was pretty self-consciously channeling physical aggression into the arts. Every single one of the original hip-hop arts—graffiti, deejaying, breakdancing, and emceeing—all of that stuff was super-competitive. For the most part, the folks who did it were competitive but sought these areas to avoid physical violence. It is something [Afrika] Bambaataa has talked about. He was a guy who had been in a gang. He came to deplore the violence. It was a conscious decision. He turned to the arts instead. Both arenas [hip-hop and boxing] are driven by testosterone-maddening competition."

Hip-hop, as evidenced by LL Cool J's song "Mama Said Knock You Out," is music made with physical competition in mind. From its rhythmic influence on training, to its metaphoric significance in videos, rap music is inextricably intertwined with boxing. The influence of LL Cool J's song is unquantifiable. Fighters from all racial, cultural, and ethnic backgrounds still find the song perfect for training.

On September 3, 2020, to celebrate the thirtieth anniversary of LL Cool J's fourth album, the rapper and his Sirius XM radio station, Rock The Bells, teamed up with Everlast to release a series of limited-edition boxing robes. Designed by Alexander-John, the collection uses the same graphic design as the album's iconic cover. "Don't Call It a Comeback" is stitched prominently on the back of the robe.

For the social media rollout, LL Cool J and Rock The Bells asked boxers Gabriel Rosado, Andre Dirrell, Andre Berto, Abner Mares, and Mikey Garcia to model the robes and reflect on what the song has meant to the sport.

"It's iconic and definitely a record that we used to play on a regular basis to get motivated for these tournaments, and to give us the inspiration to get in that gym and just put that pressure on," Andre Berto said.[34]

"My grandfather put me on to it. I was six or seven years old when this damn song came out. But we all knew it. It played in the gym often. My grandfather always played it. He loves songs by LL Cool J, Dr. Dre, you name it," Andre Dirrell added.[35]

"I feel like this is an anthem song. That's the first thing that pops in my head. I'm an '80s kid, I'm thirty-four, and all I see is Roy Jones Jr. walking in that ring playing this song. Or him working in the gym. It's boxing," said Abner Mares.[36]

Mikey Garcia, summarizing perfectly hip-hop's unique place in boxing gyms worldwide, said, "The first time I ever heard 'Mama Said Knock You Out' was in the movie *Gladiator*—not the Russell Crowe one—the boxing one. I'm watching the movie and it's about boxing so it's obviously attractive to me. In one of the fight scenes, a fighter comes out to that song. That was the first time I heard that. Once you're in the gym, you're not going to be working out to some love songs. You got to have some rhythm, some beat that can hype you up, and that can motivate you to train hard."[37]

WALK THIS WAY

For much of the late 1980s and early 1990s, the love affair between hip-hop and boxing was largely relegated to the gym. Today the energy and inspiration fighters get from the music is on full display. It would be almost impossible to watch a fight card in the United States without seeing a ring walk that features hip-hop music. Hip-hop, now more than ever, is a key component of the sport's showmanship. In my conversations with fighters, I wanted to know the thought process they used to select their songs. The formula for some was simple.

"I never put that much thought into it. I would go to the clubs. Whatever made the club go crazy. That was going to be my song for the next fight," Zab Judah said, laughing.

Judah's method isn't anomalous. Entry music often indicates what music is popular in the streets.

"I'll be honest, I just walked out to whatever was the hottest song at the time," Montell Griffin told me. "When I fought Roy [Jones Jr.] I walked out to Crucial Conflict. I had an opportunity to meet them and they were appreciative. When I fought [James] Toney, I came out to Wu-Tang; they were probably my favorite group at the time. Back in 1997, I met RZA, Method Man, Ghostface, and Rae. I was at a magic show in Vegas, and I was coming up the escalator and I heard somebody say, 'There go the guy who beat Roy Jones,' and it was Method Man. I was never no household name. I was just a regular guy. The fact that Method Man knew my name blew my mind."

As hip-hop gained global popularity in the mid-1990s, rap dominated ring-walk music in professional boxing. Fighters turned to their favorite rap artists to add drama to their entrances—with varying degrees of success.

"[Dr.] Dre actually did a song for me," James Toney recalled. "He had my name in it and all that. I was going to walk to the ring to it but back then the [Nevada] commission wouldn't allow it. It was for my fight with Prince Charles Williams in 1994. Things were different back then; they wouldn't play the records with cursing, and we didn't have an edited version."

As opposed to hyping the crowd, some boxers use their entrance music to send a message to the opponent. When it came time for sonic intimidation, Hall-of-Fame champion Bernard Hopkins often turned to his favorite rapper, Ruff Ryders' front man DMX.

"'X Gon' Give It to Ya.' I think I got like ten ring walks out of that song. DMX's first four CDs were unbelievable. I was the executioner and he was 'X' so that song just fit," Hopkins said. "I'm the champ, you're in the ring waiting, and *X Gon' Give It to Ya*. It never happened, but I was always trying some way to find a way to get DMX to come out on one of those ring walks."

In talking with some of hip-hop's pioneering legends, I also discovered that rappers pay attention to ring-walk music. Having your song selected for a ring walk is, for some rap stars, a badge of honor.

Big Daddy Kane: "Shout out to B-Hop [Bernard Hopkins] for coming out to my joint 'Young, Gifted and Black.' I will never forget that, watching it on TV. I was a B-Hop fan before we met. He was a technical beast in the ring. He confused fighters in the ring. Before one of his fights, me and Hopkins met in Vegas. He told me he used to listen to my stuff. Then, later on, he came out to my song. I felt like, 'Wow, that's love.' That meant a lot to me."

The theatrics James Toney and Bernard Hopkins couldn't achieve in the late 1990s are now, of course, commonplace in the sport. For millennials, the hip-hop ring walk has become something of an expectation.

Lil Wayne, French Montana, Rick Ross, Migos, and Kodak Black have all performed mini-concerts for boxers entering the ring for championship bouts. It would be wrong, however, to suggest that this tradition is only about showmanship. Some hip-hop entrances are more personal and symbolic.

For his first shot at the heavyweight championship, for example, Deontay Wilder walked to the ring to an original rap song titled "Bomb Squad" that was written by a childhood friend, an aspiring rapper known by his stage name Amp.

"Amp is a good friend of mine that came up in the amateurs with me. After making the national team, traveling on the way home, he was struck by a drunk driver, which paralyzed him from the waist down," Wilder told Showtime analysts during the prefight meeting.[38]

With dreams of becoming the first U.S.-born heavyweight to capture a major belt in over ten years, Wilder was escorted to the ring by Amp, who delivered the lyrics to his song from a wheelchair.

"He's a special guy. He's about to be the heavyweight champion of the world. But he thought of me. He gave me my mojo back. I will forever be grateful for that," Amp later reflected.[39]

After Deontay Wilder claimed the WBC title, the hip-hop ring walks continued. For his rematch with Bermane Stiverne, Wilder walked to the ring with 50 Cent. For his first showdown with Cuban slugger Luis "King Kong" Ortiz, Wilder was escorted to the ring by Brooklyn icon Lil' Kim. In his first bout with Tyson Fury, Wilder walked to the ring to a live performance of Jay Rock's West Coast anthem "WIN." Today, you might be pressed to find a big-time pay-per-view card that doesn't pair hip-hop and boxing in some fashion. It wasn't always this way, of course. Hip-hop's ring-walk takeover came gradually.

＊ ＊ ＊

During the late 1980s and early 1990s, playing unedited rap music at a professional boxing match was, as James Toney said, still taboo. Even among prominent Black fighters of the time, generational and cultural divides were taking place.

"I always listened to music when I trained," Tim Witherspoon, who won the WBC heavyweight championship in 1984, told me. "It got me motivated and moving in the right direction. But I didn't really like the hard rap that was becoming popular at the time. I did listen to some of it. Rap was just coming around back then. For me, it was the oldies but goodies, the Motown era. I was on the borderline of the rap era."

Former WBC heavyweight champion Chris Byrd, thirteen years younger than Witherspoon, was also drawn to the rhythm of hip-hop music but was taken aback by some of the messages being promoted in so-called gangsta rap.

Chris Byrd: "In the gym, my inspiration was Christian rap music. Rap music heavily influenced the training that I did. You had artists like Corey Red, who was my favorite. In regard to the non-Christian stuff, I was a big East Coast guy. Rakim was my favorite rapper ever. Picking my [ring walk] song, for me, was an important part of the training process. It had to be something that could move the crowd but also make them think. I've walked to the ring to Rakim's 'No Competition.' Rakim's 'I Ain't No Joke.' My favorite was 'Put Your Hands Together.' I loved the hardness of the rap, but without the cursing. I loved that era, [Big Daddy] Kane and all them. Rakim was the Mike Tyson of that era. Crushing all competition. I liked it because it was hardcore but without all of that stupid thug stuff."

Like Evander Holyfield before him, Chris Byrd didn't shy away from his Christian identity with the media. For Holyfield's 1993 rematch with Riddick Bowe, the former undisputed champion walked to the ring with MC Hammer, whose hit song "Pray" gave way to the rise of a Christian-themed subgenre of rap music. For Byrd's ring debut, earlier that same year, the slick boxer's choice in hip-hop ring-walk music was Holyfield-esque, to say the least.

"For my first professional fight, I came into the ring to PM Dawn's "After I Die." I wasn't a Christian at the time but the song must have been setting me up to be a Christian," Byrd chuckled.

Despite its persistence over the past three decades, the hip-hop ring walk continues to receive mixed reviews from boxers and rappers alike. For some, the pairing provides an extra layer of drama before the opening bell. For others, the tradition is more symbolically important than aesthetically enjoyable.

James Toney: "I love it. Hip-hop pays homage to us in the music and we pay homage to them. As a fan of both games, I love it when fighters bring out rappers."

Bronze Nazareth: "I love it. Me, as a hip-hop head, I look forward to that shit. Who is Wilder gonna bring out? Who is Floyd gonna bring out? I look for that. I even like to listen for what they play in between rounds. When you are in the arena, that shit gives you energy."

Inspectah Deck: "It's cool but I be thinking certain rappers they walk out with be jinxing them. They come into the ring gassed off that corny shit and get they legs taken. These dudes come in doing all types of craziness, like [Adrien] Broner, and get take up out of there. You gotta choose wisely."

For many detractors, it is the acoustics, not the lyrics, that are off-putting. Depending on the setup, many hip-hop ring walks are largely inaudible to those who are not in the arena

"Terrible. I don't like it at all. It's terrible. Period. The sound is off. Most of the time, it looks stupid. It's just corny to me," Bronx rapper Peter Gunz argued. "As a fan, I *do* care about the music somebody comes out to. I do care about that. But most of the time, the song doesn't match the energy anyway. I like the idea of hip-hop music at fights but I don't like the artists performing. I don't like the look of it. It isn't the proper presentation of a live hip-hop performance."

Vinnie Paz: "I still don't think they have mastered it yet. Most of the time, it sounds horrible, really bad. Most dudes are rhyming over the recorded vocals. What I think is an iller idea is playing the song and have the artist walk with the boxer. For instance, if I wanted to have Kool G Rap come out with me, I would just play his track and have him walk out as part of the entourage."

Chris Byrd: "If I could have had Rakim walk me to the ring of course I would have done it. But I wouldn't have had him rapping the track. I don't like when they rap during the ring walk. It doesn't sound as good as it does on your playlist, or whatever. It just doesn't sound good."

Others contended the prefight theatrics that come with hip-hop ring walks are an unnecessary distraction for boxers, taking their focus away from the danger that awaits in the ring.

Michael Bentt: "You don't need all the superficial stuff. Look at what happened to Wilder in the Fury rematch. You don't need the costumes and all that. Boxing is a lonely and dangerous sport. All the music and hip-hop is a distraction. You do that after the fight. Hang out with rappers after the fight. If I was training a fighter, I would advise him to go the other way."

Kermit Cintrón: "I was never that concerned with how I looked and my robe and my hair and all that. Today's fighters, they are gonna spend the money and have those guys walk them out. But that's not my style. I was focused on business."

For contemporary boxing fans, recalling the days before ring walks were part of the show isn't easy. In fact, it's almost impossible to imagine boxing minus the music.

In a 2018 *Sporting News* piece, "The Evolution of the Ring Walk," Thomas Hauser reminded readers that, "Once upon a time, even for boxing's biggest fights, ring walks were a straightforward matter. There was no entourage, no one pushing and shoving to get in front of a TV camera. The trainer led the way. The fighter put his hands on the trainer's shoulders, and they walked to the ring with the other cornermen behind them."

In the piece, Hauser cites Ralph Dupas—a welterweight from New Orleans who fought in the 1950s and '60s and was known to enter the ring to blues music—as one of the forefathers of the tradition. Hauser also notes that late in his career, for a title defense against Earnie Shavers, Muhammad Ali walked to the ring to the theme song from *Star Wars*. Mexican fighters such as Julio César Chávez and Oscar De La Hoya, who famously entered the ring accompanied by mariachi bands, are also listed as key contributors to the tradition.

In my conversation with rapper Inspectah Deck, the Wu-Tang lyricist offered a slightly different take on the origins and allure of boxing's pre-fight theatrics: "I remember Oscar [De La Hoya] coming to the ring to that authentic Mexican shit. I liked that. But a lot of this stuff you are seeing today comes from professional wrestling. As a kid, I just liked the names in boxing. 'Smokin' Joe Frazier. 'Razor' Ruddock. 'Iron' Mike Tyson. Hector 'Macho' Camacho. Roberto 'Hands of Stone' Duran. Wrestling was the other side. Kids like me loved wrestling because they had those names," Deck said. "They had the music and all that too. You watch a Duran fight and you say, 'I see why they call him that.' Tommy 'The Hitman' Hearns. I see why they call him that. 'Float like a butterfly, sting like a bee.' I get it. It's like Wu-Tang, we got more names than anybody. It's the same thing. Your name tips you. You have to live up to that. It's your calling card. Same as the entry music. The audience knows you got to live up to that sound."

Deck's argument reminded me that Muhammad Ali, as a youngster in Louisville, Kentucky, borrowed much of his act from professional wrestler Gorgeous George. As Deck correctly points out, hip-hop also keeps one eye on wrestling. Buffalo, New York, rappers Westside Gunn, Benny the Butcher, and Conway the Machine, for example, often mix wrestling clips and soundbites into their music. Westside Gunn, more specifically, has named several of his songs after legendary wrestling matches (e.g., "Undertaker vs. Goldberg" and "Flair vs. Michaels"). Virginia-based rapper Pusha T also pays homage to wrestler Ric Flair with his famous ad-lib "Wooo." Mixing boxing and professional wrestling references isn't uncommon in hip-hop. In his single "Mr. Carter," for example, Lil Wayne name-drops both Hector "Macho" Camacho and wrestler "Macho Man" Randy Savage.

For those of us who grew up in the 1980s during hip-hop's infancy, Hector "Macho" Camacho was the boxer who most closely followed the WWE playbook of self-promotion. From his flamboyant jewelry and cocky personality, to his over-the-top entrances, Camacho made the ring walk a key component of the sport. According to his son, Hector Camacho Jr., hip-hop culture held a major presence in Spanish Harlem. "Macho Time" was part of the hip-hop scene, Junior argues.

"I was born in 1978. Hip-hop was a movement for us. I grew up in the same building as Doug E. Fresh's son. I was a big hip-hop head. It was all around us. I feel proud every time I hear my father's name in the lyrics of some of the top hip-hop artists of the day. Dipset. Nas. AZ. Biggie. Lil Wayne. They have all mentioned my father in the music," Junior told me. "I believe it was my father's style that brought hip-hop to him. His Macho nameplate in the '80s. I believe he made a big impact on a lot of rappers in that time. The bling. The style. Those ring entrances in his wild gear. My father's ring walks were special. Entertainment at its best. My father even did a rap video with the Fat Boys. I recall he was into the break-dancing era. My father *was* hip-hop."

In a separate interview, boxing historian Aris Pina, who often has the best seat in the house because of his work as a CompuBox punch-counter, added to Junior's assessment of his father's role in shaping the hip-hop tradition that is now commonplace in the sport.

"Camacho was the one who originally brought the glitz and glamour. People took notice. He helped lay the foundation for what we see today,"

Pina said. "It's like any big sporting event where they have a live band. I was there, working, when French Montana brought [Adrien] Broner to the ring. People treat it like a concert and a fight. It's the whole atmosphere. That's what makes hip-hop and boxing work so well together. Fans dress up for it and get excited for it."

To better understand the impact of hip-hop music in the boxing arena, I sought the perspective of Justin Hoffman, the official live DJ of promoter Top Rank Inc. A lifelong fan of rap music, Hoffman, for well over a decade, has provided Top Rank shows with the concert-like atmosphere Pina described to me.

"It all started with Miguel Cotto vs. Zab Judah [June 9, 2007]," Justin Hoffman told me. "At the time, I was deejaying at Tryst, Todd duBoef went there all the time. He heard me play and asked the general manager if he could talk to me about music. So, we set up a meeting at Top Rank. At first, he just asked me if we could make up a CD, or mixtape, for in between rounds. I said, 'That's easy but what about having me there, live. Who's fighting?' When he told me that it would be for Cotto and Judah, I instantly said, 'Todd, this is Brooklyn vs. Puerto Rico, on the eve of the Puerto Rican Day Parade in New York City. I know exactly what to do, exactly how to play for this crowd.' We had never done it before, so everything was brand new so we were just feeling it out. So, for that fight, I just played between fights, between rounds. I got out all of my Brooklyn rappers and put it all together. My Biggie. My Jay. Black Moon. And mixed it with the Reggaeton records. That night, Todd knew it right there, what I was doing was working, and he said, 'Let's do this for every Top Rank fight.'"

In subsequent years, Hoffman has looked to perfect his formula, fusing his love for music with his passion for the sweet science. "At first, it was so different compared to the clubs. I was playing all the big clubs in Vegas. But *this* energy was different. Sometimes I play for the location of the fight, sometimes its nationality. The club has its own persona. With boxing, I always do my research. I make sure I'm aware of the ethnicities, the backgrounds, and the fan bases of each fighter. It's not always hip-hop that I'm playing. If it's a Tyson Fury crowd, it's a little bit of Oasis, Blur, mixed with hip-hop. If we are in Minnesota, for example, I'll mix in some Prince. But hip-hop artists like Jay-Z, DMX, Wu-Tang always get the biggest response from boxing fans."

Today, Hoffman does more than simply deejay in between rounds. He also works closely with Top Rank fighters, both planning and playing their walk-out theme songs.

"A lot of them [boxers] put serious thought into their walk-out music," Hoffman told me. "I love the fact that Top Rank respects this part of the show. Some fighters choose incredibly epic walk-out music. Tyson Fury, for example. With him, I don't even say a word. That guy knows how to put on a show. With some fighters I will give a suggestion. Teófimo López, when he fought Vasyl Lomachenko, wanted to come out to 'Another One Bites the Dust.' I said, 'Great idea, but you are from Brooklyn, let's let everyone know that.' I said, 'let's go into the studio and put Biggie doing 'Where Brooklyn At!!' over the track.' In the end, I think it came out beautiful."

This unique collision of cultural forces, aided by the work of DJs such as Hoffman, has helped to make hip-hop music a leading, if not *the* leading, influencer in boxing. It is a bond that transcends racial, ethnic, and cultural barriers. Dmitriy Salita, for example, once walked to the ring to the sounds of Orthodox Jewish rapper Matisyahu, hip-hop's first Hasidic emcee. For Anthony Joshua's massive ring walk for his bout with Alexander Povetkin, fans at Wembley Stadium were treated to a performance of "I See You Shining" by UK rapper Nines. In a bout televised on Fox Sports, Australian Billy Dib, who was at one point managed by 50 Cent, walked to the ring to an original track by Ruff Ryder artist Quadir Lateef. "Themes of space and place are profoundly important to hip-hop," scholar Murray Forman writes.[40] The same can be said for professional boxing.

For the hip-hop generation, one boxer stands alone. Without the influence of Mike Tyson, there would be no modern hip-hop ring walk.

"Let's put it like this, Brooklyn is a very lively place. When Mike Tyson was fighting, nobody was in the street. Nobody! That's one time when Brooklyn was quiet," Masta Killa told me. "And it didn't take long before you could get back to doing what you was doing. But, when Tyson fought, everyone was in the house watching the fight. Tyson was hip-hop's first heavyweight champion."

In a separate interview, Vinnie Paz took Masta Killa's assertion one step further, positioning Tyson instead as hip-hop's first athlete: "Mike wasn't just hip-hop's first heavyweight champion. He was hip-hop's first athlete. Mike was the first one to fully embrace it. He was fully reppin' gold fronts. He was fully reppin' Brownsville, Brooklyn. Mike was fully reppin' hip-hop in his entrance themes, to *Welcome to the Terrordome* by Public Enemy to when he got out of jail and came out to Reggie [Redman's *Time 4 Sum Aksion*] and then started coming out to Tupac later on. Mike was wearing Dapper Dan custom suits; he was at Dapper Dan's store when he beat the shit out of Mitch Blood Green. Mike was running with LL [Cool J] back then. Mike was in Harlem. If you want to be technical about it, Mike was hip-hop's first athlete. Period."

Paz continued: "You and I don't know what people were listening to when they were home. But, culturally speaking, Mike was the first. I don't know if there were some New York fighters in the early 1980s listening to Cold Crush Brothers. We will never know that. But we do know Mike was the first athlete publicly reppin' hip-hop culture. That's why hip-hop was drawn to him. Hip-hop loved [Michael] Jordan but Jordan didn't love hip-hop. Mike, on the other hand, was running with rappers. That's why hip-hop will always defend his legacy. We are talking 1985–1990, Mike is the biggest thing in the world, and at that same time we see the globalization of hip-hop. It was lightning in a bottle."

Paz's assertion is hard to refute. Born in Brownsville, Brooklyn, in 1966, Tyson's teenage years coincided with the birth of hip-hop culture. Tyson grew up with the culture taking shape around him. He witnessed hip-hop before it had ever been given a name. On his popular Hotboxin' podcast series, for example, Tyson often speaks about his lifelong love affair with the culture.

"I remember I was in a juvenile detention center when I first heard [Sugarhill Gang's] 'Rappers Delight.' We were like, 'What the fuck was that?' We'd heard the music in the street in our neighborhoods but we never thought it would be on the radio. We were all blown away," Tyson recalled. "Hip-hop gave you pride. Us being at the beginning, it gave us pride. It was on television. People were talking like we talk. I was there when hip-hop started. Those were our people. All of the street urchins, all of the thieves and criminals, the moneymakers and everything, we all listened to it."[41]

Throughout his career, Tyson was involved in news stories that blurred the lines between hip-hop and boxing. In August 1987, less than eight years after hearing the Sugarhill Gang's iconic record for the first time, he joined rap superstars Run-DMC and the Beastie Boys backstage at their groundbreaking Madison Square Garden concert. The new heavyweight champion was invited to the sold-out show as Def Jam's guest of honor. As Tyson's name continued to find its way into hip-hop music, the undefeated champion continued to find his way into the hottest hip-hop spots.

"Mike Tyson is responsible for the moment where rap met boxing," Eric B. told me. "He was the bridge. We all hung out with Tyson. He used to come to Latin Quarters. I will never forget he used to wear this red-and-black Adidas track suit. He got us all into boxing. We didn't want for nothing back then. We walked the streets of New York like dinosaurs. It would be us, all together. DJ Red Alert. Tyson. Eric B. and Rakim, chilling. We would pull up, looking like new money, we had the most expensive cars: we looked like dinosaurs walking around the city! You could see it in people's faces."

"It was an amazing time," recalled Big Daddy Kane. "At that point in the late 1980s, hip-hop had made a big impact on the world. It was like the changing of the guard from the Run-DMC, Fat Boys, Whodini era to the Eric B. and Rakim, Big Daddy Kane, KRS-One, and Public Enemy era. Then you had the emergence of Mike Tyson. All of that was happening at the same time. Everything crossed and meshed. Tyson was hanging out at the Latin Quarters and the Apollo, hanging with the hip-hop artists. The worlds started to mesh. At that time, me and Iran Barkley used to hang out every Wednesday night at the Apollo."

The headlines, of course, weren't always positive. In August 1988 Mike Tyson's infamous street fight with rival Mitch "Blood" Green brought national attention to Dapper Dan's Boutique in Harlem, a legend that is important to the history of both hip-hop and boxing.

"Tyson had adopted 'Don't Believe the Hype' as his official slogan, I remember," Def Jam's Bill Adler said. "He had hooked up with Dan to get that custom jacket. His fight with Mitch Green, outside of the boutique in Harlem, is a major moment, I think, one that helped people recognize the connection between hip-hop and boxing."

By the late 1980s, Dapper Dan, the boutique's proprietor, solidified his place in hip-hop culture by creating custom looks for rap royalty such as LL Cool J, Eric B. & Rakim, The Fat Boys, Salt-N-Pepa, KRS-One, and Big Daddy Kane. Before scrapping with Mitch Green, Tyson had purchased an $800 custom jacket embroidered with the phrase "Don't

Believe the Hype," the title of Public Enemy's hit single. The news story, for better or worse, propelled Dapper Dan into a new stratosphere of public awareness. Before the fight, Dapper Dan's was Harlem's hidden hip-hop hot spot that was open 24-7. After the scuffle, hip-hop's fashion outlaw found himself embroiled in controversy because of a string of counterfeiting raids and litigation.

Recalled Big Daddy Kane: "Back then, Dapper Dan was making all the superfly fashion for so many different rap stars and singers and boxers. Any given day you could see me in there. LL Cool J in there. You might catch Mike Tyson there. He was making the fashions we all was wearing. Something that Dap made, you might see it on a boxer. Some of it was being worn by rappers and NBA players. You would see Anthony Mason in there. We would all be there. I used to like to go in early in the morning or real late at night so that nobody else could see my shit. I didn't want anybody else to say, 'Make me one of those, Dap.' But I would come to pick up my clothes and Rakim might be there. Eric B. LL might be in there. It could be anybody. It was unfortunate that one day Mitch Green happened to be there when Mike showed up."

While Dapper Dan's Boutique was forced to close its doors in 1992, the hip-hop fashion guru has, over the years, continued to influence the boxing world. Aside from Dapper Dan's work with Tyson, contemporary fans are likely to recognize him as the designer of custom trunks and robes for high-profile champions such as Floyd Mayweather and Devin Haney. The media spotlight cast on his store in the summer of 1988 can be interpreted as the unofficial beginning of boxing's hip-hop era.

* * *

Less than a year after his street rematch with Mitch Green, Tyson showed up in his first hip-hop music video. His opponent, an unlikely foe, was a future Golden Globe and two-time Academy Award winner known as the Fresh Prince.

"We [Rush Management] managed DJ Jazzy Jeff and the Fresh Prince," recalled Bill Adler. "It wasn't hard to get press on those guys. 'I Think I Can Beat Mike Tyson' was a deliberately comical record. Will was anything but macho. He was always a good-looking comedian. Nobody back then ever dreamed he would one day play Muhammad Ali in a movie. The idea of Will beating Tyson was just a comical premise, one perfectly suited for a music video."

Long before he earned his place as one of the most prominent and powerful actors in Hollywood, West Philadelphia native Will Smith emerged as one half of the crossover rap duo DJ Jazzy Jeff and the Fresh Prince. Largely because of the success of playful and lighthearted singles such as "Girls Ain't Nothing But Trouble," and "Parents Just Don't Understand," Smith found himself in the unlikely role of a pop star. While some questioned the group's street cred, others applauded the mainstream appeal. The playful songs highlighted Smith's comedic genius, mixing suburban-friendly themes with hip-hop style and braggadocio, earning the group hip-hop's first Grammy Award in 1989.

In "I Think I Can Beat Mike Tyson," the lead single from the group's third studio album, *And in This Corner*, the Philadelphia duo stuck to the offbeat comedic formula. The video begins with the scraggily, out-of-shape Smith attempting to jog up the steps of the Philadelphia Metropolitan Museum of Art, a slapstick version of the famous scene from the Rocky Balboa franchise. The track opens with two aging fight fans, portrayed by DJ Jazzy Jeff and the Fresh Prince, sharing hyperbolic tales of Tyson's punching power.

"I seen him hit this boy, and he hit the boy so hard his head flew off into the eighteenth row! They had to get his head out of the eighteenth row!" one old-timer says.[42]

The undefeated/undisputed champion's mystique, exemplified by his unofficial title of *Baddest Man on the Planet*, is what makes the juxtaposition of his facing the rail-thin, twenty-one-year-old rapper work. In the opening verse, we find Will Smith watching another Tyson first-round knockout, frustrated by the champion's lack of a true challenge. In a moment of misguided hubris the comedic rapper will later regret, Smith makes a call to Don King (who makes a cameo in the video) and signs up as Tyson's next opponent. Tyson and members of his real-life entourage (e.g., Aaron Snowell and Rory Holloway) appear in the press conference scene as well.

In the song and in the video, Tyson's bout with the Fresh Prince doesn't last long. After a few moments of Jerry Lewis–style sticking and moving, Tyson lands one punch to the rapper's body, who soils himself and flees the ring.

"Yes. there were some rumors, stories that ran at the time. Their intention was that Will would knock Tyson out in the video, regardless of what was said on the record. But when Tyson came to the set he wasn't going for it. The answer was—*No!* Will had to take the fall," Adler laughed.

Aside from being a cornerstone moment for boxing and hip-hop, the juvenile rap song is relatively insignificant. Smith's music video wasn't even the first to include a cameo from a professional boxer. Big Daddy Kane's video for "Ain't No Half-Steppin'," for example, which features the Brooklyn rap star hitting the speed bag and battling an opposing emcee in a boxing ring, features a cameo from gold medalist and welterweight champ Mark Breland.

"Before ["I Think I Can Beat Mike Tyson"], you had me putting Mark Breland in my video," said Big Daddy Kane. "Later, MC Hammer having Evander Holyfield in his video. There was a real connection forming. You see, Mark Breland is from my neighborhood. He is a Bed-Stuy vet just like myself. He was someone kids from the neighborhood looked up to. The same way kids felt about me. When we did our first video, Lionel Martin, the director, said the concept was to have me in the boxing ring, so it was a no-brainer. I said, 'We gotta have Bed-Stuy boxing represented. Mark came down with the belts. That part was a surprise. We wasn't expecting him to grab the belts."

The historical significance of "I Think I Can Beat Mike Tyson," you might argue, is that the song and video mark the official arrival of Tyson on the hip-hop scene, the first of many Tyson-themed songs and music-video cameos spanning three decades. The Fresh Prince would serve as "Iron" Mike's first hip-hop KO victim, but not his last. Thirty years after rumbling with Smith, the former heavyweight champion decked rapper Eminem in the music video for "Godzilla" that was released in January 2020.

"Damn, is that you . . . I didn't mean that, sorry," Tyson replies after knocking out the Detroit hip-hop legend, before rushing him to the emergency room where producer Dr. Dre attempts to piece the rapper back together.

Over the years, the two-time heavyweight champion's run-ins with rappers were not strictly relegated to slapstick music videos. On April 24, 1998, fresh off his appearance on Canibus's LL Cool J diss track "Second Round Knockout," Mike Tyson launched Tyson Records.[43] Along with producer and writer Bryson Wilson and music-industry veteran Irving Azoff, Tyson sought to take on the R&B and hip-hop markets. After signing the Baltimore-based R&B duo Protégé and Donnie to the label, Tyson's team hit the streets looking for new talent.

"I didn't know what I was doing. I spent like $20 million on my record company. And nothing," Tyson reflected in 2019.[44]

While the business venture didn't provide a return on Tyson's investment, it did produce several legendary stories with rap stars, one of which was related to me by Peter Gunz, who, along with Lord Tariq, shot up the charts with the smash hit "Deja Vu (Uptown Baby)."

Recalled Peter Gunz: "It's 1998 and I got the number-one rap record in the country. Everything is good. We flying. We touring. The record is all over the place. We land in Vegas to do a show. Before the show, I'm in a lounge, people are bombarding me for pictures and autographs, wanting to talk business with me. By the time we get there, I'm getting frustrated. I'm just wanting to chill. So these artists come over to me; they say they want to do a record with me. So I pointed them to my manager. A little bit later they come back and say, 'We trying to get this done before you leave.' I tell them, 'look, I'm just trying to chill' and I send them on their way. Like five minutes later, they come back with Mike Tyson. Tyson said, 'Look, I don't know who you are, I don't care who you are, but I got a record label and these are my artists. They want to do a record with you, so stop being a fucking asshole. Go do the record and I pay you whatever you want. So, stop being a fucking asshole.'"

Gunz continued, laughing: "I gotta be honest with you, I was intimidated. That's a true story. That was the first time I met Tyson. Back then, I was a fan like everybody else. I didn't even know he had a record label. Not too many men could talk to me like that and walk away . . . but that was Iron Mike. I don't know what became of it. But they paid me a few grand to do a record."

Looking back, Will Smith's "I Think I Can Beat Mike Tyson" is a historical marker. Unbeknownst to many, this pop-cultural artifact foreshadowed the era to come, one in which boxing history and hip-hop culture would become visibly intertwined for the first time.

Hip-hop invited Tyson to the party, so to speak; and in the coming years, the champ would return the favor, bringing hip-hop to boxing.

WELCOME TO THE TERRORDOME

During the three years and three months Mike Tyson reigned as heavyweight champion of the world, hip-hop had yet to claim its place as boxing's entry music of choice. While Tyson cultivated the most menacing ring walk of his era, music had nothing to do with it. In many of Tyson's early title defenses—his showdown with elder statesman Larry Holmes, for example—the young champion chose to forgo entry music altogether. Tyson's march to war was that of a gladiator, his wardrobe spartan: no robe; no socks; black trunks, low-cut black shoes—and, on occasion, a white towel with a hole cut to fit over his head. This no-nonsense approach matched the violent and expressionless countenance Tyson wore to battle. As the knockouts piled up, Tyson's primitive ring walk became a key component of the young star's growing legacy.

It isn't until the back end of his initial reign as champion that we start to see Tyson tinker with the formula. In his 1988 pay-per-view showdown with Michael Spinks, the Brownsville native stormed to the ring amid the ominous tones of an experimental music composition, a soundscape that was like the score of a horror movie.

"It's interesting to note what Mike Tyson selected for his prefight music: just noise. Every once in a while you hear the clanging of chains—I think that's what he's got in mind to do to Mike Spinks's head. Everything that Tyson does is intimidating," boxing commentator "Colonel" Bob Sheridan told listeners.[45]

The man responsible for Tyson's nightmarish walk-out music, Tom Alonso, worked as a composer for the Trump Corporation.[46] Alonso's score was originally created to serve as the backdrop to Trump Plaza's television commercials promoting the bout. After viewing the commercial for the first time, Tyson decided to loop the music for his entrance. Alonso's eerie music lasted longer than the fight.

For his title defense against Carl "The Truth" Williams, on July 21, 1989, Tyson walked to the ring to rap music for the first time. Public Enemy's newly released single "Fight the Power" echoed off the walls of the famous Boardwalk Hall in Atlantic City. While the bout itself was forgettable—Tyson got rid of Williams in the first round—the champion's musical selection had a profound impact on the sport.

To understand the significance and context of Tyson's ring walk, you must first recognize the social and cultural meaning of the song itself. One month before Tyson's bout with Williams, Public Enemy's "Fight the Power" was prominently featured in Spike Lee's critically acclaimed, yet wildly controversial, film *Do the Right Thing*. The song also appears on the movie's soundtrack and serves as a teaser to the group's forthcoming third studio album. Conservative critics panned Lee's film, and its unofficial theme song, as a hateful expression of Black rage, one designed to incite racial violence.

"*Do the Right Thing* is the most controversial film of the year, and it only opens today. Thousands of people already have seen it at preview screenings, and everywhere I go, people are discussing it. Some of them are bothered by it; they think it will cause trouble. Others feel the message is confused. Some find it too militant," film critic Roger Ebert wrote in his review.[47]

Set in the Bedford-Stuyvesant section of Brooklyn, *Do the Right Thing* centers on a day in the life of an ensemble cast of inner-city characters, each of whom is forced to confront different degrees of discrimination, along with their own biases. The simmering racial tensions of the community are symbolized by the sweltering temperatures of the hot summer day in which the film takes place. Public Enemy's "Fight the Power" is continually injected into the film through a character named Radio Raheem, who blasts the song on his boombox wherever he goes. In the climactic scene of the film, Radio Raheem falls victim to a senseless act of police brutality. His murder, in return, incites riots and looting in the neighborhood.

For those who saw *Do the Right Thing*, "Fight the Power" quickly adopted a connotative meaning. This is, of course, precisely what Lee had in mind when he sought out Public Enemy for the project in the fall of 1988. In searching for the song that would blast through the speakers of Radio Raheem's boombox, Lee knew he needed a sound that was, as writer Dorian Lynskey points out, "defiant, angry and rhythmic, which made Public Enemy the obvious choice."[48]

Until the emergence of Public Enemy, few of hip-hop's pioneering acts had used the genre's political potential. While scholars often position "The Message," by Grandmaster Flash and the Furious Five (released in 1982), as the genesis of political rap, early hip-hop music rarely had such a focus. Until Public Enemy arrived on the scene, mainstream hip-hop lacked the political spirit found in the work of Gil Scott-Heron and the Last Poets. What Public Enemy brought to the game was a renewed sense of pro-Black politics, accompanied by an experimental sound. Public Enemy's rise to fame was just as swift as Tyson's ascension to the heavyweight throne.

The unlikely story of Public Enemy begins with the group's founder and front man, Carlton Ridenhour, better known to the rap world as Chuck D. In 1986, while working as a radio DJ on WBAU, an affiliate of Long Island's Adelphi University, Chuck released a demo track titled "Public Enemy #1," a response to those who were taking shots at him in the local hip-hop scene. The demo featured introductory vocals from the man who would later become hip-hop's most recognizable hype man, William Drayton, the zany-oversized-clock-wearing-rapper known as Flavor Flav, whom Chuck D had met while working at the radio station. Foreshadowing things to come, the demo contained a reference to boxing's newly crowned heavyweight champion. "I can go solo, like a Tyson bolo," Chuck raps in the opening verse.

Off the buzz created by "Public Enemy #1," Chuck D attracted the attention of Rick Rubin, music producer and co-founder of Def Jam, hip-hop's first independent record label, home to golden-era acts such as Run-DMC, LL Cool J, and the Beastie Boys. While Rubin initially attempted to sign Chuck as a solo artist, the Long Island emcee balked. His vision was that of a supergroup, a mix between Afrika Bambaataa's Zulu Nation and the Black Panther Party. Along with his hype man, Flavor Flav, Chuck D invited Norman Rogers, a local Long Island DJ who called himself Terminator X, to join the team he now referred to as Public Enemy.

The next, and perhaps most important, addition to the equation was that of Robert Griffin, known at the time as DJ Griff. Recently returned to Long Island after a stint in the United States Army, Griff was known in the local hip-hop community because of his security company, Utility Force, which provided services for parties. Griff's team, referred to as the S1Ws (Security of the First World), wore army fatigues and marched in choreographed military step drills, a style made famous by the security teams in the Nation of Islam, of which Griff was a member. Before signing with Def Jam, Chuck D invited both Griff and the S1Ws aboard, rounding out the formation of hip-hop's most unorthodox musical conglomerate.

On joining Public Enemy, Griff changed his stage name to Professor Griff, assuming the official title of "Minister of Information" in the group. While Griff wasn't a rapper, not in the traditional sense, his contribution was significant nonetheless.

"I am the one that set it in motion," said Professor Griff. "Back then, wasn't nobody talking like we were talking. Wasn't nobody else in the group at the mosque at that time. I was the mailman. I was bringing the information, topics to address in the music. Aside from Rick [Rubin], I debated every white person at Def Jam. They really didn't understand my role."

By Def Jam's standards, Public Enemy's 1987 debut album, *Yo! Bum Rush the Show*, was no smash hit. What the group lacked in radio play, though, they made up for in headlines. Some applauded the resurgence of a militant spirit, a stark seriousness, that had been missing from the genre. Others, particularly conservative critics and radio station pundits, feared the Black nationalist politics.

The group's follow-up, *It Takes a Nation of Millions to Hold Us Back*, released in 1988, did little to temper the fears of those who labeled the group a danger to young minds. For their sophomore effort, both the beats and the bravado would be louder than ever before, thanks to the evolving sound of Public Enemy's in-house production team, a five-man group called The Bomb Squad. Two albums and two years into the game, Public Enemy arguably became the most feared and respected rap group in America. All that was missing was the type of crossover hit that catapults emerging bands from being cult heroes to superstars.

Spike Lee's original idea for Radio Raheem's theme song involved composing a hip-hop version of the negro spiritual "Lift Every Voice and Sing," with Chuck rhyming over the track. During the initial meeting, however, brothers Hank and Keith Shocklee of the Bomb Squad encouraged Lee to reconsider his approach.

"Yo man, you've got to think about this record as being something played out of these cars going by," Hank Shocklee told Spike Lee, opening his office window and allowing the busy ambience of the nearby intersection to enter the room.[49]

Chuck D began with the title. His inspiration came from a bygone era, a song that made an indelible impact on his youth. "I wasn't the first person to write a song called 'Fight the Power.' The Isley Brothers did that in 1975. They talked about how we needed an answer to government oppression. I just built on that," Chuck D said. "If the government dictates who you are, then you're part of the power structure that keeps you down. We were going to fight that and say: 'Look at me as a human being.' The government wanted rap to be infantile, to have us talk about cookies and girls and high school shit. I was like: 'Nah, we're going to talk about you.'"[50]

Much like the film that introduced the song to the world, "Fight the Power" was filled with connotative and provocative references: Malcolm X's infamous condemnation of "We Shall Overcome" [We'd better stop singing and start swinging], the Black Panther battle cry "Power to the People," and James Brown's "Say it Loud, I'm Black and I'm Proud," for example. The music—a chaotic mix of white noise and looped, sampled, and screeching horns—was as polarizing as the lyrics.

"Elvis was a hero to most but he / Never meant shit to me you see / Straight out racist—the sucker was simple and plain," Chuck D raps.

"Motherfuck him and John Wayne," Flavor Flav adds, finishing the rhyme.

"Cuz, I'm Black and I'm proud / I'm ready, I'm hyped plus I'm amped / Most of my heroes don't appear on no stamps / Sample a look back, you look and find nothing / but rednecks for four hundred years, if you check," Chuck continues.

The 1980s were a decade of intense racial strife in New York City, particularly for Brooklyn's Bedford-Stuyvesant and Red Hook neighborhoods as well as Manhattan's Harlem. Gentrification changed the socioeconomic makeup of the boroughs, and the crack epidemic transformed communities into war zones. Those with no hope now lived close to those with just enough to get by. In the summer of 1989, Lee's film, and its lead song, shined a bold light on the strife taking place in the city. In hindsight, it's impossible to discount the significance of "Fight the Power" in *Do the Right Thing*. Never before had a hip-hop song featured so prominently in the plot of a film.

In an unconventional move, *Do the Right Thing* opens with actress Rosie Perez dancing in front a row of Brooklyn brownstones, wearing a boxing robe, trunks, and gloves, shadowboxing to Public Enemy's "Fight the Power." The song plays through to its end, the crescendo interrupted by the blare of an alarm clock. While Brooklyn's most famous boxing champion does not make a cameo in Lee's film, his presence is felt. Lee prominently features Tyson's famous Bed-Stuy graffiti mural in one scene. In another, a group of street-corner sages, in a moment of comic relief, debate the Brooklyn boxer's merit.

"Fuck Mike Tyson. Mike Tyson ain't shit. I'm remember the time he mugged that woman right there over on Lexington," says a funny, outspoken character named Sweet Dick Willie.

Tyson's mythos is equally felt in the music video for "Fight the Power," also directed by Lee. The visual backdrop, something more akin to a political rally than a hip-hop block party, features hundreds of young volunteers holding up portraits of Black heroes, boxers Mike Tyson and Sugar Ray Robinson scattered among images of activists such as Malcolm X and Angela Davis.

As Tyson was being publicly embraced by two of Black culture's most celebrated provocateurs, the twenty-three-year-old champion found himself at a crossroads, both personally and professionally. His mentor, Cus D'Amato, and co-manager, Jim Jacobs, had passed away in 1985 and 1988, respectively. The man D'Amato groomed to train the young champion, Kevin Rooney, was fired in early 1989. Steve Lott, another original member of Tyson's Catskill team, was no longer part of the camp. Added to Team Tyson were the controversial father and son promotional duo of Don and Carl King, along with friends Rory Holloway, John Horne, Aaron Snowell, and Jay Bright. Don King's desire to create a wedge between Tyson and manager Bill Cayton, the last standing member of Tyson's original entourage, has been well documented. King's rhetorical approach echoed the argumentative framework found in Public Enemy's song.

"Every ethnic group takes pride in their heroes. We have no heroes. Our heroes die. White heroes never die; they live infinitely. You know, the John Waynes. But Marvin Gaye, one of the superheroes of our time, you don't hear about him. Elvis Presley has earned more money in death than most niggas can earn in life. Mike Tyson is our hero. He is our knight in shining armor. When he strikes a blow, he strikes a blow for all those who are discriminated against," Don King told Spike Lee in a prefight featurette filmed for HBO Sports.[51]

Tyson's decision to choose "Fight the Power" as his music for the Carl Williams bout was, at the time, a bold statement for a high-profile professional athlete. The most feared boxer on the planet was entering the ring to the sounds of rap's most controversial group, both at the apex of their popularity. In the summer of 1989, a new layer of the Brooklyn champion's shifting public persona had subtly revealed itself.

"How did it feel to see Tyson walk out to your music?" I once asked Chuck D, eager for any indication of whether the endorsement held significance for him.

"We used to joke with Mike about it," Chuck replied, nodding his head in a way that indicated he had a story.[52] "We used to say that's why he lost the Buster Douglas fight. That was his next fight. He didn't come out to our music for Douglas. We used to remind him that he was undefeated with our music," Chuck continued, flashing a grin.

As Chuck D correctly pointed out, Tyson did not enter the ring to Public Enemy for his bout with 40-1 underdog James "Buster" Douglas. His entry music, a Japanese instrumental piece, held no hip-hop inspiration whatsoever. By night's end, Tyson would lose three heavyweight championship belts, along with his aura of invincibility. The knockout loss to Douglas would mark the last time Tyson would ever walk to the ring to the sounds of anything other than rap music.

✳ ✳ ✳

Superstition aside, there is reason to believe Tyson, at some level, heeded Chuck's teasing. He walked to the ring to Public Enemy in each of his next four bouts, a pair of first-round knockout victories over Henry Tillman and Alex Stewart, along with a pair of entertaining slugfests with Donovan "Razor" Ruddock. Tyson's song of choice came from Public Enemy's newly released magnum opus, *Fear of a Black Planet*, a dizzying anti-media track titled "Welcome to the Terrordome."

Just as was the case for the former undisputed heavyweight champion, the early 1990s proved to be turbulent times for Public Enemy. Professor Griff, in particular, found himself embroiled in an ugly controversy, accused of making anti-Semitic comments to David Mills of the *Washington Times*. When Griff refused to back down from his statements, Chuck D apologized for him, then called a press conference to announce that Griff was suspended from the group. As the media frenzy continued to spiral, Def Jam, in an attempt to save face, indicated that Professor Griff was no longer a member of Public Enemy. Key members of the group said Griff's comments were taken out of context, denying the expulsion.

In "Welcome to the Terrordome," released ahead of the album in January 1990, Chuck D confronts the dark cloud surrounding his group. The hectic tempo of the song is highlighted by Chuck's soulful delivery of his iconic opening lines, "I got so much trouble on my mind / Refuse to lose / Here's your ticket / Hear the drummer get wicked."

While most Public Enemy songs looked outward for inspiration, "Welcome to the Terrordome" gave listeners a window into Chuck D's psyche at perhaps the lowest point in his young career. As the song gained popularity, it came to signify more than a response to the Professor Griff controversy. Thanks to the pulse-pounding track and iconic punch lines, the song became an anthem for those who felt unjustly persecuted. Fresh off a messy divorce with actress Robin Givens, a series of public managerial disputes, and, of course, the crushing loss to Buster Douglas in Tokyo, the track likely resonated with the former heavyweight champion. Tyson's every move, much like that of Public Enemy, was scrutinized in the media.

"Crucifixion ain't no fiction / So-called chosen, frozen / Apology made to whoever pleases / Still they got me like Jesus," Chuck famously rhymes in the opening verse, playing up his own martyrdom.

In pushing back against the mainstream-media narrative, Chuck D alludes to professional boxing's most famous martyr, Muhammad Ali: "I rope-a-dope the evil with righteous / Bobbing and weaving and let the good get even."

Professor Griff, who would officially return to the group before the release of *Fear of a Black Planet*, was not surprised by Tyson's attraction to the song or Public Enemy's iconic sound. The careers of both cultural entities followed similar trajectories.

"PE's rise was at that point when Tyson's career was taking off," Professor Griff told me. "And we provided that training music. We provided that attitude. That energy. Let's be honest, that brother wasn't working out to The Whispers or an O-Jays song. Thanks to Chuck and the Bomb Squad, a song like 'Welcome to the Terrordome' helped Mike set that tone for his ring walks. Mike Tyson's style in the ring was controlled chaos and that was the Bomb Squad sound. When you drop the needle on 'Welcome to the Terrordome' it's the same feeling you get with the opening bell of a Tyson fight."

Tyson's rugged trek to the ring lined up perfectly with Public Enemy's bombastic sound. The fitting combination inspired countless boxers and rappers for decades to come, forever transforming the prefight theatrics of the sport.

"I was on a Mike Tyson undercard in Vegas [Tyson vs. Ruddock]," Bernard Hopkins told me. "It was my first fight under the Don King situation [his eleventh as a professional]. And, I remember Mike coming out with that, 'I got so much trouble on my mind, refuse to lose.' Whether wrong or right, I was always fighting with the managers and promoters. I wound up promoting myself for 80 to 90 percent of my career. I could relate to 'Welcome to the Terrordome.' I could relate to all of that, Mike coming out with no robes, no socks, like a caveman. I just loved the music and the entire entrance."

Masta Killa: "The most iconic hip-hop ring walk, to me, was Mike Tyson coming to the ring listening to Public Enemy. He had the black trunks on. The cut-out towel. No robe. And you would hear Chuck D spitting, 'I got so much trouble on my mind.' It was electrifying. When you heard that, you knew he was coming to the ring to do some damage."

Inspectah Deck: "Mike Tyson, to me, was Megatron [a character from *The Transformers*]. You didn't fuck with him. This guy was knocking grown men out at eighteen. Head movement, insane. Ability to cut off the ring, insane. He had a relentless, I want your head on my mantel, mentality. I watched damn near every Tyson fight. I even went to that Ruddock fight out in Vegas. He came out to 'Terrordome' and it just fit."

Wu-Tang producer Mathematics: "Chuck D and Public Enemy was unwavering. They were just like Tyson. Hip-hop was a voice for those who didn't have a voice. Public Enemy was talking to *us*. It manifested to man, woman, and child across the land but the message was for *us*. Tyson was champion of the world, but he was *our* champ."

Lou DiBella: "Still today, when I hear 'Welcome to the Terrordome' come on, it makes me think of Mike Tyson."

Tyson's four-fight string of "Welcome to the Terrordome" ring walks was, of course, interrupted by his arrest in July 1991 for the rape of eighteen-year-old Desiree Washington, Miss Black Rhode Island. At the time of the arrest, Tyson was scheduled to face reigning heavyweight champion Evander Holyfield, in an attempt to regain the titles he lost to Buster Douglas in Tokyo. On March 26, 1992, Tyson was sentenced to six years in prison with four years of probation, of which Tyson served less than three years.

In the months leading up to Tyson's conviction, hip-hop was changing. Just as the success of Public Enemy spawned a resurgence in Afrocentric themes in rap music, most notably in the work of artists such as Queen Latifah, Gang Starr, X Clan, and A Tribe Called Quest, the breakout success of the Compton, California-based rap group, N.W.A, gave birth to a new era. Building off a formula that originated in the works of Schoolly D and Ice-T, N.W.A (composed of Dr. Dre, Ice Cube, Eazy-E, MC Ren, and DJ Yella) introduced audiences to the street politics of South Central Los Angeles. The group's lyrics, deemed violent, vulgar, and sexually explicit by the mainstream media, unapologetically centered on the harsh realities of gang life in California. In the early days of West Coast hip-hop, the dope dealer, the pimp, Bloods and Crips alike, took center stage. These tales, both biographical and metaphorical, had no inherent moral compass, aside from holding a metaphorical mirror to brutality of life in the streets. Because of the graphic nature of the storytelling, so-called gangsta rap quickly dwarfed its highly political East Coast counterpart when it came to record sales, controversy, and media coverage.

At first, a blend between the two styles appeared. N.W.A's controversial song, "Fuck tha Police," for example, addressed political and social issues such as police brutality and racial profiling. When Ice Cube, N.W.A's lead lyricist, left the group in 1988, he selected Chuck D and the Bomb Squad to produce his solo album, *AmeriKKKa's Most Wanted*, an album that served as a unique blend of politics and street culture. In the end, the slickly produced soundscape of N.W.A's musical mastermind, Dr. Dre, carried the day.

After leaving N.W.A in 1992, Dr. Dre, along with music-industry mogul Marion "Suge" Knight, founded his own record company, rap's first gangsta-rap empire: Death Row Records. Dre's debut album, *The Chronic*, would not only launch the careers of West Coast legends Snoop Dogg, Warren G, Nate Dogg, Tha Dogg Pound, RBX, and the Lady of Rage, it would also solidify Dre's place as the number-one producer in the game. With Dr. Dre behind the boards, gangsta rap would soar to unimaginable heights.

"Just another motherfucking day for Dre, so I begin like this / No medallions, dreadlocks, or Black fists, it's just / That gangster glare, with gangster raps / That gangster shit, that makes a gang of snaps," Dr. Dre raps on his debut album, distancing the West Coast from that of its predecessor.

The three years that Tyson was away from boxing would also prove difficult for Public Enemy. Professor Griff maintained an on-again, off-again relationship with the group, both he and his bandmates publicly displaying their bitter disappointment in one another. In 1991, Flavor Flav was arrested on domestic abuse charges, lost custody of his children, and sank deeper into addiction. To compound matters, a 1994 motorcycle accident sent Terminator X into early retirement.

While Chuck D and the Bomb Squad continued to release music, the soundscape of hip-hop shifted. Even within the culture, there were those who were leery of the violent and hypermasculine direction the music had taken as a result of the rise of the West Coast. In his 1992 film *Bamboozled,* Spike Lee, for example, likened gangsta rap to the Black minstrel shows of the early 1800s, performances of the uncultured and ignorant for the entertainment of white audiences. Both conservative and liberal pundits debated the causation between West Coast gangsta rap and violent behavior. For some, mainstream hip-hop had become synonymous with the glorification of criminal activity, sexual promiscuity, and drug culture.

When Tyson left prison in March 1995, Public Enemy no longer held the title of rap's most dangerous and controversial group. That distinction now belonged to an artist signed to Dr. Dre and Suge Knight's controversial label, Death Row Records, a rapper whose friendship with Tyson would, in the coming years, forever shake up boxing and hip-hop.

ME AGAINST THE WORLD

Tattooed on his neck, a nod to Italian philosopher Niccolo Machiavelli, whose sixteenth-century political treatise outlined the amoral nature of those who rise to power. Tattooed on the right side of his chest, an image of Nefertiti, an Egyptian queen. The left side bore the hip-hop spelling of his namesake, an Indian warrior who, against all odds, led his tribe's final revolt against the Spanish inquisition. Alongside his upper abdomen, an image of an AK-47 assault rifle, the dust cover and safety compartment of the weapon replaced with the words "50 Niggaz." Scrawled along his midriff, the most famous and iconic tattoo, "Thug Life," the letter "I" replaced by a bullet.

On his right shoulder, the chilling image of a masked goon, a wad of cash in his hand, tethered to the scales of justice, an infant baby resting on one scale, a stack of gold bars on the other. Tattooed alongside his left bicep, the image of a skull and crossbones inscribed with the word "Heartless." Tattooed diagonally down his left forearm, in old English font, "Notorious." On the inside of his forearm, a seven-point crown inscribed with the phrase "Trust Nobody."

On his left shoulder, the image of a vicious black panther, symbolic of his family ties to the revolutionary socialist political organization.

Tattooed slightly below the panther, a depiction of Jesus Christ, a crown of thorns upon his head, dying on a burning cross. The inscription reads "Only God Can Judge Me." Framed by a tribal design, diagonally on his right forearm, "Outlaw."

A large gothic cross covered much of his back. Inside the cross, "Exodus 18:31," a reference to Nat Turner's 1831 slave revolt. Along his shoulders, in cursive handwriting, "Fuck the World." On each side of the cross, tattooed images of sock and buskin, ancient Greek symbols of comedy and tragedy. Appropriately listed below each figure, the words "Smile now" and "Cry Later."

Like the tattooed symbols that covered his body, Tupac Amaru Shakur was an enigma, a contradiction. Tupac was not hip-hop's first superstar, the genre's fist crossover success. Rather, Tupac was hip-hop's first legend. He was a larger-than-life cultural icon who, like figures such as Bob Marley and James Dean, lived fast and died young.

The story of Tupac's enduring legend is, for better or worse, unavoidably intertwined with that of the late twentieth-century's most famous prize fighter, Mike Tyson. Not only were the two men close friends, their lives and careers paralleled. Both were abandoned by their fathers, born into systemic poverty, escaping those daunting circumstances while also falling victim to the so-called trappings of fame and success. Each man was, at times, his own worst enemy.

First came Tyson, the youngest heavyweight champion in the history of the sport. It wasn't *who* Tyson defeated in the ring but *how* he defeated them. Even for the most violent of sports, Tyson's fire and ferocity was something new. Never had a heavyweight champion obliterated his opponents with such menace. Even after watching Tyson crawl along the canvas on his hands and knees, fumbling for his mouthpiece, it was impossible to imagine him as anything other than *the baddest man on the planet.*

Then came Tupac Shakur, a rapper whose cultural and political significance far exceeded the influence of any of his predecessors. He wasn't rap's greatest lyricist, the king of punch lines or metaphors. He didn't have the quickest flow or even the highest record sales. His influence extended beyond the record business. Tupac albums felt bigger than music; their significance attracted the attention of politicians, pundits, and presidents alike. The five bullets he'd taken in the lobby of Quad Studios would only make his music that much greater, we'd imagined.

"In one sense, Mike Tyson is Tupac in boxing shorts and Tupac is Mike Tyson with a microphone," renowned scholar Michael Eric Dyson suggests in the documentary film *One Night in Vegas*.[53]

Dyson's comparison is appropriate. In both instances, the rise to power was meteoric. The anger frightened us. The unpredictability kept us watching. The talent captured our imagination. Each man was bound by the cavernous depths of his mythmaking, mythologies that far exceeded the boundaries of their real-life accomplishments, which were indeed spectacular. Each man, not unlike the tattoos etched into his skin, lived as a symbol.

* * *

In hindsight, everything about Tupac's life appears to hold some measure of symbolic meaning, foreshadowing things to come. At the age of twenty-one, his mother legally changed her name to Afeni Shakur. *Afeni* is a West African word that translates to "lover of the people." *Shakur* is Arabic for "thankful." At age one, her son underwent an equally symbolic renaming. Lasane Parish Crooks, shortly after his first birthday, became Tupac Amaru Shakur. The mother and son relationship, immortalized in the iconic rap song "Dear Momma," is a key component of Tupac's Black Panther mythos. Even before Tupac was born, his mother appeared to be charting his destiny.

Tupac's legend begins with his uniquely symbolic family tree, a mixture of Civil Rights activists, political prisoners, and street hustlers. His mother, Afeni, worked as a section leader of the Harlem chapter of the Black Panther party, also filling in as a writer for the *Panther Post* newsletter. Six months into Afeni's tenure with the Black Panthers, in a roundup that came to be known as the "Panther 21," she was arrested and charged with conspiracy to bomb the Bronx 44th Precinct Police Station, the Manhattan 24th Precinct Police Station, and the Queens Board of Education Office.

While out on bail, Afeni became impregnated by Billy Garland, a fellow member of the organization. Until Tupac became famous, Garland had very little presence in his life. High-ranking members of the Black Panther party, Elmer "Geronimo" Pratt and Mutulu Shakur, both of whom were targeted by the U.S. government in a series of illegal covert operations aimed at discrediting Black activists, served as pseudo–father figures to the young boy.

With multiple family members on the F.B.I.'s Most Wanted Fugitives List, Tupac's childhood was anything but ordinary. When Afeni Shakur's bail was revoked, in February 1971, she was subsequently sent to the Women's House of Detention in Greenwich Village. As Tupac once famously stated in an interview with MTV News, even as an embryo, the rapper found himself behind bars. "From the start, [Tupac's] life was made-for-mythologizing," hip-hop scholar Danyel Smith once wrote, noting the rapper's symbolic origin story.[54]

The Panther 21 trial, one of the longest and most expensive in New York State history, is perhaps where Tupac's story truly begins. Despite having no law degree or legal background whatsoever, Afeni Shakur, pregnant with her first child, chose to represent herself in court, forgoing the appointed defense attorney.

"No attorney, never been to law school, facing three-hundred-and-some-odd years, one Black woman, pregnant, beat the case. That just shows you the strength of a Black woman, the strength of the oppressed," Tupac proudly stated, years later.[55]

On June 16, 1971, shortly after being acquitted of all charges, Afeni Shakur gave birth to Tupac in an East Harlem hospital. Afeni's improbable legal victory, however, was followed by years of economic struggle, personal and political disappointment, and, eventually, substance abuse. In 1975, Afeni married Mutulu Shakur, the alleged ringleader of the Black Liberation Army unit that carried out the 1981 robbery of a Brinks armored truck in Nanuet, New York. Mutulu, who famously evaded capture for six years, was unable to help Afeni provide for Tupac and their daughter, Sekywia. With Mutulu on the run, Afeni struggled to provide for her growing family. Tupac, along with his mother and stepsister, spent much of his childhood shuffling back and forth between Harlem and the Bronx, sometimes living in homeless shelters.

The story of Tupac's troubled adolescence, marred by poverty and the absence of his biological father, is also one of rich cultural opportunity. At twelve years old, Tupac played the role of Travis in the 127th Street Ensemble's production of Lorraine Hansberry's *A Raisin in the Sun* at the Apollo Theater in a fundraiser for Jessie Jackson's unsuccessful presidential bid. Despite his impoverished upbringing, Tupac's mother set out to ensure that her son had a brilliant mind. Afeni disciplined her son by forcing him to read the *New York Times* cover to cover, later quizzing him on the subject matter. Legend has it, wide-ruled notebooks were, on several occasions, Tupac's only birthday or Christmas present. Afeni envisioned a life in the arts for her son, one where the young boy would use his talent to liberate Black people.

In 1982, four years before Mutulu Shakur's capture, Afeni divorced him. In June 1986, she moved the family from New York to Baltimore, where Tupac, with dreams of becoming an actor, auditioned for the Baltimore School for the Arts. It was here that the teenager discovered his love of Shakespeare, poetry, art, and ballet, also forming a lifelong friendship with classmate Jada Pinkett (who would later go on to Hollywood stardom). For many familiar with Tupac's mythology, these experiences, coupled with his painful childhood, helped mold Tupac into the most articulate and intellectual gangsta rapper of his generation, a self-identifying Thug who quoted Shakespeare and Sun Tzu in his rhymes.

Much like the story of Tyson, who, as a troubled teenager, met Bobby Stewart in an upstate New York corrections facility, setting into motion his unlikely path to the heavyweight championship, Tupac's traumatic life groomed him, at every turn, for the role he would one day occupy. In June 1988, Tupac and his family moved cross-country, this time to live with Afeni's family in Marin City, California. Unbeknownst to the teenager, his mother was struggling with an addiction to crack cocaine. Desperate and destitute, Tupac dropped out of high school, started living with friends, and began selling drugs. Unsuited for a life of hustling on the streets of Marin City, Tupac turned to hip-hop music as an escape.

"I tried selling drugs but I couldn't do it. I wasn't good at it," Tupac remembered in an interview. "The drug dealers were like my sponsors, at first. They would say, 'Give me my drugs back, you don't need to be doing this.' They would give me a few dollars and say, 'Go do your thing. Go be a rapper. Follow your dream.'"[56]

The teenage rapper's salvation came in the form of a less-than-glamorous job as a roadie for the Oakland-based rap group Digital Underground. On tour with the band in the spring of 1990, Tupac's pre-show duties included loading the equipment and setting up the stage. During live performances, Tupac served as a backup dancer and occasionally played hype man to Digital Underground's leader, rapper Shock G. After the completion of the tour, which also featured mainstream hip-hop acts such as Big Daddy Kane, Heavy D, Kid 'n Play, and Queen Latifah, Tupac was offered a guest verse on the Digital Underground track "Same Song."

"I remember it very well," recalled Big Daddy Kane. "It was my very first tour, the Chocolate City Tour, in 1990. I took Digital Underground out. I think Digital Underground was my opening act. Me and Pac talked, we became friends. Pac was real cool. I remember he was talking about doing his solo thing. He said it wasn't gonna be no funny stuff like Digital Underground do. He said it was gonna be political, real serious. He spit some bars for me. I thought he sounded pretty good. But I admired his passion and energy more than the rhymes. He was one of the most passionate people I'd ever met. He talked about his future like nothing could possibly get in his way."

Shortly after the tour, Digital Underground began to assist with the recording of the young rapper's demo tape. It was during this time in Tupac's life, moments before his star ascended, that the young rapper first met Tyson. Over the years, Tyson has told the story on numerous occasions, and with very little variation.

"The first time I ever met Tupac, Magic Johnson was throwing a party at the Palladium on Sunset [in Los Angeles, California]. I had came outside [the club] and some friends of mine were blocking the door. I saw this young kid, I think it was Shock G and said, 'What's up, Shorty?' I told the security guard, 'Let them in, man.' Remember what it was like back when we couldn't get in the club because we weren't dressed right?" Tyson remembered.[57]

When the security guard relented to Tyson's request, Shock G returned to the front door with his entire Digital Underground crew.

Tyson continued: "He brought back like two hundred guys with him. Tupac was one of those guys."

Inside the Palladium, Digital Underground quickly made their presence known. Despite having never released an album, single, or even a music video, Tupac became a star among the stars.

"These guys come in, bully the place, and the next thing I know Tupac is rocking the mic," Mike Tyson recalled. "And the whole place is going crazy, they love it. Later, I met him and we were talking. He was just a young, shy, kid."

The irony of Mike Tyson's five-year relationship with Tupac Shakur is that the lives of both men often zigzagged. Tyson and Tupac spent very little time together as free men. Shortly after Tyson's chance encounter with Tupac in Los Angeles, he was arrested for the rape of Desiree Washington. Four months after Tyson's arrest, Tupac Shakur's debut album, *2Pacalypse Now*, was released on Interscope records. In the coming months, both men found themselves on the evening news, embattled in tabloid scandals.

✳ ✳ ✳

While *2Pacalypse Now* was not the top-selling rap album of 1991, it was most certainly the most controversial. The album's lead single, "Brenda's Got a Baby," an inner-city fable of a teenage girl who is molested by her cousin, hides her pregnancy from the family, and leaves the child in a dumpster, broke new ground for hip-hop storytelling. At the end of the song, the young girl has a change of heart, rescues the baby, but eventually turns to prostitution as a means of providing for the child. The allegory, designed to demonstrate the effects of cyclical poverty, was praised by some and misunderstood by others. Tupac's thirteen-track debut unapologetically highlights the grim realities of life in the drug-infested streets of California. Racial profiling, police brutality, and systemic racism serve as the album's primary themes. On the album, racist police are, as Tupac once stated in an interview, "the bad guys."

Tupac Shakur wasn't the first rapper to touch on racial profiling and police brutality in his music. N.W.A's "Fuck tha Police" and KRS-One's "Black Cop," both released before Tupac's debut, set the precedent for this particular hip-hop tradition. A major component of Tupac's allure was the way in which his life and art melded into one. The music video for Tupac's second single, "Trapped," for example, features graphic scenes where the rap star is being harassed and beaten by the Oakland police. Tupac delivers much of his performance from behind the bars of a jail cell.

"They got me trapped / Can barely walk the city streets, without a cop harassing me, searching me, and asking my identity / Hands up, throw me up against the wall / Didn't do a thing at all," Tupac raps in the opening verse.

Before the song could debut on the popular hip-hop music show *Yo! MTV Raps*, Tupac's art became reality. In October 1991, Tupac, on his way to a local bank to deposit a royalty check, was stopped by two Oakland police officers and asked to provide identification.

"They were sweating me for jaywalking and I swear to you I had no idea what jaywalking is, didn't until they beat me down," Tupac recalled in an interview. "They stopped me, they asked for my ID, my real name is Tupac Shakur. There is nothing fake about me. There is no stage name or a stage aura. That's my name, that's how I said it. Just because my name wasn't John Brown, it irked them. They started saying, 'What your momma name you that for?' So, I got hot. That was beyond the call of duty. So, I was like, 'Give me my citation, and let me go about my business.' And, I said the words N.W.A made famous ['Fuck tha police']. That got them too hyped. So, they put their hands on me."[58]

On January 17, 1992, as his debut album climbed the Billboard charts, Tupac and his lawyers filed a $10 million lawsuit against the Oakland police department for alleged brutality. The following month, on February 10, 1992, Mike Tyson was convicted of rape, sentenced to six years and four months in an Indiana penitentiary. At the former undisputed heavyweight champion's lowest moment, Tupac did not forget the man who opened the door to the club for him. Tyson hadn't forgotten the meeting either.

"When I went to prison, Tupac wrote me a letter and then he came and saw me," Mike Tyson recalled. "He explained to me who he was and I was like, 'I remember you.' That's how we became friends. We talked on the phone and then cultivated our relationship. And then he came and saw me again. Him coming to visit me in prison. He's so excited, he's so animated. And all the sudden he jumps up on the table. The guards didn't like him because when he came the inmates got rowdy and pumped up. He was like a bolt of energy. He demanded respect."[59]

During the early years of Tyson's prison sentence, Tupac's public profile grew considerably. Tupac's big-screen debut in Ernest Dickerson's film *Juice* once again earned the twenty-year-old a mixture of critical acclaim and additional controversy. The role fueled Tupac's outlaw image in the public eye. In *Juice*, Tupac plays Bishop, a misguided teenager turned chilling psychopath, a killer who murders his childhood friend and later hugs the boy's mother at the funeral. Tupac's performance is best encapsulated by the character's famous lines: "I am crazy. And, you know what, I don't give a fuck!"

Separating Tupac Shakur, the man, from Bishop, the film character, or even Tupac, the man, from 2Pac, the rap persona, was difficult for both fans and detractors alike. Tupac's mainstream arrival coincided with the peak of a mounting conservative political movement, one aimed at censoring the lyrics of rap artists. Those who feared the influence of violent music on young and impressionable listeners did not have to wait long to find their scapegoat.

In April 1992, a nineteen-year-old man named Ronald Ray Howard shot and murdered a Texas state trooper. The album in the tape deck of Howard's stolen truck was *2Pacalypse Now*. Howard's lawyer argued the album incited his client to kill the trooper, referencing the song "Soulja's Story" in which a similar event unfolds, resulting in the murder of a police officer.

Following the horrific murder, Vice President Dan Quayle, after meeting with the late officer's daughter, called on Time Warner and Interscope Records to withdraw Tupac's album.

"Once again we're faced with an irresponsible corporate act. There is absolutely no reason for a record like this to be published by a responsible corporation. It has no place in our society," Quayle infamously stated.[60] Presidential hopeful Bob Dole, in the coming months, echoed Quayle's argument.

The controversy surrounding *2Pacalypse Now* fanned the flames of a fire that had started a few years before the album's release. The so-called war on gangsta rap was largely spearheaded by conservative Black figures such as Civil Rights activist C. Delores Tucker, and Reverend Calvin Butts, senior pastor of the Abyssinian Baptist Church in Harlem. As a result of the media backlash, radio stations banned Tupac's music, television stations censored his videos, and copies of *2Pacalypse Now* were literally steamrolled in public demonstrations.

The campaign against Tupac's art, in hindsight, did not achieve the desired effect. Following Quayle's comments, Tupac, in the eyes of many hip-hop fans, became something of a freedom-of-speech martyr, a misunderstood antiestablishment rebel. All of this, of course, stoked the anticipation for Tupac's sophomore album.

On *Strictly 4 My N.I.G.G.A.Z. . . .* released in February 1993, Tupac predictably fires back at his critics, delivering harsh lyrics and raw street fables. With Tupac's second album, however, the stories became less allegorical and more personal. Although *Strictly 4 My N.I.G.G.A.Z.* . . . was a resounding commercial success, the album, like the artist, is best described as polarizing. With crossover singles such as "I Get Around," a song rife with traditional hip-hop misogyny, and "Keep Ya Head Up," an ode to Black feminism, Tupac brilliantly displayed his dual rhetorical sensibilities, confounding critics while, at the same time, winning over new fans. Tupac, who sought to redefine the word *nigga* (Never. Ignorant. Getting. Goals. Accomplished.) and the concept of *thug life* (The. Hate. U. Give. Little. Infants. Fucks. Everybody), inspired some and confused others.

The two sides of Tupac were also on equal display in the actor's second feature film, *Poetic Justice*. In the movie, Tupac stars opposite Janet Jackson, playing the role of Lucky, Jackson's love interest, a single father who works as a mail carrier. While the role allowed for Tupac to demonstrate his emotional range as an actor, the film was not without its own controversy. During the prerelease promotional run, Tupac told reporters that Jackson demanded he take an HIV test before kissing him on set. Tupac, who refused to comply with Jackson's demands, was eager to tell the media how he was treated, further positioning the rapper as a Hollywood outsider.

As Tupac's fame grew, so did his hubris. In a series of hotly debated interviews, Tupac expressed his disdain for a number of prominent Black celebrities who, by his estimation, were not doing enough for the Black community. The most notable names on Tupac's hit list were Spike Lee, Quincy Jones, Eddie Murphy, and Michael Jackson. His impulsive tongue, quick temper, and unpredictable demeanor soon became the stuff of pop-culture legend. Two albums and two movies into his career, Tupac earned his place as hip-hop's king of the tabloids, a brief romantic relationship with music icon Madonna further aiding the public's interest in hip-hop's thug thespian.

Much to his own dismay, Shakur's name appeared on the evening news more than any rapper of his generation. The man who famously claimed he never had a [jail] record until he made a record was arrested fourteen times during his brief career. Some of the crimes were the result of petty scuffles, others were vastly more serious. The talent and brilliance displayed in his art was sharply juxtaposed by a life of turbulence and unpredictability. As his legal woes began to mount, and his life appeared to spin out of control, Tupac received cautionary advice from the most unlikely of sources.

"His friends would call me and say, 'I saw your friend, Pac. He's just asserting himself a little bit. Being very aggressive,'" said Mike Tyson. "I would call him periodically on the phone and say, 'The word is not good out there. You need to calm down.'"[61]

In an appearance on the Arsenio Hall Show, Tupac relayed his version of the phone conversation, perhaps providing a window into their friendship: "Tyson had been calling me from before all the trouble. He would call me and say, 'I wish I was out while you was out.' He was like, 'I heard how you party, I want to be out there partying with you.' He was giving me a lot of advice. I really look up to him something horrible. For him to tell me to calm down, I was like, 'Whoa, it's time to calm down.' If Mike Tyson is telling me that he heard about me, from jail."[62]

The degree to which Tyson was able to get through to his friend is, of course, up for debate. On one hand, Tupac spoke openly about the encounter in interviews. An allusion to the conversation shows up in Tupac's song "It Ain't Easy," where he raps: "Gettin' calls from my nigga Mike Tyson ain't nuttin' nice / Yo 'Pac, do somethin' righteous witcha life."

Others close to the situation have since said that, despite Tupac's respect for Tyson, the rapper did little to make good on his promise to slow down.

"Mike Tyson cautioned [Tupac] about some of the people he was around then, that they weren't no good and that he should be careful around them," Gloria Cox, Afeni Shakur's younger sister, remembered. "Pac respected Tyson cautioning him but you got a young guy here who is *bout it-bout it* now and I'm sure he didn't want to hear it."[63]

As Tupac's career progressed, the controversy surrounding his life gradually became more serious. In October 1993, Tupac was arrested for allegedly shooting two off-duty Atlanta police officers who were said to be beating an unarmed Black motorist. The charges were eventually dropped. The following month, a nineteen-year-old woman claimed Tupac and three other men sodomized and sexually assaulted her in a Manhattan hotel. As a result of the arrest, Tupac was fired from the cast of John Singleton's *Higher Learning*. Three months after the alleged sexual assault, Tupac was sentenced to fifteen days in jail for punching director

Allen Hughes, one-half of the Hughes brothers tandem responsible for the urban cult classic *Menace II Society*. Less than six months later, two Milwaukee teens murdered a police officer, citing Tupac's music as their inspiration, further prodding critics who viewed the rapper-turned-actor as a public threat.

While on trial for sexual assault and weapons charges in New York, Tupac recorded his third studio album, aptly titled *Me Against the World*. Tupac's darkest, and perhaps most revealing album, it plays out like a grim premonition. In songs such as "If I Die Tonight," "Death Around the Corner," "So Many Tears," and "Outlaw," Tupac paints a vivid portrait of his own demise. In standout tracks such as "Me Against the World," "Temptations," "Lord Knows," and "Fuck the World," Tupac's pain and paranoia are on full display.

Before *Me Against the World* was released or the sexual assault trial was completed, Tupac was shot five times at point-blank range and was robbed of $40,000 worth of jewelry at a Times Square recording studio. As Tupac was loaded into the ambulance, his head bandaged and neck in a brace, the injured rap star lifted his tattooed arm and flipped his middle finger to paparazzi. Less than three hours after surgery, and against doctor's orders, Tupac checked himself out of Bellevue Hospital.

Two days after the shooting, on December 1, 1994, Tupac arrived at a Manhattan courtroom, heavily bandaged in a wheelchair, eager to receive his fate. The jurors did not deliver good news. Tupac was acquitted of sodomy and weapons charges but found guilty of sexual assault. A few months later, Tupac was sentenced to four-and-a-half years in prison, his term beginning immediately at New York's Rikers Island penitentiary. The rap star's turbulent career, many believed, was all but over.

Mike Tyson: "In a weird way, Tupac was like a Roman general. I say that because he took himself real serious. He had a great deal of self-respect and dignity. And a lot of people couldn't understand that. It was threatening and challenging to some people. He was really wild. I said, 'When I'm coming out, you are gonna be coming in.' And that's what happened."[64]

Just a few weeks after Tupac Shakur was handed his prison sentence, Mike Tyson was released from his three-year jail term. The two friends had missed each other by less than three months.

AMBITIONZ AZ A RIDAH

I n March 1995, Mike Tyson emerged from prison a new man. First came the news that he had converted to Islam. After being released from prison, Tyson and his entourage headed directly to a nearby mosque, where they prayed with none other than Muhammad Ali. There were also new tattoos, both controversial and puzzling. A tattoo of communist revolutionary Mao Zedong was now prominently featured on Tyson's left arm, a tattoo of Civil Rights figure Malcolm X, complete with the caption "Days of Grace," now rested on his right shoulder. An image of Marxist revolutionary Ernesto "Che" Guevara, tattooed alongside Tyson's ribs, showed up later.

In James Toback's 2009 documentary *Tyson*, the former champion discusses his postprison behavior, a reinvention of his former self.

"At first, I was too strict, too extreme, too secular, too violent," Tyson recalled. "I used Islam because I was bitter at the world. . . . When I was in prison I was so angry at society that I put a tattoo of Mao on me, I put a tattoo of Che on me because I had no faith in our government and I did that just to spite them."[65]

Equally puzzling was the news that Tyson planned to continue his promotional relationship with Don King, who was widely criticized for mishandling the champion's legal defense and personal finances. Upon announcing his return, the WBC, IBF, and WBA each granted Tyson a number-one spot in their respective sanctioning body's rankings. There were, of course, some within the sport who rolled their eyes at this move. After three years away from boxing, some boxing experts questioned whether Tyson could ever return to his previous form. The upset loss to Buster Douglas, along with surprisingly competitive bouts with Razor Ruddock, indicated to some that Tyson's skills had begun to erode before his conviction. In the spring of 1995, as the naysayers began to equal those who still believed, there was much to prove for both Mike Tyson and Tupac Shakur.

Shortly after Tyson began training for his first comeback fight, *Me Against the World* scored Tupac his first No. 1 album on the Billboard charts. Music videos for "Dear Momma" and "Temptations" were shot without the rapper being present. Going double platinum in less than seven months, the album was both a critical and commercial success. Hip-hop fans instantly branded *Me Against the World* a classic, the poignant crescendo to a three-year musical trilogy.

"The guards would be like, 'Bet you ain't gonna be rapping for you in a while. And, I was like, 'Well, actually I have the number-one album in the country. I just beat Bruce Springsteen,'" Tupac told MTV News.[66]

Although Tupac was incarcerated, no longer a fixture in the limelight, he continued to dominate news headlines. In an interview with *Vibe* magazine, published in April 1995, Tupac spoke candidly about his shooting in detail, implicating Christopher "Notorious B.I.G." Wallace, Sean "Puffy" Combs, record executive Andre Harrell, and fellow Thug Life group member Randy "Stretch" Armstrong, all of whom were present at the recording studio the night he was shot. In Tupac's version of the events, he was lured to Quad Studios under the guise of recording a featured verse on rapper Little Shawn's upcoming album. The shooting, in Tupac's eyes, was a setup, a scene not unlike something out of a Hollywood gangster movie.

"As we're walking up to the building, somebody screamed from up the top of the studio," Tupac recalled in the *Vibe* interview. "It was Lil' Cease, Biggie's sideman. That's my homeboy. As soon as I saw him, all my concerns about the situation were relaxed."[67]

Outside of the building, Tupac noticed a slim Black man, in his mid-thirties, dressed in combat fatigues, his bucket hat pulled low, unwilling to make eye contact. In the lobby, waiting to be buzzed in, Tupac noticed a second Black man, wearing similar fatigues, sitting at a table, reading a newspaper. Waiting for the elevator, Tupac—accompanied by his friend Randy "Stretch" Walker, Stretch's friend, Fred, and Tupac's sister's boyfriend, Zane—did not realize that his life was in danger. He had mistakenly assumed the two men worked security for Biggie, whom Junior M.A.F.I.A. rapper Lil' Cease had just told him was in a recording session.

"These dudes must be security for Biggie, because I could tell they were from Brooklyn from their army fatigues," recounted Tupac "But then I said, 'Wait a minute. Even Biggie's homeboys love me, why don't they look up?' I pressed the elevator button, turned around, and that's when the dudes came out with the guns—two identical 9mms . . . I'm thinking Stretch is going to fight; he was towering over those niggas. From what I know about the criminal element, if niggas come to rob you, they always hit the big nigga first. But they didn't touch Stretch; they came straight to me. Everybody dropped to the floor like potatoes."[68]

Initially, New York City police officials indicated that Tupac's shooting was merely a case of being at the *wrong place,* at the *wrong time.*

"I think anybody that walked into that studio was going to be robbed," Sergeant. James Coleman, a police department spokesperson, stated at a press conference the day after Tupac's shooting.[69]

In Tupac's version of events, his assailants had no interest in anyone but him. The two men, dressed in fatigues, had set out to kill and rob him alone, the rapper believed.

"They knew me, or else they would never check for my gun. It was like they were mad at me. I felt them kicking me and stomping me; they didn't hit nobody else," Tupac argued.[70]

After the two assailants fled the scene, Tupac's friends lifted him into the elevator, fearing for his safety. When Tupac was transported from the elevator to the studio, the rapper instantly began to suspect everyone around him. Dazed and disoriented, the rapper was unaware that he had actually been shot five times.

"We jumped in the elevator and went upstairs," recalled Tupac. "I'm limping and everything, but I don't feel nothing. It's numb. When we got upstairs, I looked around, and it scared the shit out of me. . . . Nobody approached me. I noticed that nobody would look at me. Andre Harrell wouldn't look at me. I had been going to dinner with him the last few days. He had invited me to the set of *New York Undercover,* telling me he was going to get me a job. Puffy was standing back too. I knew Puffy. He knew how much stuff I had done for Biggie before he came out."[71]

The media scandal was heightened by the fact that Tupac and Christopher Wallace had once been close friends, traveling together, visiting each other's homes, and performing on the same stage. Before Wallace's debut album, *Ready to Die*, becoming one of the most well-received rap albums of 1994, Tupac had served as something of a mentor to the up-and-coming Brooklyn rapper. Following the *Vibe* interview, both Wallace and Combs vehemently denied any involvement in the shooting.

Said Tupac: "They got different accounts of what happened and I'm the one with the bullet wounds. I was there for the whole thing. Nobody else was there for the whole thing."[72]

Meanwhile, a controversy of a different variety surrounded Mike Tyson. On August 19, 1995, Tyson officially returned to boxing in a heavily criticized pay-per-view mismatch against little-known journeyman Peter McNeeley. Although he held a professional record of 36-1 (30 KOs) and came from a notable boxing family, the outmatched McNeeley, despite a dubious number-seven ranking from the WBA, was hardly a worthy foe. In his thirty-seven professional fights, McNeeley had defeated only four opponents with winning records. The Massachusetts slugger's ring résumé lacked a single recognizable name. Many in the media felt Don King, who recognized the opportunity to capitalize on the public's curiosity, exploited fans by charging pay-per-view money for a main event that could only disappoint. Viewing the event as more spectacle than sporting contest, boxing fans and media personalities were lockstep in their criticism of the Tyson vs. McNeeley promotion.

The action in the ring, as many predicted, was anticlimactic. McNeeley, who wildly charged Tyson after the opening bell, was knocked down seconds into the fight. After a thudding uppercut dropped the free-swinging mauler for a second time, his manager, Vinnie Vecchione, entered the ring before the referee could administer the mandatory eight count. Because of Vecchione's intrusion, the grossly overmatched McNeeley lost by disqualification rather than TKO, sparing bloodthirsty fans the privilege of a highlight-reel knockout. While the pay-per-view racked up an impressive 1.5 million buys, the main event lasted only eighty-nine seconds.

Amid the ensuing the public relations backlash, King chose to take a different path for Tyson's second postprison tune-up. First, King offered up a slightly more recognizable opponent in the overweight but undefeated Buster Mathis Jr., who was, at the time, ranked in the top five by another alphabet organization. Second, King chose to air the bout on Fox Sports, all but positioning the move as a gift to those who overpaid for Tyson–McNeeley. In an equally strategic move, King also decided to host the fight at the Spectrum arena in Philadelphia, a city which had never hosted a Tyson bout.

As Tyson entered camp for the Buster Mathis Jr. fight, his friend, Tupac Shakur, launched a comeback of his own, one that shook the music industry to its core. On October 11, 1995, Death Row Records CEO Marion "Suge" Knight agreed to post Tupac's $1.4 million appeal bond. In return, Tupac signed a three-album recording contract with Knight's company, home of West Coast gangsta-rap legends Dr. Dre and Snoop Dogg.

For Knight, whose long-standing beef with Bad Boy records CEO Sean Combs had been highly publicized, the business move was the ultimate power play. Before signing Tupac, Knight and Combs experienced their own falling out. Those circumstances have, over the years, been the subject of widespread speculation and rumor.

Two months before Tupac's release from prison, at the 1995 Source Awards, held at Madison Square Garden, the match was lit. During his acceptance speech for the award for Soundtrack of the Year, Knight took the opportunity to publicly humiliate Combs in front of his hometown fans.

"I would like to tell Tupac to keep his guard up, we riding with him. And one other thing I would like to say, any artist out there that want to be an artist, and stay a star, and don't want to have to worry about the executive producer trying to be all in the videos, all on the records, dancing, come to Death Row," Knight stated, amid a chorus of boos, taunting Combs for his presence in Biggie's albums and music videos.[73]

For many, Tupac's decision to sign with Death Row was driven by a combination of desperation and revenge. Largely because of his mounting legal fees, the rapper did not have the funds to post his own bail. Knight offered Tupac a path to freedom, fame, and revenge. The controversy surrounding Tupac's *Vibe* interview, coupled with the back-and-forth between Knight and Combs at the Source Awards, solidified the public interest in the Death Row–Bad Boy rivalry. There was no question that a Tupac album on Death Row Records, regardless of its content, would be the most anticipated release of the coming year. Some close to Tupac, however, feared the repercussions of his decision.

Less than twenty-four hours after being released from Clinton Correctional Facility in Dannemora, New York, Tupac flew on a private jet to Los Angeles and immediately began recording his Death Row debut. The drama surrounding Tupac's life was nothing new for a company that, from its inception, was surrounded by controversy. Knight, a known affiliate of the Mob Piru gang, made his name in the industry by employing Mafia-style tactics to get things done. Tupac knew what he was signing up for. He and Knight were hardly strangers. In 1994, Tupac made a cameo in Death Row's first venture into independent film, *Murder Was the Case*. In that same year, he also starred in the Hollywood film *Above the Rim* and contributed music to the soundtrack released on Death Row. It has been widely speculated that Knight, who allegedly paid Tupac a large amount of money for his contribution to the soundtrack, began recruiting the rap star during this period.

Aside from Knight's willingness to pay the lofty bail bond, there were artistic incentives for Tupac to sign with Death Row. At its peak, the record company earned over $100 million a year. Dr. Dre's *The Chronic* and Snoop Dogg's *Doggystyle* were both heralded as hip-hop classics, selling over thirteen million albums combined. Along with up-and-coming West Coast acts such as Tha Dogg Pound, Nate Dogg, and the Lady of Rage, Death Row boasted one of the most talented hip-hop rosters in the business. Tupac was, to use a sports metaphor, joining a championship team.

"My mindset, at the time, was how can I make them sorry they did this to me? I'm thinking, how I can I come back ten times stronger?" Tupac stated.[74]

Tyson, who was about to embark on the second step of his own comeback, clearly fed off Tupac's ambition and energy. "We would always talk on the phone, saying we are coming out of prison to shock the world. We are gonna rule the world. Everybody is gonna know our names," Tyson recalled.[75]

Fearless and vulnerable, imaginative and shortsighted, Tyson and Tupac viewed success as a conquest. Prison had been done *to* them, both imagined. In each man's mind, he was both a ruler and a prisoner. In retrospect, however, Tyson recognized the problematic and reckless disposition of his own pursuit of redemption, a mindset he likely shared with his friend.

"I was disastrous when I came out," Tyson recalled. "Life was too fast for me when I came out. When I came out of prison I was very violent. I was real bitter. When I came out of prison in '95, I was a maniac."[76]

✳ ✳ ✳

The first signs of the Tyson–Tupac alliance took place on December 16, 1995. Although Tupac and Knight did not attend the Tyson–Mathis Jr. fight, Death Row Records made their presence felt nevertheless. The opening to Fox's broadcast featured a two-minute music video performed by Death Row co-founder Dr. Dre. Rapping from the corner of a dimly lit boxing ring, the West Coast icon delivered a remixed version of his hit single "Keep Their Heads Ringin'," released earlier that same year.

"It's a rough road back from lock down / but in the first round Mike will snatch the crown like a rebound / Ain't no trying this, fight scientist / from Brownsville to Catskill and he real with these iron fists," Dr. Dre raps, amid a montage of highlight-reel knockouts.[77]

Later that night, as Tyson made his way out of the Philadelphia Flyers locker room, those in attendance were treated to the sounds of a personalized remix of Tupac's unreleased track "Ambitionz Az a Ridah."

"I won't deny it, I'm a straight ridah / you don't wanna fuck with me / On a mission to be champ, since they let me free," Shakur's haunting voice bellowed throughout the arena, setting the tone.[78]

"When I first came home from prison, I played fucking Redman's 'Time 4 Sum Aksion' [for the Peter McNeeley fight]," Tyson recalled. "Pac came home and visited me and we were sitting down and he came over to me and said, 'Don't ever play those niggas again, they don't love you.' And I never played anybody but him again . . . his mentality was like this, we gonna kill together, we are gonna die together. We're together, we are family."[79]

Early on, Buster Mathis Jr. appeared to more than a mild upgrade in competition for Tyson, who, leading up to the McNeeley bout, had been away from the ring for more than three years. In rounds one and two, Tyson's ring rust was evident. The former champion repeatedly swung and missed with wild left and right hooks. Mathis, a slick defensive fighter, elected to stay on the inside of the onslaught and smother Tyson's counterpunches. In the third round, Tyson pivoted off the ropes, landed a vicious right uppercut, followed by two glancing right hooks. Mathis, who landed squarely on his back, was unable to beat referee Frank Cappuccino's ten count.

With these largely noncompetitive tune-up bouts out of the way, the boxing public clamored to see Tyson in a championship fight. It would be Tupac, however, who reclaimed his title first. On February 13, 1996, Tupac's *All Eyez on Me*, the first double album in the history of rap, was released to fanfare and anticipation never before experienced by a hip-hop artist. Largely off the strength of the Dr. Dre–assisted smash hit "California Love," the twenty-seven-song album, allegedly recorded in under two weeks, garnered quintuple platinum status in only a few short months.

Shortly after the album's release, Tupac continued to publicly goad his rivals Christopher "The Notorious B.I.G." Wallace and Sean "P. Diddy" Combs. In a *Vibe* article, released at the same time as *All Eyez on Me*, Tupac, once again, stoked the controversy by suggesting he had slept with Wallace's estranged wife, Faith Evans, who sang the hook on his song "Wonder Why They Call U Bitch." In the music video for his single "2 of Amerikaz Most Wanted," Tupac's highly anticipated first song with Death Row star Snoop Dogg, actors portray caricatures of Wallace and Combs—the Notorious P.I.G. and Bluff Daddy—further implicating the two in the 1994 Quad Studios shooting. As artists from New York rallied around Wallace, Combs, and their New York–based Bad Boy Records, West Coast artists sided with Tupac and the California-based Death Row camp. The ensuing war of words, played out in interviews and rap songs, would, in the coming years, lead to the full-blown media frenzy that came to be known as the East Coast–West Coast feud.

One month after the release of *All Eyez on Me*, Tyson, in his first title fight in almost six years, returned to the ring to face WBC heavyweight champion Frank Bruno. This time around Tupac and Knight were seated ringside at the MGM Grand Garden Arena. Tupac was decked out in a black tuxedo. Knight wore a burgundy suit, a black shirt and matching fedora, one red feather poking out the brim. Each man wore matching Death Row chains.

The kinetic energy building between Tyson and the Death Row camp was obvious to all who were paying any measure of attention. For the second straight fight, Tyson walked to the ring to a personalized Tupac recording, a track that later came to be known as "Road to Glory."

"Stand up Mr. Bruno, rise / Mike Tyson gonna brutalize that ass tonight / No hesitation for the whole nation / Mike gonna beat that ass so bad, he probably violate probation," Tupac rhymes on the track.[80]

"First round's for the time that I spent in a cell / The second round is for the media and the lies they tell / the third round for the pain that I felt inside, best recognize, I won't be denied," Tupac continues in the chorus.

With Tupac and Suge seated in the front row, Tyson did not disappoint. In perhaps his last great performance at the championship level, Tyson administered a brutal dismantling of the British champion. Bruno, whom Tyson had previously defeated in 1989, was cut late in the first round, penalized for holding in the second, and battered into the ropes and onto one knee in the third. Nobody in the arena was more excited than Tupac, who, on the televised Showtime broadcast, can be seen joyfully greeting Tyson, leaping into his arms in an embrace, as the champion exited the ring and made his way back to the locker room.

"You know what time it is! They can't see you, they can't see you," Tupac shouted, as Tyson grips him in a firm bear hug, the green WBC championship belt around his waist.[81]

The two men, for the first time in their friendship, were back atop the lofty cultural thrones they had once occupied. Unbeknownst to both, their furious collision course, "The Road to Glory" filled with thorns, as Tupac had dubbed it in his prefight song, would soon reveal itself as a path to self-destruction.

One week after Tyson reclaimed the WBC world heavyweight championship, Tupac Shakur and Suge Knight came face-to-face with Christopher Wallace and Sean Combs after the Soul Train Awards in Los Angeles, an incident where guns were drawn and heated words were exchanged.

Christopher "The Notorious B.I.G." Wallace: "That was the first time I really looked into his face. I looked into his eyes and I was like, 'Yo, this nigga is really buggin' the fuck out.' Pac didn't pull steel on me. He was on some tough shit, though. They made everything seem so dramatic. I felt the darkness when he rolled up that night. Duke came out the window [of the vehicle] fatigued out, screaming 'West Side! Outlaws!' I was like, 'That's Bishop [Tupac's character in the movie *Juice*]! Whatever he's doing right now, that's the role he's playing. He played that shit to a T. He had his little goons with him, and Suge was with him and they was like, 'We gonna settle this now.'" [82]

After the awards-show incident, Tupac released "Hit 'Em Up" a brutal diss track that took aim at Wallace, Combs, and several prominent New York artists who were both directly and indirectly affiliated with the Bad Boy label. On *All Eyez on Me*, Tupac had taken several veiled shots at Wallace and Combs but refused to mention either by name. For better or worse, "Hit 'Em Up" took the conventions of a hip-hop diss track in new directions. Never had a diss track featured such violent and threatening lyrics. Never had the lyrical insults been so personal. Critics were, of course, divided on the controversial song. *Billboard* magazine called the record "horrendous," others labeled the song "repugnant" and "unacceptable." Criticism aside, the song was unquestionably the biggest hip-hop story of the summer of 1996.

"[Tupac] was one of those guys who wasn't afraid of anything," recalled Tyson. "He was fearless. If he loved you, he never stopped loving you. If he was mad at you, he never stopped being mad." [83]

There were, of course, those who praised Tupac's "Hit 'Em Up" record. Fans of Death Row viewed the song symbolically, a comeback victory sealed with a knockout punch. Tupac, for lack of a better cliché, was a self-proclaimed people's champion who viewed himself as an underdog. In lyrically attacking Bad Boy Records, along with prominent East Coast figures such as Jay-Z, Nas, Mobb Deep, Tupac imagined himself as the Mike Tyson of the rap game.

"If everybody didn't like what I said about that other trick in Mobb Deep, fuck you too, nigga! If the nigga didn't want to get talked about, he shouldn't have stepped in the ring. If Tyson don't want to get knocked out, he don't step in the fucking ring. That's how the shit go. When Tyson step in the ring, he knock motherfuckers out. Well, that's what Tupac gonna do. When motherfuckers come up against me, they getting knocked the fuck out," Tupac rants at the end of his song "Why U Turn on Me."

"Nobody can ever be confused and think I'm fucking Mike Tyson and I'm heavyweight champion. I'm a little nigga but that's why it's so raw to watch me battle lions, battling niggas three times my size. Because, I'm a little skinny nigga," Tupac said to reporter Rob Marriot a few months before his murder.[84]

* * *

In the final months of Tupac Shakur's life, not all of the headlines were divisive. With his so-called comeback complete, Tupac turned his attention to building for the future. First came talk of a Tupac–Tyson joint venture, plans for an inner-city, youth-oriented organization that would provide aid and mentorship for disenfranchised youth.

"I want to be a part of the generation that builds the groundwork for us to raise each other," Tupac told *Vibe*, enthusiastic about his potential partnership with Tyson.[85]

Next came word of a Suge Knight–sponsored record label, Death Row East, an East Coast–oriented branch of the Death Row brand that would be run by Tupac himself. In an appearance on MTV, Tupac spoke of an East-West compilation album titled *One Nation*, his attempt to mend tensions between the two coasts.

Big Daddy Kane: "Me, Suge, and Pac linked up in Los Angeles before the Tyson fight. Suge was trying to sign me to this new venture called Death Row East. That's what the meeting was about. So, it started in LA and we drove to Vegas for the Mike Tyson fight. In Vegas, me and Tupac started talking about doing a song together. Suge looked at us and said, 'Shit, why y'all standing there talking about it. I put you on a flight right now.' Suge got us a flight and we went in the studio and banged out some songs."

One Nation, an album that never materialized, was to be Tupac's attempt to mend wounds between the East and West. The cross-coastal collaborations recorded for the album would, because of Tupac's untimely death, never be heard.

Big Daddy Kane: "I remember it was me, Pac, Eric B., and MC Hammer. Hammer was just signed to Death Row. The songs we recorded never made it out. Whenever there was a dispute with Death Row over Tupac's estate, after Pac passed, they [Death Row] claimed someone broke in the studio and stole the masters. These songs were some of the masters that were so-called stolen. But I remember the one me and Pac did together was called 'Wherever You Are,' the one me, Pac, and Hammer did was called 'Too Late Player.' And I wrote one for Hammer that was called 'What You Gonna Do for Me?' In the studio, Pac was a machine. He would come in there and write four or five songs back to back."

Big Daddy Kane continued: "Me and Pac actually had a long talk on the flight. We talked about being in control of what you do, about being careful. It was a beautiful conversation. But it was one of those things where, deep down in my heart, I kind of saw the end coming. There was too much going on in the brother's life. There was too much anger in his heart. He didn't have the right people around him. Didn't have the right people telling him the right things."

There were, of course, those who were skeptical of Death Row East. In aligning himself with Suge Knight and Tupac Shakur, Big Daddy Kane felt a certain level of pushback from the hip-hop community, especially in New York.

Big Daddy Kane: "It wasn't that people were warning me about Suge's negative energy. It was people saying, 'Why would you fuck with him when the East Coast and West Coast beefing? The West Coast trying to diss the East Coast,' and all that. But, at the time, I was like, Roc-A-Fella and Bad Boy ain't cut me no check. This ain't about no East Coast/West Coat thing, cats in the East Coast ain't trying to help me eat."

In the end, negative energy carried the day. After the release of "Hit 'Em Up," there was no turning back in the Death Row vs. Bad Boy beef. Artists on both coasts, with no personal connection to Tupac or Wallace, jumped on the bandwagon, trumpeting their territorial allegiance.

Christopher "The Notorious B.I.G." Wallace: "I kind of realized how powerful Tupac and I was. We two individual people, we waged a coastal beef. One man against one man, made a whole East Coast hate a whole West Coast hate each other."[86]

As Tupac and his East Coast rival further divided hip-hop's coastal allegiances, Tyson sought to unify the heavyweight titles. In signing to fight with WBA belt holder Bruce Seldon, who also boxed under Don King's promotional banner, Tyson aimed to secure two-thirds of the three-part heavyweight crown he successfully unified back in 1987. Although Seldon was hardly a marquee name, the announcement was met with great anticipation. The bout, scheduled for September 7, 1996, at the MGM Grand, marked another significant step in Tyson's comeback. Tupac, recognizing the importance of the fight, once gain cleared his busy schedule for the event, promising his friend a third consecutive original song for the ring walk.

In the documentary film *One Night in Vegas*, recording engineer Scott Gutierrez of Track Records recounted his memories of what would be Tupac Shakur's last recording session. "We got a call on a Monday or Tuesday, I think it was, that we were actually going to do a song for Mike Tyson," Gutierrez recalled. "Tupac was going to come in and lay some lyrics down on a beat we made. And we were going to ship it off to Vegas so that they could play it during the fight. We came in for a couple of days, busted out the beat. I got a call Friday morning saying, Pac is going to show up, making sure we were on point. Make sure you are ready when he comes in. He's got a tight schedule. He's going to come in for a couple of hours, he's going to lay down the lyrics, and you're going to mix it, and then we are going to send it off."

The last-minute nature by which Tupac's song was recorded concerned the heavyweight champion. His comments in *One Night in Vegas* clearly suggest Tupac's contribution was important to him.

"I called and asked him about the tape," Tyson recalled. "He made music for me to come out to for my fights. When is it going to be ready for the fight? And he said, 'I'm going to make it tomorrow.' I kept calling him because it was getting close."[87]

Tupac Shakur's final song, "Letz Get It On," was recorded at Track Studios in Northern Los Angeles on Friday, September 6, 1996, one day before the Tyson–Seldon bout. According to Gutierrez, Tupac arrived at the studio, listened to the beat three or four times, wrote his lyrics on the spot, and in less than twenty minutes from the time he entered the building completed the song. In hindsight, the lyrics in "Letz Get It On," the ring-walk equivalent of a diss track, are telling. Like much of the box-ing world, Tupac was apparently looking past Bruce Seldon and onward toward a heavily rumored, and long-awaited, Mike Tyson–Evander Holyfield showdown.

"We the real deal, tell Holyfield he next in line, tell him get his heart checked before he step to mine / Seldon, I hardly know ya, don't bother me to show ya / Don't let your head get gassed by that fast promoter," Tupac rhymes.[88]

The closing lines of the song, the final recorded words of Tupac's music career, like much of his previous work, are eerily prophetic: "This ain't gonna take long, you know how Tyson get down, everybody get ready to go to Club 662 [Suge Knight's Las Vegas Club] . . . hey, yo, Holyfield, you next!" Tupac states as the music fades out.

Tupac was, of course, correct in predicting the eventual Tyson–Holyfield showdown, as well as Tyson's quick work of Seldon. The bout lasted less than one round. The tragedy in those final lines lies in the fact that Tupac would never to make it to Club 622.

* * *

The matchup produced one of the worst heavyweight title fights in recent memory. Regardless, September 7, 1996, continues to be thought of as a pivotal moment in American sports and popular culture. The headlines the following morning blended hip-hop and boxing, exposing the links between the two seemingly disparate worlds. It was a night that all in attendance would never forget, especially for those who fought on the preliminary bouts staged earlier in the evening.

"It was overwhelming," recalled Christy Martin, a boxer there that night. "I don't think people realize that when you fight on the undercard of a Tyson fight, it doesn't even feel like a fight. The people who buy those expensive seats are NBA athletes, baseball players, actors, movie stars. You get in the ring and look around and it's Magic Johnson, Sugar Ray Leonard, Roseanne, and, on that night, it was Tupac. All kinds of celebrities. To be where I'm from, the coal miner's daughter from West Virginia, and to be fighting in front of those kinds of people, it was unbelievable."

Before Mike Tyson vs. Bruce Seldon, Christy Martin began the Tyson phase of her boxing journey as the walkout bout immediately following Tyson's knockout of Buster Mathis Jr. in Philadelphia. It was on the tele-vised undercard of Tyson's WBC showdown with Frank Bruno, however, that Martin caught her big break. In a bloody and action-packed war with Irish boxer Deirdre Gogarty, the "Coal Miner's Daughter" set the sport of women's boxing ablaze. Martin's performance, in the estimation of most observers, stole the show. Her victory resulted in a *Sports Illustrated* cover feature, along with several high-profile talk-show appearances. Following her victory over Gogarty, Don King chose to make Martin a fixture in Tyson's undercards. The night Tupac Shakur was shot in Las

Vegas, Martin fought in the first televised bout of the Tyson vs. Seldon pay-per-view undercard, scoring a fourth-round technical knockout over Melinda Robinson. As was typically her custom before Tyson bouts, Martin's plan was to take a shower, change clothes, and eventually find her ringside seat.

Christy Martin: "Everyone was talking about Tupac being there. My dressing room was right beside Tyson's. Tupac was back there with him. My sparring partner, Lil' Jimmy Malone, he was like, 'Hey Christy, look, there goes Tupac and Suge.' I was like 'Wow,' just like everyone else. But I was shy. I would never go up to him and ask for a picture. I hardly ever did that. Never in my wildest dreams did I think, in a few hours, he would be gone."

The fight itself was less than memorable. Early into the first round, Tyson threw a wild overhand right that appeared to graze the top of Seldon's head, his elbow perhaps landing flusher than his glove. Seldon crashed to the canvas, flopping on his stomach. For much of the crowd, the punch did not warrant such a dramatic reaction. Even referee Richard Steele, who initially called the knockdown a slip, seemed confused. As Seldon struggled to regain his composure, Steele picked up the count.

Actor Leon Robinson, who sat directly in front of Tupac at ringside, recalled the rap star's enthusiasm after the knockdown.

"He was sitting a row behind me. We said, 'What's up.' But, to be honest with you, he was beyond rambunctious. He was yelling to the point where the referee could hear him. He was calling the other guy a bum. He was going off. He had a lot of energy that night," Robinson reflected.[89]

When the bout continued, Tyson rushed to finish Seldon, landing a hard left hook that sent the WBA champion bouncing off the ropes and onto the canvas, facedown. Seldon made it to his feet by the count of six, staggered backward, and awkwardly shook his head in bewilderment. Steele waved the fight, the crowd booed the action, and Tyson now held two-thirds of the heavyweight championship.

The post-fight mood in the MGM Grand Garden Arena could be described as a mixture of jubilation, confusion, and bewilderment. Of all of Tyson's grossly uncompetitive postprison bouts, this was the least satisfying for boxing pundits. Seldon, many believed, was all but looking for a way out of the fight. As replays were shown on the overhead screens, some in the crowd chanted "fix, fix, fix," suggesting Seldon had taken a dive. Tyson, oblivious to the chants, looked to the heavens and spoke to his mentor Cus D'Amato.

"This one is for you Cus, two down, one to go," Tyson said at the close of his interview with Showtime's boxing analyst, Jim Gray.

Upon exiting the ring, Tyson was, once again, greeted by Tupac and Suge Knight. By all accounts, Tupac was overjoyed by Tyson's victory, literally jumping up and down with adulation.

"[Tupac] was really happy after the fight," Tyson recalled. He came to the press conference with me. We were just talking a bunch of shit. And I went home. And then he left. I was supposed to meet with him [at Club 662]. But I had just had a baby. I was supposed to join them. I was supposed to be with them."[90]

Inside the casino, camera crews captured Tupac's post-fight demeanor. In the surveillance footage, Tupac is visibly unable to contain his energy.

"Did you see Tyson do it to 'im. Did y'all see that? Fifty punches! I counted, fifty punches! I knew he was gon' take him out. We bad like that. Come out of prison and we running shit," Tupac shouted, Suge Knight coaxing him in the other direction.[91]

Moments later, in a corridor of the MGM Grand, Trevon Lane, a member of the Death Row entourage, alerted Tupac of the presence of a man named Orlando Anderson, a known Southside Crip, who was standing alone by a pillar. Earlier in the night, as Tupac and Suge made their way ringside, they had encountered a group of known Crips and exchanged words.

A few months before the Tyson fight, Orlando Anderson and three other Crip members had attempted to steal Lane's Death Row necklace during a confrontation at Lakewood Mall in California. After the encounter, rumors circulated that Sean Combs had offered a $5,000 reward for any Southside Crip who could steal a Death Row chain, which was only given out to artists and close associates of Suge Knight. If a Death Row medallion was snatched, Combs had planned to give the symbol to Wallace so that he could wear it in an upcoming music video.

When Trevon Lane brought Orlando Anderson's presence to Tupac's attention, the rap star immediately rushed over to Anderson and punched him in the face. Tupac's security pulled him away from the scuffle. Knight and other members of the Death Row entourage stomped and kicked Anderson while he was down on the ground. Knight's involvement in the incident would, in the coming months, result in a parole violation that sent the hip-hop CEO to prison for the next five years.

As MGM Grand security rushed to Anderson's aid, Tupac and Suge fled the scene of the altercation, a sea of fans following the Death Row entourage through the casino and out into the Las Vegas streets.

Christy Martin: "When the fight took place, me and my team were in a restaurant at the MGM Grand. Everyone was talking about the fight that happened. People were rushing everywhere and were scared. There were people saying a gunshot went off. The hotel locked everything down for a while. My team, they took us out through a security elevator. We left through the kitchen. When we get back to the room and we just shut it down and didn't hear anything else until the next day. After all these years, nobody has ever talked to me about seeing Tupac that night. Let me tell you, it was eerie. He was right there, right beside me. And a few hours later he was gone."

After fleeing the MGM Grand, Tupac returned to his suite at the nearby Luxor hotel, where the rapper changed clothes and readied himself for a scheduled appearance at the 662 Club after-party. Because of the scuffle with Orlando Anderson, Tupac asked his fiancée, Kidada Jones, to remain at the Luxor.

After departing from the hotel, Tupac, along with a six-vehicle caravan of security, visited Suge Knight's Las Vegas home. Upon leaving Knight's residence, Tupac elected to ride in the front passenger seat of Suge's black BMW. Tupac had asked his bodyguard to drive Kidada's car, serving as a designated driver for his return to the hotel.

On their way to 662 Club, Knight's black BMW was pulled over by Las Vegas police. The rap mogul was allegedly playing his music too loud. After being offered a warning, Suge, along with Tupac and the rest of the caravan, made their way down Las Vegas Boulevard. At an intersection of Flamingo and Koval, a white, four-door Cadillac pulled up next to Suge's car. An assailant seated in the back rolled down the window, stretched his arm out of the car, and discharged a firearm nine times, hitting Tupac with four shots.

As the white Cadillac sped away, Suge, who escaped the attack with only minor injuries to the back of his head, attempted to drive Tupac to University Medical Center. His BMW, which hopped the curb while attempting a U-turn on Las Vegas Boulevard, subsequently caught two flat tires and was halted by police on bicycles. The white Cadillac disappeared into the Las Vegas night.

Early into the morning, Tupac was rushed into surgery, which included the removal of his right lung.

Mike Tyson: "I was in my house [when I heard the news]. It's very difficult to talk about. He was just a young kid. He wanted to be great. Every time I go somewhere, it could be Africa, it could be New Zealand, everybody asks me, 'What was Tupac like?' He had an awesome energy."[92]

The following day, Tyson attempted to visit Tupac at the hospital but was denied access. On Friday, September 13, 1996, after six days in the intensive care unit, Tupac Amaru Shakur, at his mother's request, was taken off life support and pronounced dead at 4:03 p.m. The rap star was twenty-five years old.

✳ ✳ ✳

Less than two months after his tragic murder, on November 5, 1996, Tupac's first posthumous album, *The Don Killuminati: The Seven Day Theory* was released to blockbuster sales. The album cover, which depicts Tupac on a cross, naked, lists all of the cities in which the rapper had been arrested during his career.

Four days later, on November 9, 1996, Tyson walked to the ring to Tupac's posthumous single from the album, "Toss It Up." Later that night, in one of the most surprising upsets of the year, Tyson was knocked out by Evander Holyfield in the eleventh round of a mostly one-sided affair. Ironically, Tupac's death also marks the end of Tyson's career as a world champion. Iron Mike would never again win a title fight.

Following Tupac's death, a flurry of gang activity erupted in the streets of Compton, California. In a matter of ten days, eleven shootings took place between the Southside Crips and Mob Pirus. As news of Tupac's post-fight altercation at the MGM Grand became common knowledge, Orlando "Baby Lane" Anderson, who was questioned by Las Vegas police after the scuffle, shaped up as a prime suspect.

"Had Suge and other members of his entourage all been forthright and not wanted to take the matter into their own hands and handle it on the streets, Tupac's case should have, and could have, been resolved really quick," said LAPD detective Greg Kading. "Everybody knew it was Orlando. It was just getting the evidence to support that knowledge."[93]

When Anderson and his fellow gang members returned to Compton after the Tyson–Seldon fight, they quickly readied themselves for the inevitable retaliation.

"We were told Southside was responsible for the shooting of Tupac and it's coming back to Compton. So what that meant for us was that war was about to start. And, a few days after the shooting, it did," Officer Robert Land, a member of the Compton Gang Unit, recalled.[94]

At first, Anderson was unscathed by escalating gang violence. He was, however, picked up by authorities and brought in for questioning.

"We drove up, along with our other gang detectives, and he took off running into the house," Timothy Brennan, officer Robert Land's partner, recalled. "We chased him [Anderson] into the house. He went to a back room. We caught him. As we entered the house, there was AK-47s, shotguns, MAC-11s, ammunition all over the place. These guys were gearing up for a war, basically. We brought him in that day with several of the other ones from Southside."[95]

With Suge Knight and members of the Death Row entourage unwilling to participate in the investigation, the Las Vegas and Los Angeles police departments struggled to build their case against Anderson and his associates. In the streets of Compton, the violence continued.

"Baby Lane [Orlando Anderson] got shot up real bad. He got shot up in his kneecaps with AK-47s. He was wheelchair-bound for like almost a year. He had to learn to walk again. The beef was going on before that but this [Tupac's murder] kind of sparked it up because Suge got money and they [Southside Crips] got street money over there," rapper B.G. Knocc Out, Anderson's childhood friend, told VladTV in a 2019 interview.[96]

Like a scene out of a Shakespearian tragedy, the East Coast–West Coast feud all but came to a halt on March 9, 1997, when Christopher "The Notorious B.I.G." Wallace was murdered in a strikingly similar drive-by shooting in Los Angeles. In less than seven months, hip-hop lost its two biggest stars.

In October 1998, Anderson, in an unrelated gang shooting, was murdered at a Compton car wash. Conspiracy theories spread like California wildfire.

Some speculated that Suge Knight, from prison, conspired with dirty LAPD cops, David Mack and Harry Billups, to orchestrate a hit on Biggie as an act of retaliation for Tupac's murder. Other conspiracy theories suggested that the Southside Crips had shot Biggie to death because of Sean Combs's unwillingness to pay the $1 million bounty fee he had allegedly promised the gang for the Tupac shooting. In music magazines and tabloids, rumors quickly spread that Tupac, at the time of his murder, was in the process of leaving Death Row to start his own record company. Knight, some believed, had orchestrated the murders of both Tupac and Biggie. On the more fantastic side of the spectrum, conspiracy theories suggested that Tupac faked his own death to avoid jail time and get revenge on his enemies. As months turned into weeks, the rumors became increasingly far-fetched.

The downward spiral of Death Row Records was predictable. Dr. Dre, who left the company six months before the Las Vegas shooting, was no longer on board to supply hit music to the remaining artists on the label. Knight, after the fight at the MGM Grand, was back in prison for violating his parole. The label's biggest star, Tupac, was no longer alive. And, Snoop Dogg, Death Row's last man standing, was widely reported to be on his way out the door.

The release of posthumous Tupac albums, over the next few years, would not be enough to keep Death Row Records relevant in a rapidly shifting hip-hop landscape. An avalanche of controversy, lawsuits, and federal investigations would, in the end, result in the company filing for bankruptcy.

✳ ✳ ✳

In retrospect, the final months of 1996 also mark a transitional period in the sport of boxing. In their WBA title fight, Holyfield exposed the myth of Tyson's invincibility. Tyson's knockout loss to Holyfield was, of course, followed up by the biggest embarrassment of his professional career, the infamous ear-biting incident that resulted in both a disqualification loss and a one-year suspension from the sport.

After Tyson returned to boxing in January 1999, his career gradually drifted to the periphery of championship-level competition. In his final ten bouts, Tyson racked up five victories, three losses, and two no contests.

Tyson's behavior, both in the ring and in interviews, became increasingly bizarre. The Holyfield debacle, followed by back-to-back foul-filled performances, prompted the Nevada State Athletic Commission to suspend Tyson's boxing license.

No longer able to fight in Las Vegas, Tyson and his team sought opportunities abroad, securing bouts in Manchester, Glasgow, and Copenhagen. Tyson's overmatched opponents, bottom-tier heavyweights for the most part, were handpicked to match his style. Tyson, to many pundits, had become more of a promotional sideshow than an actual contender. When Tyson did get his final shot at the heavyweight title, in May 2002, he was knocked out by Lennox Lewis in a largely one-sided affair.

September 7, 1996, marked the end of two dynamic and legendary eras.

"A lot of despair, guilt. It was really, just, inconceivable to fathom that really happened. It was really sad. [Tupac] had come to see me," Tyson later recalled, fighting back tears.[97]

DIRTY SOUTH

O n the surface, it would appear that Mike Tyson's successor as hip-hop culture's symbolic champion emerged from the most unlikely of locations. Once known as "The Cradle of Naval Aviation," the sleepy Gulf Coast town of Pensacola, the western-most city in the Florida panhandle, is hardly a hotbed of rap talent. By the close of 1996, however, hip-hop had already begun to subtly move in a new direction—south.

For much of rap music's childhood, New York City maintained a cultural monopoly. Hip-hop's awkward teenage years, one could argue, belonged to Los Angeles. In both eras, Tyson maintained direct ties to the most important figures on each coast: Public Enemy (Def Jam/New York) and Tupac Shakur (Death Row/California). The firmly establish New York/California binary, by the time Tyson lost his WBA title to Evander Holyfield in 1996, had already begun to crumble.

The story of hip-hop's civil war, one could easily argue, remains the most often-misunderstood chapter in the genre's history. East Coast–West Coast tensions did not simply begin and end with Tupac Shakur and Christopher Wallace. Competitive rivalries existed between East Coast and West Coast hip-hop artists as early as 1988, when Public Enemy joined Ice Cube's solo project in an attempt to squash those hostilities. These debates primarily centered on issues of artistic authenticity and economic superiority: while New York artists, in the early days, claimed geographic legitimacy, West Coast artists, during the rise of gangsta rap, began to sell more albums.

What is often lost in our retelling of hip-hop's coastal split is a critical examination of how these performances of regional identity gave way to audience expectation. As hip-hop music continued to gain a more mainstream audience and copycat artists and producers began to regurgitate already established coastal formulas, both artists and aficionados grew weary of the East Coast–West Coast split, setting the stage for the rise of rap's unofficial third coast, "The Dirty South."

It is no coincidence that Roy Jones Jr., the four-division champion who eventually carried Tyson's metaphorical torch as boxing's hip-hop ambassador, was a direct product of the shifting geographic demographic of the post-Tupac-and-Biggie landscape. Jones did not merely attract hip-hop royalty to ringside seats. He collaborated with these artists on their albums and appeared in their videos. Jones didn't walk to the ring to original hip-hop compositions. He played his own original songs, often performing the lyrics on his way to the ring via a microphone and headset. Jones didn't simply pal around with hip-hop executives; he started his own rap label. To understand the Pensacola, Florida, native's impact on hip-hop and boxing, one must first understand the transitional period in which he became the sport's pound-for-pound best fighter. The rise of hip-hop's "Dirty South" coincided directly with the emergence and long reign of boxing's first, full-fledged pugilist turned rapper.

Long before the murders of Tupac Shakur and Christopher Wallace, budding hip-hop movements in Miami were the first to produce rap stars outside of the East Coast–West Coast binary. One of the key pioneers of this new wave of rap music was Luther "Luke Skywalker" Campbell. Born in the gang-riddled Liberty City area of Miami, Campbell rose to prominence as the leader of the controversial rap group 2 Live Crew. During a career highlighted by lawsuits, controversy, and commercial success, Campbell earned his pioneering status by become the first Southern hip-hop artist to appear on the cover of *The Source*; his group was also the first Southern act to earn a platinum plaque.

Initially viewed by music critics as an off-brand, too vulgar for some, not artistic enough for others, the 2 Live Crew sound melded the simplistic call-and-response rhyming technique made famous by early New York emcees and the potty-mouth brand of lyricism made famous in West Coast gangsta rap with a bass-heavy soundscape that was all its own. Miami Bass, as the 2 Live Crew sound came to be known (also dismissively referred to as X-rated rap, booty rap, and dirty rap), was largely written off as "party music that did not take itself seriously."[98] The enduring influence of the group, particularly in the South, is undeniable. 2 Live Crew granted the state of Florida an authenticity that did not exist before the group's success.

Over the years, Miami earned its moniker as the "bass capital" of hip-hop, with artists such as DJ Magic Mike, DJ Laz, Half Pint, Anquette, and Poison Clan following in the tradition established by Luther Campbell. The conundrum for Miami-area artists would not be commercial success. The regional style quickly took off. Instead, Miami hip-hop artists have, since the mid-1980s, struggled to get critical respect from journalists and artists from New York and California. Southern hip-hop, as a result of this history of critical backlash, adopted a regional sense of comradery.

"Miami rappers, from Vanilla Ice to Pitbull to Flo Rida, have never had trouble selling records, though it's hard to find many hip-hop fans who take any of those three seriously these days," music critic Ben Westhoff wrote in 2015.[99]

The second major Southern rap star to emerge on the mainstream scene was Brad Jordan, better known by his stage name, Scarface. Jordan's career began in his hometown of the Fifth Ward in Houston, Texas, where he signed with local upstart Rap-A-Lot Records: an independent label founded by James Prince, a natural-born hustler who began his business career as the owner of a small used-car lot. The Fifth Ward is, as most boxing fans will recognize, the adopted home of heavyweight champion George Foreman. Following in Foreman's giant footsteps, James Prince sought to make his own mark in the world. By the late 1990s, the used-car-salesman-turned-rap-mogul became the Suge Knight of the South, his underdog label growing into the pillar of Texas-based rap music.

Light heavyweight champion Reggie Johnson: "When you are young, you really don't know what is going on in the streets. I had twin sisters, my dad was locked up, my mother had me when she was fourteen years old. We lived in the apartments out in Fifth Ward. It was bad. Just like most fighters, most men of color, I came from the bottom. I found a way to rise. By age twelve, I was going down the wrong road. Cutting up in school. Fighting. My uncle took me to the Salvation Army Boxing Club, where I met the late Mr. James Carter, who became my white daddy, my father, and boxing coach. Me and Tyson kind of have the same story in that way. That's also where I first met Willie D. Me and Willie D were on the same boxing team at the Salvation Army Boxing Club. His daddy was a great boxer and he was good too. But when rap music hit our era, Willie D went that route. I stuck with boxing."

Johnson continued: "I remember right there, down the street from the Salvation Army, J. Prince used to work at a Foodland. He used to work out of an auto mechanic shop too. He was a go-getter. Lil' J's dad and my dad grew up in Fifth Ward together, they used to run the streets together. When Rap-A-Lot Records took off, he did a lot to give back to the community, started his own boxing gym. J Prince was always a huge presence in the community. The Rap-A-Lot artists became role models for kids in our community."

The Geto Boys (previously spelled Ghetto Boys), Rap-A-Lot's flagship group, at first maintained somewhat of a revolving membership. In their 1988 debut *Making Trouble*, a commercial failure, the group consisted of DJ Ready Red, Bushwick Bill, Sire Jukebox, and Prince Johnny C. The following year, James Prince found his winning formula by releasing a retooled version of the group, replacing Sire Jukebox and Prince Johnny C with local rappers Willie D and Brad Jordan, better known as Scarface. After the release of *Grip It! On That Other Level*, Jordan captured the attention of fans around the country, largely because of his unique delivery, controversial lyrics, and undeniable skill as a storyteller. Jordan, along with his label and fellow group members, also drew the ire of critics who found his lyrical content violent, misogynistic, and otherwise vulgar. Even within the Fifth Ward, some were apprehensive about the message.

"I always supported the music," Reggie Johnson told me. "Always. But I liked the more positive stuff. The Geto Boys had some songs that were out there. Crazy. But I knew Scarface. I knew Bushwick very well. When I moved back to Houston, later in my career, we lived in the same gated community. I always supported the music but I also understood the criticism."

The surreal violence found on early Geto Boys tracks was unique to the genre. Unlike early West Coast tracks, these were songs not so much focused on the harsh realities that surrounded the artists but graphic depictions of "urban paranoia," insider accounts of sociopathic impulses born out of those circumstances.[100] Jordan, the Geto Boys' strongest writer and performer, would build off the "eloquent manic" persona and "Fuck all y'all working-class chic" tropes made famous by the Geto Boys in his own solo projects.[101] Until the commercial success of the group's 1991 hit "My Mind Playin Tricks on Me," critics were quick to write off the Geto Boys' formula as relying on mere shock value, an attempt to up the rhetorical ante of vulgar West Coast lyricism. Just as was the case with 2 Live Crew, the South was quick to defend their homegrown talent, taking pride in a rapidly emerging regional hip-hop identity that held no identifiable geographic boundaries.

"There was a lot of prejudice against southerners [in hip-hop] at the time . . . a lot of people saw what the Geto Boys were doing as letting them know that if they were from the South, it was okay to be themselves. Up until that point, everything that was coming out was sounding like New York, or had to have that flavor," Rap-A-Lot co-founder James Prince reflected in an interview with *The Source*.[102]

The popularity of 2-Live Crew and the Geto Boys opened the door for the simultaneous emergence of highly influential movements in New Orleans and Atlanta, both of which set into motion what would later become a southern rap boom. Despite its immense popularity, and perhaps because of it, southern rap was slow in gaining the respect of music-industry journalists and hip-hop purists. Whether it was emergence of New Orleans bounce music, an energetic style of call-and-response rap that mixes Mardi Gras Indian chants with tales of street culture, or the eventual rise of crunk—up-tempo, bass-heavy, dance-floor-ready beats and delivery made famous in Atlanta—the story of southern hip-hop is that of marginal identity despite commercial success.

As was the case in Houston, the New Orleans hip-hop scene was defined by homebred indie labels composed of mostly homebred talent. With the swift rise of No Limit Records (home to Master P, Silkk the Shocker, Mia X, C-Murder, and Mystikal) and Cash Money Records (home to artists such as Lil Wayne, Juvenile, B.G., Birdman, and Mannie Fresh), the commercial popularity of New Orleans hip-hop paved the way for artists from other southern locations. It would be Atlanta, Georgia, in the coming years, that would quickly become the controlling city in southern hip-hop.

Within a five-year span, Atlanta's rap movement, brought on by Jermaine Durpri's So So Def imprint (home of Kriss Kross, Da Brat) and Babyface and L.A. Reid's joint venture LaFace Records (home of Atlanta hip-hop pioneers Outkast and Goodie Mob), became the overwhelmingly dominant subgenre found on the American music charts. In particular, the critical and commercial success of Outkast (a hip-hop duo made of artists Big Boi and André 3000) marked a new era of respectability for southern rap. With their third album *Aquemini,* Outkast became the first southern group to score a perfect five-mic rating in *The Source.* The group's double album *Speakerboxxx/The Love Below,* years later, would earn the South its first Diamond certification from the RIAA, indicating 10 million record sales.

The term "Dirty South," coined by Outkast's cohorts Goodie Mob in 1996, quickly became the dominant signifier for all southern hip-hop. From Atlanta to Memphis to New Orleans to Houston, southern rappers quickly began to use the term to identify themselves as part of hip-hop's so-called third-coast movement. Building off this momentum, budding hip-hop movements in Kentucky, Tennessee, Virginia, North Carolina, and Mississippi made rural identity acceptable in a genre dominated by artists form large metropolitan areas.

Roy Jones Jr., boxing's undisputed king of the Dirty South, a Florida native with direct ties to James Prince's Houston-based Rap-A-Lot Records, arrived on center stage at the perfect time. Never had southern rap music been more popular. Roy's struggle for respect, in many regards, mirrored that of his southern rap comrades; his career would be of unquestionable dominance, dampened by widespread and persistent criticism. When Roy Jones Jr. came on the scene, the Dirty South was in search of a Mike Tyson to call its own.

*   *   *

The story begins in a homemade boxing ring built in the pasture of a small farm located just seventeen miles outside the Gulf Coast town of Pensacola, Florida. It is the familiar tale of a domineering father injecting his love of boxing into the life of his firstborn son, vicariously rectifying the disappointments of his own youth through the accomplishments of his child. While the father–son narrative is all too familiar to the sport, the results, in this particular instance, were anything but typical.

Roy Jones Sr., who grew up on a small farm with his twelve siblings, was, at least in the metaphorical sense, born into a fighting family. His own father kept a pair of boxing gloves in the home to settle disputes between the boys. A standout athlete in baseball, basketball, and football at Washington High in Pensacola, Jones Sr. did not begin his own boxing journey until after a tour of duty in Vietnam, where he earned a Bronze Star for his bravery. When Jones returned from Vietnam, he briefly pursued his dream of becoming a professional boxer, earning a meager living in the process. The biggest payday of Jones's career came via a third-round knockout loss to Marvelous Marvin Hagler on the undercard of Sugar Ray Leonard's bout with Vinnie DeBarros in Hartford, Connecticut.

"I fought maybe seven fights where I didn't get but $17. I fought once in Mexico. That was the most I got, $1,500," Jones Sr. stated in a 2011 interview.[103]

After Roy Jones Sr. married his longtime girlfriend, Carol Lewis, in 1968, he set aside his dream to start a family, retiring from the sport with a record of thirteen wins, six losses, and one draw. Shortly after marring Lewis, Jones Sr. took a mechanic job at nearby Naval Air Station Pensacola. His first son, Roy Jones Jr., was born the following year. The boy, as is often the case in such scenarios, quickly became the focus of his father's ambition.

When Roy Jones Jr. was an infant, his father constructed a makeshift boxing gym in the family's garage. Strapped into his stroller, Roy accompanied his father during daily workouts. As the years passed, boxing became the centerpiece of their relationship. When Roy was just five years old, his father would get down on both knees and spar with him, roughing him up just enough to simulate an actual fight.

"Some nights he would beat me, some nights he would let me win," Roy remembered. "But, when he beat me, all day the next day at school, all I thought about was how can I get home and win tonight."[104]

Aside from boxing, it was a childhood of farm chores, hunting, fishing, raising roosters, and attending cockfights, a controversial blood sport where two roosters are bred and conditioned to fight to the death, often with razor blades attached to their thin legs. As a child, Roy accompanied his father to cockfights, road trips across state lines to Louisiana where the sport was, at the time, still legal. On countless occasions, Jones Jr. watched roosters that he loved and raised be killed in action. Amid the bloodstained canvases of the Louisiana cockpits, the young boy began to recognize the destiny being carved out for him.

"To see a game rooster and see how proud he is, that is kind of what helped me identify with what I was," Jones Jr. reflected.[105]

No doubt seeking his father's approval, Jones Jr., at nine years old, entered the ring as an amateur for the first time. To prepare his son for battle, Jones Sr. built a boxing compound on his farm, recruiting local kids in the neighborhood to train with his son. The father was a relentless and brutal taskmaster. He forced his son to box boys who were taller, heavier, and older. When Roy started to dominate the local boys in sparring, his father made him spar with one arm tied behind his back. If he dominated with his left hand, his father switched to his right.

"The methods and the techniques, you have to use to train him, are just not something that should be viewed by the general public because they would not understand," Jones Sr. once told Fox Sports.[106]

Ethics aside, the brutal training regimen produced results. Roy dominated the Gulf Coast area competition, quickly moving on to dominance at the national level. In 1984, he captured the gold medal in the Junior Olympics, an achievement followed up by back-to-back Golden Gloves titles. At just nineteen years old, he became the youngest boxer to earn a spot on the 1988 U.S. Olympic team. Winning a gold medal became something of a holy grail for the father and son. The axis of their relationship revolved around the sport of boxing.

At first, it appeared that Roy Jones Jr.'s place atop the gold-medal podium was a foregone conclusion. He blazed through the early rounds of the junior middleweight tournament without losing a single round. In the gold-medal match, against hometown favorite Park Si-hun, the action was no different. Roy used speed and footwork to bewilder his opponent, scoring a standing eight count in the second round and, according to Count-a-Punch stats, outlanded the Korean eighty-six punches to only thirty-two.

"Park Si-hun is taking a thrashing. Roy Jones building up a tremendous lead," analyst Marv Albert called in the final seconds of the fight.[107]

"If Jones doesn't win this, there is something rotten in Korea," Ferdie Pacheco joked in response to Albert's comments.

At the conclusion of the bout, NBC cameras captured Jones Sr., who traveled to Seoul Korea to witness the fruits of his labor, smiling and applauding from the stands as the decision was about to be announced, a look of adulation adorning his typically stern face. Moments later, the father–son dream was shattered. A 3-2 tiebreaker was granted to Park Si-hun—arguably the most controversial decision in the history of Olympic boxing. To hide his tears, Roy covered his face with a towel as he exited the ring.

Rumors of corruption quickly surfaced. In the Olympic boxing equivalent of a makeup call, Jones Jr. was awarded the Val Barker Trophy as the best boxer of the 1988 Olympic Games. As the result of an International Olympic Committee investigation, the three judges who voted against Jones Jr. were banned for life. The AIBA punch-counting system, which left plenty of room for both error and corruption, was abandoned in years to come.

All of this did little to lessen Roy's disappointment. He had given much of his young life to the pursuit of a gold medal. The painstaking sacrifices he had endured, coupled with the Olympic disappointment, gave way to an adversarial attitude that marked his approach to professional boxing. The irony of the high-profile Olympic scandal, which served as an embarrassment to the Korean games, is that it arguably made Roy more of a household name than would have been the case had he won the medal he rightfully deserved. The devastated nineteen-year-old, who initially told reporters that he might never box again, returned to his hometown a celebrity.

Roy Jones Jr. began his professional career in the spring of 1989, the same year Mike Tyson began experimenting with hip-hop-themed ring walks. Rather than signing a promotional deal with the likes of Top Rank or Don King Productions, Roy elected to remain loyal to his father who, for much of his early career, acted as promoter, manager, and head trainer. As a result of this decision, sixteen of Roy's first nineteen professional bouts took place in his hometown of Pensacola, many of which were hosted in local venues with no national television exposure. Roy easily pummeled the overmatched opponents his father lined up for him, building up his regional fan base but making little headway with respect to securing marquee fights. As other Olympians found their way onto lucrative televised cards in Las Vegas and New York City, Roy's frustration began to mount. Now in his early twenties, the young professional began to resent his father's suffocating presence in his life.

✳ ✳ ✳

In the years that followed, Roy Jones Jr. viewed the incident as a sign from God, a fork-in-the-road moment that shifted the trajectory of his career. Aside from his fighting gamecocks, Roy Jones Jr.'s pit bulls were his closest friends.

It happened on a hazy Florida afternoon, in June 1992. After one of Roy's dogs bit his younger sister on the arm, his father, in a fit of rage, grabbed a shotgun and killed it. When Roy came home, he was devastated by the news. The family dispute, messy by any definition of the term, resulted in Roy splitting from his father both personally and professionally. The two men would not speak to each other again for almost three years.

After the altercation, a new team was put into place. Alton Merkerson, Roy's favorite coach on the U.S. Olympic squad, was called in to serve as his new head trainer. While Merkerson, a former U.S. Army general, was no pushover, his soft-spoken demeanor and willingness to allow Roy to be his own man was a welcome change. With Merkerson, the young professional, for the first time, was permitted to listen to hip-hop music in the gym, able to explore a side of himself that he didn't share with his father.

Long before his father's departure from his corner, Roy Jones Jr. was writing his own rhymes, freestyling with friends. Rap music was Roy's only passion not born of his father's design. As a young professional, Roy drew inspiration from the rise of southern hip-hop, particularly the work of Scarface. The music was a positive space for Roy to vent and express the anger and frustration that surrounded his life.

"Everybody has their preferences," Roy said in a 2016 interview. "For me, Scarface [of the Geto Boys] is the best to ever do it. He's always got something I can relate to. And, where I grew up as a kid, understanding what I can relate to, I always knew exactly where Scarface was coming from. As a matter of fact, I was going through some of the same things at the time he made those songs. I wasn't the dope man on the street, but, in other ways, I was going through the same things in life."[108]

Until Roy Jones Jr. broke from his father and was given free rein over his career, few outside the boxer's inner circle understood the importance of hip-hop music in his life.

"Music is something [Roy Jones Jr.] has a passion for. . . . He loves fishing, chickens, music, and boxing. That would sum up Roy Jones," Deidre LaCasse of Body Head Entertainment stated.[109]

Early on, Roy Jones Jr.'s hip-hop sensibilities were relegated to his choice of ring-walk music. With his father no longer running his professional affairs, Roy began to consistently fight outside of his home state of Florida, securing matchups that fast-tracked the middleweight contender to a title shot. As he began to secure more high-profile bouts, the hip-hop side of his public persona became increasingly evident. Not unlike the "Dirty South" artists that inspired his training, success, for Roy, came before critical acclaim.

In May 1993, as the first half of an HBO co-feature with fellow Olympic teammate Riddick Bowe, Roy Jones Jr. captured his first world championship by defeating a little-known Philadelphia fighter named Bernard Hopkins for the IBF middleweight belt vacated by James "Lights Out" Toney. As is often the case with vacant title fights, especially those involving belts relinquished by elite fighters, the bout was met with tepid enthusiasm. Hopkins, who boxed under the moniker "The Executioner," entered the ring wearing the mask of a medieval headsman, accompanied by two muscle-bound executioners brandishing fake weapons. The act, at the time, was perceived as the kind of cheap gimmick fighters use to attract attention. Unlike Jones, who competed at the highest level of amateur competition, Hopkins perfected his craft during a four-year prison stint for armed robbery. After losing his pro debut via a four-round majority decision, the rugged Philadelphia boxer reeled off twenty-one consecutive wins, securing his number-two ranking by the IBF. Hopkins had, at this point in his career, demonstrated world-class perseverance but not world-class talent.

"Nowadays, people talk like I got out of prison and started knocking guys out and winning titles," Hopkins told me. "It wasn't like that. It was a long and hard road. There was no plan B and we were learning on the job. We didn't just come home and get a belt. I was grateful for the opportunity but not comfortable."

In only his third appearance on the HBO network, Roy Jones Jr.'s bout with Bernard Hopkins was viewed by many pundits as little more than a step up in competition. Fans and pundits expected from Jones a coronation, a dazzling knockout. What they got was a cautious and tactical affair. Roy, who later claimed to have entered the bout with an injured right hand, continually switched from orthodox to southpaw throughout the bout, showboating and boxing from the outside. Roy's speed and reflexes carried the day, earning him a unanimous decision victory and the first of many title belts. It would be incorrect, however, to call Roy Jones Jr.'s victory over Bernard Hopkins anything but anticlimactic.

"I've seen Ray Leonard, and Roy Jones is no Ray Leonard," HBO analyst Harold Lederman scoffed.[110]

"The irony is that while Jones may pick up his first championship, the performance is likely to diminish the luster of his image, somewhat," HBO analyst Jim Lampley added.

The true irony of this criticism, in hindsight, is that Hopkins, after losing to Roy, would go on to become the longest-reigning champion in the division's history, breaking records and unifying titles in both the middleweight and light heavyweight divisions. At the time, few experts could have anticipated the significance of Roy's accomplishment in easily outboxing the future middleweight legend.

Winning the IBF middleweight title did little to quell Roy's anger and dissatisfaction with the sport of boxing. Poor reviews dampened the Olympic redemption narrative.

After defeating Hopkins, Roy reeled off four straight victories, dominating mostly nondescript opponents. Despite building an undefeated record of 26 and 0 (23 knockouts), Roy was still viewed as an unproven commodity by most boxing experts. Questions about his unorthodox style and quality of opposition persisted.

The breakout performance Roy Jones Jr. longed for did not come until he moved up in weight to face one of boxing's pound-for-pound elites, IBF super middleweight champion James "Lights Out" Toney. For the first time in Roy's life, he found himself in the position of underdog. With a record of 44-0-2 (29 knockouts), Toney, one year younger than Roy, was already a two-division champion. His record featured victories over fighters such as Mike "The Body Snatcher" McCallum and Iran Barkley. The trash-talking Michigan native, who worked up a genuine hatred for his opponents, had a throwback style and menacing tough-guy bravado that called to mind a bygone era. Some felt, with the bigger and more experienced Toney, Roy was in over his head.

On November 18, 1994, in his first pay-per-view headlining event at the MGM Grand, Roy Jones Jr., dressed in a white tuxedo, danced his way to the ring to the sounds of Bone Thugs-N-Harmony's "Thuggish Ruggish Bone." The bout marked Roy's return to a truly grand stage, the eyes of the boxing world focused on him. From the opening bell, Roy dominated the action. His blinding hand speed and superior athleticism bewildered the champion. Roy's rapid-fire combinations negated Toney's offense throughout much of the night. The highlight of Roy's performance came in the third round when the Pensacola native, imitating a move that he learned from one of his fighting gamecocks, spread his arms like wings. As Toney attempted to mimic the move, Roy leaped in with a left hook, landing a blow that resulted in a comical flash knockdown.

For some, the performance had been too dominant. The subtext of the Toney–Jones Jr. fight centered on the champion's struggles to make the 168-pound limit. Toney, who reportedly weighed over 200 pounds at the beginning of his training camp, gained 16 pounds in the twenty-four hours proceeding the weigh-in. During the fight, HBO commentator Gil Clancy, for example, speculated that Toney's sluggish performance was, at the very least, partially due to the unhealthy rehydration tactics. Toney, himself, was happy to use this narrative.

James Toney: "I was young and dumb. I should have postponed the fight. But I went through it and paid the price. I was a jackass."

While the victory over Toney did not silence Roy's budding legion of naysayers, it did launch the boxer into a new stratosphere of celebrity. Roy was now a key figure in the sport. In true southern fashion, Roy made it a point to let his family and friends know that he had not forgotten his roots.

"I want to thank my father and Coach Merk for all the training and everything they taught," Roy stated in the post-fight interview, subtly attempting to extend an olive branch to his estranged father.[111]

Roy's hometown shout-outs, often marked by the phrase "Pensacola in the house," gradually became a staple of his post-fight interviews. Perhaps to his own economic detriment, Roy also continued to bring big-time boxing to small-town Florida. The rising superstar followed his victory over Toney with a hometown showcase against Antoine Byrd, the first world championship contest ever held in Pensacola. In an attempt to make his entrance more theatric, Roy walked to the ring to the sounds of his own original rap composition, recorded in his own home studio. Roy easily dispatched of Byrd in the first round. The song lasted longer than the fight.

The hip-hop antics continued in Roy's next big fight, a pay-per-view showdown with former junior welterweight and junior middleweight champion Vinny "The Pazmanian Devil" Pazienza, a popular all-action fighter from Cranston, Rhode Island, who, against all odds, had successfully returned to the sport thirteen months after suffering a broken neck in a car accident. During his improbable comeback, Pazienza compiled nine straight wins, highlighted by two victories over an aging Roberto Duran. For Roy, the technical matchup couldn't have been more perfect. Unlike Toney, who was a calculated counterpuncher, Pazienza was a wild character both in and outside the ring—a working-class, trash-talking brawler with an attacking style. In overcoming his brutal car crash, Pazienza played the role of the sympathetic underdog. He was, in almost every way, the perfect juxtaposition to Roy's cautious and flashy style.

For the Pazienza fight, on June 24, 1995, Roy once again entered the ring to the sounds of his own original rap song, the lyrics, this time around, aimed squarely at his brash challenger. As expected, Pazienza lived up to his reputation. From the opening bell, he fought gamely, attacking Roy, ripping body shots and wildly swinging with looping hooks. The first round was fought at a blazing pace. As the bout proceeded, however, Roy's unique combination of speed and power gradually broke down the game challenger. With each passing round, a one-sided mismatch unfolded. In the fifth, Pazienza, according to CompuBox stats, did not land a single punch. In the sixth round, beaten and bloodied, Vinny Pazienza got knocked down three times.

After obliterating "The Pazmanian Devil," Roy found himself in the unfortunate position of being out of big-name opponents. Following the resounding TKO victory, very few critics challenged Roy's greatness in the ring. And much to Roy's financial dismay, very few boxers in his weight class seemed all that eager to challenge it either.

Largely because of the lack of quality dance partners, Roy's career began to stagnate. Highlight-reel knockouts against overmatched opponents did little to advance the idea that Roy was a box-office star. At times, even Roy seemed bored with his own career. The storylines leading into his HBO televised bouts often had nothing to do with his opponents whatsoever. In his title defense against undefeated but unheralded Eric Lucas, for example, Roy played basketball for the Mississippi Mud Dogs, a minor league basketball team, on the morning of the fight. As the string of mismatches continued, Roy's hip-hop ring walks gradually became a larger part of the show. The boxing media, eager for something to talk about, began to consistently work the titles and contents of each new song into the broadcast storyline.

In search of bigger names and more competitive fights, the polarizing champion once again jumped weight classes. On November 22, 1996, almost two weeks after Mike Tyson's upset loss to Evander Holyfield, Roy Jones Jr. moved up in weight to face Mike "The Body Snatcher" McCallum. At thirty-nine years old, McCallum was a recognizable name but no longer a prime fighter. The move was significant more so because a win would catapult Roy into a division filled with potential rivals. In the buildup to the fight, Roy and McCallum showed each other nothing but respect. Unfortunately, the lack of disdain between the two fighters also showed itself in the ring. During the first nine rounds, Roy boxed McCallum cautiously, easily outpointing the once-menacing puncher. At the close of the tenth, a straight right hand put McCallum on the seat of his pants. Rather than go for the kill, Roy pulled back, coasting to an easy victory. Some speculated this reluctance was evidence of fear rather than compassion.

Roy Jones Jr: "When I fought Mike McCallum, I fought him because he told me he was in a situation and he needed a little help. And he was willing to fight for that little help. In the tenth round, Mike started to feel a little frisky, because I was really trying to carry him, and he came at me a little bit so I said, 'Okay, let me show you something Mike.' Pop. He goes down. I wasn't out there to hurt Mike McCallum."[112]

Regardless of whether Roy Jones Jr. carried Mike McCallum, there was no disputing the fact that the title fight had been, for the most part, uneventful. At one point during the closing rounds, a scuffle in the bleachers appeared to get more attention than the one in the ring. All three judges scored all twelve rounds for Roy, improving his undefeated record to 34-0 (29 KOs). Because the three-division champion had yet to take part in a closely contested fight, even his biggest supporters began to worry that their champion might never find a worthy rival. Controversy and drama, to the surprise of many, was lurking just around the corner.

Y'ALL MUST'VE FORGOT

His trunks were styled to resemble those worn by Muhammad Ali in his legendary upset over George Foreman in Kinshasa, Zaire, the words "Shock the World," sewn into his boxing robe. His headfirst lunging style, awkward and crafty, one could argue, was perhaps more suited for comparisons to Joe Frazier. At 26-0 (18 KOs), Montell "Ice" Griffin was seen by pundits as a worthy contender. Two decision victories over James Toney, both of which took place in non-title fights, validated Griffin's credentials. Yet few viewed Griffin, the son of a Chicago-area trainer, as a serious threat to the best fighter in boxing. The bout, both competitive and controversial, injected much-needed drama into Roy Jones Jr.'s unblemished career.

On March 21, 1997, almost two weeks after the murder of Christopher "The Notorious B.I.G." Wallace, Roy Jones Jr. made his way to the ring to an original rap song titled "Patience Is a Virtue." The premise of the song—good things come to those who wait—couldn't have been more ill-fitting for what was about to take place. From the outset, Griffin used his quick jab and awkward head movement to force Roy to the ropes, landing looping hooks to the head and body once the champion was cornered. Griffin's strength and physicality, coupled with his high work rate, helped the challenger dictate the pace of the early rounds. As Roy boxed cautiously, retaliating in quick spurts, Griffin landed sharp counters. After four rounds, HBO's unofficial judge Harold Lederman scored the bout three rounds to one in favor of the challenger. A gargantuan upset was brewing, it appeared.

In rounds five and six, the action continued to heat up, with each man landing flurries of power shots. Heading into the second half of the fight, Griffin had already won more rounds, done more damage, than any of Roy Jones Jr.'s previous opponents. In the closing moments of the seventh round, however, things appeared to turn. As Griffin leaned back to duck a combination, Roy landed a short left hook that sent him to the canvas. The flash knockdown, one of only eight landed punches in the round, inched Roy back into the fight.

In the eighth round, Griffin rallied back, using a shoulder bump to create space for a hard right hand that sent Roy stumbling backward into the ropes. Heading into the ninth round, there was no question that Roy Jones Jr.'s undefeated record was in jeopardy. According to CompuBox, Griffin had outlanded Roy 130 to 92 through the first eight rounds.

Roy Jones Jr.'s defeat, his first since the scandal in South Korea, came in the most improbable way. With just over a minute left in the ninth round, Roy landed a powerful lead right hand, connecting just above Griffin's ear. The effects of the punch turned Griffin's sturdy legs weak. The dazed challenger wobbled from one corner of the ring to the next as Roy relentlessly pursued the finish. Unable to clear his head, Griffin voluntarily went down to one knee to regain his composure. While Griffin was on one knee, Roy unleashed a quick right hand, followed by a whipping left hook. After a somewhat delayed reaction, Griffin slunk face-first to the canvas. Referee Tony Perez, who was too far away from the action to break up the fighters, initially declared the bout a knock-out. Roy and his cornermen celebrated the victory. After several moments of chaos and confusion, New Jersey State Athletic Commissioner Larry Hazzard overruled Perez, granting Griffin a victory by disqualification. A murmur of disbelief permeated the Taj Mahal Hotel & Casino in Atlantic City.

"They want to disqualify me and take my title, that's fine. They already stole the gold medal from me, that's fine," a distraught Roy Jones Jr. told Larry Merchant, unable to contain his emotions.[113]

The controversy surrounding Roy Jones Jr.'s first professional loss gave way to a multitude of perspectives. A robbery had occurred, some argued. Roy's supporters fervently said that Griffin faked the knockout, recognizing that if he stayed on the canvas, he would be declared the winner. Others argued that Roy had been desperate, that he was over-eager to finish Griffin, because he was losing the fight. Griffin had solved the puzzle, exposing Roy's true disposition, critics argued. At the time of the disqualification, Roy was actually ahead 76-75 on two score cards, trailing by the same score on the third. For those defending Griffin, Roy had wilted under the pressure of a tough fight. The ongoing controversy gave way to a dramatic and polarizing storyline, one that propelled Roy Jones Jr. back into the spotlight. Even in the chaotic moments after the knockdown, amid the confusion of the overturned KO verdict, a rematch seemed inevitable.

Five months later, on August 7, 1997, Roy Jones Jr. left no doubt whatsoever. Revenge came swiftly. Six seconds into the bout, Roy landed a lighting-fast left hook that sent Montell Griffin tumbling into the ropes, his left glove touching the canvas, resulting in a mandatory eight count. Griffin never recovered. With forty seconds remaining in the opening round, Roy landed a leaping left hook that put Griffin on his back. Dazed and disoriented, Griffin attempted to get up but tumbled back to the canvas on three separate occasions. Roy Jones Jr.'s brutal vindication, arguably as savage as any Mike Tyson knockout, won over even his most hardened critics.

"I wasn't coming out here to box and give y'all a show. Didn't want to give you too much to criticize me about. I wasn't gonna let you talk. I talk tonight. Roy Jones, Pensacola, we talk tonight. The Gulf Coast, Mississippi, all that era, we talk tonight," Roy said to HBO analyst Larry Merchant after the knockout.[114]

Much to the delight of his newfound supporters, Roy Jones Jr. followed up his most satisfying victory with another classic knockout performance, this time against longtime light heavyweight kingpin Virgil "Quick Silver" Hill. On April 25, 1998, dressed in a shimmering gold boxing robe, Roy performed his entry music via a hands-free headset and microphone, rapping the lyrics as he made his way to the ring.

"Roy is doing his rap number. Hard to tell the lyrics but I've read them and they all add up to *I like me*," HBO's Larry Merchant joked.[115]

In the fourth round, a brutal right-hand body shot, cracking like a shotgun blast, sent Hill, who in forty-five fights had never been knocked out, crumbling to the canvas, his face contorted in anguish.

The back-to-back virtuoso performances solidified Roy Jones Jr.'s place as one of the top billing acts in the sport of boxing. His outside-the-ring visibility and crossover appeal was also on the rise. When Roy wasn't fighting on HBO, he worked as a blow-by-blow commentator for the network. As a spokesmodel, Roy was signed to Michael Jordan's Jordan-brand apparel. The pound-for-pound boxer was also granted his own signature Jordan-brand boxing shoe.

After defeating Virgil Hill, Roy Jones Jr. moved from great fighter to pop-culture icon, a message not lost on hip-hop's Dirty South, the rapidly emerging subgenre poised for its own music-industry takeover. Bolstered by chart-topping hits from artists such as Juvenile and Master P, New Orleans–based labels Cash Money Records and No Limit Records followed Rap-A-Lot's blueprint, emerging as unlikely industry powerhouses in the rap game. The Dirty South had risen, and Roy Jones Jr. quickly became the region's champion.

* * *

After Roy Jones Jr. successfully unified all three major titles in the light heavyweight division, defeating titlists Lou Del Valle (WBA) and Reggie Johnson (IBF), the undisputed champion's hip-hop reputation became *the* dominant narrative in his career. Roy's unification bout with Johnson, held in Biloxi, Mississippi, for example, was a uniquely Dirty South affair.

Reggie Johnson: "I knew that Roy was cool with J [Prince] and Scarface and all of the Rap-A-Lot guys but this was the first time I had fought on that level of platform. I wanted to do something special. So I called up Willie D before my fight and asked him to rap me to the ring. I thought it was the ideal thing to do. I wanted to share the platform with my friend who I had boxed with at the Salvation Army Boxing Club as a kid. The Geto Boys had a new song out, 'The World Is a Ghetto,' so I asked him to rap his verse when I came to the ring."

Roy Jones Jr., as had become his custom, came to the ring to his own original recording, "Drop Bombs," the flip side to a newly released rap single titled "I Pray."

The battle of southern hip-hop entrances, in the end, proved to be more competitive than the fight, as Roy would win a lopsided unanimous decision victory. During the twelve-round tactical affair, rapper N.O.R.E. shot a music video for the single "Oh No," produced by The Neptunes and directed by Hype Williams.

After becoming the first fighter to unify the light heavyweight titles since Michael Spinks, Roy Jones Jr. achieved hip-hop celebrity status. In a television cameo on the popular *The Wayans Bros.* show, aired on May 20, 1999, for example, Roy's rap talents were worked into the script. For his bout with Otis Grant, Roy planned a Prince Naseem Hamed–style entrance, complete with a multisong mini-concert. These plans were, in the end, nixed by Foxwoods Casino.

As Mike Tyson's career began to fade, Roy's impact and influence became more apparent than ever before. Prominent artists from outside the South soon began to work Roy Jones Jr.'s name into their songs and music videos. In Nas's song "New World," the Queensbridge emcee boldly declared "the new Mike Tyson is Roy Jones."

Roy Jones Jr.'s deep connections in the hip-hop community became increasingly apparent. The undisputed light heavyweight champion was famously prone to inviting rap stars to his Pensacola training facility. For example, rapper Peter Gunz, whose single with Lord Tariq, "Deja Vu (Uptown Baby)," was one of the biggest rap hits of 1998, made the pilgrimage to Florida.

Peter Gunz: "Me and Roy Jones have the same manager so we eventually became close friends. I went to Roy Jones's camp while he was training. When I get to the gym, I worked out with him, watched him hit the bag. I was in pretty good shape but I was dead by the time they were just getting warmed up. Roy became a very good friend of mine. I'm a city boy, born and raised in the Bronx. When I got to his land I was shell-shocked. It's crazy, acres and acres of land. We went fishing. He has 'Lake Jones,' it's crazy. He just opens his home to people. He's just a beautiful person. And his impact on hip-hop was huge."

As Roy Jones Jr. entered a new phase in his career, it became clear that he planned to do more than simply pal around with hip-hop royalty. Ever the competitor, Roy's goal was to become rap royalty himself. For his bout with Richard Frazier, the undisputed champion once again performed his latest rap song with a hands-free headset. At twenty-nine years old, with a record of 39-1 (33 KOs), the unified WBC, WBA, and IBF light heavyweight champion was beginning to fully recognize his influence on hip-hop culture.

✳ ✳ ✳

On October 5, 1999, Roy Jones Jr. made his official record-industry debut. In a Rap-A-Lot Records compilation titled *J Prince Presents Realest Niggaz Down South*, Roy raps alongside Dirty South legend Scarface on the song "Stop Playin'." The track, buried on the second disc of the collection, was orchestrated by James Prince, the co-founder of the label.

Aside from hip-hop, James Prince and Roy Jones Jr. had much in common. As a teenager, Prince and his younger brother, Thelton, who rapped under the moniker Sir Rap-A-Lot, raised fighting game roosters. Prince originally founded his indie label as a means of keeping his brother off the streets of Fifth Ward. The Prince brothers, from a young age, also shared a passion for boxing.

"Ever since childhood, I've been in love with the sport of boxing," Prince wrote in his 2018 autobiography. "I never forgot the fighting techniques the older guys taught me while I was growing up in Fifth Ward. There weren't any gyms in my neighborhood, so slap-boxing with the neighborhood guys was the next best thing. As a child, having a chance to learn from the older guys and interact with them through boxing made me feel important and acknowledged."[116]

James Prince's love of boxing did not fade. After Rap-A-Lot Records became one of the most powerful hip-hop labels in the South, Prince gave back to his community by opening a boxing gym, The Prince Complex, on Jensen Drive in Fifth Ward. Opening the gym rekindled Prince's interest in the sport. When he became aware of Roy Jones Jr.'s admiration for Scarface, the hip-hop entrepreneur set things into motion, signing boxing's best fighter to an exclusive marketing deal with the Prince Marketing Group. Under Prince's guidance Roy began the process of setting up his own Pensacola-based rap label, Body Head Entertainment.

After partnering with Prince, Roy's profile in the mainstream hip-hop scene was once again taken to new heights. For his title defense against David Telesco at Radio City Music Hall in New York on January 15, 2000,

Roy was brought to the ring by rap stars Method Man and Redman, who performed their hit single "The Rockwilder." After defeating Telesco by unanimous decision, allegedly while fighting with a fractured wrist, Roy's career in the ring began to drift once more. Roy had, to a large degree, cleared out the light heavyweight division. Relatively easy victories over unheralded contenders Richard Hall, Eric Harding, Derrick Harmon, and Julio César Gonzalez lacked the same dramatic flair Roy had produced in knocking out Montell Griffin and Virgil Hill. Roy's primary interest, some speculated, was launching his Body Head record label, recruiting local talent, and recording what would be his debut rap album. With no true challengers on the horizon, boxing, it seemed, was simply a way for Roy's name to remain relevant in the public eye.

* * *

On February 2, 2002, HBO debuted Roy Jones Jr.'s first commercial single, "Y'all Must've Forgot." The music video, shown in its entirety, aired before Roy's light heavyweight title defense against little-known Australian slugger Glen Kelly.

The lyrics were straightforward, the premise simple. A retrospective on a career marked by dominance, alleged injustice, and undo criticism, "Y'all Must've Forgot" emphatically stakes Roy Jones Jr.'s claim as the best pound-for-pound boxer on planet Earth, taking jabs at former rivals along the way.

"When I beat Bernard Hopkins and won the IBF / the right was hurt, beat him with the left / Y'all must've forgot."

"You remember the left hook that James Toney got / Sucker move that I stole from a gamecock / Y'all must've forgot."

"Will there be another Roy Jones? Probably not / Stopped Virgil Hill with a body shot / Y'all must've forgot," Roy Jones Jr. rapped in the opening verse.

While the music video follows several customary hip-hop clichés— beautiful women lounging in bikinis on a speedboat, Roy Jones Jr. shadowboxing and rapping poolside—the punch lines worked. The lyrical digs were designed to remind listeners of Roy's many conquests, as well as the conditions under which those conquests were achieved, jokes that resonated with both hip-hop and boxing audiences alike.

"I got disqualified in March of '97 / After givin a whippin to Montell Griffin / Late hit—my title they had to take it / Why? I guess that's the only way I could lose."

"Five months later, rematch, I needs my crown / First round, one punch, and he sat down," Roy continues in the second verse of the song.

In a style not uncommon to hip-hop, Roy Jones Jr's song is designed to shape the parameters of his own hypermasculine persona. "Y'all Must've Forgot" redefines the arc of the boxer's legend. Just as Muhammad Ali often boasted of his conquests, Roy rapped the story of his hall-of-fame career. Later that night, after the song debuted, Roy added to his legend by placing both hands behind his back, baiting the overmatched Australian challenger, and knocking him out with a swift right hook. Both the comical knockout and the rap song received mixed reviews.

Chris Byrd: "To me, it was kinda country. I was like, you know, he's from Florida. Don't get me wrong, it was nice. But to be a full-time rapper, you gotta be creative and put work in. Especially rappers that get to the highest levels of the game. It takes a lot of writing."

Masta Killa: "That's like me jumping in the ring. I could defend myself but, on a professional level, if I jump in that ring, it wouldn't be pretty. That's not what I do. Some of these boxers grabbing the mic, it ain't pretty. I haven't seen an exception to the rule. I'm glad they love hip-hop but there are levels to this, brother."

Inspectah Deck: "Roy is gonna go down as one of the greatest. 'Y'all Must've Forgot' is the one I will always remember. I might not remember the other songs but I liked that. I did. I started off 'That Shit,' one of my songs on *The Movement,* like that. At the start of the song, I said, 'It's like Roy Jones, 'Y'all Must've Forgot' or something.'"

Among those most critical of the song, were, of course, the boxers mentioned on the track. The song, in some respects, was the equivalent of a diss track.

Montell Griffin: "At the time, we were rivals. It's like they say, 'Any press is good press.' The fact that he put my name in that song let you know how much I mean to him. If I wasn't a big deal, he wouldn't have talked about me. We cool now. I talk to him on a regular basis. But, back then, he was always on HBO sliming me. He always had something to say. And I would tell people, that's just because I'm on Roy's mind."

Bernard Hopkins: "When I heard those songs, it didn't make me mad because Roy reintroduced me to his fans, if they weren't mine already. Yes. I listened. Nobody ever asked me about it at a press conference or anything. But if they would have, I wouldn't have been upset. If Roy mention me, he's promoting me. When they were beefing, did Jay-Z mention 50 Cent's name? No. Jay-Z wasn't gonna co-sign him," Hopkins said, referencing both "Y'all Must've Forgot" and "60/40," a later Roy Jones Jr. diss track aimed at him.

James Toney, on the other hand, was far less amused. When asked about the song, the former three-division champion did not hold his tongue.

"I only heard that one song. That was it. That boy can't rap. Trash! But, it ain't just him. I ain't heard one boxer who can rap yet," Toney joked.

What the song did achieve was a noticeable cultural buzz. On February 26, 2002, a few weeks after his behind-the-back knockout of Glen Kelly, Roy Jones Jr. released his first rap album, aptly titled *Round One*. Distributed by Roy's Body Head label, the project opens with "Who Wanna Get Knocked Out?" a one-verse track that resembles the kinds of songs the boxer composed for many of his famous ring walks. For a handful of the tracks, Roy stays in this particular lane, once again taking more lyrical shots at boxing rivals Montell Griffin and James Toney. On "And Still," for example, Roy sticks to rapping about being boxing's most talented fighter.

The nineteen-track album, packed with guest appearances, did, however, offer the boxer-turned-rapper quite a bit of argumentative space to work with. On "A Real Father," Roy opens up about his relationship with his two twin boys. On "I Pray," Roy rhymes about the role of religion in his life. On "You Damn Right," Roy raps about his sex appeal. In regard to crossover success, the album's most impressive single "That Was Then," which features a hook by R&B singer Dave Hollister, tells the story of a player who turns monogamous. Peaking at number two on the Hot Rap Singles chart in the United States, the song did, in fact, attract attention from fans outside the sport of boxing. The music video, which debuted on both the BET and MTV networks, netted Roy and his Body Head clique a guest spot on the popular video show *Rap City*, where the boxer briefly freestyled for viewers.

This is not to suggest that *Round One* took the rap world by storm. The project was not treated seriously in major hip-hop publications such as *Vibe* or *The Source*. The production quality was criticized in music reviews and few left the listening experience regarding Roy Jones Jr. as a champion-level rhyme writer.

As a whole, the album was arguably a mild commercial success. What the project did achieve, however, was showcasing Roy Jones Jr.'s Body Head roster. Fellow Body Head artist Hahz the Rippa, for example, appears throughout the album, assisting Roy on many of the tracks. Dirty South heavyweights, such as Mystikal and Scarface, also make guest appearances, further validating Roy Jones Jr.'s place in the southern hip-hop scene.

With the release of *Round One*, some within the sport of boxing wondered if Roy Jones Jr. had lost his championship focus. Moonlighting as a rapper is hardly an ideal side job for a fighter. Against Clinton Woods, Roy's elaborate ring entrance featured the "Y'all Must've Forgot" dancers, complete with a mic'd up performance of his track "And Still."

Aside from the obvious distractions of promoting an album, many speculated that Roy's business dealings in the music industry might also lead to financial ruin. Roy, at the time, was *the* financial backer of Body Head Entertainment.

Bernard Hopkins: "Roy Jones made the biggest mistake of his life trying to be a rapper. I like Roy, I respect Roy. We buried the hatchet. I see him all the time. But just because you like something doesn't mean you are gonna be good at it. As of right now, nobody in boxing has been able to multitask on that level. Nobody has ever been able to do that. You have to be careful, dumping millions into studios and all that."

With respect to financial success, Roy Jones Jr.'s entry into the rap game was without question beneficial for Rap-A-Lot CEO James Prince, who was looking to make his mark in boxing. Today, Prince is likely a familiar name to boxing fans because of his various business dealings in the sport. Over the course of his managerial career, Prince has served as a manager and advisor to high-profile world champion fighters such as Floyd Mayweather Jr., Diego Corrales, Ronald "Winky" Wright, Andre Ward, and, most recently, Shakur Stevenson. Both he and Roy had, in many respects, opened new doors for each other.

* * *

Just a few short years into their partnership, James Prince guided Roy Jones Jr. in his unlikely rap career. With the tepid success of *Round One*, there was no question that Roy was going to chase his dream of turning Body Head Entertainment into Pensacola's version of Rap-A-Lot Records. Many questioned how much longer boxing might remain Roy Jones Jr.'s primary focus. In the ring, there was little left for the pound-for-pound fighter to accomplish.

Roy's next big career move was, not unlike his foray into rap music, another calculated risk. Since knocking out Montell Griffin in the first round of their rematch, Roy had flirted with the idea of jumping the cruiserweight division to challenger a smaller heavyweight contender. Back in 1997, Buster Douglas, for a fleeting moment, was rumored to be an opponent. Speculation of a Jones–Douglas fight had ironically brought Roy Jones Sr. back into his son's life, discouraging the jump to heavyweight.

As Roy's celebrity grew, speculation persisted that, despite his father's disapproval, he might still entertain the *right* offer to challenge for a heavyweight belt. With his cultural profile larger than ever before, Roy eventually found his opponent.

On March 1, 2003, Roy Jones Jr. made his long-awaited heavyweight debut, challenging John "The Quiet Man" Ruiz for the WBA portion of the heavyweight title, the same belt that Mike Tyson defended the night Tupac Shakur was killed in 1996. While Lennox Lewis was widely viewed as *the* legitimate heavyweight champion, Ruiz earned his WBA belt by going 1-1-1 in his trilogy with an aging Evander Holyfield. Despite earning the distinction of becoming the first Latino heavyweight titlist in the history of the sport, Ruiz was not a fan favorite. Unappreciated in his time, he was often criticized for his plodding style, tendency to clinch, and inability to make exciting fights. At six feet two and 226 pounds, Ruiz was, unlike the towering Lennox Lewis, a realistic opponent for the much smaller Jones, who under new strength-and-conditioning coach Mackie Shilstone bulked up to 193 pounds.

The matchup was significant for a multitude of reasons. In moving to heavyweight, Roy Jones Jr. sought to become the first boxer in history to begin his career at junior middleweight to win a heavyweight title, the first former middleweight champion, since Bob Fitzsimmons, to win a heavyweight title in 106 years, and only the second light heavyweight champion, after Michael Spinks, to accomplish the feat. In many respects, the challenge felt like something of a curtain call, the crescendo to a great magician's act.

On his way to the ring, Roy Jones Jr. was accompanied by Rap-A-Lot icons James Prince and Scarface, who performed "My Block," the lead single from *The Fix*, an album recently rated a "five-mic" classic by *The Source*.

In what was arguably the final dazzling performance of his career, Roy Jones Jr.'s speed and ring acumen neutralized John Ruiz's height, reach, and weight advantages. Throughout the night, Roy employed a crisp jab—a punch he rarely used against opponents in the past—to off-set Ruiz's aggression, while weaving in and out of danger. In the fourth round, Roy landed a snapping right hand to Ruiz's forehead, momentarily wobbling the heavyweight champion. With each round, Roy gained confidence. Consistently beating his larger opponent to the punch, he boxed and showboated his way to a lopsided unanimous decision victory.

Big Daddy Kane: "I believe if Roy had retired after he beat John Ruiz, he would have retired as the best boxer of his generation, arguably the greatest of all time. Roy was amazing. All of these shows that mix hip-hop and boxing sort of begin with Roy. Had he stopped after that fight, I think fans would have put Roy next to Sugar Ray [Robinson] and Ali."

In becoming the WBA heavyweight champion, Roy Jones Jr. improved his record to 48-1 (38 KOs), the only loss coming by way of disqualification. As Roy exited the ring with the most prized belt in boxing around his waist, few could have possibly anticipated how swift, brutal, and unforgiving his fall would be. In the coming years, success in the music industry would be the least of the Pensacola native's problems.

After defeating John Ruiz, Roy Jones Jr. celebrated his record-breaking accomplishment by contributing a guest appearance on Lil Jon & the East Side Boyz "Put Yo Hood Up (Remix)," featuring Jadakiss, Petey Pablo, and Chyna White, released later that same year. Roy had previously appeared in the music video for Lil Jon & the East Side Boyz' smash hit "Get Low." By early 2004, the Dirty South reigned supreme. To keep with the times, New York's Def Jam Recordings, for example, branched outside the company's typical demographic to establish its Atlanta-based Def Jam South, home to Atlanta artists such as Ludacris and Young Jeezy.

Scarface, the leading pioneer of rap's third coast, was recruited by Def Jam co-founder Russell Simmons to head the label, positioning Roy Jones Jr. that much closer to making his own mark in the music business.

In rap music, much like boxing, place matters. The history of hip-hop has always been that of place-based identity. Lyrical delivery, lyrical content, fashion, and even the music being sampled, remixed, and produced tends to have a regional quality. Rap artists represent themselves by claiming neighborhoods and cities and paying homage to the regional traditions established by artists from their neck of the woods. Hip-hop is competitive. It cares about authenticity, the phrase "keeping it real" was born out of the culture. Thus, Roy Jones Jr.'s improbable rise to the peak of professional boxing is a uniquely Dirty South story. His legend, captured in the song "Y'all Must've Forgot," is evidence of a parallel narrative that indelibly shifted hip-hop culture's place in professional boxing.

Had Roy Jones Jr. walked away from the sport, as Big Daddy Kane said to me, some would have heralded the Pensacola boxer as the greatest pound-for-pound champion since Sugar Ray Robinson. As a result of his nearly flawless performance against heavyweight John Ruiz, Roy's stock was at an all-time high.

It had taken Roy Jones Jr. forty-nine professional fights to reach the level of stardom he envisioned for himself. With his crossover celebrity burgeoning unlike ever before, walking away from boxing to focus on music and entertainment was simply not a smart business move. In the spring of 2003, Roy Jones Jr. found himself at a crossroads. His conundrum centered on the decision to either vacate his title and move back down to his natural weight or place all of the chips at the center of the table, in an attempt to land a heavyweight blockbuster.

"I try to make sure I'm surrounded by people as dedicated and driven as I am. Roy Jones is one of those people. We met years ago, after he said Scarface was his favorite rapper. He's someone I considered a friend because we have many things in common. We're both from the South, and share a love for hunting, fishing, music, and, of course, boxing. Roy understands the importance of good business, and we can discuss different ideas. And we almost made history together," Rap-A-Lot mogul James Prince once wrote, reflecting on *the* missed opportunity of his career as a boxing manager.[117]

LEAN BACK

At first, there was talk of Roy Jones Jr. facing some of the smaller heavyweights in the division, such as Evander Holyfield or Chris Byrd. Holyfield, whose skills were visibly declining, was still a relevant box-office draw. The four-time heavyweight champion was, however, in the eyes of many, beaten by John Ruiz in their three fights, which made a Jones–Holyfield matchup seem like a step backward.

Chris Byrd, who fought as a super middleweight in the 1992 Olympic games, was also briefly considered. Byrd's cautious, defense-first style and lack of a solid fan base eventually led Roy and his team to consider more-lucrative options. The megafight that Roy's advisor, James Prince, envisioned for his client was a clash of hip-hop's two favorite heavyweights: Roy Jones Jr. vs. Mike Tyson.

One month before Roy's victory over John Ruiz, Tyson had flattened Clifford "The Black Rhino" Etienne in the first round. The Tyson–Etienne bout, Tyson's first comeback victory since losing to Lennox Lewis, was broadcast on Showtime alongside a live Jay-Z rap concert, which also took place in Memphis. Excellent ratings for the hip-hop/boxing doubleheader clearly demonstrated that the American public, particularly the hip-hop community, was still interested in the Mike Tyson circus.

John Lepak, a member of Mike Tyson's entourage: "That event was proof that hip-hop and boxing never really separated. They just evolved. The seeds fell off the same tree and took root on their own. The seeds were fighting to survive from day one. And only the strongest survived. Bringing together Mike and Jay-Z was a major production. I was the event coordinator for that whole thing. I remember Mike wasn't coming out until Jay-Z and his crew made it to their ringside seats."

In the weeks following Roy Jones Jr.'s victory over John Ruiz, James Prince began his quest to put together the first true superfight of his boxing career.

"Roy and Mike came out to my ranch in Texas to meet with me about the idea of the fight," Prince wrote. "I showed them around the property and all three of us caught up with one another. It was a great day. Finally, we retreated to my office to get down to business. When it came down to the terms, the concern was money. Bottom line. Both men were at a premium, and we knew this fight would be the one to watch. $25 million apiece was the goal they both agreed on. We all shook on it and they left. Then we went to work to find the $50 million."[118]

In an attempt to drum up interest in Jones–Tyson, Prince sought out David Mays, owner of hip-hop's leading publication, *The Source*. With the magazine's annual-awards show on the horizon, televised on BET, Mays agreed to let Roy Jones Jr. and Mike Tyson give away an award together. During the show, Tyson and Jones engaged in a face-to-face staredown before presenting the award, an attempt to promote the *idea* of a Jones–Tyson title fight.

Behind the scenes, Prince worked with Joe and Gavin Maloof, Las Vegas businessmen with investments in the Coors beer company, Palms Casino Resort, and other lucrative businesses, to underwrite the fight. The Maloof brothers were willing to offer $17 million apiece, according to Prince. Tyson was in. Roy was not willing to budge on his price. Negotiations stalled and both fighters temporarily moved forward. With the Tyson fight on hold, Roy did not have to look far for a nemesis.

✳ ✳ ✳

Antonio "The Magic Man" Tarver had been a part of Roy Jones Jr.'s life since he was a teenager in Pensacola. The two Florida natives once fought as youngsters, thirteen-year-olds meeting in a local amateur competition called the Sunshine Games. Roy, by his account, won an easy points victory over Tarver, who at the time lived in Orlando. After the bout, the lives of both men veered in opposite directions before eventually coming back together to make history. Roy Jones Jr. went on to national fame as a result of the 1988 Olympic scandal, Tarver and his family moved from Orlando to Tampa. Because there were no gyms in Tarver's new neighborhood, he drifted away from boxing to other sports. As a high school football star, Tarver dreamed of a college scholarship that never came. After high school, Tarver, much to his own detriment, drifted toward a life of drugs and crime on the streets.

As Roy Jones Jr. went on to fortune and fame, Antonio Tarver found inspiration in the success of his one-time amateur opponent, cleaning his life up and returning to amateur boxing in his mid-twenties. At the 1996 Olympic Games in Atlanta, as the oldest member of the U.S. Olympic Boxing Team that featured Floyd Mayweather Jr., Fernando Vargas, and David Reid, Tarver won a bronze medal, an unlikely feat considering his winding path to the podium.

In 1997, the same year Roy Jones Jr. avenged his disqualification loss to Montell Griffin, Antonio Tarver made his professional boxing debut at the age of twenty-eight. From his first victory on, Tarver began relentlessly calling out Roy, attempting to craft a public interest in the Florida-based-rivalry. Defeating Roy Jones Jr., perhaps more so than even winning a world championship, appeared to be Tarver's primary ambition.

In June 2000, after sixteen straight victories, Tarver seemed poised to secure his highly coveted dream matchup. In an IBF title-eliminator shot against fellow unbeaten prospect Eric Harding, Tarver suffered a broken jaw and lost a close but unanimous decision. As a result of the outcome, Harding was granted the fight with Roy Jones Jr., eventually losing by TKO in the tenth round because of a shoulder injury.

Tarver followed his loss to Harding with five straight wins, including a devastating knockout victory over Harding in their rematch. When Roy Jones Jr. moved to heavyweight to face John Ruiz, his unified light heavyweight title splintered. One of those vacated belts, the WBC belt, was picked up by Tarver in a one-sided victory over Roy's former rival Montell Griffin. After claiming his first world championship, Tarver raised the volume on his persistent trash talk. Claiming to have run Roy out of the light heavyweight division, Tarver didn't relent. Because Roy also moonlighted as an HBO boxing analyst, escaping Tarver's verbal digs was unavoidable.

In a cinematic scene, Antonio Tarver crashed Roy Jones Jr.'s post-fight press conference following his heavyweight title victory over John Ruiz. Seated among the boxing press, Tarver boldly declared that Roy Jones Jr. wasn't even the best fighter in the state of Florida.

"I'm about to get mad," Roy warned at the podium.[119]

"Get mad, sucker. What do I have to do, come piss on your lawn in Pensacola to get your attention," Tarver persisted.

"I'm gonna get him. Before I retire, his ass is mine," a visibly frustrated Roy Jones Jr. responded.

✳ ✳ ✳

When James Prince was unable to secure a megafight with Mike Tyson, Roy Jones Jr. acquiesced to the Florida-grudge-match narrative. Roy's return to the light heavyweight division, less than eight months after capturing the WBA heavyweight title, was more about settling the grudge with Tarver than recapturing his vacated title. For many, the real drama of the buildup to Jones–Tarver centered around the issue of weight. The matchup required Roy to lose more than 25 pounds of muscle mass he had accumulated in bulking up to fight as a heavyweight. The drama surrounding the weight issue, along with Tarver's persistent trash talk, gave way to a highly anticipated pay-per-view event.

As Roy Jones Jr. prepared for his bout with Tarver, his attention also turned to Body Head Entertainment's second project, a compilation album titled *Body Head Bangerz: Volume One*. In early 2003, Roy was able to secure a distribution for the project through Universal Music Group, increasing the promotional machine behind the album. With the increased budget, Roy was able to secure guest verses by southern pioneers such as B.G., Lil' Flip, Petey Pablo, Mike Jones, Fiend, and Bun B. Writing his own rhymes and building his homegrown roster of Body Head talent became a top priority.

At thirty-four years old, Roy Jones Jr. was finally a bona fide star. On November 5, 2003, three days before his initial showdown with Antonio Tarver, Roy made his Hollywood movie debut, appearing in *The Matrix*

Revolutions, the third installment of the popular *Matrix* movie franchise. Tarver, also thirty-four, was fighting in his first pay-per-view main event.

The prefight trash talk would likely be more entertaining than the fight itself, many pundits speculated, citing Roy's physical gifts and vast experience. Aside from Tarver's height and reach advantages, there was little reason to believe the Orlando-born fighter stood a chance. Jones–Tarver wasn't about belts, or records, or even legacy. This was personal. Nobody questioned Tarver's disdain for his opponent, his Captain Ahab–like obsession with settling an old score.

In the early rounds, fans were given their first glimpse of the final stage of Roy Jones Jr.'s boxing career: slower reflexes, an inability to escape punches, and a decreased punch output. In rounds one and two, Tarver consistently cornered Roy against the ropes and aggressively swarmed with looping punches to the body and head. When Jones and Tarver boxed at center ring, fans were sporadically treated to flashes of the old Roy. Tarver's inconsistent work rate kept his visibly weakened opponent in the fight. Roy's offense, for much of the night, consisted of one or two punches at a time. By round five, swelling began to form over Roy's right eye, evidence of an accumulation of damage. He was, for the first time in his boxing life, taking a physical beating. The expression on Roy's face was perhaps the most telling sign of all. Throughout the bout, Roy gasped for air, often taking deep breaths as he backed himself into the ropes.

At certain moments, it appeared Roy was out of gas. At other moments, Tarver conceded his advantage, fighting cautiously, allowing Roy to land quick lead right hands that sent beads of sweat flying from Tarver's bald head. Most, if not all, of the rounds were closely contested, and it was difficult to clearly pick a winner.

Rounds eleven and twelve were among Roy's best in the fight. Visibly exhausted, he dug deep, outlanding and outworking Tarver. In the most grueling fight of his career, Roy Jones Jr. was forced to win by will rather than skill. For the final two rounds, the crowd remained on their feet, applauding the back-and-forth action.

When the final bell sounded, Antonio Tarver paraded around the ring as if he had just purchased a winning lottery ticket. He climbed the ropes of a neutral corner and flexed his muscles for fans, bouncing up and down on the ropes with enthusiasm. Across the ring, a look of worry blanked Roy's face as his cornermen applied an enswell to his right eye.

The decision was met with a chorus of boos from the fans at Mandalay Bay in Las Vegas, followed by chants of "bullshit, bullshit." Veteran judge Jerry Roth scored the bout 114-114, overruled by Glen Hamada and David Harris, who scored the bout for Roy Jones Jr., 117-111 and 116-112. The majority decision victory improved Roy Jones Jr.'s record to 49-1 (38 KOs), making him the three-time light heavyweight champion of the world. He had won the fight but not the drama. The controversy surrounding the decision, particularly Glen Hamada's 117-111 score, emboldened the trash-talking Tarver.

"I knew it was going to be a hard situation because of the twenty-five pounds I had to sweat. That was a hard twenty-five pounds. I had the hardest time of my whole career, making weight. That was very, very difficult for me. I was very, very tired because of the weight," Roy stated in his post-fight interview.[120]

"I gave better than a great effort. I won this fight! I showed tonight where I measure up. I am the people's champion. And there is a new face in boxing and it's Antonio Tarver. Don't listen to these commentators. Antonio Tarver beat *the man* tonight, so that makes me *the man*," Tarver responded, infuriated by the decision.

Regardless of who experts believed won the fight, there was no questioning that Antonio Tarver had given Roy Jones Jr. the most difficult test of his fifty-fight career. In the following months, Tarver persistently nipped at his rival's heels, removing any opportunity for Roy to bask in the victory.

When asked about granting Tarver a rematch, Roy initially played coy. "If I can't get Tyson, I'm probably done," he told HBO's Larry Merchant.

Behind the scenes, James Prince worked feverishly to rekindle momentum for a Jones–Tyson matchup. Believing Roy could no longer make the light heavyweight limit, Prince viewed the Tyson fight as a more lucrative risk for the thirty-four-year-old champion. Roy, according to Prince, was not willing to budge from his $25 million price tag. When negotiations came to a stalemate, Tyson and his team moved on, accepting what many believed would be an easy tune-up against British heavyweight Danny Williams. Don King, who promoted Antonio Tarver, seized the opportunity by presenting Roy Jones Jr. with a lucrative deal for a Tarver rematch, a pay-per-view showdown that sold itself. After much posturing, Roy accepted.

At the press conference to announce the fight, King and Tarver controlled the narrative. Roy, on the other hand, appeared disinterested in promoting the fight, barely acknowledged his rival's incessant taunting, choosing instead to text on his cell phone through most of the press conference. When Roy did speak, he once again emphasized that his struggle to make weight, not Tarver, was the reason for his previous sluggish performance.

"I won that fight and Roy knows it. If he didn't know it, we wouldn't be here right now. I have no pressure on me. I have nothing to prove," Tarver declared.

Aside from his body language, there were reasons for pundits to view Roy Jones Jr. as a disinterested participant. The boxer-turned-rap-CEO was being pulled in different directions. His rematch with Tarver was scheduled for May 15, 2004. The new Body Head album was slated for an August 3 release date.

Roy, who did little to build anticipation for the rematch, focused his promotional efforts, instead, on his budding hip-hop label. Tarver, working his own hip-hop connections, teamed up with Dirty South pioneers Three 6 Mafia, underground mainstays from Memphis, Tennessee. The product of the collaboration was a diss track titled "More Than Personal," featured in King's pay-per-view prefight promotional show. Project Pat of Three 6 Mafia also performed the song live during Tarver's ring walk.

"See, the weight's a poor excuse, Antonio Tarver's the truth / And your victory over him wasn't nothing but a fluke. . . ."

"Admit it Roy, the boxing world know the truth / The whole damn arena was booing when they gave the title to you."

"To the WBC, we'd thank ya for the second shot / Because this time, Tarver gonna knock him the fuck out," Project Pat raps in the song.

Roy's decision to take the rematch, to avenge a victory that was too close for his liking, was in large part due to Tarver's badgering. Before the first fight, it was Tarver who stoked public interest in the match. After his majority decision defeat, Tarver disparaged Roy all the way up to the final seconds before the opening bell of the rematch. With the two combatants standing at center ring, receiving prefight introductions, referee Jay Nady asked if either corner had any questions, a customary and largely obligatory move.

"Yeah, I got a question," Tarver responded, to the shock of those in the arena and the millions watching from home.

"You got any excuses tonight, Roy?" Tarver continued.

Despite the prefight verbal gauntlet, Tarver held back for much of the first round, posturing and feinting. Using his superior quickness to beat Tarver to the punch, Roy established himself as the aggressor, easily winning the round on all three judge's scorecards. The bad habits Roy had demonstrated from the first fight, it appeared, had been corrected. His back did not touch the ropes. In the first round, the bout was fought in the middle of the ring.

When Tarver returned to his corner, he received an earful from his head trainer, Buddy McGirt, who knew exactly how to motivate his fighter.

"Don't give him that much respect," McGirt urged.

"Stop using that word; ain't no fucking respect here," Tarver replied.

True to his word, Tarver picked up the pace. Roy continued to score with quick flurries but Tarver steadily began to close the distance. Midway through the second round, Roy landed a glancing lead right hand, followed by a left hook that missed by inches. After the exchange, Roy stepped backward, his chin up and head high. After feeling the glancing right hand, Tarver dipped forward, launching a vicious left hook, one that crashed squarely into his opponent's jaw, knocking the pound-for-pound fighter off his decade-long perch atop the sport.

Roy's body fell lifelessly to the canvas, doubled over as a result of the punishing left hook. He landed on his back, arms dangling, his head sliding awkwardly underneath the blue corner ring post. After a few seconds, he slowly rolled onto his side, ducking his head underneath the bottom rope as he crawled onto all fours. Just before the count of ten, Roy made it back to his feet. Referee Jay Nady waved off the fight regardless. Badly dazed, Roy didn't protest the stoppage. Instead, he staggered awkwardly, falling forward into the ropes, Nady catching his fall.

James Prince: "I remember the exact moment when Tarver's knockout punch landed in the second round. As Roy fell, so did our monster fight between two undisputed heavyweights. The three of us were supposed to make history together. It took one minute and forty-two seconds to lose the opportunity—and to lose $17 million. There aren't many moments in my career that I've lost sleep over, but that night, it was impossible to find rest."[121]

Prince's disappointment was, ironically, compounded further when Tyson, only a few months later, suffered his own improbable knockout loss at the hands of Danny Williams, all but ending his career as a professional boxer.

✷ ✷ ✷

Despite the shocking knockout loss, Roy Jones Jr.'s album release proceeded as planned. On August 3, 2004, Body Head Entertainment released its make-or-break project: *Body Head Bangerz: Volume One.* The album was, on the surface, a higher-quality product than the company's previous effort. Unlike Roy's debut, *Body Head Bangerz* presented itself as a straight rap album, more an ode to Dirty South hip-hop than a solo project. The compilation album was packed with notable southern rap all-stars. Bun B, Juvenile, B.G., Fiend, Petey Pablo, and Mike Jones each make cameos, rapping alongside Body Head artists Choppa, SM Bullet, Ms.Kandi, and Magic (who was previously signed to No Limit Records). Music videos for singles "I Smoke, I Drank" (featuring Lil Boosie and Young Bleed) and "Can't Be Touched" (featuring Trouble Tha Truth) scored heavy rotation on the BET network, both singles making mild dents in the Billboard charts.

"Everybody talk about 'Y'all Must've Forgot' but I think that second one [album] represented his best work. That joint, 'I Smoke, I Drank,' I loved it. That joint was hot," rapper Peter Gunz reflected.

The timing of the album's release couldn't have been worse. Roy Jones Jr.'s knockout loss to Antonio Tarver without question hampered the company's promotional efforts. With one powerful left hook, the entire story surrounding Roy Jones Jr. shifted drastically.

Following the loss to Tarver, many speculated that the Pensacola boxer, who'd successfully dabbled in fashion, movies, music, and broadcast journalism, might never return to the ring. Body Head Entertainment, it appeared, was Roy's future.

Those close to Roy, on the other hand, knew that his competitive spirit would not let him walk away from the sport after being defeated by his rival in humiliating fashion. A trilogy fight with Tarver was the only fight worth making. To the surprise of everyone, it was Roy Jones Jr., not Tarver, who returned to the ring first.

Four months after being knocked out, Roy accepted a bout with the newly crowned IBF light heavyweight champion Glen "Road Warrior" Johnson, scheduled for September 2004. As Roy returned to his Pensacola training camp for the Johnson fight, he was, once again, pulled away from his promotional duties as CEO of Body Head Entertainment. Roy's main focus, his team said, was now on boxing.

Entering the fight, few considered Glen Johnson a threat. With a professional record of 40-9-2, Johnson had earned his "Road Warrior" nickname by traveling to face opponents in their hometowns, often losing close and sometimes controversial decisions. Johnson's straightforward plodding style was, in the eyes of many, tailor-made for Roy Jones Jr. Before capturing the vacant IBF belt, Johnson avenged a disputed draw against Clinton Woods, a fighter Roy had defeated easily before moving to the heavyweight division. Because four of Johnson's nine losses were to fighters Roy had beaten (Julio César Gonzalez, Derrick Harmon, Merqui Sosa, and Bernard Hopkins), boxing analysts widely viewed the matchup as an easy bounce-back win, an opportunity for Roy Jones Jr. to pick up one of his vacated belts before rushing into a rematch with Tarver. In attempting to quickly erase the memory of his knockout loss, Roy Jones Jr. made arguably the biggest mistake of his boxing career, one that would adversely affect his record label as well.

Johnson dominated almost every second of the fight. When the opening bell rang, Johnson shot across the ring. He aggressively attacked Roy, pinning him against the ropes with a barrage of clubbing blows. Roy's defensive posture, his inability to counter, was that of a shot fighter who can't pull the trigger. In the ninth round, Johnson landed a powerful overhand right followed by a chopping left hook. The combination knocked Roy out cold; the back of his head violently smacked the canvas, resulting in a devastating concussion.

This time around, Roy Jones Jr. appeared to be in serious danger. The fallen champion remained on his back for nearly fifteen minutes. As Johnson conducted his post-fight interview, Roy sat on his stool, bent over his knees, struggling to open his eyes. When the HBO broadcast finally went off air, the great Roy Jones Jr. had yet to rise to his feet. In the crowd, seated ringside, Antonio Tarver watched as his rival was carefully led out of the ring by members of his entourage.

In less than five months, Roy Jones Jr.'s status in professional boxing had fallen like a demolished skyscraper. The back-to-back knockout losses affected other areas of Roy's business life as well. The second straight knockout loss was a public relations nightmare for Universal Records, which was banking on the boxer's fan base as a core audience. In a desperate scramble to save the project, Universal re-released *Body Head Bangerz: Volume One* on October 26, 2004, with a new cover, a modified track list, and two new songs. The album peaked at No. 38 on the Billboard charts, with record sales that steadily declined after the re-release.

To make matters worse, at the same time *Body Head Bangerz* was plummeting down the charts, one of the hottest rap songs in the United States contained a lyric that playfully poked fun at Roy's loss. In "New York," a song by Ja Rule featuring Fat Joe and Jadakiss, Fat Joe raps, "Even Roy Jones was forced to lean back." The double-edged reference was both a nod to Fat Joe's hit song "Lean Back," which dominated the hip-hop airwaves, and Roy Jones Jr.'s stunning loss to Tarver.

Fat Joe: "It didn't mean nothing. Roy Jones was like the undefeated champion and then he was knocked out twice. *Even Roy Jones was forced to lean back*. Like, the song was so powerful even Roy had to lean back."[122]

Roy Jones Jr. did not see it that way. At Ja Rule's album release party for R.U.L.E., hosted at New York's Club Exit in November 2004, Roy confronted Fat Joe over the verbal jab. News of the altercation, first broadcast by radio personality Ed Lover, quickly became the stuff of hip-hop legend. For years, several versions of the story persisted.

Fat Joe: "He came to beat me up. In real life, Roy Jones came to knock out Fat Joe. He had his getaway plan and everything."

On a 2015 episode of ESPN's *Highly Questionable*, Roy Jones Jr. spoke publicly about the altercation for the first time. Roy's version of the story is in tune with Fat Joe's account of the verbal exchange.

"We had a confrontation over the song. I thought me and Joe was cool and he put my name in a song in somewhat of a bad way. I was like, 'Wow, that's really how we gonna roll?'" Roy stated.[123]

Sensing Roy's anger, Fat Joe initially attempted to quell the animosity, arguing that his punch line in the song was no more than a clever pun.

Fat Joe: "I had to tell him, 'Please don't knock me out.' That's the story. I told him, 'Yo, it's just hip-hop,' but he persisted. I said, 'Roy, look, you are gonna knock me out. No question. But, you see those hundred and fifty guys over there? They are not gonna be cool with that. And they are not going to fight you.' So, he looks to the side and sees a hundred and fifty niggas and he says, 'So, it was just hip-hop?' I was talking to Roy like, 'Yo, we don't need to go there.'"

Roy Jones Jr: "At first, he was like 'It's just a song.' And I was like, 'No, it ain't just a song. It's me and you. I thought we were better than that.' I know he had his guys with him. He was ready to defend himself. I wasn't tripping about that. As long as I got him, I didn't care about the rest of the guys. They could have got me, too, so it could have happened that way. I was willing to die for it. He didn't have to tell me nothing. I already knew that when I came into the building. I knew the Terror Squad was there. I knew they were weaponed up. I didn't roll like that. I didn't think it was right for your friends to do you like that. We cool now, so it's over with."

"I don't regret the bar but I do regret that I was cool with him and he felt like I disrespected him. It was wrong," Fat Joe later lamented.

Regardless of the apology, the line serves as something of a cultural marker. Roy Jones Jr.'s reign as hip-hop's champion was over.

✳ ✳ ✳

In 2005, Roy took a much-needed break from competition, focusing instead on Body Head Entertainment and his career as an HBO boxing commentator. During Roy's hiatus, Antonio Tarver lost a surprising split decision to Glen Johnson, who shockingly emerged from obscurity as the unlikely Ring Magazine Fighter of the Year. Six months later, Tarver avenged the loss to Johnson with a unanimous decision victory of his own, recapturing his title. Because of his inconsistent performances, however, some speculated that Tarver, at thirty-five, might also be past his athletic prime. The two grueling fights with Johnson, some speculated, had taken some shine from his luster. Ironically, Tarver once again needed his Florida rival.

On October 1, 2005, in Tarver's home base of Tampa, Florida, Roy Jones Jr. finally returned to boxing. Forgoing a tune-up bout, Roy chose instead to face his bitter rival for the third time. In a move that many cited as an act of desperation, Roy enlisted the services of his father, Roy Jones Sr., as his co-trainer. The reemergence of Big Roy, who had not worked his son's corner since his early days as a professional, was telling. Gone was the hip-hop mini-concert. Instead, Roy opted for Notorious B.I.G.'s 1994 song "Ready to Die" as his entry music.

Roy Jones Jr.'s trilogy fight with Antonio Tarver was, as they say in hip-hop, a do-or-die affair.

Big Roy's addition to the corner made little difference in the end. While his son certainly looked better than in his previous two fights, bouncing around the ring, feinting, and occasionally clowning when Tarver scored, he struggled to consistently land counterpunches. At times, Roy looked tired, unwilling to exchange. Tarver, who also appeared physically drained at certain moments in the fight, piled up points by stalking Jones and landing the cleaner and more effective punches. In the eleventh round, during the most significant exchange of the fight, Tarver stunned Roy with a hard right hook, causing Roy to stagger into the ropes. As Tarver recklessly attacked, looking for the finish, he missed wildly, almost falling over the top rope himself. Both fighters, at times, appeared to be lesser versions of themselves. By night's end, the judges gave Tarver a unanimous decision victory.

"When you reign for as long as I did, it's hard to take going out like I did the last two times. I couldn't go out like that. I held my own for a long time. I'm not ashamed of my effort because I gave my best effort. I don't feel like I had the urge to go in there and get at it. I didn't have the hunger. I was good but I just didn't put out enough," Roy said after the fight.[124]

After his third straight loss, Roy Jones Jr.'s aura faded considerably. As a result of lukewarm sales, Universal Music dropped Body Head Entertainment from its roster. Despite the setback, Roy kept his hip-hop ambitions. In 2006, under the moniker 3D, Roy's twin sons, DeAndre (known as Dre) and De Shawn (known as DJ), along with their cousin Dyllón Burnside (known as D-Man) released an album titled *Boyz Will Be Boyz*. With the single "3D Party," a bouncy track that attempts to capitalize on the crunk-era soundscape, the teenage trio followed in the footsteps of artists such as Kris Kross, Lil' Bow Wow, and Lil' Romeo. This time around, the Body Head project was an unequivocal commercial failure, never making waves beyond the Gulf Coast region.

Along with his reflexes, Roy Jones Jr.'s boxing career continued to dissipate. In 2008, after stringing together three straight victories, Roy lost a lopsided decision to undefeated light heavyweight champion Joe Calzaghe at Madison Square Garden. By night's end, Roy's face was painted crimson. One year after losing to Calzaghe, Roy was knocked out in the first round by Australian Danny Green. Four months later, at the age of forty-one, Roy lost a lopsided decision to his longtime rival Bernard Hopkins, who had waited thirteen years for a rematch.

One year after his loss to Hopkins, Roy Jones Jr. was knocked out cold by Russian journeyman Denis Lebedev, compiling yet another string of three consecutive losses. A few years later, Roy suffered a brutal knockout loss to cruiserweight Enzo Maccarinelli. For those who grew up idolizing the brilliant feathers of Pensacola's fighting gamecock, these were images difficult to stomach.

The irony of the epilogue to Roy Jones Jr.'s masterful career is that, during his prime, he was often accused of being overly cautious. With all of his various side interests, many questioned his passion for the sport of boxing. The odds, it once seemed, favored Roy exiting the sport too early, leaving big fights on the table. Few could have imagined Roy fighting professionally at forty-nine years old. As the concussions began to pile up, and Roy continued to take punishment, even in easy victories over low-tier opponents, the narrative surrounding his career flipped. In the end, the boxing world collectively begged Roy Jones Jr. to stop fighting and focus his interests on matters outside of the ring.

Forced to enter a new phase of his boxing life, Roy Jones Jr. began a somewhat sporadic career as a part-time trainer, highlighted by gigs with the likes of Devon Alexander, Chris Eubank Jr., and Jean Pascal. Along with his business partner, Keith Veltre, the four-division champion later founded Roy Jones Jr. Boxing Promotions. In 2015, the promotional company landed a three-year streaming deal with UFC Fight Pass. Before officially retiring from the ring in 2018, Roy often fought on the UFC Fight Pass cards he promoted, performing his own hip-hop concerts before and during the events.

Hip-hop continued to be a key component of Roy Jones Jr.'s life. On August 18, 2015, Roy Jones released *Roy Jones Presents: Body Head Bangerz: The EP*, a six-song EP featuring a retooled Body Head roster. Still today, Roy is involved in many of the solo projects of his Body Head affiliates. The career of underground rapper 2piece, whose 2017 album *Business at Hand* features Roy on almost every track, was no doubt sparked by his association with the former boxing star. In recent years,

Roy has also been instrumental to the career of New Orleans–based rapper SM Bullett, promoting his music on social media and contributing guest verses to his albums.

Even after retirement, Roy Jones Jr. nostalgia continued to linger about the sport of boxing. At the Claridge Hotel in Atlantic City, for example, Roy rapped heavyweight Derrick Webster into the ring for his bout with Lamar Harris, performing a live version of "Y'all Must've Forgot." When Joseph Parker faced fellow undefeated heavyweight champion Anthony Joshua in a title-unification match at the O2 Arena in March 2018, Parker walked to the ring to the sounds of Roy's "Can't Be Touched." Parker has since continued to use the song as his official entry music.

Despite all of his accomplishments in the ring, one could argue Roy Jones Jr.'s lasting impact on the sport is best described as a profound deepening of the relationship between the boxing world and the hip-hop community.

❋ ❋ ❋

As the new millennium took shape, Don King's influence over the sport of boxing slowly began to crumble. The rise of Oscar De La Hoya's Golden Boy Promotions resulted in a redistribution of the boxing pie chart once dominated by King and Bob Arum. For a brief period of time, however, it appeared the *King* might eventually be replaced by a *Prince*.

When Roy Jones Jr. opened the door for Rap-A-Lot Records' CEO James Prince, the courtship between boxing and hip-hop shifted beyond that of a flirtation. Prince was a visible presence in Roy's career, always accompanying his fighter in the ring. Because Prince was so widely respected in the hip-hop world, it didn't take long for the Rap-A-Lot CEO to get the attention of a new generation of fighters.

Despite, or perhaps because of, the shifting promotional landscape of professional boxing, one of hip-hop's most successful moguls found himself in the role of mentor to the champion who would eventually become the richest in the history of the sport, a billion-dollar athlete, nicknamed after a bank robber—"Pretty Boy" Floyd Mayweather Jr.

The heir to Roy Jones Jr.'s throne was, uncoincidentally, the product of a rapidly changing hip-hop climate. By 1999, many of hip-hop's leading stars had already evolved from their roles as entertainers to that of music moguls. Rappers such as Dr. Dre, Sean "P. Diddy" Combs, Shawn "Jay-Z" Carter, Bryan "Birdman" Williams, and Percy "Master P" Miller, were as widely celebrated in the culture for their business acumen as they were for their musical talents. Hip-hop businessmen, such as Russell Simmons, Damon Dash, Suge Knight, and, of course, James Prince, were now just as famous, if not more so, than their artists. Gangsta rap was out, mogul talk was in. "I'm not a businessman, I'm a business, man," Jay-Z famously proclaimed, marking the dawn of a new era in rap music.

Hip-hop's corporate phenomenon occurred, as scholar Mickey Hess points out, as a by-product of a "long boom" in U.S. economic expansion where celebrity CEOs captured the country's collective imagination.[125] Hip-hop was expanding, evolving. Russell Simmons turned Def Jam Recordings into Phat Farm Clothing, Def Comedy Jam, and a number of additional spin-off companies. Wu-Tang Clan had Wu Wear, Wu Music Group, and Razor Sharp Records. Sean "P. Diddy" Combs moved from Bad Boy Records to Sean John clothing. In expanding their own Roc-A-Fella Records empire to Rocawear clothing, Jay-Z, Damon Dash, and Kareem "Biggs" Burke followed the blueprint to perfection.

James Prince was no different than his entrepreneurial peers. After partnering with Roy Jones Jr., the godfather of the Dirty South fixed his attention on becoming hip-hop's answer to Don King. Disappointment, at first, came before success.

While chasing a Jones–Tyson matchup, Prince attempted to work his way into Tyson's management team as well. Before the second set of negotiations, the two men met at Tyson's gym in Phoenix to discuss Prince's potential role in Team Tyson.

James Prince: "Boxing is a business like every other business. And just as I learned in music, the old guys don't always welcome new blood. Shelly Finkel is a longtime boxing manager who, like me, started in music. At the time, he was managing Mike and viewed me as a threat. I believe he didn't want to cut me in on the deal. When he found out Mike had taken the meeting, I think he put the brakes on the entire situation."[126]

After being allegedly blocked by Finkel, Prince focused his efforts on partnering with an undefeated twenty-three-year-old champion with whom he became acquainted during his first trip to Phoenix to court Tyson, a young lightweight from Grand Rapids, Michigan.

At first, James Prince and Floyd Mayweather Jr. centered their conversations on the boxer's desire to launch his own record company, Philthy Rich Records, a scenario strikingly similar to Prince's mentorship with Roy Jones Jr.

"Floyd wanted to talk about music. He'd been making his own songs and wanted to get into the record industry, but I knew from our first official meeting that my focus with Floyd should be in the ring," Prince recalled.[127]

Coming out of the 1996 Olympics and early into his professional career, Mayweather looked to make his mark in both worlds, boxing and hip-hop, as he aligned himself with the hip-hop clothing brand Enyce and rap-icon-turned-businessman Eric B.

Eric B.: "We [hip-hop entrepreneurs] understand the business. We did this to get out of the streets. You're talking about guys who started out counting pennies. Counting dollars is easy. James Prince understands music because it's a business. It's the same reason he understands boxing. I came in after he put Floyd's contract together. And, then him and Floyd had a falling out with his manager and I was the manager. But J Prince put together a great contract for Floyd, put Floyd on his way. It was an escalating scale, every fight it went up half a million dollars, or $750,000. J Prince did an excellent job for Floyd."

Eric B. continued: "I managed Floyd [Mayweather], Oliver McCall, and Riddick Bowe. Before Al Haymon came in, I was Floyd's manager. I was there a year or two years. Haymon came in and bought the contract. I was in charge of operations. I put some real money in his hands. We worked out of the Top Rank Gym, with Todd duBoef. I was in the gym. I was at the fights. It was an education. Floyd had his way he do stuff; we had our way. We bumped heads a lot but we came away from it having mutual respect for each other."

Before James Prince and Eric B. got involved, Floyd Mayweather Jr. shook up the sport by scoring back-to-back victories over Genaro Hernandez and Angel Manfredy to become Ring Magazine Fighter of the Year in only his second year as a professional. With a record of 22-0 (16 KOs), the WBC lightweight champion was a rising star in the sport who, at the time, was being managed by his father, Floyd Sr., and his uncle, Jeff Mayweather. Frustrated over the HBO network's seven-fight $12.5 million offer, a contract that Floyd infamously referred to as a "slave contract," James Prince stepped in to help Mayweather negotiate a new deal. An injured hand, along with the contractual stalemate, resulted in a seven-month layoff for the young champion.

The end result of the Mayweather–Prince pairing was a three-fight HBO deal that built toward a high-profile unification showdown with fellow undefeated lightweight champion Diego Corrales. In taking the short-term money, Mayweather was betting on himself to come out of the unification bout with Corrales undefeated, thus upping his value to the network. For the first fight in his new contract, Mayweather, by James Prince's estimation, was given a demotion, a slap on the wrist for bad behavior.

"We needed HBO as an ally, but HBO was ticked off. To punish Floyd, they gave him a fight against Emanuel Burton [Augustus] on a brand-new HBO boxing showcase called KO Nation,"[128] Prince recalled.

Ironically, *KO Nation*, HBO's short-lived attempt at selling boxing to the hip-hop generation, was a clear reflection of Roy Jones Jr. and James Prince's mounting influence. Hosted by broadcaster Fran Charles, former featherweight champion Kevin Kelley, and hip-hop personality Ed Lover (the original co-host of *Yo MTV Raps!*), the show, which aired on Saturday afternoons, was designed to get young viewers under the tent. The broadcast setup featured an elaborate stage, a live DJ, a hip-hop-themed soundtrack, and dancers. The show's tagline, "on the ropes and off the hook," written in graffiti-style lettering, was designed to acknowledge hip-hop culture's growing place in the sport.

Over the course of *KO Nation's* one-year life span, Ronald "Winky" Wright, Clifford Etienne, Paul Spadafora, and Lamon Brewster joined Floyd Mayweather in launching the experimental program. In his only appearance on *KO Nation*, Mayweather at times struggled against Emanuel Augustus, a talented journeyman with an ugly record and a relentless, unorthodox style. Augustus, who would have his own Fight of the Year with Micky Ward in 2001, absorbed a remarkable amount of punishment and kept coming. Over the years, Mayweather has consistently ranked the Augustus bout as one of his toughest.

Floyd Mayweather Jr: "If I was rating certain fighters out of every guy that I fought, I'm going to rate Emmanuel Augustus first compared to all the guys that I've faced. He didn't have the best record in the sport of boxing, he has never won a world title. But he came to *fight* and, of course, at that particular time I had took a long layoff."[129]

Despite suffering an injury to his right hand earlier in the bout, Mayweather was able to dig deep, demonstrating a world-class champion's resolve. In the ninth round, Mayweather landed a series of sharp left hooks that visibly dazed Augustus, prompting his trainer to throw in the towel.

Mayweather's performance against Augustus, whose record, at the time, was 22-16-4 (10 KOs), led some in the boxing media to favor the six-foot-one, power-punching IBF champion Diego Corrales, 33-0 (27 KOs) in their inevitable HBO unification showdown. Some blamed Mayweather's showing on his outside-the-ring business distractions; others cited the injury and turmoil within the family. Corrales, many pundits believed, was coming into his own, while Mayweather's career was beginning to attract controversy.

When James Prince joined Team Mayweather, a growing tension between Floyd and his father was coming to the surface. The father–son relationship, as is often the case in boxing, had a volatile dynamic. For the Augustus bout, Floyd chose his uncle Roger as head trainer, causing Floyd Sr. to leave the camp. The mounting drama between Floyd Mayweather Jr., his father, and uncle was, unbeknownst to many at the time, the by-product of violent and deeply rooted family wounds, a painful chasm unhealed.

The story of Floyd Mayweather Jr.'s rise to the top of *Forbes* magazine's prestigious list of wealthiest athletes did not begin with mansions, luxury cars, and private jets. The story of "Money" Mayweather, the hip-hop generation's first champion-turned-mogul, begins with a bullet.

GET MONEY

here is no questioning Floyd Mayweather Sr.'s claim to the title of family patriarch. He was the first of the boxing Mayweather boys to make it out of Grand Rapids, Michigan. The trail he blazed was bumpy, scattered with misfortune and squandered opportunity. Floyd Sr.'s thirty-five-bout professional career, featuring losses to stars such as Sugar Ray Leonard and Marlon Starling, resembled that of Emanuel Augustus more so than this son. Floyd Sr.'s up-and-down career, in the end, was cut short by gunfire.

In January 1979, Floyd Mayweather Sr. was shot in the leg by Tony Sinclair, the brother of Deborah Sinclair, Floyd Mayweather Jr.'s biological mother. At the time of the shooting, Floyd Sr. was holding his one-year-old son in his arms, allegedly using him as a shield, in a desperate attempt to ward off Sinclair's attack.

"This family controversy, it all started with my mother's brother, Tony Sinclair," Mayweather Jr. stated on HBO's 24/7 program. "He and my dad had a difference. I don't really know what happened, you're always gonna get different sides of the story."[130]

"My father said he was holding me and he said, 'If you're going to shoot me, you're going to shoot the baby, too.' But my mother said he used me as a shield to keep from getting shot. Either way, I'm just happy I didn't get shot and I'm still here," Mayweather Jr. reflected in a 2007 interview with Tim Smith of the New York *Daily News*.[131]

As a child, Floyd Jr. moved back and forth between his mother, father, and grandmother. Instability was the only constant in his young life. After the shooting, he and his mother moved from Grands Rapids to the Hiram Square neighborhood of New Brunswick, New Jersey, where his mother had family.

Floyd Mayweather Jr: "When I was about eight or nine, I lived in New Jersey with my mother and we were seven deep in one bedroom and sometimes didn't have electricity. When people see what I have now, they have no idea of where I came from and how I didn't have anything growing up."[132]

By his own admission, Floyd Jr. raised himself. His mother was addicted to heroin and his aunt died of AIDS as a result of her own drug use. When his father came around, boxing defined their relationship. Floyd Sr. aimed to mold his son into his own pugilistic image. As both a trainer and a father, he was a brutal taskmaster, quick to punish his son for anything less than perfection. At ten years old, Floyd Mayweather Jr. entered a boxing ring as an amateur for the first time. According to Floyd, his ambitions were driven by the poverty, desperation, and abuse that surrounded his life.

"The home that I come from, I had a father who was a hustler and a mother who was on drugs. That's one of the reasons I had to fight," Mayweather Jr. recalled.

After retiring from boxing, Floyd Mayweather Sr. returned to the streets. When Mayweather Jr. was sixteen years old, his father was convicted of smuggling cocaine and sent to federal prison in Milan, Michigan, for five and a half years. With his mother struggling with her own addiction, Mayweather Jr. was sent to live with his grandmother in Grand Rapids. Boxing, for the troubled high school dropout, was the only viable path to salvation.

"My father is a strong man but he is bitter about me and my mother's relationship," Mayweather Jr. recalled. "When I was a kid, he used to beat me. Beat me for no reason. And all I wanted was that one-on-one time. And that's probably the reason I take it out on my opponents to this day."[133]

In 1993, the same year Floyd Sr. was sent to prison on drug trafficking charges, Floyd Jr. captured his first National Golden Gloves title, an accomplishment he would repeat in 1994 and 1996. As Floyd Jr. dominated the amateur ranks, his uncle, Roger, was, at the very same time, making his mark as one of the top junior welterweight contenders in professional boxing. Following in his brother's footsteps, Roger Mayweather, nine years younger than Floyd Sr., bolstered the family name by winning the WBA super featherweight championship in 1983, widening the door for future generations of Mayweathers.

In a colorful, up-and-down career highlighted by title victories over Samuel Serrano, Rene Arredondo, Vinny Pazienza, and Livingstone Bramble, Roger Mayweather earned two of the most colorful nicknames in the sport—"The Black Mamba" and "The Mexican Assassin." Largely because of his ability to defeat top Mexican fighters with his shoulder-roll defense and sneaky right hand, Roger Mayweather became a respected commodity in the sport. Often playing the role of the heel, he regularly entered the ring wearing a poncho and sombrero. Like that of his brother, moments of confounding disappointment permeated Roger Mayweather's professional career, one that was marred by drug problems, money problems, and managerial disputes. Roger's brilliance was, in the end, juxtaposed with losses to Hall of Fame fighters such as Julio César Chávez, Freddie Pendleton, and Pernell Whitaker. In 1999, two years after his nephew turned professional, Roger Mayweather retired with a record of 59-13 (34 KOs).

Roger Mayweather's success, like that of his older brother, widened the path of opportunity. Six years after Roger Mayweather captured his first world-title belt, his younger brother, Jeff, also turned professional. Over the course of his own journeyman career, Jeff Mayweather built a professional record of 32-10-5, losing spirited bouts against high-profile fighters such as Oscar De La Hoya and Jesse James Leija.

For all of the socioeconomic disadvantages that plagued his childhood, Floyd Mayweather Jr. had one key advantage in his turbulent life: a wealth of boxing experience ran through his blood.

With Floyd Sr. locked away in prison, Roger and Jeff Mayweather became advisors, and even father figures, to their talented nephew, helping guide him to the professional ranks. When Floyd Mayweather Jr. secured his place on the 1996 U.S. Olympic boxing team, becoming the first in the family to do so, critics predicted big things for the young amateur star.

Floyd Mayweather Jr. lived up to the hype. In the opening round of Olympic competition, Floyd scored a technical knockout over his over-matched opponent from Kazakhstan. In his second bout, Floyd easily outpointed his Armenian opponent by a score of 16-3. In the third round of competition, Floyd cleared his path to gold, many believed. By out-pointing Lorenzo Aragón, Floyd became the first U.S. boxer to defeat a Cuban opponent in twenty years. Controversy, rather than a gold medal, was waiting just around the corner.

Because of a scorecard travesty similar to the verdict given to Roy Jones Jr. in 1988, Floyd Mayweather Jr.'s dreams of winning gold were dashed in the semifinal round when judges granted a controversial decision to Serafim Todorov of Bulgaria, the eventual silver medalist.

After the announcement, referee Hamad Hafaz Shouman of Egypt accidentally raised Floyd Mayweather Jr.'s hand during the announce-ment, thinking the American had just won the fight. In hindsight, the gesture is laughably ironic, for it would mark the final loss of Floyd's career.

* * *

After being awarded a bronze medal in the 1996 games, Floyd Mayweather Jr. ended his amateur career with an impressive record of eighty-four wins and only nine losses. Floyd's pedigree and impressive showing got him a contract with Bob Arum's promotional company, Top Rank. Floyd Sr., who was serving the final years of his sentence in Michigan, paid a big price for his crimes. Not only did he miss seeing his son in the Olympics, he was also absent for the first fourteen fights of Floyd's professional career. Upon his release, Floyd Sr. reunited with his son, taking over the role of head trainer and manager. Seven fights later, the relationship was already shaky.

While Floyd Sr. was incarcerated, his son had become his own man. Rumors indicated that Floyd Mayweather Jr. preferred his uncle's training style to his father's. As the young champion grew in stature, the family drama became a reoccurring subtext to his early title fights.

While Floyd Sr. was absent for his son's *KO Nation* bout with Emanuel Augustus, he was, to the surprise of many, brought back into the camp for Floyd Mayweather Jr.'s fifth defense of his WBC title, a mandatory defense against tough Mexican Gregorio "Goyo" Vargas, the second fight of Mayweather Jr.'s new HBO contract. The thin ice on which Floyd Sr. stood was hardly a family secret.

As Floyd made his way to the ring, flanked by his father and new manager James Prince, many speculated Floyd Sr. was no longer the dominant voice in his son's entourage.

"Yesterday, when Floyd went to the boxing commission, they asked him what color trunks his son was wearing and in an embarrassed and almost hurt way he said, 'I'm sorry, I don't know.' That's how big the rift is between them outside of the ring and the gym," HBO analyst Larry Merchant commented during Floyd's ring walk.[134]

When James Prince joined Team Mayweather, a renewed hip-hop vibe was injected into Floyd's brand. With his Ken-doll smile, many likened Floyd to Sugar Ray Leonard, the kind of fighter who can be marketed to the American public via his good looks and nonthreatening image. As Prince joined the fold, things quickly changed.

For the first time, Floyd Mayweather's ring walk featured a live hip-hop performance. For the Vargas fight, Wu-Tang Clan rapper Raekwon, who performed his song "100 Rounds," accompanied the boxer and his entourage to the ring. The theatrical move, now commonplace in the sport thanks to Roy Jones Jr., was a signal to many in boxing that Prince was now a force to be reckoned with.

"He's out to grab all of the young superstars in boxing. Mayweather is just the beginning. I think you are gonna see other young stars be bought up by James Prince," HBO commentator Emanuel Steward said as Raekwon delivered his trademark gritty vocals.

The mounting business upheaval did little to distract Floyd Jr., who, despite another hand injury, defeated "Goyo" Vargas in a lopsided decision. Diego Corrales, who fought in the HBO co-feature, scored another impressive knockout, leading critics to suggest he was the division's most dangerous champion.

Heading into the biggest fight of his career, Floyd Mayweather Jr. initially indicated that his father would remain as head trainer. In the months before his win over Vargas, however, the father-and-son duo finally made their inevitable split official. Roger Mayweather, once again, was promoted back to the role of head trainer. James Prince now guided the young champion's business affairs.

At first, Mayweather–Prince appeared to be a lucrative partnership.

"Before I met with James Prince, I was making six figures. Now I'm making seven figures. Before I hooked up with J Prince, I was staying in a $250,000 home. Now I'm staying in a million-dollar home. Before James Prince, I had a Lexus. Now I've got a Benz and a Corvette. James Prince has helped me manage my money and make the right moves," a young Floyd Mayweather told Karl Preltag of *Fight News* after the Vargas fight.[135]

Leading into Mayweather–Corrales, James Prince was hardly the dominant conversational sidebar. Floyd wasn't the only participant surrounded by controversy. The skeletons in Diego Corrales's closet, at the time, proved more gruesome than that of Mayweather.

In the summer of 2000, Diego Corrales had been arrested on charges that he assaulted his 98-pound pregnant wife, Maria. Sacramento police claimed the boxer broke Maria's collarbone, jaw, and a rib. On February 1, 2001, just two weeks after his career-defining bout with Mayweather, Corrales, free on $100,000 bail since his arrest, was scheduled in court. In an attempt to deflect attention away from Floyd's in-house family drama, James Prince advised his fighter to seize the psychological opportunity.

James Prince: "I had a plan to not only prepare Floyd but also to get inside Diego's head. Always know who you're fighting, no matter the arena. A little bit of homework can give you the advantage and make the difference between a big win and a big loss. Diego was a champion inside the ring, but outside he was in some trouble. He'd been arrested for a domestic battery incident; he allegedly fractured the skull of his pregnant wife during an argument. I tried telling Floyd to take the opportunity to beat Diego for every battered woman in America."[136]

At the prefight press conference, Floyd Mayweather Jr. did just that—dedicating his performance to all the battered women in America. Corrales, clearly irked by the move, responded with his own personal digs.

Diego Corrales: "As a person . . . it's a shame, a crying shame the things he's done, like kicking his own father out of his house. Something like that is uncalled for. Floyd's a guy who acts tough when he has seven or eight of his buddies around him. But this time it's going to be just him and me."[137]

Although Mayweather vs. Corrales wasn't a pay-per-view bout, it was indeed a high-stakes affair, with a lucrative multiyear HBO contract on the table for the winner. Both champions were twenty-three years old, undefeated, and untested. Neither champion had been knocked off his feet. On the promotional side of the equation, both fighters were surrounded by controversy; the bad blood between camps was real. Because of Mayweather's history of hand problems, inactivity, and distractions outside the ring, several high-profile boxing personalities, such as Max Kellerman and Dan Rafael, picked Corrales to win, despite Mayweather being the slight betting favorite.

From the ring walk on, the night belonged to Floyd Mayweather Jr. Accompanied by his father, who carried Floyd's infant daughter, Team Mayweather marched to the ring in a symbolically unified front. For a second straight fight, Floyd entered the ring to a live rap concert. This time around, Floyd's fans were treated to a performance from P-Reala and Postaboy, upcoming artists signed to the boxer's Philthy Rich record company. The song lyrics contained a variety of personal insults toward Corrales. The lyrical jabs from P-Reala and Postaboy, however, would be the least of Corrales's problems.

In what some have deemed the greatest performance of his career, Floyd Mayweather Jr. completely outclassed his lightweight rival. Floyd's hand speed, quickness, and defensive agility left Corrales befuddled. After six rounds, Mayweather had outlanded Corrales 121-32, according to CompuBox. To call Mayweather's victory dominant would be an understatement. In the opening seconds of round seven, Corrales was dropped, for the first time in his career, by a laser-quick left hook. Mayweather attacked his disoriented opponent, knocking him down two additional times in the seventh. In the tenth round, Mayweather scored two more knockdowns, prompting Ray Woods, Corrales's father and trainer, to throw in the towel. Before the fight was stopped by referee Richard Steele, Floyd Mayweather Jr. had won every round of the fight on every judge's scorecard.

The gamble paid off. Mayweather's knockout victory over Diego Corrales resulted in a long-term deal with HBO. Floyd's impressive victory also propelled the young champion to a new level of public visibility. With fame came new business opportunities. Following the Corrales bout, Mayweather began wearing an oversized, diamond-encrusted necklace etched with the Philthy Rich logo. The record company's namesake also began showing up on the back of Floyd's boxing robes. During public appearances, Mayweather touted his new label as if it were the next Def Jam or Death Row Records.

As Floyd Mayweather Jr. began to assemble the pieces to what he believed would be his crossover venture into the music business, many in boxing speculated that the foray into music might lead to nothing more than outside-the-ring distractions, hampering Mayweather's focus. While the label was highly publicized at Mayweather events, the company, for the first few years of its existence, had yet to produce an actual rap album. Some feared the investment might even lead to Mayweather's financial ruin.

"Mayweather spent at least $2 million developing his own record label, Philthy Rich Records, and the investment has yet to pay dividends," Tasha Robinson-White, Floyd's one-time assistant, told the *Detroit Free Press*.[138]

Floyd Mayweather Jr. came out of the Diego Corrales fight a hot commodity, yet his star dimmed significantly over the next two years. After defeating Corrales, Floyd faced mandatory challenger Carlos Hernandez in his hometown of Grand Rapids, gritting through the pain of yet another devastating hand injury to win a hard-fought unanimous decision. The inactivity, due to injury, was compounded further by Floyd's inability to get another Corrales-level matchup. In the 130-pound division, few, if any, blockbuster fights could be made. Frustrated by Bob Arum's inability to make his brand a household name, Floyd began to publicly express his disapproval of Arum and Top Rank. Fighting lesser-known opponents in front of less-than-capacity crowds was not what Mayweather had envisioned for himself after dominating Diego Corrales in his breakout performance.

* * *

On April 20, 2002, the outside-the-ring turmoil finally seeped into Floyd Mayweather Jr.'s professional life. In moving up in weight to face WBC lightweight champion Jose Luis Castillo, Floyd endured the toughest challenge of his young career, eking out a controversial but unanimous decision. While the early rounds had gone to Mayweather, Castillo gradually lured the young star into a toe-to-toe brawl, cutting off the ring, applying relentless pressure, and landing vicious body punches. The MGM

Grand crowd loudly objected to the verdict, and HBO's commentators questioned the decision. After the fight, Floyd claimed to have injured his left shoulder during training, which rendered him unable to effectively throw jabs or left hooks during the final six rounds. In winning his second world title, Floyd faced widespread criticism that all but forced his hand to accept an immediate rematch.

Because of Floyd's shoulder surgery, his rematch with Castillo didn't happen until eight months later. Fighting as the co-feature bout to Wladimir Klitschko's headlining heavyweight title defense against Jameel McCline, Mayweather Jr. used his superior hand speed and footwork to outbox Castillo, defending his title with a second straight unanimous decision. Floyd silenced the critics who believed Castillo had beaten him in their first fight, yet the boos came nevertheless—this time because the bout lacked action. Pundits labeled Floyd's defense-first approach as one that might win him more world titles but would never translate into pay-per-view success.

"I'm fighting against the odds. I feel like everyone is against Floyd Mayweather. You have to give respect where respect is due, Floyd Mayweather is the best pound-for-pound out there," the boxer said in his post-fight interview.[139]

Floyd's problems in the ring, however, were dwarfed by those in his personal life. Over a five-month span in 2001 and 2002, Floyd Mayweather Jr., according to *Business Insider*, pled guilty to two separate counts of domestic battery, receiving forty-eight hours of community service and two days of house arrest. Three other charges—stalking, obstruction of a police officer, and violation of a protective order—were dismissed. According to the *Las Vegas Review-Journal*, Melissa Brim, the mother of Mayweather's oldest daughter, was the victim. In November 2003, Mayweather was arrested and later convicted of two counts of misdemeanor battery for allegedly fighting with two women at a Las Vegas nightclub.

Controversial statements, legal trouble, recurring injuries, and an unexciting style all played a role in stunting Mayweather's plans to become the sport of boxing's leading man.

In November 2003, in front of a small crowd in Grand Rapids, Michigan, of just over four-thousand, Floyd Mayweather Jr. was set to face yet another obscure contender in hard-punching, South African

Phillip Ndou. Mayweather's fame had dwindled, his record company had yet to flourish, and he was now questioning the value of keeping James Prince as his manager. For the Ndou fight, Mayweather was set to make $3.05 million, $600,000 of which would be allocated to Prince. During the final days of the Ndou negotiations, Floyd made a call to Top Rank that would, in the end, have dire consequences.

"Floyd had asked us not to do a fight in October but to do it in December, after his contract with James Prince had run out," Bob Arum reflected.[140]

When word of Mayweather's move got back to Prince, the hip-hop mogul allegedly took matters into his own hands.

James Prince: "Things between us became distant. Communication was at an all-time low, and he was trying to avoid paying my $600,000 fee, so I flew to Las Vegas to settle it in person."[141]

On September 11, 2003, Prince and several men showed up to the Top Rank Gym in Las Vegas. A violent encounter ensued that resulted in Mayweather's advisor, Leonard Ellerbe, and ex-camp member Thomas Summers being taken to the hospital with serious injuries.

James Prince: "Together we were able to flip their original $12 million [HBO] offer into a contract that's worth anywhere from $24 to $50 million, factoring in the incentives. At the very least, we'd doubled their original offer. Floyd had no complaints, and that's why I'm not sure why he had such an issue paying me. Floyd didn't want his last fight to happen under contract with me because he flat-out didn't want to compensate me for all of the hard work I put in. He mistook my kindness for weakness and was fooling himself. When I arrived at the training facilities where Floyd was working out, the mood was tense. After his training, he and I stepped aside and I attempted to talk with him man to man. I wanted to know why he wasn't paying me. Floyd mentioned settling in court, and I told him I was there to hold court."

In an appearance on ESPN eight years later, Bob Arum reflected on the violent incident, one that continues to be talked about in both boxing and hip-hop circles: "We were at dinner. We got a call one night that there was a disturbance in my gym. The disturbance in my gym was, some people came over, with or without the knowledge of James Prince, and proceeded to break a couple of heads of people in Mayweather's camp with baseball bats. So, the gym was splattered with blood."

According to Arum, Floyd Mayweather Jr. came to his office the next day requesting that Top Rank pay James Prince the money he would have been owed as manager for the Ndou fight. When Arum suggested a letter of credit, Floyd insisted he write Prince a check for $600,000.

"To his credit, Floyd kept his word, and he had Bob Arum pay his debt. It was done," James Prince wrote in his 2018 biography.

By early 2004, the Rap-A-Lot CEO found himself at a boxing crossroads. Floyd Mayweather Jr. was no longer his client. Roy Jones Jr.'s reign as boxing's pound-for-pound best fighter was about to collapse. Partly because of the incident that occurred at Arum's Top Rank Gym, hip-hop's place in boxing was beginning to draw close scrutiny. James Prince's reputation was that of a mob boss more so than an entertainment mogul.

"There are stories about Prince that sound like hip-hop fables. Tall tales, like the rumor that Scarface was able to set foot in dangerous Chicago hoods because of Prince's relationship with Gangster Disciples' founder Larry Hoover. . . . It's hard to believe that a man who may not stand any taller than 5'9" is arguably the most feared figure in the history of Southern hip-hop," journalist Brandon Caldwell wrote.[142]

While Rap-A-Lot Records served as the blueprint for southern labels such as No Limit Records, Cash Money, and Suave House Records, controversy had always surrounded James Prince's various business enterprises. For naysayers, the details surrounding the Top Rank incident were strikingly similar to that of an evolving pattern in hip-hop business, one in which street entrepreneurship clashed with corporate America in both a literal and metaphorical sense. Hip-hop's mogul era, branded a mafioso-style takeover, frightened much of the mainstream media."[143]

Patterns of street violence were not uncommon in the rise of hip-hop moguls. In May 1999, for example, Bad Boy Records CEO Sean "Puff Daddy" Combs—along with two bodyguards—was charged with attacking Steve Stoute, president of Universal Records' urban division, in his New York City office. In December 1999, Roc-A-Fella Records co-founder Jay-Z was charged with felony assault in the second degree for allegedly stabbing Lance "Un" Rivera, CEO and co-founder of Untertainment Records, at a record-release party. In the early 1990s, Death Row co-founder Marion "Suge" Knight was accused of hanging rapper Vanilla Ice over the railing of a hotel balcony, forcing him to sign over the rights to "Ice Ice Baby" to his client. A few years later, Knight and his associates allegedly beat up Ruthless Records co-founder Eazy-E in an attempt to get Dr. Dre out of his contractual obligation to the label.

Just as the Mob had once controlled boxing for much of the 1950s and early 1960s, many feared the rise of a hip-hop mogul in boxing was simply an old phenomenon with a new twist.

"A lot of people that are scared of me are wrongdoers," James Prince told Philadelphia's Power 99 radio station. "A lot of those people don't mean right and they got things up they sleeve. And, if that's the case, they should be."[144]

Wrongdoer or not, Mayweather eventually gravitated toward the role of *bad guy*. The reinvention of his public persona was, to a large degree, made possible by his decision to align himself with an emerging rap villain in his own right. Together, the two formed the most controversial boxing and hip-hop pairing since Mike Tyson and Tupac Shakur.

GET RICH OR DIE TRYIN'

He was a stick-up kid who earned his reputation on the streets of Brooklyn by robbing rap artists. At five feet two and 120 pounds, Kelvin Martin wasn't imposing—not in the physical sense. He'd earned his nickname because of indiscriminate criminal practices. He'd rob you for a mere "50 Cent."

Kelvin Martin's life, like those of many career criminals, was cut short by gunfire. On October 20, 1987, in the stairway of his girlfriend's project building, Martin was gunned down at twenty-three years old. At the time of his death, Kelvin "50 Cent" Martin could not have possibly imagined a scenario where his nickname would become famous around the world.

"He was respected on the streets, so I wanted to keep his name alive," Curtis "50 Cent" Jackson wrote in his 2005 autobiography. "Other rappers were running around calling themselves Al Capone and John Gotti and Pablo Escobar. If I was going to take a gangster's name, then I wanted it at least to be that of someone who would say, 'What's up' to me on the street if we ever crossed paths. I couldn't see Gotti or Escobar giving me the time of day."[145]

Much like the original "50 Cent," Curtis Jackson was born into hellish circumstances. Jackson's mother, a neighborhood drug dealer, was murdered when he was just a child, and his father was absent from his life completely. Raised by his grandparents, hip-hop's "50 Cent" also gravitated toward gang life. At twelve years old, he began selling drugs and was arrested multiple times during his youth. On the streets of Jamaica, Queens, Jackson earned his own tough-guy reputation. At first, it appeared boxing might be 50 Cent's salvation. At eleven, the wayward child had wandered into a Queens boxing gym and found temporary shelter from his turbulent and unpredictable life.

50 Cent: "Boxing was the great equalizer. And it was the one sport that I could take part in where I had no one to blame for my success or failure other than myself. I liked that. Before I boxed, I was more likely to fight mad. I was reacting more on emotion than being conscious of my opponent's movements, and that took me off point. I realized that if I stuck with it and stayed calm enough, everything else would fall into place inside and outside the ring. I was able to deal with my problems for what they were without having my feelings take over."[146]

As 50 Cent progressed in his amateur boxing career, eventually competing in the Junior Olympics and New York Golden Gloves, he continued with one foot in the ring and the other in the streets. After dropping out of high school, 50 climbed his way to the top of the local drug-dealing hierarchy, sacrificing any opportunities the sport of boxing might have given the troubled teenager.

50 Cent: "I actually did better in the streets than I did in the ring. In the gym, I was going toe-to-toe with more-accomplished fighters who knew what they were doing. The guys on the streets had no technique. I picked up a few tricks from my street fights, but, for the most part, winning in the street just gave me confidence in the ring. That began a serious cycle, because my confidence from the street wins led to more wins in the ring. And the more I won in the ring, the more fights I picked in the streets."[147]

While boxing served as an escape for 50 Cent, the sport couldn't compete with the Queens native's first love—hip-hop. Just as the young teenager rode the violent waves of the 1980s crack epidemic, he would also follow the path provided by the record-industry boom of the 1990s, seeking an unlikely career as a rap artist in his late teenage years. The rules 50 Cent learned in the drug game, fueled by a relentless ambition and desperation, guided his work ethic, shaped his hip-hop persona. Broken and black hearted, fearless and lawless, 50 Cent fashioned himself as the walking personification of the Machiavellian street hustler. His underground buzz on the streets of New York City was legendary.

* * *

50 Cent's ability to network within New York hip-hop circles gave way to a rapid ascension. In 1996, 50 Cent was introduced to Jam Master Jay of Run-DMC, who was, at the time, attempting to establish his own record label. Under Jam Master Jay's tutelage, 50 learned the craft of writing songs rather than simply spitting freestyle verses. Just two years after meeting Jam Master Jay, 50 Cent was signed by record mogul Steve Stoute to a management contract with platinum-selling producers Trackmasters, who guided the young rapper to a recording contract with Columbia Records.

One could easily argue that it was the most controversial debut song in the history of hip-hop. Featured on the soundtrack of *In Too Deep*, released on August 10, 1999, "How to Rob," 50 Cent's introduction to the rap game, instantly roiled the industry.

In "How to Rob," 50 Cent plays up the origins of his rap moniker, fantasizing about mugging a variety of hip-hop and music-industry figures (over forty specific celebrities are mentioned in the song's three verses). The rhetorical style, comical in nature, was designed as a tribute to Kelvin Martin, introducing 50 Cent to American audiences as the metaphorical bully of the rap game.

"The bottom line is, I'm a crook with a deal / If my record don't sell, I'm gonna rob and steal / You better recognize, nigga, I'm straight from the street / These industry niggas starting to look like something to eat," 50 rhymes in the opening lines.

These hypothetical scenarios, filled with insults aimed at the artists 50 dreams about robbing, got deep underneath the collective skins of those referenced in the fictitious robberies. On the track "It's Hot," Jay-Z, who rarely responds to diss tracks, returned fire with the line: "I'm about a dollar, who the fuck is 50 Cent?" Always an opportunist, 50 began playing the Jay-Z soundbite at the beginning of his concerts. Other notable artists, such as Kurupt (of Tha Dogg Pound), Sticky Fingaz (of Onyx), Wyclef (of the Fugees), Ghostface Killah (of Wu-Tang Clan), and Big Punisher (of Terror Squad) each responded to "How to Rob" with return fire, further adding to 50 Cent's underground buzz. Many rappers felt the insults were unnecessarily cruel.

"I'll rob Pun without a gun, snatch his piece and run / That nigga weigh four hundred pounds, how he gon' catch me son?" 50 rapped about Bronx emcee Big Punisher, who suffered from obesity.

The controversial song gave way to several competing debates in hip-hop circles. Some worried that in hip-hop's post-Tupac–Biggie era, 50's strategy, if successful, might encourage upstart rappers to disrespect high-profile artists to bolster their own public profile, which could lead to further violence in the streets.

One song into his music career, 50 Cent had earned the reputation as hip-hop's newest bad guy, twice as bold and intimidating as many of his predecessors.

"People love the bad guy. I watch movies all the time and root for the bad guy and turn it off before it ends because the bad guy dies. It's cinematic law: the bad guy has to die. But sometimes the bad guy gets a record deal and becomes a superstar," 50 Cent told *The Guardian*.[148]

As 50 Cent began work on his debut album for Columbia Records, his focus was twofold. Still in the streets, still selling drugs, 50 Cent held tightly to his position in the world of organized crime. He missed gang meetings to record rap songs and missed recording sessions to handle business in the streets, an impossible balancing act. Beefs in the streets began to overlap with those in the music business, the most famous example being 50 Cent's long and drawn-out feud with Queens rapper Ja Rule and members of his Murder Inc. record company.

50 Cent: "A friend of mine robbed Ja Rule. That's how the beef originally started. My man robbed him for a chain, and then this guy named Brown came and got the chain back for Ja. Later, Ja saw me in a club with the kid who had robbed him. I went over to say, 'What's up' to Ja, and he acted like he had a problem with me."[149]

After the club incident, the two men experienced a second encounter, volatile in nature, during the taping of a music video on Jamaica Avenue in Queens. The rivalry turned physical when 50 Cent and Ja Rule once again crossed paths in a Miami club where 50 allegedly punched Ja in the face after a brief exchange of words. In an act of relation, 50 Cent was later ambushed and stabbed in the stomach during a Hit Factory recording session in Manhattan.

As a result of their burgeoning feud, Ja Rule, who was four albums deep into his career, began working his connections within the music industry to discourage producers and rappers from working with his rival.

"He was sabotaging my fan base . . . he was leveraging relationships he had in the industry to keep people from working with me," 50 Cent reflected in his 2005 memoir.[150]

Even before the release of a full-length LP, 50 Cent's propensity for mixing street culture and hip-hop music got the young rapper a list of enemies. In "Ghetto Qu'ran," a leaked song from 50 Cent's unreleased debut album, 50 references his experiences with a variety of drug dealers from his neighborhood in Southside Queens, most notably drug kingpin Kenneth "Supreme" McGriff and members of his notorious gang "The Supreme Team."

The references to McGriff were significant at the time because of the drug kingpin's alleged ties to Ja Rule's record company Murder Inc. After being released from prison in 1994, McGriff had, according to the FBI, connected with hip-hop producer Irv Gotti, who founded Murder Inc. with the hope of legitimizing his business interests. 50 Cent, some speculated, was attempting to pull the curtain back, exposing Murder Inc.'s illegal ties. In 2003, the record company's offices were raided by the FBI and McGriff was indicted on counts of money laundering. To his fans, 50 Cent was hip-hop's realest gangster—to his detractors, he was a snitch.

Rap beefs aside, 50 Cent's biggest problems were in the streets. At 11:22 a.m. on Wednesday May 24, 2000, 50 Cent left his grandmother's home on 161st Street in the Jamaica section of Queens and entered a parked car driven by his friend Curtis Brown. Because Brown's girlfriend was seated in the front passenger seat, 50 Cent sat in the rear passenger side of the car. Moments later, a masked assailant crept up to the window, reached his arm into the backseat, and shot 50 Cent nine times with a 9-mm handgun, repeatedly in the leg and hip area and once in the hand. The most gruesome wound, a fragment that tore into 50 Cent's mouth, exploded his left cheek. After the gunman fled the scene, Curtis Brown drove his friend to Jamaica Hospital, where he underwent surgery and was admitted for thirteen days.

Both of 50 Cent's legs were broken. His hip was fractured in several places. Pins were inserted into his hand because of a bullet that had penetrated his thumb and grazed his pinky finger. As a result of the bullet wound to his face, 50's jaw was wired shut for six weeks. His tongue, which also contained bullet fragments, was left permanently swollen. His normal speaking voice was altered as well. Even after therapy, 50 Cent spoke with a slight lisp. After being released from the hospital, the troubled rapper escaped New York City for the Poconos, laying low, recovering, and trying to find out who was responsible for the hit.

50 Cent: "The situation with those shots going off didn't have anything to do with hip-hop. It stemmed from me not cooperating with the niggas in the streets. I was on my own page and felt like niggas should do what I wanted them to do. They felt like I should be doing what they wanted to do. And that's when the shots went off. . . . He was from Brooklyn, and the guys I knew from Brooklyn knew who it was. He wasn't even down with the crew that shot me—he was a freelancer. Had I paid him first, he would've shot those other niggas for me. I knew everything about the situation right after it happened."[151]

A few years later, 50 Cent did, in fact, immortalize his shooter's name in a song. In "Many Men (Wish Death)," 50 names his assailant by briefly referencing his street moniker, one that is likely to be familiar to Mike Tyson fans.

"Hommo shot me, three weeks later, he got shot down / This is how I know I'm here for a real reason / Cus, he got hit like I got hit, but he ain't fucking breathin," 50 raps.

50 Cent's alleged attacker, Darryl "Hommo/Homicide" Baum, was a known presence in the streets of Brooklyn. A childhood friend of Mike Tyson, Baum at one point worked as a bodyguard for the undisputed heavyweight champion. When 50 stated the name "Hommo," hip-hop fans, and many boxing aficionados, knew exactly who the rapper was talking about.

Boxing fans will likely recall the name Darryl Baum because it was explicitly referenced in one of Tyson's more bizarre, emotional, and intimidating interviews with Showtime's Jim Gray. On June 10, 2000, just a few weeks after 50 Cent was shot in Queens, Darryl Baum was shot in the back of his head. Fourteen days later, Tyson took on Lou Savarese in Glasgow, Scotland, winning with a thirty-eight-second knockout.

"I dedicate this fight to my brother, Darryl Baum who died, I'll be there to see you. I love you with all of my heart," Tyson said, before launching to one of his most famous post-fight soliloquies.[152]

"I didn't train for this fight. I only trained probably two or three weeks, I had to bury my best friend. I wasn't going to fight but I dedicate this fight to him," Tyson continued before declaring that he wanted to "eat" Lennox Lewis's children.

When asked about the "Hommo" lyric, over the years, 50 Cent has largely played coy, neither confirming nor denying any involvement in what appeared to outsiders as an act of retaliation.

"How many times people say I did things I didn't do? People been saying that my whole career. I didn't do any of that. I'm a businessman," 50 Cent stated to Power 99.1, a slight smirk on his face.[153]

In a 2020 interview on Lil Wayne's podcast, twenty years after the shooting, the Southside Queens rapper finally held nothing back.

"When I got shot, Hommo pulled the trigger. Hommo was a part of Mike Tyson's camp," 50 admitted.[154]

At the time of the shooting, 50 Cent's debut album *The Power of the Dollar* was slated for an August 1 release. As a result of the incident, and the swirling rumors of the retaliatory attack, Columbia Records shelved the album and eventually released 50 Cent from his recording contract, leaving the injured rapper to pick up the pieces of his shattered rap career.

* * *

Columbia's decision to drop 50 Cent from the label was, in the end, a blessing. By surviving the shooting, 50 Cent gained priceless street authenticity in the eyes of fans. By being dropped by his record label, 50 Cent concretized the notion that he was a music-industry outsider, a threat to the hip-hop establishment, not unlike N.W.A, Public Enemy, and Tupac Shakur. 50 Cent was now in the ironic position of being too dangerous for hip-hop.

After recovering from his injuries, 50 Cent returned to his old neighborhood, hitting the gym, building back his body, and recording mixtape verses on other rapper's beats. Partnering with his childhood friends Sha Money XL, Lloyd Banks, and Tony Yayo, 50 rebranded his crew "G-Unit" (short for Guerrilla Unit). Together they became the hardest-working underground entity in the New York City hip-hop scene, mainstays on the popular mixtapes of DJ Whoo Kid. Despite his buzz in the streets, signing the rapper, many believed, was a risk not worth taking. As rumors circulated that Ja Rule and his Murder Inc. camp were attempting to block record companies from signing 50 Cent, there was no doubt that any potential suitor would inherit the beef. 50's ultimate power move, in the end, was announced to shock waves.

Andre "Dr. Dre" Young knew controversy. Each phase of his career was marked by both unprecedented success and turmoil. As the leader of N.W.A, hip-hop's first all-star gangsta-rap group, he was at the center of hip-hop's conservative political backlash. As the co-founder of Death Row Records, he was tethered to the real-life dangers of heading a gangsta-rap empire. After leaving Death Row, however, Dr. Dre, for the first time in his music career, stumbled. From an artistic perspective, Dre pushed back, attempting to deflect the East Coast–West Coast tensions, aiming instead for a message of bicoastal unity and positivity, a post–gangsta-rap version of himself. The reinvention failed.

Dr. Dre's new company, Aftermath Entertainment, was for a brief period without a centerpiece artist. The label's first release, a compilation titled *Dr. Dre Presents . . . the Aftermath*, received mixed reviews and had modest sales. The label's second offering, The Firm (a rap group comprised of New York emcees Nas, Foxy Brown, AZ, and Nature) was, given the level of star power on the album, a commercial and critical flop. The hip-hop equivalent of a shot fighter, Dr. Dre was finished many said. Gangsta rap was over. The Dirty South had risen. And hip-hop had changed.

Dr. Dre's comeback occurred in an unlikely way. In signing an unknown white rapper from Detroit, Michigan, named Marshall "Eminem" Mathers, Dr. Dre took a huge risk. This isn't to suggest Eminem was hip-hop's first white rapper. Def Jam's Beastie Boys had long broken that color barrier. Post-Beastie acts such as 3rd Bass, Vanilla Ice, House of Pain, and even Mark Wahlberg of Marky Mark and the Funky Bunch, had also proved to be commercially successful. Many of these artists were seen as cultural outsiders, however, even as one-hit wonders who commodified the culture by mimicking Blackness. White rappers sold records, many argued, but would never get respect in authentic hip-hop communities.

Eminem instantly turned rap music upside down. First and most important, the white boy could rap. His compound-syllable rhyme scheme was akin to the legendary Rakim. His R-rated sense of humor borrowed from the zany and intentionally inappropriate tradition established by artists like Redman. His talent as a storyteller, one could argue, was equal to that of the great Slick Rick. His self-deprecating and almost cartoonlike depictions of taboo subjects (such as rape, murder, and drug usage) were cultivated by Detroit's underground acid rap scene. Eminem's rhetorical style, which combined all these previous traditions into one artist, brought in a new era, giving way to competing notions of what it means to be white in the rap game. Unlike his predecessors, Eminem confronted his whiteness head on. He made fun of himself before listeners could get a chance to. Eminem's backstory—a poor white boy raised in the predominantly Black neighborhoods of Detroit—became a key component of his records. His mother, Debbie, and girlfriend/ex-wife, Kim, both depicted as so-called white-trash drug addicts, became recurring targets in his songs. Fans of all colors flocked to the music.

Eminem's Aftermath Entertainment debut, *The Slim Shady LP*, released in February 1999, not only saved Dr. Dre's new record company but also shot Dre back into the forefront of rap music and served as a powerful building block to his own comeback album *The Chronic 2001*. With the release of Eminem's next album, *The Marshall Mathers LP*, in May 2000, Eminem became the most popular artist in rap music. The album, which sold just under two million units in its first week, broke records and made headlines.

Like Dr. Dre's other artists, Eminem's rise was controversial. For all of his underdog qualities, Eminem was something of a rap bully. He picked on pop stars. He panned politicians. He made fun of dead and crippled celebrities. He lyrically murdered family members and rival emcees alike. When using the alter-ego "Slim Shady," Eminem's rapped about topics other artists simply could not.

While the album was criticized by women's rights organizations and LGBTQ rights groups, particularly for violent imagery against women and the use of homophobic language, the controversy surrounding Eminem's career without question propelled the rapper into a new level of fortune and fame. Vice President Dick Cheney, for example, drew a connection between the Columbine massacre and violent music and mentioned Eminem by name. By 2002, Eminem was rap music's most polarizing figure. Not only was he the genre's number-one selling artist, he was a budding movie star and the head of his own record label, Shady Records. What Shady Records needed was an Eminem, a rapper who could sell records and stir up controversy, a void that 50 Cent would soon fill.

✳ ✳ ✳

When news broke that Dr. Dre and Aftermath Entertainment had teamed up with Eminem's Shady Records to sign New York's most controversial underground artist, 50 Cent, to a joint record deal, the balance of power in rap music shifted instantly. Like a chapter in a comic book, hip-hop's supervillains were teaming up.

50 Cent's debut album, aptly titled *Get Rich or Die Tryin'*, was considered an instant classic. Off the success of the Dr. Dre–produced lead single, "In Da Club," which spent nine weeks at the top of the Billboard charts, 50 Cent purchased Mike Tyson's fifty-two-room Connecticut mansion for $4.1 million. The rapper who had once fantasized about mugging Tyson on his debut track "How to Rob" was now moving into the house the former heavyweight champion could no longer afford.

50 Cent: "I came off the tour and was like, 'How much money I got?' I'll buy whatever the fuck I want. I bought the property in a direct wire transfer. Mike Tyson owed the IRS $30 million when I bought the property. I did it. Monica was his wife at the time. I got the property and boom."[155]

At the same time 50 Cent was moving into the Connecticut mansion formerly owned by Tyson, a new boxing star was rising to the top of the sport.

On May 22, 2004, one week after Antonio Tarver knocked out Roy Jones Jr., Floyd Mayweather defeated DeMarcus "Chop Chop" Corley in his first fight in the 140-pound division, the undefeated boxer's third weight class. Floyd's entrance music was 50 Cent's hit single "Many Men (Wish Death)." Before the fight, Mayweather and 50 Cent had met at a club and struck up an instant friendship.

"The two men were tight. They hung out daily, partied, and were on an upward trajectory in their careers around the same time," wrote journalist Kourtnee Jackson about the duo's early days together.[156]

With Roy Jones Jr. dethroned, it was Floyd's time to reign as boxing's king. In most of his early championship bouts, however, Floyd attracted crowds of under ten thousand spectators. He was respected, he was paid, but he was not loved—or even liked—by the masses. Floyd had yet to cross over into pay-per-view status. Like 50 Cent, who, by his own assessment, "put the rap game in a choke hold," Floyd wanted more. The grandiose level of fame he envisioned for himself had, to this point, escaped him.

"I'm not worried about being popular, I'm worried about being a legend in boxing. Twenty years, thirty years from now—mark my word—they will say Floyd Mayweather was the best ever," Mayweather told HBO Sports before the Corley fight.[157]

During the second half of Floyd Mayweather's career, his relationship with 50 Cent, as well as his visibility within the hip-hop scene, became a larger component of the boxer's public persona. For his bout with undefeated Puerto Rican challenger Henry Bruseles in January 2005, Mayweather once again entered the ring to 50 Cent's music. As the months went by, the two stars were spotted at nightclubs and courtside at NBA games acting like childhood friends. As had been the case with Mike Tyson and Tupac Shakur, the pairing gave way to headlines that crossed pop culture's boundaries.

Before 50 Cent joined Floyd Mayweather's inner circle, the boxer's sidekick—or hype man—was rapper and Philthy Rich CEO P-Reala, born James McNair.[158] P-Reala's path to Mayweather began in the streets of Harlem, where hip-hop music was his first love. P-Reala's knack for poetry and love of language helped him excel in school, which perhaps saved him from the dangers in the streets.

After graduating high school, P-Reala received a full scholarship to Virginia State University in Petersburg, Virginia. While in college he studied sociology and continued to make music, producing college mixtapes. After he graduated from Virginia State, McNair returned to Harlem and got a job with the Department of Social Services. Back in his old neighborhood, McNair hooked up with a childhood friend who rapped under the name Postaboy. After reuniting, the two friends soon began recording music, underground mixtapes that eventually caught the attention of Floyd Mayweather Jr., who signed both acts to his record label. Postaboy's stay on Philthy Rich was brief, but P-Reala eventually became the company's CEO.

P-Reala: "Me and Postaboy was doing a lot of music. We had a friendship. And they [Postaboy and Mayweather] didn't see eye to eye on a business level, and some other things. Floyd and myself, we kept communication and he offered me the position of CEO at the label, and I took the opportunity given to me. Unfortunately, some people don't do that. But I gotta do what is best for me and my family."[159]

As Mayweather focused on his day job, P-Reala worked to saturate the underground market with Philthy Rich mixtapes and guest features. As CEO of Mayweather's label, P-Reala signed an Atlanta-based artist named Land Lord, along with an up-and-coming Brooklyn rapper named SL 500. For P-Reala, Mayweather's newfound proximity to one of hip-hop's biggest superstars was just one of the many perks of rolling with the champ.

"[Our music] gonna be on ThisIs50 [50 Cent's official website] first. Because, you know, he's someone who really supports our music and gets behind us. Teaching me the business. I'm gonna listen to someone that sold fifty million records. Why not? I don't know everything," P-Reala told CiseTV.

Floyd Mayweather's new partnership with 50 Cent represented what was taking place on a larger scale across the sport. Just as Lennox Lewis regularly wore custom-designed FUBU boxing trucks, the "For Us, By Us" hip-hop apparel company, fighters like Zab Judah, Ronald "Winky" Wright, and even Marco Antonio Barrera now wore Rocawear (Jay-Z's clothing line) into the ring. Promoter Cedric Kushner's *Heavyweight Explosion* series featured rap stars who performed in between fights, first-rate acts such as Xzibit and Eve.

Just a few weeks after Mayweather's TKO victory over Henry Bruseles, in January 2005, former Roc-A-Fella Records co-founder Damon Dash held a press conference in New York during which he announced a partnership with boxing promoter Lou DiBella. The first three boxers signed to the company, Dash/DiBella Promotions, were blue-chip prospects—Andre Berto, Jaidon Codrington, and Curtis Stevens—which demonstrated the potential of such a partnership.

"I think Lou [DiBella] and I will make the promotion dream team. I will bring my marketing expertise and will treat these boxers like my artists; I want them to not only be the best fighters, but entrepreneurs. Lou has the savvy to make them champions," Dash said at the press conference.[160]

"I have always admired Damon for what he's accomplished and his ability to market. Young fighters, particularly African American fighters, need greater exposure, especially in the young, urban market," DiBella added.

To a degree, Damon Dash was following in James Prince's entrepreneurial footsteps. After Floyd Mayweather beat Diego Corrales, Prince ramped up his efforts to become a key player in the sport. Jilted by Floyd, Prince took a page out of Don King's promotional playbook, visiting Diego Corrales during his two-year prison sentence. At first, Corrales was reluctant to meet with Prince because of his connection to Mayweather's persistent domestic-violence taunts before their fight.

James Prince: "I reached out to Diego's fiancée Michelle and told her flat out that I wanted to be in business with him. She told me Diego hated me and it would never happen; she said Diego would try to fight me if he ever saw me again. Nevertheless, I convinced her to take me to the prison to meet Diego face to face to explain my actions."[161]

When Corrales was released from prison, he shocked people in the fight game by signing a management contract with Prince, who, to his credit, guided his fighter to his two legendary wars with José Luis Castillo. When James Prince upset Don King by beating a $20 million lawsuit launched against him by Don King Promotions—who sued the rap mogul for "interference in [King's] relationship with former WBA welterweight champion James Page,"—boxing critics no longer questioned his managerial savvy.

After signing Diego Corrales, James Prince built on his momentum by signing Winky Wright to a joint venture with Roy Jones Jr.'s Square Ring Promotions. Later, Prince famously guided U.S. Olympic gold medalist and two-division world champion Andre Ward (32-0, 16 KOs) through his thirteen-year undefeated career, a relationship that helped Prince land a new generation of high-profile boxing prospects.

Today, former U.S. Olympic silver medalist and WBO featherweight champion Shakur Stevenson—who is named after Tupac Shakur—is represented by the Rap-A-Lot Records co-founder. Prospects Gabriel Flores Jr., Efe Ajagba, and Jared Anderson also fight under Prince's managerial company, wearing the Rap-A-Lot logo on their trunks and robes. Anderson even got a tattoo of the Rap-A-Lot logo underneath his chest. Because of James Prince, the idea of a rap mogul making it in the fight game is no longer taboo, or even surprising.

Andre Ward: "James Prince, I feel, is the best manager in the business. I talked to all of them. Prince is the kind of guy who gonna go to bat for you when it comes to negotiations. And he's gonna teach you the game. That's what I like about Prince. What he does other than boxing is his business."[162]

Back in 2005, however, many questions remained about hip-hop's place in the business of boxing. For better and for worse, 50 Cent and Floyd Mayweather Jr. found themselves at the center of the debate. Thanks to an ugly, reality-television-style feud, business opportunities were lost and a friendship fractured. What began as the most important cross-cultural pairing since Tyson and Tupac quickly turned into boxing and hip-hop's most bitter rivalry.

13

WHAT'S BEEF?

By 2007, the so-called urban youth market, driven by hip-hop trends, values, and spending habits, affected all aspects of American business. With increasing regularity, rappers-turned-businessmen began testing the entrepreneurial waters in new arenas. A fast learner, 50 Cent studied the successes of his peers and forged new career paths outside the vocal booth. Like his rival Jay-Z, 50 Cent now served as CEO of his own record company, G-Unit Records. After doing a $50 million deal with Reebok, 50 Cent founded his own clothing line, G-Unit Clothing. At thirty-two years old, the Queens rapper, like his label-mate Eminem, starred in a Hollywood movie based on his life story, releasing and executive producing the soundtrack on his own label.

50 Cent's ambitions grew larger than dominating the hip-hop marketplace. When Coca-Cola purchased Vitamin Water in 2007, for an estimated $4.1 billion, according to the *Washington Post*, 50 Cent, an early investor in the company, walked away with a figure somewhere between "$60 million and $100 million, which put his net worth at nearly a half billion dollars."[163] 50 Cent, the rapper, had become 50 Cent the businessman.

In retrospect, 2007 also proved to be a pivotal year for Floyd Mayweather Jr., who, like 50 Cent, was also striking out on his own. No longer under Bob Arum's Top Rank, Mayweather now fought under his own banner: Mayweather Promotions. In early 2007, Floyd also opened his own boxing gym, Mayweather Boxing Club, located just off the Las Vegas Strip. The newly founded "Money Team," guided by longtime Mayweather confidants Leonard Ellerbe and Al Haymon, looked to build upon the business blueprint established by Oscar De La Hoya's highly successful Golden Boy Promotions.

In the ring, Floyd Mayweather Jr. had nothing left to prove. With a professional record of 37-0 (24 KOs), he found himself considered by most to be the best boxer on Earth. In the business world, however, there were still those who simply didn't see "Pretty Boy Floyd" as a crossover star. To Floyd's dismay, only three of his first thirty-seven bouts took place on HBO's pay-per-view platform.

Phase one of Mayweather's master plan to dethrone Golden Boy Promotions began with facing the company's namesake. In Oscar De La Hoya (38-4, 30 KOs), Floyd Mayweather Jr. found a fitting box-office costar, his antithesis. De La Hoya, the WBC junior middleweight champion, was boxing's "Golden Boy," the sport's richest star south of the heavyweight division. Aside from the obvious good guy versus bad guy dichotomy, the matchup featured several interesting subplots. Some argued that Mayweather, who had previously struggled to knock out opponents in the welterweight division, simply didn't possess the size or power to dominate fighters in the 154-pound division. On the other hand, De La Hoya, at thirty-four years old, was no longer in his prime. The matchup's greatest subplot, however, had nothing to do with the tale of the tape.

In the years leading up to the pay-per-view megafight, Oscar De La Hoya's career had been extended under the tutelage of head trainer Floyd Mayweather Sr., who guided the Golden Boy to victories over Fernando Vargas, Felix Sturm, and Ricardo Mayorga. The public soap opera between Floyd Sr. and his son, regardless of Floyd Sr.'s decision to remove himself from De La Hoya's team before the fight, figured heavily in the promotional hype, family drama brilliantly captured on HBO's reality series, *De La Hoya–Mayweather 24/7*, which provided fans with an all-access look into the lives of both fighters.

On 24/7, "Money" Mayweather, as the boxer chose to label himself for the cameras, flaunted his material wealth as if auditioning for a hip-hop music video. The mansion, the luxury cars, the diamonds, the large stacks of cash all became a key component of Mayweather's new persona. Throughout the series, Mayweather's trash talk was more venomous than ever before. At this point in his career, most boxing fans were aware that he wasn't going to knock out De La Hoya with one fierce blast. He was no Mike Tyson. Aficionados also understood that, because of his cautious counterpunching style, Mayweather wasn't going to engage in a war either. He was no Arturo Gatti. Mayweather could, however, make fans hate him, make them pay to see him get his comeuppance, a move that Muhammad Ali used often in his early days.

In preparing to face one of boxing's most popular celebrities, Floyd followed 50's Cent's lead and played the villain role perfectly.

"Can't be two good guys, somebody gotta be the bad guy," Floyd boldly stated on the first episode of *De La Hoya–Mayweather 24/7*.[164]

Hip-hop's favorite villain was also a key component of the HBO reality program. In fact, Mayweather's relationship with 50 Cent served as an underlying theme on the series for years to come. For the De La Hoya fight in particular the contrast worked perfectly. Segments that featured De La Hoya's relationship with his wife Millie and their children were masterfully bookended with clips of Mayweather partying with one of rap music's most notorious figures.

"Don't nobody understand 50 Cent. We talk about things that he don't talk about with nobody else. He's the villain in rap music, I'm the villain in boxing," Mayweather stated.

"I'm the Floyd Mayweather of hip-hop," 50 Cent interrupted, riding an electronic scooter around the boxer's mansion.

As expected, "Money" Mayweather brought his newly perfected bad-guy act into the ring. At a sold-out MGM Grand Garden arena crowd, on Cinco De Mayo weekend, Floyd walked to the ring wearing a Mexican sombrero and a robe and boxing trunks draped in the colors of the Mexican flag, just as his uncle and head trainer, Roger Mayweather, had done during his days as "The Mexican Assassin." There would be no mariachi band. As the crowd booed, 50 Cent provoked De La Hoya's supporters with a live performance of his latest single "Laughing Straight to the Bank."

Unfortunately, the prefight drama proved more compelling than the fight itself. In a largely tactical match, Floyd Mayweather took Oscar De La Hoya's WBC junior middleweight title via a split decision, which earned Mayweather the distinction of becoming only the third boxer in history to win titles in five different weight classes.

According to most experts, the bout wasn't as close as the scorecards indicated. Thanks to an impressive work rate and strong left jab, De La Hoya hung with his younger opponent for the first six rounds. As the fight progressed, however, Mayweather took over. Floyd's superior defense, speed, and accurate counterpunching ultimately proved to be the difference.

As 50 Cent's entry music augured, Floyd Mayweather Jr. got the last laugh. At the time, on May 5, 2007, Oscar De La Hoya vs. Floyd Mayweather Jr. was the most lucrative pay-per-view event in the history of boxing, pulling in over $130 million in total revenue. The victory, despite the lack of action in the ring, catapulted boxing's bad guy to the forefront of the sport.

* * *

While Floyd Mayweather Jr's stock surged, 50 Cent's career was about to experience a downturn. Just a few months after the De La Hoya fight, 50 Cent released his third studio album, *Curtis*. The buildup to the album largely centered on 50's record-sales rivalry with hip-hop's newest star, rapper and producer Kanye West. While 50 Cent maintained a rare street authenticity, Kanye West was the son of an English professor, a rapper whose production style and lyrical content shifted the temperature of the culture completely. 50 rhymed about slinging crack. Kanye rhymed about dropping out of college and folding jeans at The Gap. 50 Cent, who had bullied his way into the rap game, would, in the end, be outpaced by the most unlikely of competitors.

On September 11, 2007, *Graduation*, Kanye's third studio album, was released on the same day as 50 Cent's *Curtis*. Before this showdown, 50 Cent jokingly vowed to retire if Kanye's album outsold his.

"Mine will sell and his will still be on the shelf. He should be terrified. What should I do? Do I send flowers? Do I send condolences?" 50 Cent told *Rolling Stone*, leading up to the release date of both records.

While both records were commercially successful, *Curtis* received mixed reviews and was surpassed by Kanye's album in first-week sales and total sales, which perhaps signaled a shift in hip-hop music. Back in 2005, *The Massacre*—50 Cent's second effort under Shady/Aftermath—produced the highest sales of the year for any album, according to Nielsen SoundScan numbers. Just two years later, it now appeared that Kanye West ruled hip-hop.

As 50 Cent battled Kanye West, Floyd Mayweather looked to capitalize on his new appeal by increasing his profile. First came a series of appearances on WWE's professional wrestling series *Monday Night Raw*, which culminated with a WrestleMania XXIV showdown with wrestler "The Big Show," one of the company's stars. Mayweather's 24/7 sidekick, 50 Cent, was also worked into the storyline—he was present for Mayweather's wrestling match and accompanied his friend to the ring just as he had done for the De La Hoya fight.

A few months after WrestleMania, in December 2007, Floyd Mayweather Jr. added to his crossover celebrity by appearing on the fifth season of ABC's popular show *Dancing with the Stars* while also training for his upcoming pay-per-view fight against the undefeated and popular British boxer Ricky "The Hitman" Hatton (43-0, 31 KOs).

Hatton, like De La Hoya, proved the perfect foil for Mayweather—a wild, free-swinging brawler who considered himself an everyman and enjoyed darts and pints of Guinness at his local pub. In a sequel of sorts to the original four-part series, HBO's *Mayweather–Hatton 24/7* once again captured the dysfunction of the Mayweather family, Mayweather's growing rivalry with Golden Boy Promotions [which also represented Hatton], as well as the boxer's growing partnership with hip-hop's bad guy, 50 Cent. All of this set up a second straight pay-per-view blockbuster.

While Floyd Mayweather Jr. got eliminated early in *Dancing with the Stars*, the boxer had few problems in the ring. In the tenth round, a perfectly timed Mayweather check hook sent Hatton careering into the turnbuckle and onto his back. Mayweather wasted little time in finishing off Hatton with a barrage of punches, capped off by a left hook that sent the Hatton back down to the canvas. As Floyd Mayweather Jr. improved his record to 39-0 (25 KOs), once again defeating one of the sport's most popular fighters, there seemed was no debate—"Money" was number one in the ring and at the box office.

"[My team] got me two of the biggest fights in boxing history. And it's just truly a blessing. Now I need a vacation. I'm not trying to call out no welterweights. I've done what I had to do in the sport. I've accomplished what I had to accomplish. It's time for me to focus on being a promoter. . . . I'm not going to let the sport of boxing retire me, I'll retire from the sport," Floyd told HBO's Larry Merchant after the fight.[165]

In both boxing and hip-hop, retirements rarely stick. Yet as 2007 ended, both Floyd Mayweather Jr. and his friend 50 Cent began to tease their eventual career transitions. Unhappy with the cool reception of *Curtis*, 50 Cent allegedly threw a cell phone through a window in the G-Unit offices. After learning the music video for his fifth single from the album had been leaked to the internet, he reportedly ripped a television off the wall.[166] Hip-hop had slipped away from him, some argued. Kanye West's exploratory sound, a mix of soul sampling and EDM music, had brought something new to a genre looking for a post–gangsta-rap trailblazer. 50's latest record, according to most critics, followed closely the formula he established on his debut record *Get Rich or Die Tryin'*.

Now a hip-hop mogul, 50 Cent, in the coming years, began to focus much of his attention on ventures outside the music industry. As promised, Floyd Mayweather Jr. also stepped away from his craft and focused on growing Mayweather Promotions. His absence from the ring would be just under two years in total. Ironically, it was during this hiatus that a worthy rival to his throne finally emerged.

✳ ✳ ✳

By demolishing Floyd Mayweather Jr.'s previous two opponents in back-to-back fights—Oscar De La Hoya (December 2008) and Ricky Hatton (May 2009)—Manny "PacMan" Pacquiao (48-3-2, 36 KOs) of General Santos City, Philippines, quickly supplanted "Money" Mayweather as boxing's new star. With his all-action southpaw style and inspirational life story, Pacquiao proved to be an underdog hero unlike anything the sport had seen. To his irritation, Mayweather had exited the sport on top only to be immediately replaced by a shooting star who many though was more entertaining and perhaps more popular than he ever was.

Though Pacquiao's rise may have felt like an overnight phenomenon to casual boxing fans, his road, as it is for all champions, was arduous. Manny Pacquiao's troubled childhood in the Philippines was marked by the kind of poverty few can imagine. Stories of the young Manny Pacquiao eating once a day, sleeping in the street, living in a tin shanty, and fighting other children for money gave way to a mythical rags-to-riches narrative.

Just as brilliantly as Mayweather played the villain, Pacquiao, in both style and story, played the role of hero just as skillfully, carrying an entire country on his back each time he entered the ring.

Manny Pacquiao's story was remarkable. In a desperate attempt to feed his family, Pacquiao, in January 1995, turned professional at just sixteen years old, weighing only 98 pounds in his first match.

"The malnourished Pacquiao weighed just 98 pounds for his [first] fight and filled his pockets full of heavy objects (reportedly rocks and ball bearings) to make it to 106 pounds," boxing writer Ryan Songalia writes.[167]

For the first six years of his career, Manny Pacquiao worked in obscurity. Thirty-one of his first thirty-five fights took place in the Philippines, Thailand, and Japan. Battle-tested but relatively unknown in Europe and the United States, Pacquiao, at twenty-four years old, walked into the Wild Card Boxing Club in Los Angeles in early 2001, looking for the spark that might ignite his stagnant boxing career. What he found was a mentor.

Freddie Roach: "I was doing the mitts in the ring with one of my fighters. This guy walks through the door, this small kid with a couple of managers. I come down and say hi. He asked me if he could hit the mitts with me. He says, 'I hear you're pretty good (on the mitts); I'm good, too.' We went into the ring and after the first round, I thought to myself, 'Wow, this kid can fight.' At the same time, Manny says to his manager, 'We have a new trainer.' That was the very beginning of our [. . .] together."[168]

The pairing of unlikely underdogs, in years to come, became the main subplot of Manny Pacquiao's story.

Before Pacquiao, the mild-mannered Roach had been an understudy of the legendary trainer Eddie Futch, a gig that eventually led to Roach working with a variety of top-level fighters such as Olympic silver medalist and eventual light heavyweight champion Virgil Hill. With Pacquiao, however, Roach found the boxing prodigy that would single-handedly transform his gritty Wild Card Gym into a household name and confirmed his status as a world-class trainer.

As destiny would have it, the duo's big break came in equally surprising fashion. On June 23, 2001, the little-known Pacquiao served as the stand-in opponent for WBA bantamweight champion Lehlohonolo "Lehlo" Ledwaba (33-1-1, 22 KOs), a hard-punching South African who was seen by most as the top fighter in the division. In a fight taken on only two weeks' notice, Pacquiao and Roach made an instant splash. Pacquiao's sixth-round technical knockout over Ledwaba, whom he dropped to the canvas three times, marked the emergence of a new star in the sport, earning the first of many world titles for Team Pacquiao.

Over the next six years, Pacquiao became Roach's chief pupil. Aside from his work with stars such as Mike Tyson, James Toney, and Oscar De La Hoya, Roach earned his reputation as a trainer by transforming the hard-punching southpaw from a one-handed reckless brawler into to a complete fighter.

While there would be setbacks along the way, a draw with Juan Manuel Marquez and a unanimous decision loss to Erik Morales, few could ignore the results of the pairing. As Pacquiao climbed one weight class after another, racking up impressive wins over future Hall of Famers such as Marco Antonio Barrera (twice), Erik Morales (in a rematch), and Juan Manuel Marquez (in a rematch), he gained new fans with each action-packed performance.

By 2009, Roach, who had previously replaced Floyd Mayweather Sr. in Oscar De La Hoya's corner for his fight with Mayweather Jr., found himself entangled in what would soon become a bitter rivalry. During HBO's *De La Hoya–Mayweather 24/7* reality series, for example, Roach was relentlessly taunted by Mayweather and his team. After Pacquiao became a force in the welterweight division, however, many speculated that Roach had a fighter who could deliver the comeuppance the boxing world wanted to see. As Pacquiao steamrolled Oscar De La Hoya and Ricky Hatton—much more easily than Floyd Mayweather Jr. did—it was now Roach's turn to talk.

"The whole world wants to see him fight Mayweather, and I want Mayweather," Roach stated boldly, arguing that his man could do what others could not.[169]

✳ ✳ ✳

As predicted, Mayweather Jr.'s retirement didn't last. In September 2009, Floyd returned from his "extended vacation" to face Juan Manuel Marquez (50-4-1, 37 KOs), who in two fights with Pacquiao proved to be one of the "PacMan's" toughest opponents, earning a draw and a split decision loss in their two previous bouts.

Floyd's choice in opponent was not popular. Despite Marquez's pedigree, this was not the fight fans wanted. In a now-infamous interview with ESPN's Brian Kenny, Floyd Mayweather Jr., for the first time in his career, became unraveled, and was visibly perturbed at having to share the spotlight with boxing's newest hero.

"We welcome into *SportsCenter* the former number-one pound-for-pound fighter in the world," Kenny said in his introduction.

"I'm not no former pound-for-pound fighter. Nobody has dethroned me. How am I not the best pound-for-pound fighter in the world? You tell me," Floyd interrupted, his face grimacing at Kenny's audacity.[170]

"Because you retired. You retired, Floyd. What do you want to become champion emeritus forever?" Kenny rebutted.

"Have I ever been beat? Well, once again, I already forgot who I was talking to . . . Brian Kenny, a guy who never laced up gloves in his life," Mayweather scoffed.

"You always come back and face the best. Why not face the guy who won the Pacquiao vs. Marquez fight? Why not face the winner? Is it because of Bob Arum, Pacquiao's promoter?" Kenny responded, in a heated back-and-forth exchange.

"We already know, me and Bob Arum have a problem, some issues," Mayweather responded. "So, that's gonna be hard to make. If Pacquiao want it, he can get it. You know that. I've never ducked and dodged no opponent, so stop that. Stop! Stop it! The guy won a couple of fights. You wasn't saying that when he got his ass kicked by Erik Morales. You wasn't saying put him in there with Floyd Mayweather. All the sudden he got a couple of wins now you saying throw him in there with Mayweather. Where was Pacquiao in '98, '99, '00? I'm in a whole new era dominating fighters. When I beat him, it'll be 'Oh, we knew this was gonna happen, Floyd is the bigger fighter.' It's always excuses."

In the months that followed, the animus continued. On hip-hop personality Lord Sear's *All Out Show*, rapper R.A. the Rugged Man accused Mayweather of ducking both Antonio Margarito and Manny Pacquiao. When 50 Cent, listening to the radio show in New York, made Mayweather aware of the rapper's comments, he, to the surprise of everyone listening, called in.

"Brother, you ain't no more special than Aaron Pryor, you ain't no more special than Pernell Whitaker. You ain't more special. You gotta prove you're the greatest ever to call yourself that." R.A. the Rugged Man goaded Mayweather in their twenty-four-minute dustup.

Aside from battles with boxing pundits, Mayweather's return was filled with controversy outside the ring. Most believed, despite his choice of opponent, the comeback had nothing to do with Pacquiao and reasserting his place in the sport. Leading up to the fight, rumors of Mayweather's mounting tax problems loomed.

Just as was the case for Mayweather, 50 Cent's time away from the rap game also produced new rivals. Public beefs with rappers The Game, Fat Joe, and Rick Ross kept 50's name in the news, despite a lack of new music. For this new phase in his career, however, the rapper was much more likely to insult his foes on social media than on diss tracks. For example, in February 2009, 50 invited Tia, the mother of Rick Ross's baby, and their son on a trip to Floyd Mayweather Jr.'s Las Vegas mansion, posting videos of the get-together on social media to taunt his rival. In response to the viral video, Rick Ross fired back in his 2009 single "Mafia Music," where he rhymed, "That Mayweather money lookin' funny in the light," poking fun at the alleged $6 million that Mayweather allegedly owed the IRS before his bout with Marquez.

Regardless of the outside turmoil, Floyd Mayweather Jr.'s performance in the ring was spectacular. In a technical masterpiece, Mayweather dropped Juan Manuel Marquez twice en route to a lopsided unanimous decision victory.

After the fight 50 Cent continued to provoke Rick Ross with the diss track "Officer Ricky," which dug deep into his rival's past and revealed his previous career as a correctional officer.

Ross quickly fired back with diss records of his own: "Kiss My Pinky Ring, Curly" and "Push Em Over the Edge."

As 50 Cent and Floyd Mayweather looked to get back on top, fans picked sides and joined the debate on social media. Winning back popularity, for both 50 and Floyd, would not come easy.

In easily beating Juan Manuel Marquez, a fighter who pushed Manny Pacquiao to the limit, Floyd Mayweather Jr. made a strong case for himself. Two months later, in the same arena, Manny Pacquiao fanned the flames by knocking out Puerto Rican superstar Miguel Cotto (34-1, 27 KOs) in the eleventh round, earning his first title at welterweight. In becoming a six-division champion, "PacMan" provided a strong response to Mayweather's comeback win. Chants of "We Want Floyd" rang throughout the MGM Grand as Pacquiao delivered his post-fight remarks.

In 2010 there was only one fight boxing fans wanted to see. Unfortunately, a Mayweather vs. Pacquiao fight would not happen for another five years. At first, negotiations stalled because of Mayweather's insisted on a 60/40 split of the purse. Next came Mayweather's insistence on Olympic-style drug testing. When negotiations finally broke down and Pacquiao and his team moved forward with a bout against Joshua Clottey, Mayweather aired his grievances publicly, accusing Pacquiao of using performance-enhancing drugs.

"All I'm asking is give a little blood, give a little urine. Is that a crime? You go back and look at the pictures. First, his head is small and then his head grew. C'mon, this is basic common sense. This man probably went from a 7¼ to an 8 in a hat, a fitted hat. C'mon, man. This is basic common sense. I went up in weight but I didn't just walk through fighters. This nigga 106 pounds and now he just walking through fighters," Mayweather taunted, leading into his bout with WBA welterweight champion "Sugar" Shane Mosley (46-5, 39 KOs), scheduled for May 1, 2010.

The Mayweather–Mosley fight for the most part played out as predicted by boxing insiders. Using his superior ring generalship, Mayweather outpointed the thirty-eight-year-old Mosley by a comfortable margin. The Mosley bout, however, had given Pacquiao fans a glimpse of what they wanted to see—a chink in Mayweather's armor. In the second round, Mosley buckled Mayweather's knees with a powerful overhand right that forced the undefeated fighter to grab his opponent to avoid going down. While Mayweather dominated virtually every second of the fight from that point forward, the brief flash of vulnerability was enough to make

Pacquiao supporters wonder, *What if Manny Pacquiao had landed that punch?*

"If Manny Pacquiao can take a blood and urine test, we have a fight. If not, no fight," Mayweather told HBO commentators in his post-fight interview.

As tensions between the camps grew stronger, and the accusations grew harsher, both Mayweather and Pacquiao went their separate ways. After defeating Mosley, Mayweather would not return to the ring until the following year. Pacquiao, on the other hand, chose to stay busy. In the fall of 2010, Pacquiao dominated a much larger foe in Antonio Margarito, an opponent many had accused Mayweather of ducking earlier in his career. In May of the following year, Pacquiao would push things further by also defeating "Sugar" Shane Mosley by unanimous decision, dropping Mosley in the third round en route to an easy victory. If not for a disputed majority decision win over Juan Manuel Marquez in their trilogy fight in the fall of 2011, Pacquiao might have captured the popular vote with ease.

Meanwhile, rap's bogeyman was in middle of his own comeuppance. 50 Cent's battle with Rick Ross had, to this point, produced negative results. In a string of diss tracks and deeply personal social media threats, 50 clearly won the war of words. Ross, however, came out of the feud more commercially viable than ever. While Ross's music was surging on the charts, 50's career—as measured in record sales—was heading in the other direction. His fourth album, *Before I Self Destruct*, released in late 2009, was a flop.

Rick Ross: "At this point, my relationship with Curtis is amusing, because of the fact that I'm the biggest 'L' [loss] he ever took. A lot of these guys, they're one-trick ponies, so they're going to be gone. In hip-hop, they say it's not what have you done, but what have you done for me lately."[171]

Rappers, unlike boxers, don't have their hands raised. Rap beefs typically rely on public perception. At the time of the 50 Cent–Rick Ross rap battle, artists such as Kanye West and Drake, both emotional and boastful, fused R&B and pop and brought forth a new type of masculinity to the rap game, one without the street ethos that had dominated the genre for almost three decades. In choosing to hold on to his gangsta-rap image, 50 Cent perhaps overstayed his welcome as the music moved in new directions. 50 appeared aware of the demographic shift.

"I'm trying to fit in and I can't fit in, damn," the rapper mockingly rhymed on the 2011 mixtape track "Suicide Watch."

Aside from trolling Ross, 50 Cent's main focus now was to build a professional relationship with Mayweather, whose own *bad boy* image was also beginning to exhaust boxing fans. Before Mayweather's bout with Victor Ortiz (29-2-2, 22 KOs), the boxer's first fight in sixteen months, 50 Cent announced the two had started a film production company called Mayweather Productions. Later that summer, Mayweather, along with Mike Tyson, appeared in a commercial for 50 Cent's Street King energy drink. In November 2011, 50 Cent and Mayweather appeared on the cover of the popular hip-hop magazine *XXL*, the first and only time the two stars would be featured together.

On the night of the Victor Ortiz fight, 50 Cent accompanied Mayweather to the ring, wearing his WBC belts around his chest and waist. The rumored Mayweather–50 Cent promotional venture, called "The Money Team," was all but inevitable, many believed.

"As far as boxing, I think [50 Cent] is going to be involved with the promotion side. . . . We might even have him fight on pay-per-view one time. We don't know what the future holds, but he is getting involved with boxing," Mayweather told *XXL* after the fight, a controversial fourth-round knockout over Ortiz that many fans believed came from a sucker punch.

Aside from his questionable behavior during and after the Ortiz fight, Mayweather's crumbling popularity had little to do with his boxing career. As Business Insider reported, Mayweather, over the course of his career, was accused of violence against women several times. In December 2011, the latest in a string of allegations, Mayweather pleaded guilty to one count of misdemeanor battery [domestic violence] and no contest to two counts of harassment for hitting Josie Harris, the mother of his three children. The mounting pressure to take on Manny Pacquiao, for a brief period of time, proved to be the least of Mayweather's problems.

＊ ＊ ＊

In early 2012, when negotiations with Mayweather Promotions and Top Rank once again fell through, Floyd Mayweather Jr. chose to move up in weight to face WBC junior middleweight champion Miguel Cotto, who had reestablished himself in the division. Mayweather's upcoming incarceration, delayed only by a Las Vegas judge who allowed the boxer to fulfill his previously booked fight date, quickly became the dominant narrative surrounding the matchup.

On HBO's 24/7, Mayweather's relationship with 50 Cent was worked into the coverage as a way of addressing the damning charges that hung over the promotion. In the first episode, 50 Cent, who also spent time behind bars as a young man, assessed Mayweather's imminent ninety-day bid at the Clark County Detention Center.

"One day is too many. Two days is too many to spend without being able to get up and move as you please. What's interesting is going to be what you see next from Floyd," 50 said.

At least in front of the 24/7 cameras, it appeared that Mayweather drew strength from 50 Cent's presence in the training camp. For the second straight fight, 50 accompanied Floyd to the ring, wearing his championship belts as if they were hip-hop accessories.

"[50 Cent] has a very busy schedule but I like to have him around, for that inspiration. Going into this fight, this reminds me of that *Get Rich or Die Tryin'*," Mayweather stated on the show.

As predicted, Mayweather dominated the early rounds, outboxing Cotto and using his defensive skills to avoid punishment. In the middle rounds, however, the proud Puerto Rican champion launched a comeback, using a powerful jab and sharp body punching to back Mayweather against the ropes. Sensing an upset, the crowd came alive as Mayweather's nose and mouth became bloodied, an unfamiliar sight.

"What a determined effort by Miguel Cotto . . . this fight is evening up," HBO's Jim Lampley called at the end of the eighth round.

"Mayweather hasn't lost a round as clearly, as solidly, as he did this one, in a long time. The cheering you are hearing in the background is for the blood on Mayweather," Larry Merchant added.

To the disappointment of the thousands of Puerto Rican fans watching around the world, there would be no upset. In the final rounds of the fight, Mayweather picked up the pace and Cotto began to fade, his eyes swollen and battered from Mayweather's pinpoint counterpunching. After twelve surprisingly hard-fought rounds, Mayweather was given a close but unanimous decision victory.

"And now, of course, fans will fixate on a viable comparison between what Cotto was able to do against Pacquiao, not much, and what Cotto was able to do against Mayweather, a little more," Jim Lampley said moments after the decision was announced.

While the promotion had been lucrative, and the fight excellent, Mayweather had little time to enjoy his win. On June 1, 2012, 50 Cent accompanied him as he turned himself into the Clark County Detention Center. According to 50 Cent, he immediately began working on the duo's previously planned business merger, acquiring talent and completing legal paperwork for a company that would merge hip-hop and boxing like no other.

Eric B.: "Back then, 50 and Floyd had the right idea. This was way before Triller. That merger would have been major. It is a shame how that played out because it would have been major. That was an opportunity lost for hip-hop and boxing."

Eight days later, as Mayweather sat in his Las Vegas jail cell, Manny Pacquiao's seven-year winning streak was snapped in a controversial split-decision loss to former junior welterweight champion Timothy Bradley (28-0, 12 KOs).

Even though public opinion favored Pacquiao, the loss shocked the boxing world and perhaps took something away from the potential dream matchup. The bizarre Las Vegas scorecards were an omen for the chaos to come.

After serving sixty days of his ninety-day sentence, Mayweather was released from jail and greeted by a small group of family and friends. 50 Cent was there. The day before Floyd's release, 50 had posted a message to fans, declaring the two "back in business and ready to get TMT [The Money Team] off the ground."

The following month, September 2012, the first signs of a frayed relationship appeared. In an appearance on *The Rickey Smiley Morning Show*, 50 Cent surprised listeners by replacing Manny Pacquiao as Floyd Mayweather's chief rival.

"Everybody around him is waiting on the next time he feels generous. And I have a lot, so I don't wait for nobody," 50 said.

When pressed about the apparent delay in launching TMT, 50 Cent didn't hold back.

"He changed his mind. As he was going into jail, he asked me to help him with Mayweather Promotions. As I took a look, I realized there was no Mayweather Promotions. There was no LLC, no corporation. It's just a name. Technically, Floyd is a Golden Boy fighter. He fights on every Golden Boy card. They do all the footwork. They build the whole show. So, when he says help me with Mayweather Promotions, and it's not there, I go . . . I know what he means, he wants me to put it together for him. I do TMT Promotions. I get it all together. Sign the actual fighters, we get the acquisition of Gamboa. I had to negotiate his release, 1.2 million. Andre Dirrell. IBF champion, Billy Dib. WBA champion Celestino Caballero. I brought them over while Floyd was incarcerated. When Floyd came home, there is the 'let's get Floyd back in pocket campaign.' Three-hundred-thousand-dollar chains being bought, new Lambos. And, I'm sitting there going, 'When are you going to give me the money?'"

Boxing fans would also become increasingly frustrated with Mayweather in the coming months, but for far different reasons. After being released from jail, the pay-per-view cash cow announced that he had left the HBO network in favor of a thirty-month, six-fight deal with Showtime Sports and its parent company CBS, one of the richest television deals in boxing history. Because Manny Pacquiao fought exclusively on HBO, many felt the move to Showtime all but ended any chance of a Mayweather–Pacquiao blockbuster. 50 Cent, perhaps, felt equally jilted.

50 Cent: "I wanted my half of the money back, but I ain't trying to press him because he just got out of jail. When he actually does bring up the situation, he acted like he didn't know anything. Like, I didn't tell you to do that. Floyd will say he doesn't know how we fell out. Like I never said anything to him, like I woke up one morning and just had a problem with him. But that's not what happened. What happened was that he asked me to help him. I could stop them from using TMT as their logo, right now. But to be honest with you, I incorporated TMT in Delaware while he was incarcerated. Just because he didn't sign the paper doesn't mean the corporation isn't valid. I could tell him, you can't have them TMT socks, that TMT shirt you got on."

Soon after 50 Cent's shocking radio interview, Mayweather responded via Twitter.

"A male boxing groupie. Hold my belts because your album sales have declined," Floyd tweeted, including a picture of 50 Cent holding his championship hardware.

50 Cent, in typical fashion, countered swiftly by referencing Floyd's history of domestic violence and making fun of his failed hip-hop aspirations.

While some speculated the bickering was a publicity stunt, others feared the war of words might escalate into actual violence.

To the surprise of many, 50 Cent continued with his fight-game ambitions, dropping the TMT moniker and forming SMS Promotions, a name the company shared with 50's popular line of Studio Master Sound headphones and electronic equipment.

"I didn't come to [Floyd] saying, I want to be a boxing promoter. I'm around [boxing], and I love it. I loved it before I ever met Floyd," 50 said.

On December 8, 2012, the *Get Rich or Die Tryin'* rapper officially began his career as a boxing promoter. On the undercard of Manny Pacquiao's fight with his longtime nemesis Juan Manuel Marquez, Yuriorkis Gamboa, 50's fighter, defeated Michael Farenas, which marked the debut of SMS Promotions.

To make matters worse, 50 Cent had joined two of Mayweather's chief rivals, Bob Arum and Manny Pacquiao, for the event, perhaps deepening the tension between him and his one-time friend.

The following morning, few would be writing about the growing 50 Cent–Mayweather rivalry, as the main event became the boxing headline of the year.

In choosing to face Juan Manuel Marquez for a fourth time—as opposed to a rematch with Timothy Bradley, who most believed he defeated earlier in the year—Manny Pacquiao made a grave mistake. In the sixth round of a back-and-forth war, Marquez landed a perfect right hand as Pacquiao charged headfirst into an exchange. The instant the punch landed, Pacquiao was out cold.

After the back-to-back losses, even the most passionate Pacquiao fans were forced to concede that their man was no longer boxing's biggest attraction.

As Mayweather prepared for his Showtime debut, he found himself back in the metaphorical driver's seat. During promotional events leading up to the fight, Mayweather largely deflected the Pacquiao questions. When it came to 50 Cent, however, Mayweather let loose.

Floyd Mayweather Jr: "50 be at my house every day. We go to the gym. We kick it. We cool. I come home on a little vacation [his ninety-day jail term]. When I was on my vacation, I got the newspaper and it said he started TMT Promotions. When I came home, I guess he wanted to become fifty-fifty partners in the boxing business. And my thing was, I was happy and comfortable with what I was already doing. I guess he wanted to be a part of what I was doing. We have a good relationship, we friends, let's just keep it like that. Then one day, I don't know if he got upset, they showed me on the internet, they was like, 'Look what 50 said.'"

Mayweather continued: "I'm a fighter, you shoot at me, I'm gonna shoot back. It took me a lifetime to build the Mayweather brand in boxing, me and Al Haymon working hand in hand. We got PBC [Premier Boxing Champions] and Mayweather Promotions. We got 300 to 400 fighters that we are working with. I never asked him to get a part of G-Unit or whatever he was doing. We just had a genuine friendship, that's what I thought."

A few months later, in an appearance on ESPN's *First Take*, 50 Cent openly accused Mayweather of ducking Manny Pacquiao back in 2010.

"Yes. That's a $100 million and he just left it. . . . At this point, it's about him sorting out who is the perfect opponent as opposed to who is the toughest fight," 50 said.

The year 2012's biggest loser was HBO. Mayweather's nine HBO pay-per-view events generated the network just under ten million buys and $543 million in television revenue. During his time with the network, Mayweather co-starred in four of the richest non-heavyweight pay-per-view events in boxing. With Pacquiao now taking his own much-needed hiatus from the sport, because of his brutal knockout loss to Marquez, Mayweather was, once again, boxing's king.

The real question following Pacquiao's loss was whether 50 Cent and the SMS brand could take on Mayweather Promotions.

50 Cent: "We can bring youth culture back to the sport. Boxing's demographic, I believe, is thirty and up. The UFC, 56 percent of them are fifteen to thirty-four. To reignite that excitement, I believe there is a possibility for us to merge music culture, to bring some of the showmanship they see in WWF, some of the theatrics. We can create cards that have a lot more than the actual main event."

With the possibility looming of Andre Dirrell, 50's fighter, taking on Andre Ward, who was represented by James Prince, some forecasted a hip-hop boxing invasion.

"When that fight is made, there's going to be excitement from areas and people who don't usually tune in to it. Because they're going to feel it's 50 Cent vs. J Prince, not just Ward vs. Dirrell," 50 told *USA Today*.[172]

50 Cent continued: "A lot of people expected me to pull out immediately after Floyd decided not to. Fighters didn't come to TMT [now SMS] Promotions feeling secure about Floyd's business acumen. They respect Floyd as an actual fighter and where he's at in his career, but they're excited about my knowledge and brand extension opportunities, because they're aware that George Foreman made more money selling a grill than boxing."

As 50 Cent, now licensed to promote in New Jersey and Nevada, continued to sign notable fighters, such as middleweight James Kirkland, some speculated that the rap mogul might be the right man for the job, when it came to skewing the sport young again.

For Showtime and Floyd Mayweather Jr., easy money awaited.

14

HATE IT OR LOVE IT

On May 4, 2013, in his first bout since being released from jail, Floyd Mayweather Jr. outclassed underdog Robert Guerrero (31-1-1, 18 KOs), who had not lost in over eight years. By timing Guerrero's aggressive style, Mayweather cruised to a unanimous decision victory. The cautious approach Mayweather used in the ring was, one might argue, the opposite of how the boxer lived outside the ring.

Before the Guerrero bout, Showtime, which pulled out all the stops for their new franchise fighter, debuted *All Access*, a reality-television-style documentary series narrated by rapper Common, one that served as a spin-off of HBO's *24/7*. At this stage in Floyd's career, the outside-the-ring drama, more so than the action in the ring, had become a major component of his appeal.

"What I do is not reality TV, because a reality show is watered down. What I am going to give you is raw and uncut," Mayweather said in the first episode.[173]

In ponying up to land "Money" Mayweather, Showtime had indeed bought a ticket to the circus. Some speculated that signing the thirty-six-year-old fighter might, in the end, result in a bad case of buyer's remorse. In his second fight with the network, however, Mayweather silenced the nonbelievers and proved himself to be a worthwhile investment.

Outside of the Mayweather–Pacquiao dichotomy, one name clearly stood alone as the sport's most lucrative champion. Groomed by Oscar De La Hoya and Golden Boy Promotions, WBC and WBA junior middleweight titleholder Saul "Canelo" Alvarez (42-0-1, 30 KOs), over the course of his eight-year pro career, steadily carved out a place as the sport's fastest-rising superstar. Because of the Mexican star's size and punching power, many believed Alvarez was Mayweather's most significant challenge in years. ESPN analyst Teddy Atlas, for example, was not alone in picking the twenty-three-year-old Alvarez to win the fight.

Mayweather–Alvarez, which took place on September 14, 2013, in the end proved to be big money but with minimal risk. In front of a sold-out MGM Grand Garden Arena, Floyd Mayweather Jr. rolled to an easy points victory over his younger opponent. Despite judge C. J. Ross's questionable 114-114 scorecard, everything had gone according to plan. Using his superior timing, defense, and ring generalship, Mayweather controlled the distance and won decisively.

Never a model of humility, Mayweather used his late career resurgence to disparage old adversaries. In interviews, Mayweather labeled Manny Pacquiao a "desperate dog" chasing a payday to fix his tax problems, a "broke fighter" whose pay-per-view numbers were a joke. For his May 3, 2014, bout with WBA welterweight champion Marcos Maidana, Mayweather also sent a clear message to 50 Cent by inviting Rick Ross to the prefight weigh-in, broadcast live on ESPN.

By June 2014, age appeared to be catching up with both Mayweather and 50 Cent. In his bout with Maidana, Mayweather, to the surprise of many, didn't dominate. Maidana's awkward angles and high work rate gave Mayweather problems throughout the fight, which resulted in his second straight majority decision win. The thirty-seven-year-old Mayweather, some speculated, was finally declining.

A few weeks later, 50 Cent and SMS Promotions suffered a worse setback. Because of a knockout loss to rising star Terence Crawford, Yuriorkis Gamboa, SMS's top fighter, was no longer undefeated or a champ.

The same month as Gamboa's loss, 50 Cent released his fifth studio album, *Animal Ambition*, to little acclaim and low sales. In his first project since being released from his deal with the Shady/Aftermath conglomerate, 50 no longer played up the bogeyman motif, the last gang-sta rapper standing. By this point, 50 Cent was seen in the culture as more mogul than murderer. The message of *Animal Ambition*, therefore, was simple: "I have more money than you do." Lost in a rapidly changing hip-hop demographic, *Animal Ambition* felt painfully out of step.

After his fight against Maidana, some predicted Mayweather's downfall as well. Because of his slim victory, many speculated that Mayweather's focus was now on *ballin'* rather than boxing. During press opportunities, many of the questions aimed at Mayweather's had more to do with love triangles, TMZ rumors, and hip-hop beefs than his upcoming rematch. At the time, 50 Cent wasn't the only rapper taking shots at Floyd on social media. Rappers Nelly and T.I. also got involved and disrespected the boxer on Twitter. In an appearance on ESPN's *Highly Questionable* on June 24, 2014, St. Louis rapper Nelly, who was dating Mayweather's former fiancée Shantel Jackson, addressed the situation.

Nelly: "I don't have a beef with Floyd Mayweather. For me, for the most part, I think the whole thing is misunderstood. I try to understand where he is coming from, which is hard to do. He's one of those people who doesn't like the word 'no' said to him. If anybody does that, that's what gets underneath his skin a little bit. It's kind of hard talking to a guy who hasn't graduated from high school."

Following Nelly's appearance on ESPN, 50 Cent took to Twitter, teas-ing his former friend. "DAMN da nigga really took your lady Champ," 50 tweeted, also warning Mayweather to stay away from Tameka "Tiny" Cottle, the wife of Atlanta rap star T.I., who some speculated was having an affair with the boxer, thanks to TMZ reports.

In an interview with hip-hop magazine *XXL*, published on August 21, 2014, Mayweather addressed his feuds with 50 Cent, Nelly, and T.I., taking the opportunity to mock the falling record sales of all three artists.

Floyd Mayweather Jr: "I don't really focus on nothing like that. I'm relevant. My life is the shit. I'm something to talk about. What's so crazy is this: You know, when people are not relevant, and they're not moving units like they were once moving . . . you've got to realize, I've been rele-vant for eighteen years. God has blessed me with unbelievable talent, with fast feet, fast hands, unbelievable defense and a very, very sharp mind. So I'm thankful of that. Of course, hip-hop artists, they come and go. They come and go. But I'm still here."[174]

50 Cent responded on social media the next morning.

"I woke up. Looked at the computer. The computer say Floyd say 'Fuck T.I. Fuck Nelly. Fuck 50.' I'm like what he say fuck me for. Nelly fucked your first baby mama Melissa. Then took your fucking fiancée [Jackson]. Say fuck that nigga," 50 said in the short Instagram video.[175]

Hours after his initial comments, 50 Cent continued his assault on Twitter.

"Floyd will you except [sic] my ALS/ESL Challenge: I will donate $750,000 to a charity of your choice, if you can read a full page out of a Harry Potter book out loud without starting and stopping or fucking up. Lmao," 50 posted, tagging Mayweather's account.

Following the tweet, 50 Cent posted a video on Instagram in which he challenged Mayweather to appear on Jimmy Kimmel's television show to prove, once and for all, that he can read one page of a children's book.

"We don't wanna put pressure on you. We know you can't pronounce those words in the Harry Potter book, so we are gonna let you read *Cat in the Hat*," 50 laughed.

The next morning, the beef took another ugly turn when hip-hop radio host Charlamagne tha God, of *The Breakfast Club,* played a video clip of Mayweather struggling to read a series of ten-second radio "drops."

"He was the greatest defensive fighter of all time. But I got a show to do. I gotta sell tickets too, baby. Just like he likes to put on a show. I like to put on a show too," Charlamagne said, defending his actions.[176]

In September 2014, Mayweather combatted the invective, taking his rivalry with 50 Cent up a level by questioning the rapper's relationship with his estranged son, Marquise Jackson, posting a photo of himself and Marquise.

"Last time I checked, I think [50 Cent] was a boxing promoter. Hopefully, I want to see him sell records. I think he had an album? I don't know when the last time 50 Cent had an album. But best of luck to him for everything," Floyd Mayweather responded.

Ten days before the Marcos Maidana rematch, only the second rematch of his career, Mayweather made what appeared to be his final social media statement regarding his reading ability, posting an image of two checks that totaled over $72 million. The caption below the image: "Read This."

Just like in his second fight with Jose Luis Castillo back in 2002, drama outside the ring didn't affect Mayweather's tactical approach. He won his rematch with Maidana with relative ease, boxing cautiously and keeping the action at center ring. Better prepared for the Argentinian fighter's aggressive style the second time around, Mayweather's defense was flawless. According to CompuBox, Maidana connected on only 22 percent of his 572 punches thrown. Throughout the night, Mayweather picked apart his opponent from the outside and coasted to a unanimous decision victory, one that would, to the surprise of many, finally set up the overdue fight everyone wanted to see.

✳ ✳ ✳

For some, Mayweather–Pacquiao could be considered a huge disappointment, one that represents all that's wrong with boxing. Money, politics, and egos had gotten in the way of what, in 2010, looked like a historic matchup. By 2015, Pacquiao was campaigning as a senator in his native Philippines, moonlighting as both a politician and a pugilist. After an eleven-month absence from boxing, Pacquiao and Freddie Roach had slowly reestablished their place in the sport. In beating fighters such as Brandon Ríos, Timothy Bradley (in a rematch), and Chris Algieri, each by unanimous decision, Pacquiao rekindled interest in the Mayweather fight. To his millions of fans, the Filipino champion was the only man who posed a true threat to the controversial boxer who now branded himself as "TBE" (The Best Ever).

When Mayweather–Pacquiao was announced on February 20, 2015, the sports world fell victim to irrational exuberance. The promotion was called "The Fight of the Century." ESPN, broadcast many of its daily programs live from Las Vegas during the week, despite having no direct network ties to either fighter.

Even 50 Cent appeared to be overcome with anticipation. On the day of the fight, May 2, 2015, 50 posted a photo of himself and Mayweather on Twitter, with a caption that read, "THE original Money Team, you gotta love it. My brother ready."

Despite being six years too late, Floyd Mayweather vs. Manny Pacquiao resulted in a financial colossus for all involved. The event surpassed all previous pay-per-view and live gate numbers, earning Mayweather a reported $230 million payday. The fight, however, was a disappointment.

Early on, Mayweather dictated the pace and controlled the distance with his jab and lead right hand. Despite a brief rally in the fourth round, when Pacquiao finally broke through Mayweather's guard, the fight inevitably turned into a copy of so many cautious Mayweather performances. Flummoxed by Mayweather's defensive skill, Pacquiao spent much of the second half of the fight chasing, swinging, and missing. Those who daydreamed of Pacquiao running roughshod over Mayweather, humbling the cocky champion once and for all, were treated to a less spirited attack. Pacquiao, according to CompuBox had landed only 19 percent of his punches.

As Mayweather was awarded a unanimous decision by scores of 118-110, 116-112, and 116-112, boxing shifted to a new era. In beating Pacquiao, Mayweather earned the largest payday in boxing history but not the adulation of the millions of fans who considered the fight painfully anticlimactic. No one, outside of Pacquiao's team, wanted a rematch.

50 Cent, like most boxing experts, criticized the action. The rapper's reconciliation with Floyd would be short-lived.

"It's obviously huge business. [They made] $200 million in thirty-six minutes. I don't think the response he got from the fight was positive. I don't think people were jumping up and down and demanding a rematch," 50 Cent told ESPN.

The widespread criticism of the bout did little to bother Mayweather, who had, in many respects, outlasted his rivals. Just twenty-four days after Mayweather–Pacquiao, 50 Cent's SMS Promotions filed for Chapter 11 bankruptcy.[177] Later, Pacquiao compounded the disappointment surrounding his performance by revealing that he had gone into the bout with a torn rotator cuff, a claim that some viewed as an excuse.

Just as it appeared Mayweather had run out of rivals to disparage, he quickly found himself back in the headlines, this time as a result of a brawl that occurred at a Fat Burger restaurant on the Las Vegas Strip. According to TMZ, Mayweather was confronted by rapper T.I. for the second time in a matter of weeks.

In an interview published by *Bleacher Report*, Floyd addressed the altercation, detailing the backstory of his budding feud with the Atlanta rapper.

Floyd Mayweather Jr: "[T.I.] came to me when I was in New York. He stepped to me when I was at the jewelry store like, 'Yo, let's go outside and talk.' We went outside to talk, but he talked about, basically, 'These girls tryna play us against each other.' I said, 'I don't know what you're talking about. You're talking about your wife?' I never put up a picture of her on Instagram, Twitter, or Facebook. I was basically like, 'Listen. I'm letting you know I ain't got . . . me and your wife don't have nothing . . . if you think so."

In the same interview, Mayweather also spoke about the Las Vegas altercation.

Floyd Mayweather Jr: "So Memorial Day Weekend, a lot of people come out to Las Vegas. Tiny and Shekinah was out here. They come to my party last night. They cool. Everything is cool. We was at the strip club. Everything was cordial. We having fun. I throw my daughter [Iyanna] a big birthday bash today. I'm eating at Fat Burger and, next thing you know, he walk in talking about we need to talk again. And then I told him, 'You need to get the fuck outta my face. That's what you better do.' And then he said, 'I ain't talking to all these people so you ain't gotta talk loud.' I said, 'Listen, don't come to my face with no disrespectful shit. Like I told you before, you must've forgot what I did for a living.' He said, 'You do it in the ring, I do it in the streets.' I said, 'My man, I do it everywhere. You can find out if you want to.'"

Mayweather continued: "Then a couple of words exchange and people got to pushing and a riot kinda broke out. And then a bunch of chaos and that was basically it. Because, like I said before, he probably does some foolish things, but he ain't no damn fool to swing on me. Like, you must've forgot what I do for a living. He had a totally different look on his face."[178]

In the coming years, Mayweather's rap rivals, 50 Cent, T.I., and Nelly, consistently proved more difficult than his opponents in the ring. That said, on September 12, 2015, Mayweather defended his welterweight championship for the final time and easily outpointed former champion and massive underdog Andre Berto (30-3, 23 KOs).

"My career is over. It's official. You gotta know when to hang it up. It's about time for me to hang it up. I'm knocking at the door now, I'm almost forty. I've been in the sport nineteen years, been a champion eighteen years, I've broke all the records. There is nothing else to prove in the sport of boxing," Mayweather told Showtime's Jim Gray after the fight.

Two years later, Mayweather returned to boxing for a circus-like-bout with UFC star Connor McGregor, who had never boxed as an amateur or professional. The bout itself was as strange as the promotion. To the surprise of most, Mayweather abandoned his typical cautious style.

Flat-footed and plodding forward with his guard high, the forty-year-old boxer walked down McGregor who, in the UFC, was also known as a counterpuncher. After five rounds of relatively spirited action, Mayweather began to attack with more frequency. As the fight progressed, McGregor ran out of gas. In the tenth round, Mayweather swarmed his overmatched opponent and referee Robert Byrd stopped the fight.

The circus got Mayweather another $200 million payday and was the second-largest pay-per-view event in combat sports history.

✳ ✳ ✳

After the McGregor bout, Mayweather's rap feuds flared up.

In July 2018, Mayweather hosted an event with reality-television star and R&B singer Teairra Mari at his Las Vegas strip club Girl Collection. Before Mari's performance at the club, she had sued 50 Cent for allegedly posting "revenge porn" on his Instagram. 50 Cent, who by several accounts had been instrumental in setting up negotiations between UFC president Dana White and Mayweather, was furious at the news of his former friend socializing with his accuser.

"Somebody please tell me why Floyd would be doing this right now? I don't understand this one," 50 tweeted before posting screenshots of a text string between him and Mayweather.

In a nasty exchange, 50 Cent accused the boxer of disloyalty and reminded his followers of similar accusations made against the boxer by his former fiancée, Shantel Jackson.

Mayweather responded to 50 Cent by posting an open letter to his hip-hop rival, titled "Curtis 'Confidential Informant' Jackson."

The letter read as follows: "You're mad because your oldest son Marquees mother doesn't want to be with you! Your Son, your own flesh and blood don't want nothing to do with you! You haven't had a hit song on radio in who knows when and you're definitely not hot enough to even sell records anymore so Interscope dropped you. You are jealous of any rapper, athlete or entertainer that's hot or got something going on for themselves. You are a certified snitch and we got the paperwork to prove it."[179]

Never to be outdone, 50 posted a mock rough draft of the same letter, with almost every word misspelled, joking that it was written by Mayweather.

A few weeks later, the reignited feud worsened. On July 23, 2018, 50 Cent accused Mayweather of sleeping with late rapper Earl Hayes's wife, Stephanie Moseley, leading Hayes to kill himself and Moseley. In 2014, Hayes had reportedly FaceTimed the boxer before committing the murder-suicide. While rumors had previously suggested R&B star Trey Songz was the man with whom his wife had committed the infidelity with Moseley, 50 Cent claimed it was Mayweather.

"Tell everybody why you was on FaceTime when he killed Stephanie and himself. Because he was confronting you about fucking his wife," 50 wrote on Instagram, before accusing Mayweather of also sleeping with rapper P-Reala's ex-girlfriend.

When Mayweather ignored the allegations, 50 Cent needled him further. The next day, 50 posted a police report written by Floyd's son Koraun, which read: "I came out [of my room] and dad was hiting my mom. It happed at 4:00 a.m. in the morning."

As Mayweather stayed silent, 50 Cent pushed more, stirring rumors that suggested Mayweather's money was running low.

On February 14, 2019, T.I. joined in, releasing a song titled "Fuck Nigga." The cover art for the song featured a picture of Mayweather wearing a controversial blackface Gucci sweater. Provoked by Mayweather's dismissive comments amid a growing call for Black celebrities to boycott Gucci for the allegedly racist imprint, T.I.'s song accuses the boxer of being tone-deaf to the struggles of the Black community, especially in his home state of Michigan.

"I ain't made as much as you have, purses you grab / Could feed some countries out in Africa, you just go buy a Lam / Or Bugatti, or something else that depreciate when you drive it off the lot," T.I. raps in the opening bars.

"Give you the chance, you showing your ass / I don't give a fuck how much money you have / What did you do with it? How did you use it? / To make an impact and influence the world for the better? / You rather go buy some jewelry, whatever / But never should you ever think / That it's gon' last forever as soon as you blink / It'll be gone as quick as it came," T.I. continued.

Hours after the song dropped, Mayweather responded on Instagram.

Floyd Mayweather Jr: "Why wouldn't we agree to a permanent boycott of Gucci as well as all other merchandise that fall under the Kering ownership such as YSL, Balenciaga, Alexander McQueen and more? I'll tell you why . . . it's because in this day, celebrities and failing artists pick and choose the hottest trending topic as a means of seeking attention and using fake advocacy as their platform when their 'talent' no longer benefit[s] them."[180]

In July 2019, the taunting continued as 50 Cent posted an embarrassing clip of Mayweather during a recent celebrity basketball game.

"What the fuck champ, are you alright?" 50 tweeted.

Mayweather responded by poking fun at 50 Cent's recent foray into the liquor business, Effen Vodka.

Floyd Mayweather Jr: "Jay-Z been killing the champagne game with Ace of Spade selling worldwide at premium prices for well over a decade. While Curtis got a bottle with a cheap chess piece on it that taste like shampoo . . . Diddy got Ciroc and its still selling worldwide and you can't find Effen in no stores and it's well known the shit taste like rubbing alcohol."

50 Cent replied to Mayweather's comments by calling a mock truce to their social media beef.

"Tell Floyd I said he won he is the greatest of all time and nobody I mean nobody can ever take that away from him what he's done with his life is amazing. I'm done will all of the back and forth. Now Can Someone Please Read This To Champ," 50 tweeted.

Looking back, the venomous beef between Floyd and 50 Cent can only be viewed as a low point in boxing and hip-hop's sometimes-turbulent marriage, a massive crossover opportunity wasted. This, of course, has nothing to do with money. Both men amassed fortunes during their careers.

The tragedy is that both Mayweather and 50 Cent were as brilliant as they were vulgar, as calculated as they were impulsive. Both were natural winners, unapologetic bad guys. Neither man asked for love, only respect. Had they merged, using their talents to maximize hip-hop's foothold in boxing, the duo might have been able to pull off what others couldn't.

Instead, we were left with the story of two self-made villains, each reaping the benefits and drawbacks of such a performance.

"Villains provide an interesting window into learning about parts of the self that we normally don't explore," scholar Rebecca Krause writes, a theory that perhaps speaks to the impulse that attracted people to the lives and careers of both men.[181]

Part of 50 Cent's legacy is that of a bully. When the bully stumbles, we, like his enemies, enjoy the *schadenfreude*.

Floyd Mayweather Jr., midway through his career, branded himself similarly and suffered a similar fate. When Mayweather was trolled by rap stars, either on social media or in hit songs, we paid attention because we wanted to see the bully humbled.

In this respect and in the end, the story of Floyd and 50 gave us precisely what we wanted, consciously or unconsciously.

They're the bad guys, after all, and we couldn't wait to see them fail.

WATCH THE THRONE

Before he won the first season of the Netflix music competition *Rhythm + Flow* or released his acclaimed debut album, *Black Habits*, rapper D Smoke, born Daniel Anthony Farris, dreamed of becoming a world champion boxer. This ambition was born in the streets of his hometown of Inglewood, California, a place known more for producing rap stars than pugilists. West Coast notables Mack 10, Skeme, AMG, Shade Sheist, and Big Syke (from Tupac's Thug Life collective), for example, all come from the city,

The Inglewood of D Smoke's childhood was also known for its staggering amount of gang activity. By the early 1980s, the Avenue Piru Gang, the Crenshaw Mafia Gang, the Queen Street Bloods, and the Inglewood Family Gang Bloods all laid territorial claim to the city. Growing up in such an environment, physical confrontations happened daily. Learning how to *throw hands*, the California-based rapper told me, was a prerequisite for survival. Compton, Long Beach, and East LA had more-notable boxing communities, but Inglewood also possessed some of the same energy.

"Boxing, for me, started with two thirty-dollar pair of Everlast Big 5 Sporting Goods boxing gloves. The ones in the red pack," Smoke reflected.

During childhood summers, when D Smoke and his friends were playing in the streets, his uncle, the family's instigator, often showed up with Everlast gloves draped over his broad shoulders.

"Who locking up?" he'd call to the children.

D Smoke: "My uncle would make me fight my best friends at like six years old, my older brothers too. That's what gets people in the gloves in the hood. It's always someone's uncle. Around here, if you gonna be *scary*, then you better be super paid, or super funny, or something. When I was little, my older brothers and my uncles would get us to fight each other, then it became us boxing everybody in our neighborhood. I'ma keep it a hundred percent. I really didn't have an option when I was young. If you didn't volunteer, they started calling people out. You had two choices, you better be really funny and come with some jokes; otherwise your reputation was destroyed."

D Smoke's dreams of winning a world title never materialized. His path in life was guided by the Farris family trade. He was, in every way, the product of a musical family, raised in a strong ministry background. His mother was a well-known gospel singer who, at one point in her career, performed background vocals for Michael Jackson and Anita Baker. His cousin, Tiffany Couche, a singer and songwriter, has worked with the likes of Ty Dolla $ign, Solange, Anderson Paak, Jill Scott, Lauryn Hill, and Missy Elliott. Smoke's older brothers, Darryl and Davion, are also professional musicians. Darryl, who records under the stage name SiR, is currently signed to Kendrick Lamar's Top Dawg Entertainment. Aside from his skill as a rapper, D Smoke also played the piano, drums, and lead guitar, musical talents that served him well on Netflix's *Rhythm + Flow*.

D Smoke's world has always revolved around music. The family garage, at one point during the rapper's adolescence, was converted into a recording studio. WoodWorks Records, the rapper's current label, is also family owned. In hindsight, music was D Smoke's destiny. The sport of boxing, however, was his muse.

D Smoke: "When I was a kid, Roy Jones Jr. was my hero. I loved "Y'all Must've Forgot." I loved Roy's style in the ring when he would come to the ring rapping. I loved the way he carried himself. Last year, I saw [Antonio] Tarver in Vegas, told him that myself. I said, 'You broke a young kid heart, man." I even put a line about that fight [Jones Jr. vs. Tarver II] in my song 'Bullies.'"

After graduating from Inglewood High School, Smoke enrolled at UCLA, where he double-majored in Spanish and music theory. After college he got a job at his high school alma mater, teaching Spanish and music, and often used hip-hop as a teaching tool in the classroom.

During his brief time as an educator, D Smoke continued to work on his music. On occasion, Smoke would play new tracks for students, gauging their reactions. To his family's dismay, D Smoke also continued to flirt with boxing, the dangerous trade he had long wanted to pursue.

D Smoke: "When I started boxing, my family was very against it. I was twenty-four. I was an educator. I had a degree. I was good at music. But it was my decision. When I was a kid, we had one boxing gym in Inglewood, at Rogers Park. It was in the cut. There were a couple of other gyms nearby. But, in college, I got serious about wanting to do it. I went over to Broadway Boxing, in another hood. It's a historic gym on 100 and 8th. That's where I got consistent sparring, at a high level. Anywhere you have gang banging, where you have that threat of being confronted, you are gonna have that pressure to learn self-defense. That energy brought me to Broadway Boxing."

At Broadway Boxing, D Smoke became a licensed USA amateur boxer, competing in the junior middleweight division. A speedy southpaw, with quick hands and a defensive, counterpunching style, Smoke won all three of his amateur bouts, each by unanimous decision. While the full-time teacher, part-time boxer was victorious in the ring, it was sparring high-level talent that eventually made him see that he'd come to the sport too late.

D Smoke: "At first, I was serious about it. I actually wanted to go pro. I used to spar Chris van Heerden, who fought [Errol] Spence. We had some *real* sparring. He caught me with some heavy shots. I was like whoa. Okay. These are *professional punches*. Chris had *professional hands*. My family didn't want me to box. I messed up a knuckle. Hurt my ribs once. They continued to discourage it. Like I said, I had a degree. I was an educator. I was doing my music. I finally realized you don't *play* boxing. It's all or nothing."

After only three amateur fights, D Smoke decided to focus his outside-the-classroom efforts on music. The breakthrough opportunity he had long dreamed of came from Netflix's *Rhythm + Flow*, which was hosted by T.I., Cardi B, and Chance the Rapper. The music competition show, hip-hop's answer to *American Idol*, borrowed heavily from the reality-television formula. Auditions took place in Chicago, New York, Atlanta, and Los Angeles, where the celebrity panelists worked with guest judges, such as Snoop Dogg, Fat Joe, and Killer Mike, to find hip-hop's next big star.

During the competition, the personal stories of cast members were highlighted before performances. One of D Smoke's featurettes had footage of the rapper hitting the hand pads, jumping rope, and showing off his boxing skills. Hector Diaz and Henry Walker of Broadway Boxing were both interviewed for the segment.

On October 23, 2019, D Smoke emerged as *Rhythm + Flow*'s inaugural champion, winning $250,000 in prize money and making a variety of top-shelf music-industry connections. A month after winning the Netflix competition, Smoke attended Deontay Wilder's title defense against Luis Ortiz at the MGM Grand in Las Vegas, a rematch to Wilder and Ortiz's thrilling 2018 bout. The event marked D Smoke's first time attending a heavyweight championship. To his surprise, he discovered that Wilder was a fan of both his music and backstory.

D Smoke: "Our friendship began with the Wilder–Ortiz rematch. That's when we first met. Deontay and his wife approached me and said they were fans of mine; they loved the show [*Rhythm + Flow*]. After the fight, we met and chopped it up. It was me, him, and DJ Bay Bay from Dallas. They let us on *that* side of the rope. And that's when I put a bug in his ear. I said, 'Let me know if you need someone to walk you out for your next fight.' I really didn't think much of it after I said it."

A few weeks after the Ortiz fight, Wilder took D Smoke up on the offer. He and his team had already begun planning the entrance for their upcoming fight against Tyson Fury, a match that had been contractually agreed upon before Wilder–Ortiz II.

D Smoke: "Wilder's team contacted me through Marcus Watson, DJ Quest, who deejays at all the big fights. He deejayed at the Shawn Porter vs. Errol Spence fight. So it was the Watson brothers and DJ Quest. They told me, 'Wilder wants a poem to start it off.' And they told me Wilder selected my song 'Black Habits' for the ring walk. The rematch [with Tyson Fury] was gonna be at the end of February. And the ring walk was going to be a Black History Month tribute. So I sent him a draft of the poem and we went from there."

On Saturday, February 22, 2020, just six years after D Smoke gave up his boxing dream to focus on music full time, the former high school teacher found himself standing center ring at the MGM Grand Garden Arena for one of the biggest heavyweight championship fights in recent years, the last big fight to take place before the COVID-19 pandemic.

D Smoke: "When we look back, considering all that's changed in the world since that night, I think we will continue to kind of realize what that particular moment meant in history, regardless of the outcome of the fight. I can actually say that I was a part of boxing history, sports history really. That [ring walk] might go down as one of the most controversial and talked about entrances in heavyweight history. It was the last big fight before the world was turned upside down by the pandemic."

✳ ✳ ✳

Statement-making ring walks were nothing new for Deontay Wilder. Long before his rematch with Fury, people expected elaborate, over-the-top entrances from him. In the past, Wilder had recruited rappers like Lil' Kim, 50 Cent, and Jay Rock to perform his entry music. He'd also recruited hip-hop deejays, dancers, and even contortionists. Wilder's gaudy apparel was also part of the act, a routine that began after a visit to a New Orleans costume shop in 2013. Browsing the store, killing time before a celebrity basketball tournament, Wilder came across a golden Venetian mask. For fun, Wilder placed the mask on his face.

"With the mask, it was like the revealing of me. Deontay Wilder is no longer here. What you are witnessing is the *Bronze Bomber*," Wilder told Showtime's *All Access*.[182]

Wilder wore the Venetian mask for his first championship fight against WBC champion Bermane Stiverne, and the gimmick continued through each fight of his seven-year title reign. At the time, wearing a mask, or even a costume, into the ring was nothing new in boxing. What set Wilder apart, however, was the amount of money that he pumped into his masks. With each new knockout victory, his masks and ring-walk costumes became more elaborate. In his rematch with Luis Ortiz, for example, Wilder wore a diamond-encrusted mask and custom armor made of gold crystal and Italian leather. His outfit had "90,000 gems and stones affixed to it," the *Los Angeles Times* reported.[183]

During Wilder–Fury II fight week, which conjured the WWE hype, rumors of absurdly extravagant ring walks spread. D Smoke, however, remained tight-lipped.

D Smoke: "We didn't let anybody know it was going down. Wilder wanted to maintain that element of surprise for the fans. So, we didn't promote it on social media or talk about our involvement leading up to the fight."

Fury, who held the division's lineal title, entered the MGM Grand Garden Arena first. Dressed like a king and brought to the ring on a throne, Fury milked the moment and blew kisses to his subjects while Patsy Cline's 1961 country hit "Crazy" played.

Moments later the MGM Grand house lights went down. The camera operator, positioned directly behind D Smoke, slowly circled the rapper, dressed in all black, as he delivered the poem:

> *Born in Tuscaloosa*
> *Pledged his days to lay the pavement for brighter futures*
> *Set ablaze like lighter fluid*
> *He fights the ruthless*
> *They tried to beat 'em and can't defeat 'em*
> *Their fight is useless*
> *Because on the canvas landed every man that stood in his way*
> *And, he is still devastating opponents, till this day!*

The last line of D Smoke's poem refers to a 2018 interview before the first fight, where Wilder lashed out at boxing reporter Radio Rahim for what he saw as a race-baiting question. Earlier in the week, Fury had said his *people*, referring to his Irish Gypsy traveler heritage, were *fighters*. As Fury taunted Wilder further, suggesting that he had only come to boxing because he wasn't good at football or basketball, Wilder countered Fury's trash talk by suggesting his *people*, African Americans, had been fighting for over four hundred years, and were still fighting—"Till this day."

Shortly after the press conference, Wilder's "Till this day" comments went viral. In the coming months, particularly on Showtime's *All Access* series, Wilder became increasingly vocal on issues of race relations in the United States, and in particular on police brutality and racial profiling.

His vision for a Black History Month tribute had begun with those three words.

As D Smoke finished his poem, the music to his debut single "Black Habits" slowly began to build. The video screens lined the walls, which guided Wilder's path from the locker room to the ring, came to life with a montage of Black cultural icons. Images of Harriet Tubman, Martin Luther King Jr., and Malcolm X were interwoven with shots of iconic sports stars such as Jackie Robinson and Muhammad Ali. Images of the late Tupac Shakur, who lost his life after attending a fight at the MGM Grand some twenty-four years earlier, were also featured.

"You'll notice that Deontay is honoring Black History Month with some of the iconic figures he holds so dearly," ESPN's Joe Tessitore said during the broadcast.[184]

D Smoke's "Black Habits," the title track to his debut LP, which was released just two weeks before the fight and inspired by the Black Lives Matter movement, was a fitting selection. The song celebrates what it means to be Black in modern America. Like Wilder's montage, it is a tribute to D Smoke's cultural heroes.

"Rapidly, happily, I look back on Afeni Shakur / Her son paved the way, now all eyes on me / Cause I'm young, black and gifted, Nina, all eyes gon' see," Smoke raps in the opening verses, channeling the inspiration of powerful Black women such as Afeni Shakur and Nina Simone.

Looking back, you could argue that Wilder set the stage for the Black Lives Matters protests that showed up in the post-lockdown demonstrations of athletes in the NBA, NFL, MLB, NHL, and NCAA—powerful moments in sports history that were a response to the deaths of George Floyd, Freddie Gray, Ahmaud Arbery, and Breonna Taylor. D Smoke saw the prefight performance as a potential moment of healing.

D Smoke: "When I wrote the song, I didn't know what 2020 had in store for us, with all the marches and riots and political movements. Police brutality ain't nothing new in Inglewood. That song was just where I was at, that song was true to my life experience, reaching back into my upbringing. It's special that art can do that. I'd recorded half of the album before the [Netflix] show was finished but Deontay obviously felt it was the right song for the moment, an opportunity to bring people together under something positive," Smoke said.

Poetic symbolism aside, Wilder received a harsh welcome from the thousands of British fans who had traveled to Las Vegas to support Fury.

D Smoke: "Waiting around all day, at the MGM, it felt like waiting around on a fight. It felt like we were playing an away game, right at home. Walking through the MGM, I felt that energy all through the hallways. Somehow all those people came over from the other side of the pond. It reminded me of that Mayweather vs. Hatton crowd; it was that level of energy. So many British fans, talking trash all through the hotel. It was like, 'the dosser is going down,' all that. As we set up for the performance, and I'm about to walk him out, the booing started, little kids cussing you out and all that."

In response to the boos, D Smoke, mid-performance, lifted his fist into the air, mimicking the Black Power gesture made by track-and-field stars John Carlos and Tommie Smith in 1968.

D Smoke: "I hadn't planned on putting the fist in the air and all that stuff, I was just going to perform. The fans were yelling 'fuck you' and all that so I wanted to match that energy. So I put the fist up."

Any attempt by Wilder to make a political statement was overshadowed by his elaborate costume. As D Smoke finished the first verse of his song, Wilder, emerged from the shadows. His oversized skull mask featured a large, florally bejeweled crown and illuminated eyewear. The shimmering skulls resting on both of Wilder's shoulders matched his mask. Of all of the champion's prefight costumes, the onyx ensemble was, without question, the most shockingly gaudy.

D Smoke, who led Wilder into battle, was equally surprised by the outfit.

D Smoke: "I hadn't seen the mask. I'd just seen the body armor. I didn't see the mask until he walked past me to go into the ring. I saw it out of the corner of my eye, at one point. If you watch my performance, you'll notice that I checked my spacing a few times, to see if I was too far ahead of him. There was no dress rehearsal or any of that. I saw the costume just like you did. Out of the corner of my eye I saw it and thought, 'Oh shit, he looks like the Shredder [from the Teenage Mutant Ninja Turtles]."

The shimmering all-black costume, designed by the Los Angeles duo Cosmos GlamSquad, instantly became a trending topic on Twitter. This, however, would be his only victory of the night. Fury, to the surprise of many, kept his word and walked down Wilder. Fury dominated almost every second of the rematch and scored knockdowns in the third and fifth rounds.

"Wilder's legs look gone; they look shot," former super middleweight and light heavyweight champion Andre Ward said after the first knockdown, which came from a Fury right-hand shot that landed on Wilder's left ear.

Early in the seventh round, Fury cornered his battered opponent and landed several combinations. As Wilder covered up and threw nothing back, his trainer, former U.S. gold medalist Mark Breland, threw in the towel.

Moments after the fight, the controversy shifted to an argument between Wilder's trainers, Breland and Jay Deas, who disagreed with the stoppage.

When Wilder was interviewed by ESPN's Bernardo Osuna, the former champion added to the confusion.

"I had a lot of things going on coming into this fight. But it is what it is. My legs were already weak coming into this fight. We can't make excuses tonight, [but I] had a lot of complications," Wilder said.

A few days later, Wilder shed light on his post-fight comments in an interview with Yahoo! Sports, making an excuse that would draw criticism.

Deontay Wilder: "[Fury] didn't hurt me at all, but the simple fact is my uniform was way too heavy for me. I didn't have no legs from the beginning of the fight. In the third round, my legs were just shot all the way through. But I'm a warrior and people know that I'm a warrior. A lot of people were telling me, 'It looked like something was wrong with you.' Something was, but when you're in the ring you have to bluff a lot of things. I tried my best to do so. I knew I didn't have the legs because of my uniform. I was only able to put it on [for the first time] the night before, but I didn't think it was going to be that heavy. It weighed forty, forty-some pounds with the helmet and all the batteries. I wanted my tribute to be great for Black History Month. I wanted it to be good and I guess I put that before anything."[185]

Criticism of Wilder's costume excuse was widespread.

"It wasn't the weight of the costume, it was the weight of the [self] doubt," boxing analyst Teddy Atlas argued.[186] Popular sports commentator and radio host Stephen A. Smith also castigated Wilder the next day on ESPN.

"[Wilder] needs to get with a publicist to make sure he never makes a statement like the one he made blaming his outfit . . . it was one of the most embarrassing excuses for a loss in the history of boxing," Smith argued.[187]

Debates about Wilder's costume, and lackluster performance, were also waged on social media, particularly in hip-hop circles.

"Damn, Blood, what about the gang. smh [shaking my head]," 50 Cent posted to Twitter, underneath an image of a Tyson Fury right hand that split Wilder's lip.[188]

"Nah you not gon beat me up & lick my blood off me, no Sir," rapper Joe Budden tweeted, referencing what appeared to be Fury's attempt to lick blood off Wilder's shoulder at the end in the sixth round.[189]

D Smoke found himself caught up in the post-fight controversy and was inadvertently forced to defend himself.

D Smoke: "I didn't understand the criticism. Ring walking is nothing new. I remember back when Lil Wayne started walking out Mayweather. Back then, it had everybody thinking like ring walking was the thing to do. Hip-hop is a big part of boxing. I like all types of music, I come from a musical background, but Celine Dion isn't going to get a boxer in a winner's mindset, that warrior spirit. I don't think I was a distraction. I was just trying to get Wilder into that warrior spirit."

✳ ✳ ✳

Much of the criticism of Deontay Wilder in the aftermath of his knockout loss to Tyson Fury had been percolating for some time. Since the emergence of the hip-hop ring walk, there have been plenty of people who belittle the tradition. This is nothing new. Had Floyd Mayweather Jr. been knocked out during the later stages of his career, a similar criticism might have emerged. This newest wave, however, can, in part, be seen as evidence of a shifting cultural mindset in the sport. Ring walking, to borrow a phrase from rapper D Smoke, was under fire like never before.

During the course of my research, for example, Wilder's name often found its way into the conversation, used as evidence of why the tradition should be thrown out of the sport altogether. Promoter Lou DiBella, a steadfast supporter of hip-hop's place in boxing show business, is, for example, not alone in pointing to Wilder's controversial entrance as the potential end of an era.

Lou DiBella: "Roy Jones Jr. had probably the best hip-hop ring walk of all time. The ring walk with Method Man and Redman at Radio City Music Hall was one of the most theatrical ring walks in the history of the sport. Not to mention it was one of the most beautiful settings I've witnessed at a boxing match. I loved it. But, today, I think the hip-hop ring walk is getting played out a little bit. I don't like the idea of a fighter thinking of the ring walk as a performance. David Telesco [Roy Jones Jr.'s opponent at Radio City Music Hall] was an opponent that I barely approved [at HBO]. I didn't give Telesco much of a chance. But if it was *my guy* walking to the ring, facing someone who can actually kill him, I wouldn't want my guy worrying about the celebrity guest or singing and dancing along to the music. Deontay needed to forget about D Smoke and the costume and the ring walk and focus on Tyson Fury. Overall I think everyone in boxing feels like the mini rap concerts are getting played out."

Boxer and CEO of Christy Martin Promotions, Christy Martin: "I was at the fight [Wilder–Fury II]. I came away from it feeling like there are too many fighters worried about what they are wearing, how they are going to get to the ring, the rapper, and the entrance, instead of concentrating on the fight. From the outside looking in, it seems like they get so caught up on the entrance and they lose focus. As a promoter, I understand the hoopla. It's all about the fans. It makes the event feel bigger than it is. But if you are my fighter, trust and believe you will never come in the ring like that."

Boxing's current wave of hip-hop fatigue may be connected to the current state of mainstream rap music. Before trainer Mark Breland threw in the towel and ended Wilder's reign as WBC heavyweight champion, hip-hop music had already started to wear on people, even those who admire it. The rise of the so-called mumble-rap era, as Lou DiBella told me, is at least partially to blame.

Lou DiBella: "Many of my closest friends are in the hip-hop world. Eric B. is a friend. Melle Mel is a friend of mine. [Big Daddy] Kane is a friend. 50 Cent is, of course, a friend. Dame [Dash] is a friend. But I'm not a fan of mumble rap. Even some of my closest friends [in the hip-hop world] agree with me on that, about the mumbling and the auto-tune. In boxing, there have been too many low-level rappers doing that kind of music before fights. You can't understand a word they are saying. If a fighter can get a major artist, I suppose I'm for it. But over the past few years there haven't been many *major rap artists* doing those performances anymore."

In pointing to mumble rap's effect on boxing, DiBella moves us closer to understanding the criticism aimed at Wilder after his loss to Fury. Local rappers, friends of fighters, and SoundCloud emcees have, for the most part, taken over the tradition. Style, as DiBella suggests, also plays a part in this recent cultural shift.

Mumble rap is a derivative of southern-style trap music, an Atlanta-based subgenre (marked sonically by simple snare drums and triple-time hi-hat patterns) that focuses on narratives involving drug dealing, street life, and violence. Mumble rap, therefore, is essentially the by-product of an already maligned tradition. The term itself is often used pejoratively.

Mumble rap can be loosely defined as a youth-driven hip-hop movement, marked by catchy beats, singsong hooks, and simplistic rhymes, which are often delivered in a mumbled or slurred fashion (often through an auto-tune voice modulator). While the genre's name is widely attributed to rapper Wiz Khalifa following a June 2016 interview on Hot 97 FM, artists such as Gucci Mane, Chief Keef, and Future had been shaping the style for several years. The breakout success of Kanye West protégé Desiigner, who in 2015 scored a number-one hit with "Panda," a song many loved but couldn't understand, gave way to a new generation of mumble rappers. Today, Lil Uzi Vert, 21 Savage, Lil Yachty, Playboi Carti, and Lil Pump are prominent artists in the genre.

Both lyrically and semantically, mumble rap differs from the work of pioneering hip-hop artists. Mumble rap's omission of clever, eloquent storytelling and word play, as scholar Adam de Paor-Evans has written, serves as the genre's most often cited criticism.[190]

Despite the genre's popularity among millennial listeners, some have argued that the subgenre is a caricature of the culture. The sociopolitical messages found in the work of rappers such as Chuck D and Tupac Shakur are noticeably absent in mumble rap. For critics, mumble rap offers style but no substance, focusing its empty subject matter on hip-hop clichés such as cars, cash, drugs, and the objectification of women. When asked to define the movement for leading hip-hop magazine *XXL*, Lil Uzi Vert simply said, "It's lit. It's all about being lit."[191]

"The merit of mumble rap has grown to become one of the most divisive topics in today's hip-hop industry. Although some fight to fiercely protect the sanctity of rap as a voice for society's marginalized groups, others agree that hip-hop has expanded to upbeat, pop-inspired production that serves to express artists' bravado to the masses," cultural critic Ankita Bhanot writes.[192]

While Inglewood rapper D Smoke can hardly be classified as a mumble-rap artist, mumble rap is partially to blame for the fact that few people publicly applauded Deontay Wilder's Black History Month statement. Mainstream hip-hop, you might argue, is less political, less Afrocentric, and yet more commercially popular than ever.

The popularity of trap music, and mumble rap, shifted the hip-hop paradigm. This new-school persona shows up in boxing as well. Once again, this reciprocal pattern is nothing new. For over thirty years, emerging hip-hop trends have visibly altered the personas of some of boxing's biggest superstars.

In the later days of Mike Tyson's undefeated reign, for example, his rage echoed the political message made famous by hip-hop's most controversial act, Public Enemy. For the postprison era of his career, Tyson's tattooed ethos was perhaps more in line with the persona of his close friend, Tupac Shakur. Public Enemy and Tupac thus serve as a window into understanding these changes in Tyson's public demeanor.

What's more, it's no coincidence that Roy Jones Jr.'s popularity coincided with the rise of hip-hop's third coast, the Dirty South. Jones, who made his mark in both arenas at the same time, fed off this energy. During the height of Jones's rise to the top of the sport, southern pride, in the hip-hop world, was in style like never before.

An even stronger example, perhaps, is Floyd Mayweather Jr.'s progression from "Pretty Boy" to "Money" Mayweather. Mayweather, more so than any of his contemporaries, embodied the capitalist fantasies of hip-hop's twenty-first-century mogul era. Boxing's answer to Jay-Z or Sean "P. Diddy" Combs, he flaunted the material excess that marked hip-hop's corporate takeover, inspiring new generations of fighters to follow his entrepreneurial lead.

For those who understand hip-hop history, and its deep connection to professional boxing, it should come as no surprise that trap music and mumble rap have changed the game. This new movement had, for a brief period, its own champion, a boxer who represented this cultural trend both in the ring and in the vocal booth.

MO' MONEY, MO' PROBLEMS

The story begins at the Millvale Recreation Center in West Cincinnati. Funded by the Cincinnati Recreation Commission, the facility long served as a home for underprivileged city youth.

Or maybe the story truly begins at English Woods, a housing project in North Cincinnati, where, as early as five years old, a boy named Adrien and his twin brother, Dre, boxed local kids as their father recorded the sparring sessions on a VHS camcorder, a childhood story not unlike D Smoke's.

"I was like, c'mon. Ain't gonna be no more of that fighting in the house. So we came up with that fighting in the yard. He got eight brothers so he had to learn how to fight," Thomas Knight, Broner's father, told *Showtime Sports*.[193]

"No kids in the neighborhood could beat us, they didn't want to box with us, so we always had to fight older and bigger guys," Adrien added.

Adrien Broner's story, like those of many rap artists, starts at the bottom. The Cincinnati of Broner's troubled youth was plagued by a drug epidemic, a spike in regional gang activity, and the highest child poverty rate in the nation. As street gangs from larger cities moved into the West Cincinnati, the city quickly became, as Broner once said, "treacherous."

Adrien Broner: "It was different than a lot of cities. I was schooled by the older dudes. If you had it and I didn't have it, *I had to have it. I need that.* 'Hey, nice hoodie, bruh, let me get that.' I went knee-deep. I was shoulder-deep in the game. And, I had to swim my way out. I've been in there with the sharks and I made my way out."[194]

The hypermasculine narratives of impulse found in trap music/ mumble rap are, of course, fueled by this same violent reversal of authority. Swimming with sharks, as a metaphor, comes to represent a set of masculine cultural expressions emanating from the lower rungs of America's social hierarchy.

Mumble rap, in particular, can be seen as the wild and reckless celebration of overcoming insurmountable odds. Flaunting of material possessions, visible representations of class ascension, *is* the rhetorical aim of the music. In mumble rap, *celebration* is the message. Stacks of money, luxury vehicles, designer clothes, and multimillion-dollar homes serve as the spoils of having navigated shark-infested waters.

Like many subgenres of rap music, trap music/mumble rap focuses its content on extremes. Holding on to the protective mantle of poverty and victimization, mumble rap champions a particular path to the top, one in which morals and ethics are suspended. Adrien Broner's life and career, for better or for worse, play like a trap-music/mumble-rap record. Understanding the conventions of the hip-hop subgenre provides a starting place for understanding the masculine, materialistic, and often morally ambivalent public persona the boxer created for himself in the media.

As is often the case in hip-hop origin stories, Broner's cautionary tale is tied to regional identity. Had Broner been born in New York City, Los Angeles, or Atlanta, his path to fame and fortune may have begun with trap music. Cincinnati, for all of its socioeconomic problems, did offer one advantage: It was a fight city. Following in the tradition of Ezzard Charles and Aaron "The Hawk" Pryor, a long list of hometown Cincinnati Olympians—Tony Tubbs (1980), Tim Austin (1992), Larry Donald (1992), Ricardo Williams Jr. (2000), and Dante Craig (2000)—forged a path for aspiring boxers. When Adrien Broner's father brought him to the Millvale Recreation Center for the first time, the scrappy youngster once again found himself swimming with sharks.

According to coach Michael Stafford, Broner's first sparring session, outside those organized by his father in English Woods, came against a young man who would become the first U.S. amateur boxer to compete in three separate Olympic games: Rau'shee Warren.

Michael Stafford: "Adrien's dad brought him down to the gym when he was about seven years old. Because Adrien was supposed to be tough, I put him in there with Rau'shee [Warren]. Both were fifty-five pounds at the time and Rau'shee was eight or nine years old. Rau'shee had fought everyone in the country and a lot of them were bigger than him. So he and Adrien sparred all the time. Rau'shee made Adrien cry a lot. He was the test of the gym back then. If you could make it three rounds with Rau'shee, you were on my team."[195]

As the sparring sessions gradually became more competitive, Stafford recognized Broner as a boxing prodigy. Keeping the hyperactive youngster busy in the ring, and off the streets of Cincinnati, became his main objective. If needed, Stafford took it upon himself to spank Adrien and his twin brother. Boxing was their ticket out of poverty, a vehicle that would provide structure, discipline, and, most important, purpose. In subsequent years, Adrien, more so than Dre, realized his potential, dominating local, and eventually national, competition.

"In Cincinnati we had a very good amateur system. We used to fight almost every week," Broner reflected.[196]

In Midwest boxing circles, a buzz surrounded Stafford's group of Olympic hopefuls. At twelve years old, Adrien Broner was interviewed for a segment featured on *The Early Show*, broadcast on a local Cincinnati news station. The child's words are prophetic.

"What do you think you guys would be doing, if not for boxing?" the reporter asked.[197]

"A lot of bad things," Broner replied.

"Like what?" the reporter asked.

"Trying to rob people. Break into cars," Broner answered.

"Oh, come on, you would not be doing that," the reporter laughed.

"Probably. If you hang out with some of the people like that you probably will," Broner said, grinning.

Five years later, in 2007, Broner found the trouble he mentioned in the interview. Just seventeen years old, he was arrested by Cincinnati police and charged with aggravated robbery and felonious assault. According to Broner, he spent a full year in the county jail fighting the case, which involved charges that could carry a maximum penalty of fifty-seven years.

Adrien Broner: "Allegedly, it was assault, guns, robberies, a lot of shit. I was seventeen. You gotta think, growing up, our mom and dad tried to take care of us. I started getting older and started wanting shit. So, it was either go take for it or go hustle for it. At that time, I didn't give a fuck. They bound me over and tried me as an adult. I was seventeen, locked up with the grown-ups. Everybody in my pod that was going to court and going back. *I got eighteen [years]. I got twenty-two. I ain't tripping.* We was young and dumb; all we knew was trouble."[198]

As Broner sat in a Hamilton County jail cell, awaiting the sentence that would dictate the course of his adult life, he briefly imagined hip-hop music as his key to freedom but then reconsidered.

Adrien Broner: "My trial date was coming up, I had like a week left. I was doing twenty-three hours in my room and one out a day. And I was writing raps. Then, I just stopped and looked out the window, it was like this little bitty window. 'What the fuck am I gonna do if I get out? I'ma sell drugs?' Then I was like, 'Nah, I'ma be back in here.' Then, I was like, I'ma box.' And I got up and started shadowboxing."[199]

While Broner eventually beat the charges in October 2007, much was lost. The Cincinnati boxing prodigy with three hundred amateur wins and only nineteen losses missed his opportunity to join his teammate and child-hood friend Rau'shee Warren at the Olympics and Pan American Games. Unfortunately for Broner, more legal trouble awaited. According to the *Cincinnati Enquirer*: "A separate charge was filed against [Broner] that same year, but it too was dismissed. In 2008, [the following year] Broner was arrested again. Cincinnati police said he was unlawfully carrying a .32-caliber Smith and Wesson revolver and intimidating a witness in separate incidents. Both cases were dismissed by Hamilton County Common Pleas Judge Robert Ruehlman. A domestic violence charge against Broner was also dropped that year."[200] The troubled boxer, it appeared, had not learned his lesson.

✳ ✳ ✳

Branding himself "The Problem," Adrien Broner turned professional at eighteen years old and, proved himself as a serious prospect, knocking out his first sixteen opponents by the end of the sixth round. As the knockouts accumulated, Broner's stock rose. In the ring, his defense, quick hands, reflexes, and star quality were comparable to that of a young Floyd Mayweather. Outside the ring, Broner's incessant trash talk, flamboyant style, and brash demeanor came off as a parody of Mayweather's "Money Team" persona.

Big Daddy Kane: "Floyd clearly appealed to millennial rappers, his attitude matched up with millennial rappers. He was fly, flashy. The stacks of money. The cars. All that. His persona fit that era in hip-hop and you can see his influence in the mannerisms of other boxers that followed him."

After signing with Oscar De La Hoya's Golden Boy Promotions, it looked like Broner was headed toward crossover stardom, the heir to Mayweather's throne, some said. Broner's breakout performance came against former junior featherweight champion, and hometown favorite, Daniel Ponce De Leon, 41-2 (34 KOs), in Anaheim, California, a ten-round bout televised on the undercard of a Canelo Alvarez HBO headliner.

"At the moment, [Broner] is just a big-talking, fast prospect, but tonight we find out if he's something more than that," HBO's Max Kellerman said as Broner made his way to the ring, escorted by Cincinnati's Aaron "The Hawk" Pryor.[201]

By the end of the night, Kellerman's question was, at least partially answered. In a fight marked by sporadic, back-and-forth action, Broner carried many of the middle rounds, while Ponce De Leon rallied late. To the dismay of the hometown fans, Broner, who had yet to go past eight rounds, won a close but unanimous ten-round decision. Harold Lederman, HBO's unofficial judge, narrowly scored the fight for Ponce De Leon.

After being given the thin victory, Broner jokingly refused to answer Kellerman's first post-fight inquires and instead asked his father, Thomas Knight, to brush his hair. The fans booed and Broner played the heel, enjoying the disapproval of his opponent's supporters.

With Golden Boy Promotions fueling his momentum, the cocky young boxer didn't have to wait long for a title shot. Two fights later, Broner faced Vicente Martin Rodriguez, 34-2-1 (18 KOs), at the U.S. Bank Arena in Cincinnati for the vacant WBO world junior lightweight title, which was televised on HBO's *Boxing After Dark* series.

This time, Broner dazzled. In the third round, a whipping Broner uppercut followed by a hard body shot and a sharp hook sent Rodriguez tumbling to the canvas, blood streaming from his broken nose. Bloody and beaten, Rodriguez made no attempt to beat the count.

"Cincinnati has a new problem and it's a good one," ring announcer Michael Buffer called to the fans before introducing Broner—who had occupied a lonely Hamilton County jail cell, shadowboxing and writing rhymes—as a world champion, the second-youngest in the sport.

"Left right, good night," Broner, already branding himself an aspiring rapper, rhymed in the post-fight interview.

After he won the world title, setbacks came quickly. In early 2012, Broner was once again arrested in Cincinnati on assault charges. Although the case was later dismissed, Broner's public image took another serious hit.

Against battle-tested contender Vicente Escobedo, on July 21, 2012, Broner lost his WBO belt on the scales, failing to make weight for the contest. Later that evening, Broner tweeted an image of a Twinkie snack cake, a move that many boxing analysts interpreted as a nonchalant attitude toward the WBO ruling. To nonbelievers, Broner's long pattern of problematic behavior, the ambivalent persona, had more to do with emotional immaturity than clever marketing.

On the outside, Broner showed no signs of distress. As he walked to the ring to face Escobedo, in what was now a non-title affair, the precocious boxer, draped in diamond jewelry and platinum chains, danced his way to the ring, accompanied by mumble rapper Waka Flocka Flame, who performed his song "Work."

"At twenty-two, Broner is already trying to come off the page as a *big personality*," HBO's Jim Lampley said flatly during the performance.[202]

Against Escobedo, Broner's apparent lack of focus did not show itself in the ring. In a brutal, one-sided contest, Broner defeated Escobedo by a fifth-round stoppage. After the fight, the high jinks continued. Once again refusing to answer the first of Max Kellerman's post-fight questions, Broner grabbed the microphone and took over the show.

"I'm sorry, I have to do this, I have to do this on national television, worldwide, international. I just got into a relationship. But I know true love at first sight. Baby, come here," Broner called to his girlfriend, getting down on one knee, as if ready to propose marriage.

"On national TV, in front of the whole world. Arienne Nicole Gazaway . . . can you brush my hair?" Broner joked, pausing to build anticipation.

"That was a good one, you got me," said Kellerman, bewildered.

"I want everyone to follow me on Instagram and on Twitter @AdrienBroner. I do cut up like scissors," Broner continued, not interested in talking about the fight, his legal problems, or his not making weight.

As the number of Broner's followers grew, so did the list of pundits who said his penchant for nightlife and apparent immaturity were the biggest threats to his career. The flashy ring walks, the pre- and post-fight antics, and often lewd behavior on social media served as foreshadowing devices for those who believed Broner's success might be of the "too much too soon" variety. Never one to back down from controversy, Broner grew more and more loquacious with each new victory. In his post-fight interviews, Broner often tiptoed the line between good-natured bravado and racist/homophobic discourse.

"They call me 'The Problem' but you can call me 'The Can Man' . . . because anybody can get it. Africans. Americans. Dominicans. Mexicans. Anybody can get it. I should have fought with my jewelry on because I don't think I got hit," Broner stated.[203]

There were few subtleties when it came to boxing's "Problem Child." Fans either loved or hated the persona. As Broner's star rose, he continued to talk about his dreams of making it in the hip-hop music business and said his initials stood for "About Billions." Many in the boxing community argued that Broner lacked the discipline necessary to walk the same tightrope as fighters such as Mike Tyson, Roy Jones Jr., Zab Judah, and Floyd Mayweather, all of whom founded hip-hop record companies during the height of their boxing careers. Broner, more than any of his predecessors, sought to make it as a rap artist.

A few months after the Vicente Escobedo bout, Broner moved up in weight to challenge WBC lightweight champion Antonio DeMarco (28-2-1, 21 KOs) at Boardwalk Hall in Atlantic City. In one of the best performances of the boxer's career, Broner temporarily silenced his critics by stopping DeMarco in the eighth round. After this impressive outing, comparisons to Floyd Mayweather were unavoidable. In the post-fight interview, when asked if he wanted to be known as a *fighter*, as opposed to a slick boxer like Mayweather, Broner refused to be serious.

"If I had a choice, I'd be a playboy, Larry [Merchant]," Broner joked.[204]

"As you can see, once I'm in there, and I got a game plan, I go after it. I shake 'em, bake 'em, cook 'em, and eat 'em . . . no homo,"

Broner continued, using a homophobic phrase that often gets rap artists in trouble.

While Broner's talent was undeniable, many people in boxing had already grown weary of him. Unlike Mayweather, who could switch off his "Money" persona, Broner seemed determined to push the boundaries of acceptable behavior. For some, Broner's act was a cheap imitation. For others, the undefeated Cincinnati kid was quickly becoming must-see entertainment. Either way, there was no denying Broner's box-office potential.

* * *

Unable to secure a bout with Ricky Burns, the most lucrative match in his division, Broner chose to jump two weight classes to face WBA welterweight champion Paulie Malignaggi at the Barclays Center in Brooklyn, moving him a step closer to his idol, Mayweather, who, at the time, competed in the same division.

Aside from conquering the welterweight division, Broner had other goals.

A few weeks before the Malignaggi fight, Broner released "On Everything," the aspiring rapper's official debut single. On a bouncy, auto-tune-heavy track devoted to the fruits of his success, he created a song that fit hip-hop's current soundscape. In the song's music video, shot in the same style as the popular MTV show *Cribs*, Broner's rags-to-riches story was visually represented by the love story of his well-documented relationship with his fiancée, perhaps winning him fans outside the sports world. During the week of the Malignaggi fight, however, Broner reverted back to his darker side and tried some psychological warfare.

At the prefight press conference, Broner took his vulgar antics up a level, taunting Malignaggi by attempting to bring his former lover to the event. When the young woman was refused entry, Broner took over.

"[Saturday night] I'm gonna bring a guest that is really one of my closest friends, Jessica. Jess, as he [Paulie] used to call her. His ex. She is my sweetheart now," Broner told the media, launching into a rambling story that playfully accused Malignaggi of hitting his ex-lover but not having the punching power to knock her out.[205]

"They broke it off. Paulie wasn't hitting hard enough and now she's with a heavy hitter," Broner joked. He then called Jessica on his cell phone and put her on speakerphone for all to hear.

Irked, Malignaggi spoke last.

Paulie Malignaggi: "This guy better be grateful he is a Floyd Mayweather imitation, otherwise he wouldn't be getting laid at all. . . . Stop trying to talk like Floyd. . . . He has the imitation down pat—he doesn't just fight like him; he talks like him. You're not Floyd Mayweather, you are Adrien Broner."

The bout, much like the press conference, was tense. Malignaggi, who, at thirty-two years old, was seen by most as past his prime, started aggressively, using a sharp left jab to set up quick flurries. As the fight progressed, Broner timed Malignaggi with sharp right crosses and counter left hooks and regained the momentum in the middle rounds. Heading into the championship rounds, the fight was even. Broner's low punch output left many speculating how seriously he had trained. When the fight ended, both fighters paraded around the ring as if they believed they had won.

Broner was given a split decision victory over Malignaggi: one judge scored the bout 115-113 for Malignaggi, which was overruled by 117-111 and 115-113 scores from the other judges. Among ringside experts, the prevailing notion was that Broner had done enough to eke out a victory over Malignaggi but ultimately failed to live up to his own hype.

"Any regrets over everything that went on in the prefight news conferences?" Jim Gray asked Broner soon after the decision was announced.[206]

"Negative. I left with his belt and his girl," Broner bragged, wearing an eighteen-karat gold grill as he delivered his post-fight remarks.

Despite his boorish behavior before and after the fight and average performance, the split-decision victory made Broner, at twenty-three years old, the youngest three-division champion in boxing history. The hip-hop community in particular seemed poised to recognize Broner, at 27-0 (22 KOs), as their champion, Floyd Mayweather's likely successor.

As Broner's popularity grew, his name, like Mayweather's, began to show up in hip-hop songs.

"I got the whole hood with me. I got the whole hood on my back. I'm doing it for them. I'm the hood's champion," Broner often said to the media.

In retrospect, Broner's victory over Malignaggi was a turning point in both his life and career. After Broner's contract with Golden Boy Promotions expired, he became the hottest free agent in the sport. While rumors suggested that Jay-Z's Roc Nation Sports and 50 Cent's SMS Promotions might land the star, most believed he would join forces with Mayweather Promotions.

Adrien Broner: "I never met [Floyd Mayweather Jr.] until I beat Paulie. I was actually talking to him while I was fighting Paulie. I was talking shit to Floyd [who was sitting ringside] while I was fighting Paulie. That's when I started taking trips [to visit Mayweather] and shit. We was in Cali, we was in Greystone [Mansion] they came to my booth and was like, 'Floyd want to meet you.' We meet Floyd, we was supposed to be leaving but Floyd was like . . . 'Come with us.' He kidnapped me for like two months, I went everywhere with Floyd, for like two months."[207]

The Broner–Mayweather partnership never materialized. To the surprise of many, Broner instead signed with Premier Boxing Champions and formed his own promotional banner titled About Billions Promotions, allegedly spurning Mayweather's courtship.

Adrien Broner: "I think that's where the problems came. When I met him, I was already rich; I had millions of dollars already. You my idol. I fucks with you. But I don't need you. That's when things got shaky. People started saying he's gonna be better than Mayweather. If I would have signed to him, there wouldn't have been problems."[208]

After the Malignaggi fight, Broner's hip-hop profile grew. In an impressive social media campaign that spanned several platforms, Broner and his Cincinnati-based rap collective Band Camp launched a series of lifestyle videos and online mixtapes. Mostly composed of Broner's childhood friends, Band Camp followed in the tradition of Mike Tyson Records, Body Head (Roy Jones Jr.), Super Cartel (Zab Judah), and Philthy Rich Records (Floyd Mayweather Jr.). With the advent of online audio distribution platforms and music-sharing websites such as SoundCloud, Spotify, and later Tidal, Band Camp, unlike its predecessors, capitalized on the music industry's move toward streaming services. In an era where rap stardom no longer required record contracts, distribution, marketing, or even radio play, Band Camp used Broner's social media following to carve out a place in the emerging trap-music/mumble-rap landscape.

Using his celebrity and new connections in the industry, Broner took to the road. As an opening act on the Most Wanted Tour, featuring head-lining artists Lil Wayne, T.I., and Soulja Boy, Broner sought to have an unprecedented year as both a performer and a prize fighter.

As expected, Broner's hip-hop aspirations figured heavily in the pro-motional campaign for his first title defense at welterweight, a crossroads bout with hard-punching Argentinian challenger Marcos Maidana (34-3, 31 KOs), scheduled for December 14, 2013. While Maidana was respected in the sport for his granite chin and aggressive style, against top fighters such as Devon Alexander and Amir Khan, the rugged Argentinian had in the past come up short. In promoting the matchup, Showtime high-lighted Broner's hip-hop career to hype what many experts believed to be a stepping-stone fight for him.

"I love [hip-hop]. I've been into rap since six years old. We used to rap as kids. And I never stopped. It's just another way to relieve my stress. It's another way to communicate with somebody that I don't know. You can listen to one of my songs and see why I act the way I act. I don't know why God gave me all this talent. One day I will be great at this, I'm still learning, I'm still a sponge, but my last few raps been off the chain," Broner said on Showtime's *All Access* program before the fight.[209]

To the delight of Broner's detractors, his comeuppance came fast. Maidana swarmed Broner from the opening bell, using a relentless mix of stiff jabs, wild left hooks, and powerful overhand rights. Early on, Broner was staggered by a looping right hand. For much of the first round, Broner covered up on the ropes as the Argentinian pounded away at his defensive guard. The highlight moment of the first round, however, did not come from a punch. In the closing moments, Broner wrestled with Maidana, turning him around and pushing his face into the ring ropes. While Maidana was pinned against the ropes, Broner pretended to hump him from behind. The fans at the Alamodome in San Antonio, Texas—a markedly pro-Maidana crowd—booed the crude act. It would be Broner's final vulgarity of the night.

In the final minute of the second round, it happened. A leaping left hook from Maidana struck Broner's chin, sending him careening half-way through the bottom two ropes, his arms dangling helplessly. Broner, who rose to his feet perhaps too quickly, stumbled into the corner. The knockdown, the first of his career, electrified the crowd. When the action resumed, Maidana launched a brutal attack, pummeling Broner for the remainder of the round. The fight had changed instantly.

To the cocky champion's credit, he survived, showing toughness and guts. Broner eventually worked his way back into the fight, but by his own admission he never recovered from the punch.

Adrien Broner: "That bitch hit hard. He hit me with a good shot early. I was moving, I was cool. I was cool. But he threw a weird shot, it looked like he was coming to the body but he came up top. And, I was like, 'Oh shit. Good shot.' But I got up though. And I don't remember nothing until the seventh or ninth round. It all went blank but I was still fighting my ass off. Everything was all slow motion."[210]

The crescendo of Broner–Maidana came in the ninth round. Midway through, Maidana landed a brutal right hook to Broner's ribs, followed by a short left hook to the head. The combination rocked Broner and he stumbled backward and to the canvas, stemming any chance of a rally.

"He caught me again with another big shot [in the ninth]. I had to thug it out. I was like, c'mon. Now you gotta kill me. I did what I had to do. I was fucked up," Broner reflected.

After twelve rounds of brutal action, Marcos "Chico" Maidana claimed his first world championship via a unanimous decision victory. More important, perhaps, Maidana was the first man to shut Broner's mouth.

"Problem solved," boxing analyst Mauro Ranallo called after Jimmy Lennon Jr. read the verdict.

This time, there would be no hair brushing or lewd quips. Broner left the ring with his head low, refusing to do a post-fight interview with Showtime's Jim Gray. Rowdy audience members tossed cups of beer and other debris at the former champion as he made his way to the locker room.

While Maidana was given credit for executing a brilliant game plan and for delivering a gritty performance, the subtext of the upset revolved around Broner's decision to participate in the Most Wanted Tour before training camp.

Adrien Broner: "You think I would be able to stand in there with Maidana for twelve rounds, as a lightweight, and not be in shape? I took training camp very seriously. It's just, I was coming off tour. I was on the Most Wanted Tour with T.I., 2 Chainz, and Lil Wayne. We came off the last city, Las Vegas, and I went straight to camp. Coming from that life-style [hip-hop] to this lifestyle [boxing] takes time."[211]

In the months following the Maidana bout, many boxing writers debated whether "The Problem" was underprepared or overhyped, more of a reality-television star than an elite fighter. Unlike Roy Jones Jr. and Floyd Mayweather, who both cemented their greatness before they incorporated hip-hop into their business plans, Broner now found himself in the same spot as Zab Judah—a talent who didn't reach his potential because he liked hip-hop nightlife. For those who called Judah and Broner underachievers, the lesson was simple: Boxers can't live like rappers.

* * *

Why Adrien Broner's downfall was framed as a hip-hop issue is easy to understand. At the height of his popularity, Broner's ring walks were rap concerts. In 2013, Broner walked to the ring with rapper French Montana for his fight against Paulie Malignaggi. Montana performed his song "Ain't Worried About Nothin." The next year, Broner walked to the ring with Rick Ross for his fight against John Molina Jr. at the MGM Grand in Las Vegas. The Miami rap star performed his hit song "Box Chevy." In his next fight, Broner walked to the ring with Young Thug, Birdman, and Rich Man Quan, as the trio performed their song, "Lifestyle." When Broner faced Khabib Allakhverdiev at the U.S. Bank Arena in Cincinnati, he was escorted to the ring by trap-music supergroup Migos. Less than two years later, in the same arena, Broner walked to the ring with rap-per Kodak Black for his fight against Adrian Granados. Broner's loss to Maidana, in the view of many, served as evidence of an already estab-lished precedent. Broner's hip-hop lifestyle was, at the very least, a key component of the fight's subtext.

Some people in the rap world also poked fun at his comeuppance.

Just like when Roy Jones Jr. lost to Antonio Tarver, the hip-hop com-munity, on social media and in the music, reacted to Broner's upset loss. In "The Hope," featured on *The Soul Tape 3* mixtape, Brooklyn rap-per Fabolous, for example, rhymed, "Niggas looking washed up, it's something in the soap / You looking like Adrien Broner in the ropes," referencing the first knockdown in the Maidana fight.

After the mixtape was released online, Broner quickly fired back on social media, tweeting directly to Fabolous: "Nigga had a bad night and you jumped ship my nigga. I thought you watched my fight to see me win."[212]

Unable to get a rematch with Maidana—who scored a huge payday against Floyd Mayweather because of his upset victory—Broner chose instead to drop down to junior welterweight, the division he skipped to fight Malignaggi.

On the pay-per-view undercard of Mayweather–Maidana, on May 5, 2014, Broner faced Carlos Molina (17-1-1, 7 KOs) and won a one-sided unanimous decision. Broner followed up the Molina victory with back-to-back wins over journeyman Emanuel Taylor (18-2-1, 12 KOs) and John Molina Jr. (27-5, 22 KOs), each by a points victory. The three-fight winning streak, made up of solid but not great performances, got Broner an intriguing catchweight fight against fellow Ohioan "Showtime" Shawn Porter (25-1-1, 16 KOs), a crossroads matchup that would help launch the newly formed *Premier Boxing Champions* series.

Billed as "The Battle of Ohio," both Adrien Broner and Shawn Porter were at similar points in their careers. Both were in their mid-twenties and coming back from the first defeats of their careers. While most experts viewed the matchup as a toss-up fight, Broner refused to see Porter as a threat. At the final press conference, for example, Broner refused to speak to the media first, believing that he was the A side of the promotion.

"This is the AB show. The AB show starts now. I'm fighting Shawn Porter, a football player, and I'm fighting his dad. It's like I'm fighting his dad because when the check come, it come in his dad's name and then he pays Shawn and then he make Shawn sign the check and go deposit it in their joint account. I see him spending Shawn's money, that's why he got better cars, while Shawn is catching an Uber or hopping out his 2011 CTS, the little one, that's the difference between me and him," Broner clowned.[213]

Broner's strategy, to needle Porter about his relationship with his outgoing father and trainer, Kenny Porter, drew laughs from some and criticism from others. Throughout fight week, the taunts were incessant.

"After this fight, I'm gonna sign Shawn to About Billions, we will get him better cars than his dad's. I already wrote out the contract, it's ready for him to sign," Broner continued.

Shawn Porter would do his talking in the ring. From the outset, it was clear that Porter had prepared better. Using a powerful jab to set up a relentless body attack, Porter dominated much of the action, bullying Broner around the ring. Using a defensive posture for much of the night, Broner often threw only one or two punches at a time, which gave some the impression that he was fighting merely to survive. His low work rate once again fueled speculation that his focus was no longer on boxing.

Outworked by Porter for most of the night, Broner scored a flash knockdown in the final round but couldn't capitalize on it. After he lost for the second time as a professional, in a mostly one-sided affair, Broner looked indifferent.

"This time I didn't get the decision, but it's okay. At the end of the day, everybody in here will take my autograph and take my picture," Broner said in the post-fight interview, drawing boos from the crowd.[214]

Broner's indifference toward defeat was rooted in some measure of economic reality. His high jinks and persona outside the ring had become the reason he drew fans to his fights. His most talked-about moments in the years to come would take place before and after his bouts. Despite his diminished skills, Broner's personality could sell a fight, even lopsided mismatches against outclassed opponents.

Coming off Broner's second loss in four fights, Al Haymon looked to dump his controversial fighter's plummeting stock, quickly matching Broner with Russian Khabib Allakhverdiev (19-2, 9 KOs) for a vacant junior welterweight world title, hosted in Broner's hometown of Cincinnati.

"I'm still AB," Broner assured fans after he won the fight by a twelfth-round TKO. "This next half of my career, I'm going to be about boxing and billions," he added.

Claiming to be rededicated to the sport, Broner rebranded himself as an older, wiser, and more dangerous version of himself, a man who had seen the error of his ways.

"[The Shawn Porter fight] is the only time ever that I bullshitted in camp. I bullshitted in camp, I swear. I did a camp in Vegas, I was out gambling all night, losing $30,000, might win $500,000. Then I would train at night. I was out at clubs with Chris Brown. It was too much, I was tripping. Shawn Porter won. But he didn't dominant me. I didn't have a scratch on me. I just wasn't in shape to do what I needed to do," Broner argued.[215]

Broner's reawakening proved to be just talk. Following his victory over Allakhverdiev, his legal problems snowballed. Before his bout with Ashley Theophane (39-6-1, 11 KOs), a British journeyman who was at the time managed by Floyd Mayweather's Money Team, Broner made headlines again. In late January 2016, a few months before the scheduled bout with Theophane, Broner was taken into custody and charged with beating a West Chester, Ohio, man and robbing him of $14,000 during a gambling dispute outside a Madisonville bowling alley. In a separate incident soon after, Broner was jailed for reckless driving. Though wanted on two charges, Broner's April 1 fight in Washington D.C., broadcast by Premier Boxing Champions, was allowed to proceed.

The negative publicity surrounding the event wasn't "The Problem's" only problem. At the prefight weigh-in for the Theophane bout, Broner was stripped of his WBA world title for not making the 140-pound weight limit. While Broner only exceeded the limit by 0.4 pounds, he refused to get weighed again and instead chose to vacate his belt. Broner's actions prompted Floyd Mayweather, who promoted the event, to publicly question his focus and professionalism, speculating to reporters that the troubled boxer likely suffered from alcoholism.

Broner, who often referred to Mayweather as "Big Bro," was visibly hurt and likely embarrassed.

Adrien Broner: "If you really feel like that, and one minute you like, 'You Baby Bro, I want you to do good,' then you can tell me that in person. That's how a real big brother would do a little brother."[216]

Despite the distractions, Broner dominated Mayweather's Money Team pupil, staggering the Theophane in the third and eventually stopping him via TKO in the ninth round. Broner's comments in the post-fight interview went viral.

"Y'all probably know about this but somebody that I look up to, somebody that I admire, took the chance to do an interview and talk all bad about me. Now, I don't know how y'all look at it, but I don't like it. I wasn't gonna do this but I'm a man that learns shit from physical activity so me and Floyd, he gotta see me. Point. Blank. Period. I'm a man at the end of the day. And I come from the streets. The trenches. From the bottom to nothing. I'm talking about water and cornflakes. I come from nothing. And I will never let a man disrespect me like that. So he got to see me. I don't care if we spar or we fight, let's get it on," said Broner, as Floyd Mayweather stood ringside and appeared to laugh off the challenge.[217]

Three days after beating Theophane, Broner turned himself in to Cincinnati police to serve his ten-day sentence for reckless driving. While the charges from the bowling alley incident eventually got dismissed, Judge Robert Ruehlman sentenced Broner to an additional thirty days in jail for showing up to a hearing "three hours late and drunk."[218]

After getting out of jail, Broner and members of his Band Camp crew headed straight to a Cincinnati recording studio to lay down vocals for "Slammer," a remix to Desiigner's 2015 hit "Panda." A music video for the song was shot on-site during the recording process.

From the outset, it was clear that Adrien Broner's wanted to taunt Floyd Mayweather, framing the remix as something of a diss track. "Slammer" is bookended with audio clips of Broner's post-fight challenge to Mayweather.

Imitating the flow and cadence of Desiigner's chart-topping mumble-rap hit "Panda," Broner begins by referencing his legal issues.

"I just got up out the slammer, they say they got me on the camera / F-1's, I got several, you try to sue me, I won't settle / Niggas be, telling / And, now a days they be accepting / I bought a Bugatti and wrecked it," Broner rhymes in the chorus.[219]

In the second verse, Broner calls out Mayweather.

"I got Floyd going against me, I ain't trippin / Turned over for some business / Found out I couldn't get him, so I knocked out his nigga," Broner rhymes.

While the song caused waves in both boxing and hip-hop circles, Mayweather didn't take the bait. After months of back-and-forth on social media, the trash talk cooled and Broner finally moved on.

Unable to lure Mayweather out of retirement, Broner resumed his boxing career, choosing to face brawler Adrian Granados (18-4-2, 12 KOs), winning a split decision that many observers felt he didn't deserve. After the fight, Broner cited his ten-month layoff and an injured left hand as the reasons for his sluggish performance. At the time, it appeared that Broner's actual in-ring performances mattered little. "Slammer," and the attendant social media beef with Mayweather, had, for better or worse, injected new interest in Broner, increasing the reach of his celebrity. Five months later, for example, Broner followed the Granados victory with a lopsided unanimous decision loss to three-division star Mikey Garcia (36-0, 30 KOs) at Barclays Center. After being outworked and out-classed by the smaller Garcia for most of the night, Broner no longer appeared to be a top talent. The poor performance did little to temper his post-fight bravado.

"I gotta thank all the people who came to see me lose, all the people who came to see me win, because, at the end of the day, y'all the reason I make all this money. If I fight in this motherfucker tomorrow, everybody still gonna come see me. At the end of the day, I'm still AB, I'm still About Billions, I'm still the Can Man," Broner told Showtime's Jim Gray.[220]

After the Garcia loss, it became clear that Broner's unique brand of hip-hop sports celebrity was now the driving force behind his cultural relevance. The defeat did little to slow him down. Three months later, Garcia Broner released his debut rap album, *Wanted*. A mug shot served as the cover art for the album.

Containing thirteen original songs and featuring production from hip-hop veterans Zaytoven, Metro Boomin, Chaz Guapo, and Young Chop, as well as guest features from Cook LaFlare and B. Luck, Broner's *Wanted* got modest streaming numbers and mixed reviews. *Vibe* maga-zine, for instance, wrote that the album "wasn't terrible." Released at the height of the mumble-rap craze, Broner's vocals and bravado did, in many ways, mesh with the times. In songs such as "Millionaire," "Bag Talk," and "Horses," Broner plays up his lavish outlaw lifestyle, delivering punch lines and vocals that are, as *Vibe* suggested, not all that differ-ent from those dominating the Billboard charts. Shortly after releasing *Wanted*, Broner once again hit the road, touring and collaborating with a variety of hip-hop artists, such as Philadelphia Freeway (formerly of Roc-A-Fella Records) and Rick Ross.

Despite the downward spiral of his boxing career, Broner continued to maintain a certain amount of respect within hip-hop. Yet even in the rap world, AB, the rapper, had his detractors.

Peter Gunz: "I was a fan of Broner at first. And, then the stuff he started to do outside of the ring started getting to me, bothering me. Stuff he would say and do. And I'm not one to normally judge people. I went on TV and acted like an asshole [*Love & Hip-Hop*] so I get it. But when I saw him flushing $100 on social media. Some of the stuff coming out of his mouth. Nah. From that point forward, there was no way I could be a fan."

Leading up to Broner's fight against former two-division champion Jessie Vargas (28-2, 10 KOs), held at the Barclays Center in Brooklyn in April 2018, Broner was trolled relentlessly on social media by rapper Tekashi 69, a trap-music newcomer known for his aggressive lyrics, rainbow-colored hair, numerous tattoos, and long list of public feuds on social media.

"This pussy ass Nigga, what's his name, Broner? I got $300,000 you gonna lose the fight," 69 taunted in one video, violently tossing stacks of $100 bills toward the ceiling.[221]

The trolling worked. Largely because of his ongoing feud with Tekashi 69, who was rapidly becoming a major figure in the music industry, the topic of Broner–Vargas was discussed on a variety of leading hip-hop radio shows, such as Sway Calloway's *Sway in the Morning* on Sirius XM and Power 105.1 FM's *The Breakfast Club*. Leading up to the Vargas fight, some speculated that Broner and Tekashi 69 faked the social beef. The boxer himself later said this was indeed the case. Regardless of his promotional intentions, Broner's focus, once again, became a topic of conversation in the boxing world. Even though Broner had hired the no-nonsense trainer Kevin Cunningham—who replaced his childhood mentor, Michael Stafford—most saw his involvement in the hip-hop world as self-destructive.

Broner and Vargas turned out to be a surprisingly entertaining fight that resulted in a twelve-round majority draw. One card had the bout 115-133 for Broner and two cards scored the bout 114-114. While Broner had been the more accurate fighter, connecting with 44 percent of his power punches, compared to 27 percent for Vargas, his inactivity was the key factor in the fight. Vargas, who had been the more active fighter by 300 punches, was widely viewed as the more deserving of the two, having outworked Broner in the final rounds. Broner continued with his familiar post-fight routine, regardless of the outcome.

"Hey man, fuck all that, I beat him. Look at his face," Broner shouted after the fight, attempting to wrestle the microphone away from Showtime's Jim Gray.[222]

"I'm an honest man, we went at it for twelve rounds, can do it again," Vargas replied, interrupting the childish rant.

"That's gay. Going at it is gay. I beat yo ass like you stole some-thing . . . you need peroxide and alcohol . . . yo face on 69, you a blood" Broner interrupted, referencing Tekashi 69's alleged gang affiliation.

Jim Gray attempted to temper Broner's lewd comments but failed.

"I beat him, no homo. You watching? You got cataracts? Your eyes fucked up? Did you see?" Broner said.

"Final thought . . . would you want to fight Vargas again, based on this draw?" Gray replied, doing his best to appear unnerved.

"Hell yes . . . but let's go to my town. I want to fight him where I'm from. There is hella Mexicans in here, everyone keeps booing and shit, they want rice and beans," Broner responded.

Despite losing his last two fights, "The Problem" still got lucrative opportunities because he could fill arenas. In October 2018, for exam-ple, Broner signed to fight a forty-year-old Manny Pacquiao at the MGM Grand in Las Vegas. At twenty-nine years old, Broner, for the first time in his boxing career, was granted a headlining pay-per-view event, an oppor-tunity many felt he didn't deserve.

As expected, Broner's personal life sold the show. The promotion before the Pacquiao fight played out predictably. The prefight legal drama that surrounded Adrien Broner's life became a key component of the Pacquiao vs. Broner narrative. On January 7, 2019, twelve days before the pay-per-view card, Broner faced two separate allegations of sexual misconduct in two courtrooms in two separate states. The first case, stemming from an incident that took place in February 2018 at an Atlanta shopping mall, alleged that Broner assaulted a woman, groping her against her will. In June of that same year, Broner was again arrested, this time in Cleveland, for forcing himself on a woman in a nightclub. Facing multiple felony counts, including gross sexual imposition and abduction, hearings for both cases were scheduled for January 7, 2019. Broner's lawyer attended the hearing in Cleveland. Broner, himself, skipped training camp to attend the hearing in Atlanta. The in-ring action also played out as expected. Manny Pacquiao, although past his prime, won a workmanlike unan-imous decision, retaining his WBA world welterweight championship by scores of 116-112 (twice) and 117-111. The issues Broner had in the Pacquiao bout didn't differ from the ones he had in his previous two fights. He couldn't or wouldn't throw enough punches to win rounds. After being staggered by a straight left hand from Pacquiao in the seventh round, Broner mostly retreated into survival mode the rest of the fight, landing only one punch in the twelfth and round.

"Bring your motherfuckin' ass over here, I got a lot to say," Broner shouted as Showtime's Jim Gray approached him with the microphone after interviewing Pacquiao after the fight.[223]

"We are going to conduct this professionally, or we are not going to have an interview. It's your decision. What did you think about the fight?" Gray responded sternly.

"Everybody out there know I beat him . . . they are trying to get that money again for Pacquiao vs. Floyd, everybody know it," Broner clapped back.

"You averaged eight punches a round," Gray flatly injected.

"It already sound like you against me. I don't appreciate that. . . . I wanna thank the whole hood for coming out here. I'm doing it for the hood," Broner said.

"You are 3-3-1 in his previous seven fights. What will you do next?" replied Gray.

To this, Broner quickly replied, "I may be 3-3-1 in my last seven fights but I'd be 7-0 against you." Jim Gray cut off the interview.

The customary boos, which often rang loud and clear after both victories and defeats, served as a fitting end to Adrien Broner's night.

Mostly because of his mounting legal troubles, Broner didn't fight in 2019 or 2020. Still trying to navigate his place in both hip-hop and boxing, Broner continually popped up at high-profile fights, making his presence known—and often embarrassing himself in the process.

At the Danny Garcia vs. Shawn Porter fight at Barclays Center, in September 2019, for example, Adrien Broner appeared intoxicated during a media appearance.

On November 2, 2019, AB allegedly showed up drunk and attempted to breach security to get into Canelo Alvarez's dressing room before his light heavyweight debut against Sergey Kovalev. After an altercation with security officials, Broner was arrested and transported to the Clark County jail, processed, and released with a misdemeanor trespassing charge.

Three months later, Broner got arrested at the weigh-in for Deontay Wilder's rematch with Tyson Fury, at the same arena, and was cuffed and removed from the property by Las Vegas police.

Less than a month after Wilder–Fury II, in March 2020, Adrien Broner was found passed out in his black Rolls-Royce SUV with the engine running. After being woken by police and given a sobriety test, the troubled boxer was arrested and charged with a DUI.

Soon after, Broner temporarily disappeared from social media, prompting some to speculate that he had finally hit rock bottom.

In the spring of 2020, amid the peak of the COVID-19 pandemic, Broner emerged from his self-imposed seclusion, breaking his silence in an erratic two-minute video posted to Instagram. The rant, recorded on Broner's cell phone as he drove down the street, conjured a bizarre 2016 incident where the troubled boxer alarmed fans by threatening to commit suicide in a series of cryptic countdown posts, one of which featured an image of a gun.

"I ain't gonna lie, I been staying in Cincinnati for like the last month. And this shit done changed me all the way back. When you see me, don't call me AB no more. I'm Twin. This shit changed me all the way back to Twin. If they ain't talking about my $10 million, Al Haymon, Stephen Espinoza, they ain't hit me up. They ain't talking about my 10. This shit over with," said Broner as he sped down the street, occasionally fixing his eyes away from the camera, his long, unkempt beard showing signs of gray for the first time.[224]

Broner continued: "I'm at the point now where, I might rob you. Say something stupid to me, I might rob you. Just because. I dare one of you rappers to try me. I'm gonna knock one of y'all out on camera and put it up [on social media]. What y'all gonna do, sue me? Then your career will be over. If you want to go into some extra street shit, I'ma shoot the fuck out of you. If they ain't talking about my 10, fuck that, I'm Twin. I'm a rapper, I'm a full-time rapper. . . . Until they talk about my 10 million, I ain't gonna be in the ring, I'ma be in the studio. I'm a rapper now."

A few days after posting the video to Instagram, on May 10, 2020, Broner, and Cincinnati rapper Cook LaFlare, released a surprise EP titled *ABC*. The six-track album featured all of the stylistic moves you might suspect from the trap-music/mumble-rap era. Broner's vocals are delivered through auto-tune. Most of the songs on the EP focus on street life and flaunting material wealth. Broner's ambivalence toward his legal issues are on full display throughout.

"Couple of months I had to lay low / Dropped a 100 now the case closed," Broner rhymes on "Something New."

As expected, *ABC* wasn't a hit. It hardly registered on hip-hop's radar, prompting critics to mock the boxer's full-time shift toward rap music. Bad reviews and low record sales would be the least of Broner's concerns, however. Following the release of *ABC*, he was arrested in Miami and charged with his second DUI of the summer. Two months later, on November 2, 2020, Cuyahoga County Common Pleas Court Judge Nancy Margaret Russo held Broner in contempt of court as part of a civil lawsuit filed by the woman he allegedly assaulted in a Cleveland nightclub back in 2018. On multiple occasions, the thirty-one-year-old boxer failed to make deadlines the judge had set for him to present documents and other evidence demonstrating why he was unable to pay the more than $800,000 judgment. Citing videos posted the previous week on Instagram, showing Broner flaunting stacks of money, the judge ordered Broner to remain in jail until he could provide "complete and truthful information about his finances" to the victim's attorney.

Broner attempted to convince the court that he was flat broke, claiming the stacks of money featured on his Instagram account had been wired to him by wealthy friends in the boxing world. It didn't work. Broner's attorney stated that his client had "issues of mental illness and alcohol abuse and relied on others, namely his mother and his manager and promoter, to handle his finances,"[225] adding that Broner relied on them so heavily that he did not know whether he owned or leased his vehicles or whose name his house in Florida was under. The desperate plea was, in the end, ignored. Officers led Broner out of the courtroom in handcuffs.

During his turbulent career, Adrien Broner built a record of (34-4-1-1, 24 KOs) and captured world titles in four weight divisions. All of this will likely be seen as a disappointment. Almost by himself Broner redirected popular notions about hip-hop's place in the boxing. "The Problem," for many, continues to be an enigma.

Eric B.: "You can be a plumber one day and a rapper the next. So I had no problem with a world champion boxer like Broner rapping. When it comes to Broner, outside the ring, I don't think you throw the baby out with the bath water. You gotta go back and look at all the other troubled boxers. I loved Pernell Whitaker but he definitely got in trouble often. You can't put that all on Broner and say he was a bad ambassador for boxing or bad for hip-hop. He didn't bring the sport down, he didn't make hip-hop look bad. He was only embarrassing to his family and his team and to himself. It wasn't that hip-hop was a bad influence on Broner or that boxing went down the drain because of him. Adrien talked a lot, brought a lot of attention to himself, but he is also the one that had to pay the price for all that in the end."

Adrien Broner's rise marked a pivotal, and perhaps problematic, shift in both boxing and hip-hop history. The question is whether Broner's fall marks the end or the beginning of a new era. For New York emcee R.A. the Rugged Man, the answer is the latter.

R.A. the Rugged Man: "Back when Roy Jones Jr. released 'Y'all Must've Forgot,' none of us [in hip-hop] took that music seriously. It was cool but it wasn't really competition. It wasn't topping the charts. It wasn't being played in the clubs. We didn't think of him as a rapper. But now, looking back, I think the song was ahead of its time. It came at a unique time in hip-hop, a moment of change. In the 1980s you had a lot of uplifting music. Brand Nubian. Public Enemy. KRS-One. The Poor Righteous Teachers. You had a lot of antidrug records as a response to the New York City crack epidemic. But by the time Floyd Mayweather Jr. became champion, hip-hop culture had already become this dumbed-down, get-the-money, flash-money-at-the-camera type of era. Floyd wanted to embody that persona and be around those people. But at that point guys like Roy and Floyd really couldn't have been taken seriously as rappers. They couldn't have actually made the transition despite everybody having a record company back then."

R.A. the Rugged Man continued: "Now, today, we are in this non-lyrical era where nobody has to actually rhyme, you don't have to be a dope rapper anymore. The door is open for boxers like Broner to make that leap. If you come up with a catchy hook and repeat it over and over again, you can be a rapper. We live in a celebrity-obsessed culture now. In today's [hip-hop] world, all you have to be is a celebrity, you don't have to spit lessons like an Inspectah Deck."

The decline of Adrien "The Problem" Broner's boxing career shouldn't be seen as a sign of the demise of boxing's hip-hop era. It is unlikely that bombastic ring walks and inaudible prefight concerts are, even in a post-COVID-19 landscape, going to disappear anytime soon, as evidenced by Gervonta "Tank" Davis's entrance against Leo Santa Cruz at the Alamodome in October 2020, the first high-profile boxing match to feature fans after the pandemic lockdown. Colombian reggaeton star J Balvin's performance before Canelo Alvarez's ring walk for his defense against Avni Yildirim at Hard Rock Stadium in Miami in February 2021 also demonstrates the continued cross-cultural allure of the tradition. Fighters will always want to become rappers and rappers will always admire fighters. Some, as boxing history shows, will try to be both.

Adrien Broner's life story is a testament to the depths of hip-hop's connection to the sport of boxing. Broner's life and career, like those of Floyd Mayweather Jr., Zab Judah, Roy Jones Jr., Mike Tyson, and so many others, remind us that boxing and hip-hop will always maintain an intimate relationship because of the proximity in which both art forms draw their talent pools.

Both fighters and rappers are bound by struggle. As long as cyclical poverty, economic exploitation, and marginalized peoples exist, there will be boxing. And in those communities, there will always be fathers who take their sons to rickety boxing gyms as a means of survival, uncles who coax their nephews into backyard boxing matches. Hip-hop, as the stories of D Smoke and Adrien Broner attest, operates under these same parameters.

Lou DiBella: "Boxing and hip-hop aren't from different worlds. Think Bed-Stuy, Brownsville, the South Bronx, Washington Heights, and Spanish Harlem. All of Harlem, really. Those areas produce great rappers and great fighters. The common denominator is the struggle, fighting or rapping your way out of those circumstances. It is not an accident these guys are hanging together. If you come from not much, you come from the streets, and you are trying to better yourself. There is no accident there is crossover."

"Think about it. *Get Rich or Die Tryin'* . . . ain't that boxing?" DiBella continued, pausing briefly to consider his own argument.

AFTERWORD

DON'T CALL IT A COMEBACK

I n both hip-hop and boxing, retirements are rarely taken seriously. In 1996, Too Short became one of the first rappers to officially announce his retirement from the game. His decision would, of course, not last. The same can be said for Jay-Z who, on a few occasions in his career, marketed albums as being his last. Boxing history is full of stories like this. And like the remix to a collaboration that never materialized, 2020 offered fight fans the most surprising and unlikely of nostalgic throwback jams, one that reignited conversations about hip-hop's effect on the fight game.

On May 1, 2020, former two-time heavyweight champion "Iron" Mike Tyson shocked the world by posting a brief snippet of training footage on his social media platforms. In the footage, Tyson appeared in prime shape, cracking the hand pads with snapping force, demonstrating impressive hand speed.

Three days later, MMA trainer Rafael Cordeiro, who had been conducting private workouts with the former heavyweight champion, stoked the public's curiosity by stating that Tyson, at fifty-four years old, was indeed ready to make a comeback. Six days later, Tyson's team released a second, extended, training montage on the boxer's Instagram page. At the end of the twenty-one-second video, a rapid-fire series of training clips, Tyson, drenched in sweat, turns to the camera and boldly states, "I'm back!"

Few knew what to make of the cryptic message. While there was no denying that Tyson, who had reportedly lost over a hundred pounds, was in spectacular condition, many viewed the social media posts as part of a calculated rebranding effort. Following the release of the training videos, for example, Tyson made two appearances on *All Elite Wrestling* on TNT. In back-to-back episodes, Tyson took on professional wrestler Cody Rhodes and engaged in a face-off with former WWE rival Chris Jericho.

After appearing on the professional wrestling series, Tyson continued to release training footage on social media, pitching the urban clothing brand Chinatown Market while doing so. The Instagram endorsements, coupled with the news that Tyson would star in the Discovery Channel's upcoming Shark Week program *Tyson vs. Jaws: Rumble on the Reef*, tempered expectations that any real comeback would happen.

On July 23, 2020, an unofficial announcement was made public via a twelve-second video clip posted to both fighters' Instagram accounts. In the video, Mike Tyson and Roy Jones Jr. connected via a conference call, each appearing to sign contracts.

Somewhere in Houston, Texas, rap mogul James Prince, the Rap-A-Lot CEO who had worked tirelessly to stage a Tyson–Jones megafight seventeen years before, must have been, like the rest of us, filled with mixed emotions.

✳ ✳ ✳

The Tyson–Jones Instagram video was a viral sensation, attracting the attention of mainstream-media outlets across the globe. From MTV to ESPN, E! News to BET, the event's crossover potential was clear from the start. For the hip-hop community, perhaps more so than any other sector of American subculture, the improbable matchup held nostalgic significance.

Eric B.: "Before it was announced, when I started hearing things, I called up Nas. I was like, 'Yo, Nas, they talking about Mike fighting Roy.' He said, 'C'mon E., Roy ain't gonna fight Mike. You must be out your mind.' Then, a few weeks later, when it was announced, Nas hit me back up. He said, 'E. you was right again.' I told him, 'You know I'm a boxing insider."

Hosted on the social media app Triller and broadcast on traditional pay-per-view, the eight-round Tyson–Jones exhibition was originally scheduled to take place at Dignity Health Sports Park in California on September 12, 2020. Both men would wear twelve-ounce gloves but neither would wear protective headgear. To account for the age of the participants, two-minute rounds were instituted. The California State Athletic Commission, which did not officially appoint judges to score the fight, contended that if either fighter was cut or suffered a knockdown, the fight would be stopped.

While the buzz was undeniable, reactions to the particulars of the event were varied. Roy Jones Jr., at fifty-one years old, had not competed in a boxing ring for over three years. The fifty-four-year-old Tyson, aside from a 2006 public sparring session against heavyweight Corrie Sanders, had been away from the sport for over fifteen years. Some saw the exhibition as an unnecessarily dangerous risk for two aging fighters. Others speculated as to how *real* the action would really be.

When the co-feature to the Tyson–Jones exhibition was announced, a six-round professional fight pitting three-time Slam Dunk Contest Champion Nate Robinson, a former NBA player with no boxing experience whatsoever, against YouTube influencer Jake Paul, naysayers quickly labeled the event nothing more than a spectacle. The addition of hip-hop stars Lil Wayne, French Montana, Wiz Khalifa, and YG, each slated to take part in multi-song performances during the pay-per-view telecast, did little to temper skepticism among those who considered the event a circus act.

There were also those who believed Triller could not pull it off. When the company released an announcement, on August 9, 2020, postponing the event until November 28 of that year, stating organizers needed more time to iron out the details of the international TV deals, rumors swirled that Roy Jones Jr. wanted additional compensation for the delay. Tyson, reports suggested, was slated to make $10 million. Roy was guaranteed $3 million. With no possibility of a live gate because of COVID-19, a strange mix of hoopla and trepidation surrounded the promotion.

From a marketing standpoint, the buildup to the promotion was a disaster. In the weeks leading up to the exhibition, California State

Athletic Commission executive director Andy Foster, in an attempt to stave off critics, classified the action as nothing more than "hard sparring." Triller, on the other hand, worked to assure fight fans the action would be intense. Both Tyson and Jones did their part in promoting the event, talking the talk, so to speak.

"Listen, I don't know what you're talking about. My objective is to go in there with the best intentions of my life and disable my opponent. You've got Mike Tyson and Roy Jones Jr. and I'm coming to fight. I hope he is," Tyson said when asked about Foster's statements.

"Last guy that did an exhibition with Mike got dropped in the first round. If you don't know that, something wrong with you. Who goes in the ring with the great, legendary Mike Tyson and think it's just an exhibition? Twelve-ounce gloves. No headgear. C'mon, bruh," Jones added.

✳ ✳ ✳

The delay, despite the ongoing confusion, only served to build more interest in the event. Eventually moved to the Staples Center, home to the Lakers, the Tyson–Jones exhibition proved to be a box-office success, generating over 1.2 million buys.

In something of an upset, Tyson–Jones did not turn out to be the black eye for the sport many predicted. By all accounts, the production quality of the event was superb. Emmy-winner Mario Lopez played host during the countdown show, also introducing rap artists before their performances. Showtime veteran Jim Gray played the role of roving reporter. The play-by-play duties were superbly handled by Showtime's Mauro Ranallo, Sugar Ray Leonard, and UFC middleweight champion Israel Adesanya. Ring announcer Michael Buffer delivered his trademark "Let's Get Ready to Rumble," emerging from his brief COVID-19-induced hiatus from the sport. The three undercard bouts were action-packed and superbly matched. The empty Staples Center, transformed into a visually stunning set, also worked as both a high-tech concert venue and futuristic boxing stage.

The successful infusion of hip-hop music into the telecast was perhaps the biggest upset of the night. While boxing/hip-hop–themed promotions such as *KO Nation* and ThunderBox were, in the past, widely panned for their forced approach to mixing music and sport, the performances by French Montana and Swae Lee, Wiz Khalifa, YG, Saint Jhn, and Snoop

Dogg, who replaced Lil Wayne on the bill, were received positively on social media, overcoming the perceived cultural and generational gap the all-hip-hop lineup presented to viewers.

Snoop Dogg, a last-minute addition to the broadcast, stole the show. As a lead-in to the main event, Snoop Dogg performed a montage of his greatest hits, many of which were chart-topping hits during the Tyson and Jones eras. For the final two bouts of the night, Snoop joined the play-by-play crew as an analyst, where the rap star sent Twitter ablaze with his hilarious, impromptu commentary.

"Precious Lord, take my hand, lead me home, let me stand," Snoop sang, invoking a hymn to describe his reaction to Nate Robinson as he struggled to pick himself up off the canvas after suffering a thunderous right hand from YouTuber Logan Paul.

Moments later, after a second overhand right sent the former NBA star tumbling face-first to the canvas, Snoop alluded to another well-known song.

"Good night, Irene," Snoop joked. "Oh, Lord!"

Impressed celebrities, including LeBron James, 50 Cent, Stephen A. Smith, Steph Curry, Flea (of the Red Hot Chili Peppers), Blake Snell, Jemele Hill, Frank Thomas, Adrian Peterson, Dwyane Wade, Zach LaVine, Tyus Jones, and Donovan Mitchell, lit up Twitter with praise and calls for more Snoop Dogg broadcasts. Among those impressed by Snoop's skills was hip-hop star Eric B., with whom I spoke with over the phone the following week.

"Snoop's commentary was second to none. It was the highlight of the night for me. Some boxing network needs to sign him up. Snoop had all of us in hip-hop texting back and forth," Eric B. said.

Snoop's prefight concert set the nostalgic tempo for a cross-cultural matchup seventeen years in the making.

"Hearing those songs kind of took you back to those years. The Tyson–Jones years. Snoop was phenomenal. It was a smart move on [Triller's] part," Eric B. added.

As expected, Roy Jones Jr. walked to the ring to his own original music, a track titled "Never Switch Sides," featuring Body Head recording artist SM Bullett. Roy's trunks and robe, embroidered with a fighting gamecock insignia, paid tribute to fallen NBA star Kobe Bryant, who was tragically killed in a helicopter crash in January 2020.

Tyson's ensemble also held symbolic significance. His trademark black towel paid homage to the neighborhood where his journey first began, Brownsville. His black trunks were embroidered with the name of his four-year-old daughter (Exodus Tyson) who died in a tragic accident involving a treadmill in 2009.

With both Tyson and Jones in the same boxing ring, for the first time, pacing back and forth, the importance of the event for both men was clear. It was an exhibition only on paper. For many of us who enjoyed their brilliance in the ring, it was more—an imperfect sense of closure but closure just the same.

* * *

At first, Tyson provided brief glimpses of his former self, using side-to-side head movement as he moved forward, throwing hooks to Roy Jones Jr.'s ribcage. Jones, displaying slightly faster hand speed, played matador, snapping his jab as he moved around the ring, attempting to use footwork and angles to slip punches, occasionally switching to a southpaw stance.

"This shit like two uncles fighting at a BBQ . . . look at my uncles out there fighting. Grandma gonna have to break this one up," Snoop called, in one of the most talked-about moments in the rapper's debut as a boxing commentator.

"Grandma, they out there fighting again," Snoop continued.

"Snoop phrased it just right. Hip-hop loves Mike. We love Roy. It was like hip-hop's two uncles out there fighting in the backyard," Eric B. said.

While neither Tyson nor Jones were physically capable of recapturing their youth, the exhibition wasn't without sporadic moments of action. In the second round, for example, Tyson crouched low and landed a solid right hand.

"That was a lowrider move right there, he dipped real low," Snoop Dogg joked.

As one might suspect from two men in their fifties, the bout was mostly sloppy. In between rounds, both men looked exhausted. Tyson occasionally landed powerful double left hooks to the body. Jones, who spent much of the night clinching, occasionally landed jabs and check hooks.

To the delight of all involved, the sixteen-minute exhibition produced no serious injuries. In going the eight-round distance, both Tyson and

Jones were able to save face, providing their fans with one final glimpse of what made them special. The final verdict was inconsequential.

Scored by former WBC champions Christy Martin, Chad Dawson, and Vinny Paz, the bout was unofficially ruled a draw. At a post-fight press conference, both fighters were awarded custom WBC belts. Tyson, who was widely seen as the actual winner of the contest, cared little about the decision. In the post-fight interview, both men showed glimpses of their one-of-a-kind personalities. The post-fight interview, like the pay-per-view promotion, did not disappoint.

"Mr. Tyson, what did you think of that? Did you think you won the fight?" Jim Gray asked.

"Yeah, but I'm good with a draw. I'm good with that. Because I entertained the crowd and they enjoyed it," Tyson replied.

"Hell naw. I ain't never satisfied with a draw. I wear draws, I don't do draws," Jones injected.

As the interview continued, Tyson playfully took exception to Jones, who had suffered several devastating knockouts in the latter stages of his career, being asked whether he was afraid of getting hurt before the fight.

"I was afraid I might get hurt!" Tyson injected, slightly redirecting Jim Gray's microphone.

"I didn't fight in twenty years, he only stopped fighting for three years. . . . Why'd nobody care about my ass?" Tyson continued.

Most viewed Tyson–Jones as an entertaining spectacle. Had it been anyone else, the event might have predictably played out as a disaster. Boxing purists, however, viewed Triller's success as an ominous sign of things to come. Following the exhibition, Snoop Dogg revealed plans to partner with Triller for "The Fight Club," a boxing league that fuses rap entertainment into its broadcasts. The "Triller effect," as it came to be known in the pejorative sense, had its detractors. In April 2021, for example, the company's second pay-per-view event, featuring YouTuber Jake Paul in the headlining bout, was heavily criticized by boxing's old guard. In June 2021, Floyd Mayweather Jr. joined in the fun, making his own nostalgic return to the ring, facing Jake Paul's brother, Logan, in an eight-round exhibition broadcast by Showtime. The Mayweather–Paul exhibition proved to be nothing more than a glorified sparring session. Mayweather himself referred to the matchup as "legalized bank robbery." His flashy ring walk, complete with back-to-back live performances by

Migos and Moneybagg Yo, served as a reminder of the event's core demographic appeal.

The winding path to Mike Tyson vs. Roy Jones Jr., like the four-decade-long relationship between boxing and hip-hop, is perhaps best described in the words of Snoop Dogg, who, before his broadcast debut, took a moment to reflect on the enduring cultural bond.

"Watching Mike Tyson fight we was inspired. When he heard our music, he was inspired. It was a brotherhood. It was like we was raised by different mothers but it was all one family. It's crazy how hip-hop and boxing is so connected," Snoop Dogg said.[226]

ACKNOWLEDGMENTS

"Shout-outs" are a staple of both hip-hop and boxing because no rap star, or fighter, views their success as individual. Listen to any outro track, or post-fight interview, and you will know exactly what I mean. "It wouldn't be hip-hop without a ton of shout-outs," scholar Jeff Chang once wrote. I agree.

This book, as has been the case with each of its three predecessors, is dedicated to my wife, Stephanie, and son, Huntington Jay. If I have done anything right in life it has been to know my passions and follow them. Doing so has brought both of you into my world. Thank you for inspiring me.

BeatBoxing would not have been possible without the support of my family. I want to thank my mother, Cheryl, for ordering those subscriptions to *The Source* and *The Ring* back in the day. Consider this book a late return on your investment. I want to thank my father, Mike "Lo" Snyder, for introducing me to the sport of boxing. I am grateful that we share this bond. I also want to thank my sister, Katie; my brother-in-law, Zach Tonkin; and my nephew, Carter Daniel, for their unwavering love and support. To my aunt, Michele, a special thank you for bringing hip-hop into my orbit back in 1987. I love the Nutter fam with all of my heart.

To those who have put up with my endless boxing/hip-hop chatter over the years: Johnathan "Hollywood" Winkler, Billy "The Pittsburgh Kid" Greer and the Greer Fam, Ryan "Monk" Greene and the GreenE clique, Bradley Bennett, Matt Clayton, Leonard Boggess, Jeff "Flex" LeMasters, Josh Iddings, Jesse Moya, Erich Hertz, Paul Ciullo, "The Mayor" Bill Womer, Devesh Chandra, and Roman Jaquez—thank you. I consider each of you a part of this journey.

Next I would like to thank the boxing luminaries and hip-hop icons who agreed to be interviewed during a global pandemic. In a time of unparalleled fear and uncertainty, you took hours out of your busy lives to share your stories with me. For this, I will be forever grateful. I couldn't have written this book without your insight.

On the boxing side, I want to thank Zab "Super" Judah, James "Lights Out" Toney, Bernard "The Executioner" Hopkins, Montell "Ice" Griffin, Michael Bentt, Sergio "The Latin Snake" Mora, Chris Byrd, "Terrible" Tim Witherspoon, DeMarcus "Chop Chop" Corley, Hector Camacho Jr., Heather "The Heat" Hardy, Kermit Cintrón, Reggie Johnson, Lou DiBella, Lee Groves, Michael Woods, Justin Hoffman, John Lepak, Aris Pina, Manouk Akopyan, and "The Coal Miner's Daughter" Christy Martin.

On the hip-hop side, I want to thank Bill Adler, Rakim, Big Daddy Kane, Eric B., Professor Griff, Vinnie Paz, D Smoke, Peter Gunz, R.A. the Rugged Man, Khalid el-Hakim, and Akil Houston. To my Wu-Tang Clan brethren Inspectah Deck, Masta Killa, Mathematics, and Bronze Nazareth, a special thank you.

I also want to thank those who have been critical to the success of Siena College's Hip-Hop Week program (and to my career as a hip-hop scholar). To Kareem "Biggs" Burke, Grandmaster Flash, Chuck D, Biz Markie, Titan Fredericks, Sha-Rock, Ben Ortiz, Alfredo Medina, Brother George Camacho, Christa Grant, and Valencia Gomez, I owe much gratitude.

On the publishing side, I want to thank Kyle Sarofeen and Andy Komack for believing in my vision. As writer, I couldn't possibly hope for a better home. Hamilcar is the squad: #WU93. We did it again, my brothers. Thank you.

On the academic side, I am thankful for the influence of my colleagues at Marshall University: Mary Moore, Katherine Rodier (R.I.P.), Kathy Seelinger, Thelma Isaacs, Edmund Taft, Roxanne Kirkwood Aftanas,

Kelli Prejean, Kristen Lillvis, and Jana Tigchelaar; Ohio University: Dinty W. Moore, Sherrie Gradin, Jennie Nelson, Mara Holt, George Hartley, Candace Stewart, Albert Rouzie, Matthew Stallard, and Ayesha Hardison; and Siena College: Jack Collins, Holly Grieco, Nate Leslie (R.I.P.), Keith Wilhite, Meg Woolbright, Chris Farnan, Chingyen Mayer, Stacey Dearing, Shannon Draucker, James Belflower, and Tim Cooper.

I am also grateful for the brilliant students who occupy my "Rhetoric(s) of Hip-Hop Culture" courses each spring. You continually remind me of how much I love hip-hop.

And finally, I would like to thank every single person who has ever asked how a trailer-park boy from Cowen, West Virginia, the son of a coal miner, could possibly fall in love with hip-hop. Your inquiries, regardless of their intentions, have, over the years, helped me articulate the allure. In conducting research for this book, I discovered just how connected we all are.

"I was born in New York but my people from West Virginia, too. Beckley. My dad, John Abraham Griffin, worked in the mines. He died of black lung disease. We have a lot in common, man," Public Enemy's Professor Griff said to me, moments into our first interview.

When Grandmaster Flash visited my hip-hop course at Siena in March 2015, we spent most of our time arguing whether Floyd Mayweather Jr. was ducking Manny Pacquiao. Boxing, even more than our mutual love for hip-hop, was the spark. The same thing happened when Chuck D, Masta Killa, and Biz Markie visited my campus in later years.

I am not from the hip-hop community. But I am from the bottom. This is of course where most of us in boxing and hip-hop start our journeys. This is our bond.

Aside from my family, boxing and hip-hop are what I enjoy most in life. I am humbled and grateful for the opportunity to write this book.

To all of the writers and fighters who have most inspired my work, I am grateful for your talent and courage.

—*Todd D. Snyder*

APPENDIXES: A COMPILATION OF HIP-HOP & BOXING SONGS

APPENDIX A: SONGS THAT REFERENCE BOXING PERSONALITIES

As stated in the introduction, Appendix A does not pretend to be a comprehensive list. Rather, it is a snapshot of five hundred moments in music history where boxing personalities (fighters, trainers, promoters, ring announcers, managers, etc.) show up in hip-hop. The database is meant to demonstrate the frequency by which boxing shows up in hip-hop discourse, nothing more. The songs listed in Appendices B, C, and D were not included in the data analyzed in the introduction. I list this information separately for future researchers, to help provide a clear picture of hip-hop's impact on professional boxing.

Laila Ali: Five songs
AZ (feat. Consequence). "Heavy in Da Game." Anthology: B-Sides & Unreleased. BEC Music, 2008.
Eminem & Royce da 5'9". "Take from Me." *Hell: The Sequel.* Shady Records, 2011.
Jim Jones (feat. Cam'ron, Juelz Santana, and Max B). "Pin the Tail." *Hustler's P.O.M.E.* Kotch Records, 2006.
Lil' Romeo. "The One." *Romeoland.* The New No Limit, 2004.
Yo Gatti. "Shorty Violatin." *Back 2 Da Basics.* TVT Records, 2006.

Muhammad Ali: Eighty-five songs
Above the Law. "Clinic 2000." *Time Will Reveal.* Tommy Boy, 1996.
Beastie Boys. "Alive." *Anthology: The Sounds of Science.* Capitol, 1999.
Benny the Butcher. "Legend." *Burden of Proof.* Griselda, 2020.

Big Boi (feat. Jay-Z and Killer Mike). "Flip Flop Rock." *Speakerboxxx/The Love Below*. Arista, 2003.

Biz Markie. "Party to Da-Break-A-Day." *Weekend Warrior*. Tommy Boy, 2003.

Busta Rhymes (feat. Jamal, Redman, Keith Murray, and Rampage). "Flipmode Squad Meets Def Squad." *The Coming*. Elektra, 1996.

Camp Lo. "B Side Hollywood." *Uptown Saturday Night*. Profile, 1997.

Chance the Rapper. "Missing You." *10 Day*. Chance LLC, 2012.

Child Rebel Solider. "Don't Stop." *Good Fridays Mixtape*. Good Music, 2010.

Chino XL. "Have 2." *Ricanstruction: The Black Rosary*. Viper, 2012.

Common. "The Game." *Finding Forever*. Good Music, 2007.

Conway the Machine. (feat. Pete Rock). "Piper." *Everybody Is F.O.O.D.* Griselda, 2018.

Diplomats. "Bigger Picture." *Diplomatic Immunity*. Koch Records, 2004.

Dogg Pound. "Don't Sweat It." *Cali Iz Active*. Doggystyle, 2006.

Dr. Dre (feat. Snoop Dogg and Jon Connor). "One Shot, One Kill." *Compton*. Aftermath, 2015.

Drake. "Under Ground Kings." *Take Care*. Young Money, 2012.

Eminem. "Chloraseptic (remix)." *Revival*. Aftermath, 2017.

Eminem. "Groundhog Day." *The Marshall Mathers LP 2*. Aftermath, 2013.

Eminem. "My Darling." *Relapse*. Aftermath, 2009.

Eminem. "The Greatest." *Kamikaze*. Aftermath, 2018.

EPMD. "Blow." *We Mean Business*. RBC, 2013.

EPMD. "Only a Customer." *Strictly Business*. Priority, 2010.

Erick Sermon. "Payback II." *No Pressure*. Def Jam, 1993.

50 Cent. "Many Men (Wish Death Upon Me)." *Get Rich or Die Tryin*. Aftermath, 2003.

Freeway (feat. Beanie Sigel). "Roc the Mic." *State Property*. Roc-A-Fella, 2002.

French Montana (feat. Tyga and Ace Hood). "Thrilla in Manilla." *Mac & Cheese 3*. Evil Empire, 2012.

Fugees. "Ready or Not." *The Score*. Ruffhouse, 1996.

Game (feat. Rock Ross and 2 Chainz). "Ali Bomyae." *Jesus Piece*. Interscope, 2012.

Game. "New York, New York." *The Documentary 2.5*. One Music, 2015.

Gucci Mane. "Classic." *The State vs. Radric Davis*. Warner, 2009.

Ice Cube. "Stop Snitchin." *Laugh Now, Cry Later*. Lench Mob Records, 2006.

Jay-Z. "F.U.T.W." *Magna Carta Holy Grail*. Roc Nation, 2013.

Jay-Z. "Some People Hate." *The Blueprint 2: The Gift and the Curse*. Roc-A-Fella, 2002.

Jay-Z. "We Family FUTW." *Magna Carta Holy Grail*. Roc Nation, 2017.

Jay-Z and Beyonce (feat. Childish Gambino). "Mood 4 Eva." *The Lion King: The Gift*. Columbia, 2019.

Jay-Z and Kanye West. "Primetime." Watch the Throne. Roc-A-Fella, 2011.

Jim Jones (feat. Cam'ron and Game). "Certified Gangstas." *Ryder Musik*. Birds Fly Inc., 2004.

Juelz Santana (feat. Razah). "Back Again." *From Me to U*. Roc-A-Fella, 2003.

Kanye West (feat. Raekwon). "Glorious." *My Beautiful Dark Twisted Fantasy*. Roc-A-Fella, 2010.

Kendrick Lamar. "Backseat Freestyle." *Good kid, m.A.A.d city.* Aftermath, 2012.

Kendrick Lamar. "Rigamortis." *Section.80.* Top Dawg, 2011.

Kevin Gates. "Fly Again." *I'm Him.* Bread Winners, 2019.

Kevin Gates. "Wish I Had It." *By Any Means.* Kevin Gates, 2014.

Kodack Black (feat. Gucci Mane and Rick Ross). "Pull a Caper." *Grateful.* Epic, 2017.

KRS-One. "True School." *DJ Jean Maron Presents . . . True School.* Bring Back Yesterday, 2014.

Lil Dicky. "Truman." *Professional Rapper.* BMG, 2015.

Lil Dicky. "Would You Believe That." *Hump Days.* BMG, 2014.

LL Cool J. "Momma Said Knock You Out." *Momma Said Knock You Out.* Def Jam, 1990.

Lloyd Banks. "Not Without My Glock." *The Big Withdraw.* G-Unit, 2005.

Logic. "Hallelujah." *Everybody.* Def Jam, 2017.

Lucas Joyner (feat. Mystikal). "FYM." *508-507-2209.* Atlantic, 2017.

Lupe Fiasco. "The Champ Is Here." *Fahrenheit 1/15: Part I.* Atlantic, 2005.

Mac Miller. "One Last Thing." *Blue Side Park.* Rostrum, 2011.

Master P. "Whole Hood." *Ghetto Bill: The Best Hustler in the Game.* No Limit, 2005.

Metro Boomin (feat. Offset and Drake). "No Complaints." *Not All Heroes Wear Capes.* Republic, 2017.

Migos. "Built Like Me." *No Label 2.* Quality Control, 2014.

Migos. "M&M's." *No Label 2.* Quality Control, 2014.

Mos Def. "Love." *Black on Both Sides.* Rawkus, 1999.

Nas (feat. Damian Marley). "My Generation." *Distant Relatives.* Republic, 2010.

Nas. "The Message." *It Was Written.* Columbia, 1996.

Nicki Minaj. "Win Again." *The Prinkprint.* Young Money, 2014.

Nipsey Hustle. "Rose Clique." *The Marathon Continues.* All Money In, 2011.

Ol' Dirty Bastard (feat. The Clipse and Pharell Williams). "Operator." *A Son Unique.* Def Jam, 2005.

Outkast (feat. Killer Mike and Jay-Z). "Flip Flop Rock." *Speakerboxxx/The Love Below.* Arista, 2003.

R.A. the Rugged Man. "The People's Champ." *Legends Never Die.* Nature Sounds, 2013.

Raekwon. "Shells Kitchen." *The Appetition.* Red Bull Music, 2020.

Rakim. "It's a Must." *The Master.* Universal, 1999.

Redman (feat. Ready Roc). "Coc Back." Single. Def Jam, 2009.

Reflection Eternal (feat. Jay Electronica). "Just Begun." *Revolutions per Minute.* Warner, 2010.

Rhymefest. "Can't Make It." *Man in the Mirror.* Allido Records, 2007.

Royce da 5'9". "Black Savage." *The Allegory.* Heaven Studios, 2020.

Slick Rick. "I Own America." *The Art of Storytelling.* Def Jam, 1999.

Spice 1. "Ghetto Star." *Ghetto Star.* Thug World, 2013.

Sugar Hill Gang. "Rapper's Delight." *Sugar Hill Gang.* Sugar Hill Records, 1979.

Talib Kweli (feat. MF Doom). "Right About Now." *Right About Now: The Official Sucka Free Mix CD.* Koch Records, 2005.

T.I. "No Matter What." *Paper Trail.* Grand Hustle, 2008.

T.I. "Rubber Band Man." *Trap Muzik*. Grand Hustle, 2003.

T.I. (feat. Lil Wayne). "Wit Me." *Wit Me*. Grand Hustle, 2013.

Timbaland & Magoo. "Clock Strikes." *Welcome to Our World*. Atlantic, 1997.

Vic Mensa. "Dynasty." *There's a Lot Going On*. Roc Nation, 2016.

Wale (feat. DJ Money). "Cassius Clay (Excellency)." Self-promotion EP. MMG, 2018.

Will Smith. "Getting Jiggy Wit It." *Big Willie Style*. Columbia, 1997.

Wu-Tang Clan. "7th Chamber." *Enter the Wu-Tang 36 Chambers*. Loud, 1993.

Wu-Tang Clan. "Slow Blues." *Wu-Tang Meets Indie Culture*. Babygrande, 2005.

YG. "Up." *Just Re'd Up*. Pu$haz Ink, 2011.

Riddick Bowe: Fourteen songs

Cru. "The Ebonic Plague." *Da Dirty 30*. Violator, 1997.

De La Soul. "Rock Co. Kane Flow." *The Grind Date*. Sanctuary Urban, 2004.

Dr. Dre (feat. Eminem and Xzibit). "What's the Difference." *Chronic 2001*. Aftermath, 1999.

Eminem (feat. Gwen Stefani). "Kings Never Die." *Southpaw: Original Soundtrack*. Shady, 2015.

Keith Murray (feat. Erick Sermon). "Pay-Per-View." *The Most Beautiful Thing in This World*. Jive, 1997.

Lupe Fiasco (feat. Travis Barker and Lil' Ron). "Joaquin Phoenix." *Friends of the People: I Fight Evil*. The Orchard, 2011.

Master P. "Something Funky for the Street." *The Ghetto Tryin' to Kill Me*. No Limit, 1997.

MC Breed (feat. 2Pac). "Comin' Real Again." *The New Breed*. Ichiban, 1993.

Onyx. "Flip That Shit." *Cold Case Fives*, Vol. 2. Major Independent, 2014.

Oukast. "Millennium." *ATLiens*. LaFace, 1996.

Sean Price. "Prisoner." *Imperius Rex*. Ruck Down, 2017.

Smif N Wessun. "Wreckonize." *Dah Shinin*. Wreck/Nervous, 1995.

Souls of Mischief. "A Name I Call Myself." *93 'Till Infinity*. Jive, 1993.

Tech N9ne. "Make Waves." *Strangulation*. Strange Music, 2014.

James Braddock: One song

R.A. the Rugged Man. "Bang Boogie." *Legends Never Die*. Nature Sounds, 2013.

Shannon Briggs: Three songs

Public Enemy. "Shake Yo Booty." *He Got Game: Official Soundtrack*. Def Jam, 1998.

Royce da 5'9". "Dead Presidents Heads." *Trust the Shooter*. Heaven Studios, 2016.

Sean Price. "Prisoner." *Imperius Rex*. Ruck Down, 2017.

Adrien "The Problem" Broner: Two songs

Fabolous (feat. Jadakiss). "The Hope." *The Soul Tape 3*. Def Jam, 2013.

Migos (feat. Rich Homie Quan). "Falicia." *Back to the Bando*, Vol. 2. Quality Control, 2015.

Michael Buffer: Five songs
Big Tymers. "Broads." *How You Luv That*. Cash Money, 1998.
Dogg Pound. "Heavyweightz." *Cali Iz Active*. Doggystyle, 2016.
Game (feat. Young Jeezy). "Paramedics." *The R.E.D. Album*. Interscope, 2011.
Juelz Santana. "Violence." *What the Game's Been Missing*. Def Jam, 2005.
Lupe Fiasco. "Much More." *Fahrenheit 1/15: Part II: Revenge of the Nerds*.
   Lupe Fiasco, 2006.

Hector Camacho: Six songs
AZ (feat. Nas). "The Essence." *Aziatic*. Motown, 2002.
Cam'ron. "Come Kill Me." *S.D.E.* Epic, 2000.
Lil Wayne. "I'm Raw." *The Carter III Mixtape*. Cash Money, 2008.
Lil Wayne (feat. Jay-Z). "Mr. Carter." *Tha Carter III*. Cash Money, 2008.
Notorious B.I.G. (feat. Eminem). "Dead Wrong." *Born Again*. Bad Boy, 1999.
The Diplomats. "Dipset Anthem." *Diplomatic Immunity*. Roc-A-Fella, 2003.

Julio César Chávez: Two songs
Jedi Mind Tricks (feat. GZA). "On the Eve of War." *The Best of Jedi Mind
   Tricks*. BabyGrande, 2016.
Wu-Tang Clan. "The MGM." *Wu-Tang Forever*. Loud, 1997.

Gerry Cooney: Two songs
Erick Sermon. "Payback II." *No Pressure*. Def Jam, 1993.
Fu-Schnickens. "True Fuschnick." *F.U. Don't Take It Personal*. Zomba, 1992.

Miguel Cotto: Six songs
50 Cent. "Put Your Hands Up." *The Big Ten Mixtape*. G-Unit, 2011.
Lil Wayne (feat. Gudda Gudda). "It's Young Money." *We Are Young Money*.
   Young Money, 2009.
Pusha T. "Lunch Money." Single. Good Music, 2014.
Remy Ma. "Another One." Single. Terror Squad, 2017.
Wale (feat. Meek Mill and J. Cole). "Black Grammys." *Self Made Vol. 3*. MMG,
   2013.
Westside Gunn. "Lil Cease." *Flygod Is an Awesome God 2*. Griselda, 2020.

Cus D'Amato: Two songs
Cam'ron. "Bubble Music." *Purple Haze*. Roc-A-Fella, 2004.
Nas (feat. Foxy Brown). "Watch Dem Niggaz." *It Was Written*. Columbia,
   1996.

Gervonta "Tank" Davis: Two songs
Conway the Machine and Big Ghost Ltd. (feat. Flee Lord). "Sicarios." *No One
   Mourns the Wicked*. Big Ghost Ltd. Music, 2020.
Westside Gunn. "No Vacancy." *Pray for Paris*. Griselda, 2020.

Jack Dempsey: Ten songs
Craig Mack. "Real Raw." *Funk da World*. Bad Boy, 1994.
Das EFX. "Real Hip-Hop." *Hold It Down*. East West Records, 1995.
Dogg Pound. "Me In Your World." *Doggy Bag*. Death Row, 2012.
Kool G Rap. "Let the Games Begin." *Roots of Evil*. Downlow Records, 1998.
Meek Mill. "Intro." *Dreamchasers 2*. Warner Brothers, 2012.
MF Doom. "New Beginning." *On the Ropes: Original Motion Picture
   Soundtrack*. Milan Records, 1999.

Nas. "Loco-Motive." *Life Is Good*. Def Jam, 2012.

Raekwon. "Came Up." *Lost Jewelry*. Ice H20 Records, 2013.

Salt-N-Pepa. "Swift." *Blacks' Magic*. Next Plateau Records Inc., 1990.

Slaughterhouse. "House Gang." *Funk Flex: Who You Mad At? Me or Yourself?* Loud, 2013.

James "Buster" Douglas: Seven songs

A Tribe Called Quest. "Vibes and Stuff." *The Low End Theory*. Zomba, 1991.

Consequence (feat. Rhymefest). "Yard 2 Yard." *Take 'Em to the Cleaners*. Sure Shot, 2004.

Fugees. "Blunted Interlude." *Blunted on Reality*. Ruffhouse, 1994.

Phryme (feat. Slaughterhouse). "Microphone Preemee." *Phryme*. Phryme Records, 2015.

Pitbull. "I Wonder." *M.I.A.M.I.* The Orchard, 2004.

Rapsody. "New Black Love." *A Tribute to Black Dynamite*. Jamla, 2014.

Vinnie Paz. "And Your Blood Will Blot Out the Sun." *God of the Serengeti*. Enemy Soil, 2012.

Angelo Dundee: One song

Too Short. "Short Dog's Wedding." *The Pimp Tape*. Dangerous Music, 2017.

Roberto Duran: Four songs

Kool Keith. "Black Elvis." *Black Elvis/Lost in Space*. Ruffhouse, 1999.

Missy Elliot (feat. Jay-Z). "One Minute Man" (remix). *Miss E . . . So Addictive*. Elektra, 2001.

R.A. the Rugged Man (feat. Vinnie Paz). "Sam Peckinpah." *Legends Never Die*. Nature Sounds, 2013.

Redman (feat. Busta Rhymes). "Da Goodness." *Doc's Da Name 2000*. Def Jam, 1998.

Lou Duva: One song

Jedi Mind Tricks. "When the Body Goes Cold." *The Bridge and the Abyss*. Enemy Soil, 2018.

George Foreman: Fifteen songs

Common (feat. Bilal). "Gladiator." *Universal Mind Control*. Good Music, 2008.

Ghostface Killah. "Barber Shop." *Fishscale*. Def Jam, 2006.

Jadakiss. "Knock Yourself Out." *Kiss the Game Goodbye*. Ruff Ryders, 2001.

Kanye West. "Family Business." *The College Dropout*. Roc-A-Fella, 2004.

Kendrick Lamar. "The Art of Peer Pressure." *good kid, m.A.A.d city*. Aftermath, 2013.

Lil Wayne. "Banned From TV." *No Ceilings*. Cash Money, 2009.

Migos. "Struggle." *Rich Ni**a Timeline*. Quality Control, 2014.

Nas. "Queens Get the Money." *Nas*. Def Jam, 2008.

Nelly. "Grillz." *Sweatsuit*. Universal, 2005.

Obie Trice (feat. Eminem). "Hands on You." *Cheers*. Shady, 2003.

Quavo (feat. Lil Uzi Vert and Shad Da God). "200,000." *ATL*. 916% Ent., 2017.

Royce da 5'9". "Black Savage." *The Allegory*. Heaven Studios, 2020.

RZA. "We Pop." *Birth of a Prince*. BMG, 2003.

Sheek Louch (feat. Method Man and Redman). "2 Tears in a Bucket." *Ryde or Die*, Vol. II. Ruff Ryders, 2000.

Showbiz & A.G. "Diggin in the Crates." *Soul Clap* EP. Payday, 1992.

Joe Frazier: Eleven songs

Above the Law. "Clinic 2000." *Time Will Reveal*. Tommy Boy, 1996.

Big L (feat. Big Daddy Kane). "Platinum Plus." *The Big Picture*. Rawkus, 2000.

Diplomats. "Bigger Picture." *Diplomatic Immunity*. Koch Records, 2004.

Dogg Pound. "Don't Sweat It." *Cali Iz Active*. Doggystyle, 2006.

Eminem. "Groundhog Day." *The Marshall Mathers LP 2*. Aftermath, 2013.

French Montana (feat. Tyga and Ace Hood). "Thrilla in Manilla." *Mac & Cheese 3*. Evil Empire, 2012.

Gangstar. "FALA." *Hard to Earn*. Chrysalis Records, 1994.

Ice Cube. "Crack Baby." *Raw Footage*. Lench Mob Records, 2008.

Wu-Tang Clan. "Protect Your Neck." *Enter the Wu-Tang 36 Chambers*. Loud, 1993.

Wu-Tang Clan. "7th Chamber." *Enter the Wu-Tang 36 Chambers*. Loud, 1993.

Wu-Tang Clan. "Slow Blues." *Wu-Tang Meets Indie Culture*. Babygrande, 2005.

Arturo Gatti: Three songs

Czarface & Ghostface Killah. "Mongolian Beef." *Czarface Meets Ghostface*. Silver Age, 2019.

Jay Electronica. "Cool, Relax." *Victory*. Dogon Society, 2010.

Vinnie Paz. "M.O.B." *No Sellout*. Ground Original, 2009.

Mitch "Blood" Green: Two songs

Cam'ron (feat. Jim Jones and Juelz Santana). "Come Home with Me." *Come Home with Me*. Roc-A-Fella, 2002.

DJ Muggs (feat. Dr. Dre and B. Real). "Puppet Master." *Muggs Presents . . . The Soul Assassins Ch. I*. Sony, 1997.

Marvin Hagler: Seven songs

Benny the Butcher (feat. Royce da 5'9"). "Who Are You." *Tana Talk 3*. Griselda, 2018.

Canibus. "Wreck Room." *Fait Accompli*. RBC, 2014.

Helta Skeltah. "Perfect Jab." *Magnum Force*. Priority, 1998.

MF Doom (feat. Raekwon). "Yessir." *Born Like This*. Lex Records Ltd, 2009.

Styles P. "Space Ghost." *The Phantom Menace*. D-Block, 2007.

Tech N9ne. "Fresh Out." *Planet*. Strange Music, 2018.

The Alkaholics. "Da Da Da Da." *X.O. Experience*. Loud, 2001.

Naseem Hamed: Two songs

Easy Mo B. "Sunstroke." *Now or Never: Odyssey 2000*. Priority, 2000.

Nas. "You Won't See Me Tonight." *I Am*. Columbia, 1999.

Al Haymon: One song

Wu-Tang Clan (feat. Redman). "People Say." *The Saga Continues*. 36 Chambers, LLC, 2017.

Tommy "The Hitman" Hearns: Four songs

Donald D. "Dope Jam." Single. Rockin' Hard Records, 1987.

Game. "State Yo Name, Gangsta." *Westside Story: Compton Chronicles*. Black Wallstreet, 2004.

Royce da 5'9". "Rock City." *Rock City*. Risa, 2002.

Smoke DZA. "Hollywood Smoke Hogan." *Cuz I Felt Like It*. 916% Ent., 2012

Larry Holmes: Eight songs

Desiiner. "Outlet." Single. Good Music, 2017.

Drake (feat. Bun B and Lil Wayne). "All Night Long." *Thank Me Later*. Young Money, 2010.

Drake (feat. Lil Wayne). "Miss Me." *Thank Me Later*. Young Money, 2010.

Eminem (feat. 50 Cent and Busta Rhymes). "Hail Mary." *DJ Green Lantern: Invasion Part 2—Conspiracy Theory*. Shady Records, 2003.

Inspectah Deck (feat. La the Darkman and Killa Priest). "9th Chamber." *Uncontrolled Substance*. Loud, 1999.

Joe Budden. "Keep On." *The Escape Route*. E1 Music, 2010.

2Pac. "Against All Odds." *The Don Killuminati: The 7 Day Theory*. Death Row, 1996.

Vinnie Paz. "Slum Chemist." *God of the Serengeti*. Enemy Soil, 2012.

Evander Holyfield: Eighteen songs

August Alsina (feat. Rick Ross). "Benediction." *Testimony*. Def Jam, 2014.

Bizzy Bone. "What Are We Seeing." *Thugs Revenge*. B-Dub, 2006.

Cappadonna. "Everything Is Everything." *The Pillage*. Razor Sharp, 1998.

Da Brat. "Funkdafied." *Funkdafied*. So So Def, 1994.

Da Brat. "Mind Blowin." *Funkdafied*. So So Def, 1994.

Dr. Dre (feat. Snoop Dogg). "Nuthin' But a G' Thang." *The Chronic*. Death Row, 1992.

Master P (feat. No Limit Soliders). "Hot Boys and Girls." *MP Da Last Don*. No Limit, 1998.

MC Hammer. "Sleeping on a Master Plan." *The Funky Headhunter*. Giant, 1994.

Outkast. "SpottieOttieDopaliscious." *Aquemini*. Arista, 1998.

Rick Ross (feat. Wale). "Act a Fool." *Act a Fool*. Maybach Music, 2019.

Rick Ross (feat. The Weekend). "In Vein." *Mastermind*. Def Jam, 2014.

Scarface. "Funky Lil Aggin." *The World Is Yours*. Rap-A-Lot, 1993.

69 Boyz. "Get Together." *199 Quad*. Lil Joe Records, 2006.

Snoop Dogg. "The Shiznit." *Doggystyle*. Death Row, 1993.

Vanilla Ice. "Prozac." *Hard to Swallow*. Universal, 1998.

Wale (feat. Travis Scott). "Fish N Grits." *Shine*. Maybach Music, 2017.

Whiz Khalifa. "Holyfield." *Rolling Papers 2*. Atlantic, 2018.

Yung Joc. "Knock It Out." *New Joc City*. Bad Boy, 2006.

Bernard Hopkins: Five songs

Knock-Turn'al. "Str8 West Coastin." *LA Confidential Presents: Knock-Turn'Al*. Elektra, 2002.

Lloyd Banks (feat. Styles P). "Predator." *The Cold Corner 2*. G-Unit, 2011.

Migos. "China Town." *Young Rich N*ggas*. Quality Control, 2013.

Sean Price. "Hush." *Mic Tyson*. Duck Down Music, 2012.

The Clipse (feat. Kanye West). "Kinda Like a Big Deal." *Til the Casket Drops*. Star Trak, 2009.

Jack Johnson: Five songs
Apollo Brown & Ras Kass. "Drink Irish." *Blasphemy.* Mello Music, 2014.
Mos Def. "Ghetto Rock." *Sex, Love, & Money.* Geffen, 2004.
Mos Def. "Zimballabim." *The New Danger.* Geffen, 2004.
Run the Jewels. "Report to Shareholders." *Run the Jewels 3.* Run the Jewels Inc., 2016.
U-God (feat. Ghostface Killah). "Train Tussle." *Dopium.* BabyGrande, 2009.

Roy Jones Jr: Eight songs
D Smoke. "Bullies." *Black Habits.* Woodworks, 2020.
Drake (feat. Lil Wayne). "Ignat Shit." *So Far Gone.* Young Money, 2009.
Inspectah Deck. "That Shit." *The Movement.* Koch Records, 2003.
Ja Rule (feat. Fat Joe and Jadakiss). "New York." *R.U.L.E.* Murder Inc., 2004.
Mystikal. "If You Could." *Let's Get Ready.* Jive, 2000.
Nas. "New World." *Nastradamus.* Columbia, 1999.
Tyga. "Make It Nasty." *Careless World: Rise of the Last King.* Rap-A-Lot, 2010.
V Don (feat. Dark Lo and Benny the Butcher). "Roy Jones." *Timeless.* Serious Soundz, 2018.

Zab Judah: Fifteen songs
Busta Rhymes (feat. Notorious B.I.G.). "I Knock You Out." *Back on My B.S.* Motown, 2011.
G Dep. "Special Delivery." *Child of the Ghetto.* Bad Boy, 2005.
Game (feat. Lil Wayne). "Red Nation." *The R.E.D. Album.* Interscope, 2011.
Jay-Z. "All I Need." *The Blueprint.* Roc-A-Fella, 2001.
Juelz Santana (feat. Diplomats). "Squala." *From Me to You.* Roc-A-Fella, 2003.
Lil Flip (feat. Z-Ro). "Get It Crunk." *Kings of the South.* Rap-A-Lot, 2010.
Lil' Kim (feat. Method Man). "Knock 'Em Out the Box." *La Bella Mafia.* Atlantic, 2003.
Ludacris (feat. Lil Flip). "Screwed Up." *Chicken-N-Beer.* Def Jam, 2003.
N.O.R.E. (feat. Styles P and Raekwon). "Google That." *Crack on Steroids.* BabyGrande, 2012.
Ol' Dirty Bastard (feat. Rhymefest). "Dirty, Dirty." *Osiris.* Sure Shot, 2005.
R.A. the Rugged Man. "Supa." *Street Life: The Best of Underground Hip-Hop.* Zen La, 2015.
Sean Price. "Prisoner." *Imperius Rex.* Ruck Down, 2017.
Talib Kweli. "Rock On." *Right About Now.* BabyGrande, 2005.
Wale. "Staying Power." *Staying Power.* Maybach Music, 2018.
Wu-Tang Clan. "Uzi (Pinky Ring)." *Iron Flag.* Loud, 2001.

Don King: Thirty-seven songs
Beastie Boys. "Remote Control." *Hello Nasty.* Capitol Records, 1998.
Benny the Butcher. "Sly Green." *Burden of Proof.* Grislenda, 2020.
Big Sean. "So Much More." *Finally Famous.* Good Music, 2011.
Black Moon. "One-Two." *War Zone.* Duck Down Music, 1999.
Cam'ron. "Get Em Daddy." *Killa Season.* Asylum Records, 2006.
Cam'ron. "Halftime Show." *Purple Haze: Harlem Diplomats.* Dynasty Records, 2004.

Cappadonna (feat. Raekwon). "Life's a Gamble." *Wu South Welfare*. Wu South, 2010.

Cypress Hill. "Killafornia." *Temples of Boom*. Sony, 1995.

Dialated Peoples. "Soundbombing." *Rawkus Presents: Soundbombing 2*. Rawkus, 1999.

E40. "Tell Me When to Go." *Tell Me When to Go*. Black Market, 2005.

EPMD (feat. Keith Murray and Redman). "That's My Thing '99." *DJ Clue: The Professional*. Roc-A-Fella Records, 1999.

Erick Sermon. "Home" (Intro). *Chilltown, New York*. Def Squad, 2004.

Erick Sermon. "Swing It Over Here." *No Pressure*. Rush, 1993.

50 Cent. "Smile." *Curtis*. Aftermath/Shady/Interscope, 2007.

GZA. "Fame." *Legend of the Liquid Sword*. MCA Records, 2002.

Ice Cube (feat. WC and Jayo Felony). "Life in California." *I Am the West*. Lench Mob Records, 2010.

Jay-Z. "I Know What Girls Like." *In My Lifetime*, Vol. 1. Roc-A-Fella, 1997.

Killer Mike. "American Dream." *Pledge*. SMC Entertainment, 2011.

Lupe Fiasco. "Put 'Em Up." *Food & Liquor II: The Great American Rap Album*. Atlantic, 2012.

Mac Dre (feat. Andre Nickatina). "U Breezy." *A Tale of Two Andres*. Thizz Entertainment, 2008.

Mase. "All I Ever Wanted." *Double UP*. Bad Boy Records, 1999.

Masta Killa (feat. Method Man and Redman). "Therapy." *Therapy*. Nature Sounds, 2017.

Missy Elliot. "Ching-a-Ling." *Step Up 2: The Streets*. Atlantic, 2008.

Missy Elliot. "Go to the Floor." *Under Construction*. Elektra, 2002.

Nicki Minaj. "Chung Swae." *Queen*. Young Money, 2018.

Pete Rock & CL Smooth. "Tell Me." *The Main Ingredient*. Eletkra, 1994.

Pharoahe Monch. "The Hitman." *W.A.R.* Duck Down Music, 2011.

Redman. "Jam 4 U." *Whut? Thee Album*. Def Jam, 1992.

Rick Ross & Birdman (feat. Gudda Gudda). "Justice." *The H: The Lost Album*. Maybach Music, 2013.

Rick Ross. "Heavyweight." *Hood Billionaire*. Maybach Music, 2014.

Rick Ross. "Ice Cold." *God Forgives, I Don't*. Maybach Music, 2012.

Riff Raff. "Only in America." *Peach Panther*. BMG, 2016.

Royce da 5'9". "Anything Everything." *Book of Ryan*. Eone Music, 2018.

The Roots. "Table of Contents." *Things Fall Apart*. MCA Records, 1999.

Theodore Unit (feat. Ghostface Killah). "Gurrilla Hood." *Theodore Unit: 718*. Sure Shot, 2004.

2 Live Crew. "Living in America." *Music from and Inspired by Jerry Springer's Ringmaster Soundtrack*. Lil Joe Records, 1999.

Xzibit (feat. Snoop Dogg). "DNA." *Restless*. Loud, 2000.

Vitali and Wladimir Klitschko: Six songs

Conway the Machine and Big Ghost Ltd. "Bricks to Murals." *No One Mourns the Wicked*. Big Ghost Ltd. Music, 2020.

French Montana (feat. Lil Wayne and Drake). "Pop That." *Rap Force One*. Bad Boy, 2014.

R.A. the Rugged Man. "Lessons." *Die, Rugged Man Die*. Nature Sounds, 2004.

Royce da 5'9". "Tired of Ya'll." *The Bar Exam 4*. 916% Ent., 2017.
Snoop Dogg. "Back Up." Single. SCSD Music, 2015.
Wu-Block (feat. Ghostface Killah and Sheek Louch). "Coming for Your Head." *Wu Block*. E1 Music, 2012.

Oscar De La Hoya: Six songs
AZ (feat. Nas, Foxy Brown, and Cormega). "Affirmative Action II." *Decade*. EMI, 2004.
Chino XL (feat. Big Punisher). "Kings." *Ricanstruction: The Black Rosary*. Viper, 2012.
504 Boyz. "I Can Tell." *Goodfellas*. No Limit, 2000.
French Montana. "Don't Waste My Time." *Coke Boys*. Bad Boy, 2014.
Lil Wayne (feat. Brisco and Busta Rhymes). "La, La." *The Carter III*. Cash Money, 2008.
Meek Mill. "Forever." *Phillystyles*. Hustle Team, 2013.

Jake Lamotta: One song
House of Pain. "X-Files." *Truth Crushes to Earth, Shall Rise Again*. Tommy Boy, 1996.

Mills Lane: Four songs
M.O.P. "G Building." *Warriorz*. Loud, 2001.
Naughty by Nature. "The Shivers." *19 Naughty III*. Arista, 1999.
Wale (feat. Lady Gaga). "Chillin." *Attention Deficit*. Interscope, 2009.
Yukmouth. "Regime Killers." *Thug Lord: The New Testament*. Rap-A-Lot Records, 2001.

"Sugar" Ray Leonard: Nine songs
A Tribe Called Quest. "One Two Shit." *Midnight Marauder*. Jive, 1993.
D12. "Chance to Advance." *The Underground EP*. D12, 1996.
Fat Joe. "Bet Ya Man Can't." *Don Cartagena*. Big Beat, 1998.
Grandmaster Flash and the Furious Five. "The Message." *The Message*. Sugar Hill, 1982.
Ice Cube. "Soul on Ice." *I Am the West*. EMI, 2010.
Method Man & Redman. "4 Minutes to Lockdown." *Blackout 2*. Def Jam, 2000.
Redman (feat. Busta Rhymes). "Da Goodness." *Doc's Da Name 2000*. Def Jam, 1998.
Snoop Dogg. "A Bitch I Knew." *The Blue Carpet Treatment*. Doggystyle, 2006.
Snoop Dogg (feat. Dogg Pound). "Doggy Dogg World." *Doggystyle*. Death Row, 1993.

Lennox Lewis: Two songs
Mac Miller. "Watching Movies with the Sound Off." *Watching Movies with the Sound Off*. Rostrum, 2013.
Vic Mensa. "Crazy." Single. Roc Nation, 2015.

Sonny Liston: Nine songs
Anderson Paak. "The Chase." *Oxnard*. Aftermath, 2018.
Bronze Nazareth (feat. RZA). "Carpet Burns." *School for the Blindman*. Black Day July, 2011.
Chance the Rapper. "I Got You Forever." *The Big Day*. Chance LLC., 2019.

De La Soul. "Long Island Degrees." *Stakes Is High*. Tommy Boy, 1996.
Kool Keith (feat. Sadat X). "Static." *Black Elvis/Lost in Space*. Ruffhouse, 1999.
Lil Wayne. "Swag Surf." *No Ceilings*. Cash Money, 2009.
The Roots. "Don't Feel Right." *Game Theory*. Def Jam, 2006.
Travis Scott (feat. Young Thug). "Pick Up the Phone." *Birds in the Trap*. Epic, 2016.
Wu-Tang Clan. "Triumph." *Wu-Tang Forever*. Loud, 1997.

Joe Louis: One song
Anderson Paak. "Winner's Circle." *Ventura*. Aftermath, 2019.

Ray "Boom Boom" Mancini: One song
La the Darkman. "Shine." *Heist of the Century*. Wu-Tang Productions, 1998.

Rocky Marciano: Four songs
Anderson Paak. "Winner's Circle." *Ventura*. Aftermath, 2019.
Da Lench Mob. "You and Your Heroes." *Guerillas in the Mist*. Street Knowledge, 1992.
Lil Wayne (feat. Birdman). "All About That." *Like Father, Like Son*. Cash Money, 2006.
9th Prince. "100 Degrees." *Grandaddy Flow*. BabyGrande, 2010.

Floyd Mayweather Jr: Thirty-four songs
Conway the Machine & Big Ghost Ltd. "Icon." Big Ghost Ltd., 2020.
Dizzy Wright. "Floyd Money May." *Lost in Reality Mix*. Funk Volume, 2015.
Drake (feat. Jay-Z). "Light Up." *Thank Me Later*. Young Money, 2010.
Eminem (feat. Slaughterhouse). "Em360." *BET Rap City*. Shady Records, 2014.
Eminem. "Rap God." *The Marshall Mathers LP 2*. Aftermath, 2013.
Flee Lord (feat. Westside Gunn). "Ain't Hit Nobody." *Griselda & BSF: Conflicted*. Griselda, 2021.
Future. "Never Gonna Lose." *Purple Reign*. Gold Cartel, 2017.
Game (feat. Kendrick Lamar). "The City." *The R.E.D. Album*. Interscope, 2011.
Ghostface Killah (feat. Action Bronson). "Meteor Hammer." *Wu Tang Legendary Weapons*. E1 Music, 2011.
Hoodie Allen. "Show Me What You're Made Of." *Show Me What You're Made Of*. ADA, 2014.
J. Cole. "I'm On It." *Truly Yours, J. Cole*. Roc Nation, 2017.
J. Cole. "Who Dat?" *Cole World: The Sideline Story*. Roc Nation, 2011.
Jay Rock. "Parental Advisory." Single. Top Dawg, 2014.
Jay Rock and Kendrick Lamar. "Money on Mayweather." Single. Top Dawg, 2010.
Joey Bada$$. "Belly of the Beast." *B4.Da.$$*. Cinematic, 2015.
Lupe Fiasco. "SLR." *Extra Laser*. Atlantic, 2011.
Mac Miller (feat. Kendrick Lamar). "Fight the Feeling." *Macadelic*. Rostrum, 2018.
Mez. "The Allure." *My Everlasting Zeal*. Dreamville, 2012.
Migos. "Aight." *Still On Lock*, Vol. 1. YRN Music, 2018.
Nicki Minaj. "Anaconda." *The Pinkprint*. Young Money, 2014.
Nicki Minaj. "Shanghai." *The Pinkprint*. Young Money, 2014.

Prodigy. "Told Ya'll." *The Bumpy Johnson Album*. Infamous, 2012.

Raekwon. "100 Rounds." *Immobilarity*. Loud, 1999.

Rick Ross. "I.D.F.W.U." (remix). *Straight Out Da Trap*, Vol. 1. Maybach Music, 2016.

Rick Ross. "Mafia Music." *Mafia Music*. Def Jam, 2009.

Rick Ross. "911." *God Forgives, I Don't*. Def Jam, 2012.

Riff Raff (feat. Dolla Bill Gates). "Air Canada." *Jumpin Out the Gym*. Grizz Lee Arts, 2013.

Royce da 5'9". "Psycho." *The Bar Exam 3*. MIC Records, 2010.

Smoke DZA. "Kenny Powers." *Rugby Thompson*. High Times, 2012.

T.I. "Fuck Nigga." Single. Grand Hustle, 2019.

Travis Scott (feat. Migos and Pewee Longway). "Sloppy Toppy." *Travi$ La Flame*. TSLF Ent., 2019.

Wu Tang Clan. "Why, Why, Why." *The Saga Continues*. E1 Music, 2017.

Young Cris (feat. Freeway). "Red Eye." *Gunna Season*. State Property, 2014.

Young Thug (feat. Travis Scott, Gucci Mane, and Gunna). "Floyd Mayweather." *Jeffery*. 300 Entertainment, 2016.

"Sugar" Shane Mosley: Eleven songs

Buddah Monk. "Play the Game." *Zu-Chronicles, Vol. 2: Like Father, Like Son*. Duk-Lo Ent., 2005.

D12. "King Kong." *Return of the Dozen*, Vol. 2. Marcyville, 2011.

Foxy Brown (feat. Spragga Benz). "Oh Yeah." *Broken Silence*. Def Jam, 2001.

Freeway (feat. Lil' Chris, O. Sparks, and Beanie Sigel). "It's Not Right." *State Property*. Roc-A-Fella, 2002.

Kool Keith. "Mane." *Diesel Truckers*. DMAFT Records, 2004.

Lil' Kim (feat. Method Man). "Knock 'Em Out the Box." *La Bella Mafia*. Atlantic, 2003.

Lil Wayne. "Groupie Gang." *Dedication 6: Reloaded*. Young Money, 2018.

Migos. "Bags." *No Label 2*. Quality Control, 2012.

North Star. "Break Bread." *West Coast Killer Beez*. Chambermusik, 2008.

Paul Wall. "I Ain't Hard to Find." *Get Money, Stay True*. Atlantic, 2007.

Snoop Dogg. "Back Up Off Me." *The Last Meal*. Priority, 2000.

John "The Beast" Mugabi: One song

Vinnie Paz. "Monster's Ball." *Season of the Assassin*. Enemy Soil, 2010.

Ken Norton: Two songs

Jay-Z. "S. Carter." *Vol. 3: The Life and Times of S. Carter*. Roc-A-Fella, 1999.

Mac Dre. "Screw-E-Boo-Boo." *The Game Is Thick*. Sumo Records, 2004.

Manny Pacquiao: Twelve songs

A$AP Rocky. "Phoenix." *Long.Live.A$AP*. RCA, 2013.

Ab-Soul (feat. Black Hippy). "Black Lip Bastard." *Control System*. Top Dawg, 2012.

Eminem and Royce da 5'9". "Lighters." *Hell: The Sequel*. Shady Records, 2011.

French Montana (feat. Rick Ross and P. Diddy). "Shot Caller." *Mister 16: Casinon Life*. Bad Boy, 2012.

J. Cole. "Sideline Story." *Cole World: The Sideline Story*. Roc Nation, 2011.

Jay-Z. "Thank You." *The Blueprint 3*. Roc Nation, 2009.

Nicki Minaj (feat. Ciara). "Roman's Revenge." *Pink Friday.* Young Money, 2012.

Rick Ross. "High Definition." *Rich Forever.* Maybach Music, 2012.

Slaughterhouse. "Sound Off." *Slaughterhouse.* Gracie Ent., 2009.

Vic Mensa. "Orange Soda." *Innanetape.* Roc Nation, 2013.

will.i.am (feat. Britney Spears). "Scream & Shout." *#willpower.* Interscope, 2014.

Wu-Tang Clan (feat. Redman). "People Say." *The Saga Continues.* 36 Chambers LLC, 2017.

Willie Pep: One song

Jedi Mind Tricks. "The Sacrilege of Fatal Arms." *Violence Begets Violence.* Enemy Soil, 2001.

Hasim Rahman: Two songs

Cam'ron (feat. Memphis Bleek and Beanie Sigel). "The Roc (Just Fire)." *Come Home with Me.* Roc-A-Fella, 2003.

Royce da 5'9". "Chopping Block." *The Bar Exam 4.* 2019 Records, 2019.

Freddie Roach: Two songs

Eminem. "Asshole." *The Marshall Mathers LP 2.* Aftermath, 2013.

Tony Yayo (feat. Too Short). "Break a Bitch." *Sex, Drugs, & Hip-Hop.* G-Unit, 2012.

"Sugar" Ray Robinson: Four songs

Anderson Paak. "Winner's Circle." *Ventura.* Aftermath, 2019.

Eminem. "Groundhog Day." *The Marshall Mathers LP 2.* Aftermath, 2013.

Usher (feat. Nas and Bibi Bourelly). "Chains." Single. RCA, 2015.

Vinnie Paz (feat. R.A. the Rugged Man). "Nosebleed." *Season of the Assassin.* Enemy Soil, 2010.

Donovan "Razor" Ruddock: One song

R.A. the Rugged Man (feat. M.O.P and Vinnie Paz). "The Slayer's Club." *All My Heroes Are Dead.* Nature Sounds, 2020.

James "Bonecrusher" Smith: One song

Das EFX. "Baknaffek." *Straight Up Sewaside.* Atlantic, 1993.

Leon Spinks: Six songs

Crash Crew. "High Powered Rap." *High Powered Rap.* Old Skool Flava, 1986.

Dogg Pound (feat. Lady of Rage). "Do What I Feel." *Dogg Food.* Death Row, 1995.

Kool Keith (feat. Sadat X). "Static." *Black Elvis/Lost in Space.* Ruffhouse, 1999.

Lupe Fiasco. "Dumb It Down." *The Cool.* Atlantic, 2007.

Scarface. "Who Are They." *Emeritus.* Rap-A-Lot, 2008.

Westside Gunn (feat. Black Thought). "Ishkabibble's." *Who Made the Sunshine.* Griselda, 2020.

Michael Spinks: Three songs

Eminem. "Drop the Bomb on 'Em." *Relapse: Refill.* Aftermath, 2009.

Masta Killa. "All Natural." *Selling My Soul.* Nature Sounds, 2012.

Twista (feat. Ab Soul). "3rd Eye." *Reloaded.* GMG Ent., 2017.

Richard Steele: One song
Wu-Tang Clan. "MGM." *Wu-Tang Forever.* Loud, 1997.

Johnny Tapia: One song
South Mark Mexican. "I Must Be High." *The Soundtrack.* Silent Giant, 2001.

Antonio Tarver: One song
D Smoke. "Bullies." *Black Habits.* Woodworks, 2020.

James Toney: Five songs
Lil Flip. "Black Money." *I Need Mine.* Warner Records, 2007.
Pimp C. "I'm Free." *Pimpalation.* Rap-A-Lot, 2011.
Riff Raff. "ICU." *ICU.* Empire, 2009.
Royce da 5′9″. "I'm a Let You Tell It." *The Bar Exam.* MIC Records, 2017.
Slim Thug (feat. Scarface and M.U.G.). "Chase." *Slab Soldierz Radio 2.* Slab
 Soldiers, 2012.

Felix Trinidad: Three songs
Cormega. "Get Out of My Way." *The Realness.* Legal Hustle Music, 2001.
Jay-Z. "Lyrical Exercise." *The Blueprint.* Roc-A-Fella, 2001.
LL Cool J. "Put Your Hands Up." *Violator: The Album.* Violator, 2001.

Kostya Tszyu: Two songs
Lil' Kim (feat. Method Man). "Knock 'Em Out the Box." *La Bella Mafia.*
 Atlantic, 2003.
R.A. the Rugged Man. "Supa." *Street Life: The Best of Underground Hip-Hop.*
 Zen La, 2015.

Mike Tyson: Seventy-three songs
Asher Roth. "Amperstand." *Pampst and Jazz.* Retrohash, 2016.
AZ. "Back to Myself." *Back to Myself.* EMI, 2015.
Big Sean and Metro Boomin. "Pull Up and Wreck." *Double or Nothing.*
 Republic, 2017.
Bone Brothers. "No Rules." *Bone Brothers.* Koch Records, 2005.
Busta Rhymes. "What It Is Right Now (pt. II)." *Dr. Doolittle: Original
 Soundtrack.* Def Jam, 2001.
Conway The Machine. "They Got Sonny." *LuLu.* ALC/Empire, 2020.
Czarface (feat. Method Man). "Night Crawler." *Every Hero Needs a Villain.*
 Brick Records, 2015.
Eminem. "Just Don't Give a Fuck." *The Slim Shady LP.* Aftermath, 1999.
Eminem. "Shady XV." *Shady XV.* Shady Records, 2014.
Eminem. "You're Never Over." *Recovery.* Aftermath, 2010.
Fetty Wap (feat. Nicki Minaj). "Like a Star." Single. 300 Ent., 2016.
50 Cent. "How to Rob." *In Too Deep: Original Soundtrack.* Sony, 1999.
Future. "Draco." *Future.* Epic, 2017.
Future. "Keep Quiet." *Hndrxx.* Epic, 2017.
Geto Boys. "Scarface." *The Geto Boys.* Rap-A-Lot, 1990.
Ghostface Killah (feat. Bronze Nazareth). "Majestic Accolades." *Ghost Files—
 Bronze Tapes.* X-Ray Records, 2018.
Ice Cube. "Hood Mentality." *Raw Footage.* Lench Mob Records, 2008.
Ill Bill (feat. Vinnie Paz). "A Bullet Never Lies." *The Hour of Reprisal.* Uncle
 Howie Records, 2008.

Jay-Z. "Can I Live." *Reasonable Doubt*. Roc-A-Fella, 1996.

Jay-Z (feat. Justin Timberlake). "Holy Grail." *Magna Carta Holy Grail*. Roc Nation, 2013.

Jay-Z and Kanye West. "Niggas in Paris." *Watch the Throne*. Roc Nation, 2011.

Joe Budden. "Inception." *Mood Muzik 4*. Mood Muzik, 2010.

Joel Ortiz. "Nursery Rhyme." *Free Agent*. E1 Music, 2011.

Juicy J. "Still." *100% Juice*. Lean Ent., 2016.

Kanye West. "My Way Home." *Late Registration*. Roc-A-Fella, 2005.

Kanye West (feat. Big Sean and 2 Chainz). "The One." *Cruel Summer*. Good Music, 2012.

Lil' Kim (feat. Method Man). "Knock 'Em Out the Box." *La Bella Mafia*. Atlantic, 2003.

Lil Pump (feat. Smokepurpp and Rick Ross). "Pinky Ring." *Lil Pump*. Warner Brothers, 2017.

Lil Uzi Vert. "Money Mitch." *The Perfect Luv Tape*. Atlantic, 2016.

Lil Wayne. "I'm That Nigga." *FWA*. Cash Money, 2015.

Lil Wayne. "Oh No." *The Carter II*. Cash Money, 2005.

Lil Wayne. "Sick." *Dedication Reloaded*. Young Money, 2018.

LL Cool J. "I'm Bad." *Bigger and Deffer*. Def Jam, 1987.

LL Cool J. "The Ripper Strikes Back." Single. Def Jam, 1998.

Mac Miller. "Two Matches." *GO:OD AM*. Warner, 2015.

Machine Gun Kelly. "Street Dreams." *Black Flag*. Cavalere Ent., 2016.

Migos. "Get Right Witcha." *Culture*. Quality Control, 2017.

Migos (feat. Nicki Minaj and Cardi B). "Motorsport." *Culture II*. Quality Control, 2018.

Migos. "Say So." *Back to the Bando,* Vol. 2. Quality Control, 2017.

Mystikal. "Here I Go." *The Mind of Mystikal*. Jive, 1995.

Mystikal. "You Would If You Could." *Let's Get Ready*. Jive, 2000.

Nas. "Nas Is Like." *I Am*. Columbia, 1999.

Nas. "New World." *Nastradamus*. Columbia, 1999.

Naughty by Nature. "The Hood Comes First." *19 Naughty III*. Tommy Boy, 1993.

Nelly. "Don't It Feel Good." *Five*. Universal, 2010.

Nicki Minaj. "Barbie Dreams." *Queen*. Young Money, 2018.

Notorious B.I.G. (feat. Jay-Z). "I Love the Dough." *Life After Death*. Bad Boy, 1997.

Ol' Dirty Bastard (feat. The Alkaholics and Xzibit). "Hip-Hop Drunkies." *Wu-Tang vs. Shaolin*. Wu Music, 2011.

P. Diddy (feat. Notorious B.I.G. and Busta Rhymes). "Victory." *No Way Out*. Bad Boy, 1997.

Pitbull. "I Wonder." *M.I.A.M.I.* The Orchard, 2004.

Public Enemy. "Public Enemy No. 1." *Yo! Bum Rush the Show*. Def Jam, 1987.

R.A. the Rugged Man. "All Systems Go." *All My Heroes Are Dead*. Nature Sounds, 2020.

R.A. the Rugged Man. "Midnight Thud." *Die, Rugged Man Die*. Nature Sounds, 2004.

Raekwon. "Guillotine (Swordz)." *Only Built 4 Cuban Linx*. Loud, 1995.

Rick Ross (feat. Drake). "Made Men." *Welcome to 2011*. Maybach Music, 2011.

Rick Ross (feat. John Legend and Lil Wayne). "Maybach Music VI." *Port of Miami 2*. Epic, 2019.

Run the Jewels. "Job Well Done." *Run the Jewels*. Run the Jewels Inc., 2013.

Sean Price. "What's the Deal." *Master P*. Duck Down Music, 2007.

Snoop Dogg (feat. Xzibit and Nate Dogg). "Bitch Please." *No Limit Top Dogg*. No Limit Records, 1999.

Styles P (feat. Sheek Louch). "Creep City." *Phantom and the Ghost*. Phantom Records, 2014.

The L.O.X. "Yonkers Tale." *Money, Power, & Respect*. Bad Boy, 1998.

TRU. "Gangstas Make the World Go Round." *Tru 2 Da Game*. Priority, 2007.

2Pac (feat. Richie Rich). "Lie to Kick It." *R U Still Down?* Interscope, 1997.

2Pac. "It Ain't Easy." *Me Against the World*. Interscope, 1995.

2Pac. "The Lunatic." *2Pacalypse Now*. Interscope, 1991.

2Pac. "The Uppercut." *Loyal to the Game*. Death Row, 2004.

2Pac. "Why You Turn on Me." *Until the End of Time*. Amaru Entertainment, 2001.

Westside Gunn. "Broadway Joes." *Hitler Wears Hermes 7*. Griselda, 2019.

Westside Gunn (feat. Fat Joe). "Kelly's Korner." *Hitler Wears Hermes 7*. Griselda, 2019.

Westside Gunn. "Michael Irvin." *Flygod Is an Awesome God 2*. Griselda, 2020.

Will Smith. "I Think I Can Beat Mike Tyson." *And in This Corner*. Jive/Word UP, 1989.

Wu-Tang Clan. "Bells of War." *Wu-Tang Forever*. Loud, 1997.

XXXtension. "Going Down." Single. Bad Vibes, 2018.

Fernando Vargas: Three songs

AZ (feat. Nas). "The Essence." *Aziatic*. Motown, 2002.

Lil Wayne. "Grew Up a Screw Up." *The Greatest Rapper Alive*. Cash Money, 2007.

OG Kid Frost. "Where My Es'es At?" *Still Up in This Shit!* Koch Records, 2002.

Andre Ward: One song

Rittz (feat. Jelly Roll). "Sound Check." *Put a Crown on It*. CNT Records, 2019.

Micky Ward: One song

Czarface and Ghostface Killah. "Mongolian Beef." *Czarface Meets Ghostface*. Silver Age, 2019.

Pernell "Sweat Pea" Whitaker: Four songs

Eminem (feat. Black Thought and Royce da 5'9"). "Yah Yah Yah." *Music to Be Murdered By*. Aftermath, 2020.

Jedi Mind Tricks. "When the Body Goes Cold." *The Bridge and the Abyss*. Enemy Soil, 2018.

The Clipse (feat. Famlay). "Famlay Freestyle." *Lord Willin*. Arista, 2009.

Wu-Tang Clan. "MGM." *Wu-Tang Forever*. Loud, 1997.

Deontay Wilder: Two songs
Benny the Butcher. "Dirty Harry." *The Plugs I Met*. Black Soprano, 2019.
Conway. "Land O' Lakes." *Everybody is F.O.O.D*. Griselda, 2018.
Paul Williams: One song
Pusha-T. "Can I Live Freestyle." *Fear of God Mixtape*. Good Music, 2011.
Ronald "Winky" Wright: Five songs
Consequence. "Night, Night." *Don't Quit Your Day Job*. Good Music, 2007.
Game. "Scream pn 'Em." *Doctor's Advocate*. Geffen, 2006.
Migos. "Bakers Man." *Young Rich Niggas*. Quality Control, 2013.
Tony Yayo. "We Don't Give a Fuck." *Thoughts of a Predicate Felon*. G-Unit, 2005.
Twista. "Check that Hoe." *The Day After*. Atlantic, 2005.

APPENDIX B: NOTEWORTHY HIP-HOP COLLABORATIONS WITH BOXERS
Adrien Broner (feat. Rick Ross). "40." *Soundcloud*. Adrien Broner, 2014.
Canibus (feat. Mike Tyson). "2nd Round KO." *Can-i-bus*. Universal, 1998.
Freeway (feat. Adrien Broner and Sir Wooda). "Steve Young Jerry Rice." *Black Santa EP*. Babygrande, 2014.
Ludacris (feat. Floyd Mayweather). "Undisputed." *Theatre of the Mind*. Def Jam South, 2009.
Reflection Eternal (feat. Lennox Lewis). "Lennox Lewis Skit." *Train of Thought*. Rawkus, 2002.
Roy Jones Jr. (feat. B.G.). "You Know My Kind." *Body Head Bangerz, Vol. 1*. Body Head, 2004.
Roy Jones Jr. (feat. Bun B and Mike Jones). "24's." *Body Head Bangerz, Vol. 1*. Body Head, 2004.
Roy Jones Jr. (feat. Feind and Petey Pablo). "Keep It Moving." *Body Head Bangerz, Vol. 1*. Body Head, 2004.
Roy Jones Jr. (feat. Juvenile). "Don't Start It." *Body Head Bangerz, Vol. 1*. Body Head, 2004.
Roy Jones Jr. (feat. Lil Boosie and Y.B.). "I Smoke, I Drank." *Body Head Bangerz, Vol. 1*. Body Head, 2004.
Roy Jones Jr. (feat. Lil Flip). "Ballers." *Body Head Bangerz, Vol. 1*. Body Head, 2004.
Roy Jones Jr. (feat. Mystikal). "Get Started." *Round 1*. Body Head, 2002
Roy Jones Jr. (feat. Scarface). "Invincible." *Round 1*. Body Head, 2002.
Roy Jones Jr. (feat. Young Bloodz). "I Smoke, I Drank" (remix). *Body Head Bangerz, Vol. 1*. Body Head, 2004.
Scarface (feat. Roy Jones Jr.). "Stop Playin." *J Prince Presents: The Realest N****s Down South*. Rap-A-Lot, 1999.

APPENDIX C: NOTEWORTHY HIP-HOP SONGS SPECIFICALLY CRAFTED FOR BOXING
Chuck D. "Get Used to Me." *Ali Rap*. ESPN, 2006.
Eminem. "Phenomenal." *Southpaw: Soundtrack*. Shady Records, 2015.
Fugees (feat. A Tribe Called Quest and Busta Rhymes). "Rumble in the Jungle." *When We Were Kings: Original Soundtrack*. Columbia, 1996.
Future. "Last Breath." *Creed: Soundtrack*. MGM, 2015.

Mike WiLL Made-it and Lil Wayne. "Amen (Pre Fight Prayer)." *Creed II: The Album*. Interscope, 2018.

Mike WiLL Made-It and Nas, Rick Ross. "Check." *Creed II: The Album*. Interscope, 2018.

Nas. "Legendary." *Tyson: A James Toback Film*. Sony, 2009.

Public Enemy. "Hit Em, Mike Get Em." *Soundcloud*. ESPN Films, 2001.

R.A. the Rugged Man. "Boxing Freestyle." Online Video. Nature Sounds, 2009.

Three 6 Mafia. "It's a Fight." *Rocky Balboa: The Best of Rocky. Original Motion Picture Soundtrack*. Capitol, 2006.

APPENDIX D: NOTEWORTHY HIP-HOP SONGS BY BOXERS

Adrien Broner. "Bag Talk." *Wanted*. Band Camp, 2017.

Adrien Broner. "Millionaire." *Wanted*. Band Camp, 2017.

Adrien Broner. "On Everything." Single. Band Camp, 2013.

Adrien Broner. "Slammer (Panda Freestyle)." Band Camp, 2016.

Adrien Broner (feat. Cook Laflare). "Something New." *ABC*. Band Camp, 2020.

Roy Jones Jr. (feat. Body Head Bangerz). "Can't Be Touched." Single. Body Head, 2002.

Roy Jones Jr. (feat. Dave Hollister). "That Was Then." *Round 1*. Body Head, 2002.

Roy Jones Jr. "Ya'll Musta Forgot." *Round 1*. Body Head, 2002.

Floyd Mayweather Jr. "Yep." Music Video. Philthy Rich Records, 2007.

Mike Tyson. "If You Show Up." Online Video. Mike Tyson, 2012.

NOTES

1 I am referencing six iconic hip-hop albums that shaped my passion for the culture: Grandmaster Flash and the Furious Five. *The Message*. Sugar Hill Records, 1982; Afrika Bambaataa & the Soul Sonic Force. *Planet Rock*. Tommy Boy Records, 1982; Run-DMC. *Tougher Than Leather*. Profile Records, 1988; Slick Rick. *The Great Adventures of Slick Rick*. Def Jam Records, 1988; Eric B. and Rakim. *Paid in Full*. 4th and B'Way, Island, 1986.

2 Hip-hop scholars describe the culture as consisting of four key elements: graffiti, break-dancing, DJing, and MCing (rapping). These elements were originated in the South Bronx during the 1970s. Most scholars suggest the actual birthplace of hip-hop culture is 1520 Sedgwick Avenue, the project building where pioneering figure, DJ Kool Herc (Clive Campbell) lived as a child. In this section, I am tracing the lineage of hip-hop's evolution. I am highlighting the cities where cornerstone hip-hop movements took place. The term, *Dirty South*, is being employed to describe the key movements that took place in the southern portion of the United States of America. In this section, I am explaining how hip-hop found its way to the Appalachian region.

3 I have listed some of the key Appalachian stereotypes that have been promoted by the culture industries. I bring these stereotypes into the conversation as a way to explain how my identity was impacted by them.

4 Small portions of this introduction are borrowed from my recent biography of Drew Bundini Brown, *Bundini: Don't Believe the Hype* (Hamilcar Publishing, 2020). In my introduction to the book, "Requiem for a Hype Man," I write about Muhammad Ali's vicarious impact on my childhood. My research on the life and times of Bundini Brown, as one might suspect, stirred up so many memories from my childhood. I wanted to share these memories once more in this collection because they so vividly outline my pathway to this research.

5 Roy Jones Jr. and Adrien Broner are not the only boxers who have rapped. Floyd Mayweather tried his hand at rap with the 2007 song "Yep." Mike Tyson did the same in 2017, crafting "If You Show Up" a playful diss song aimed at rapper Soulja Boy, who, at the time, was set to take on Chris Brown in a celebrity boxing match. Even Fernando Vargas and Victor Ortiz have rocked the mic.

6 Rodriguez, Ranaldo. "The 5 Worst Musical Careers by Professional Boxers." *Houston Free Press*. May 4, 2012. https://www.houstonpress.com/music/the-5-worst-musical-careers-by-professional-boxers-6777218

7 Throughout this book, all citations for hip-hop lyrics can be found in Appendix A, Appendix B, and Appendix C. Rather than duplicate the citations, I have separated these entries from the other sources listed in the Works Cited page.

8 "Max Kellerman the Pale White Rapper Back in 1994." YouTube video. https://www.youtube.com/watch?v=9cV2ngGSmQg

9 "Muhammad Ali Daughter 'May May' on Being a Rapper (1992)." YouTube video. Uploaded by Relentless Rick on December 5, 2018.

10 Haylock, Zoe. "Everything We Know About Pop Smoke's Death." *Vulture.* https://www.vulture.com/2020/03/pop-smoke-death-what-to-know.html

11 DJ Vlad. "Zab Judah on Floyd Mayweather, Mike Tyson, Pernell Whitaker, Big Meech." VladTV. YouTube video. March 20, 2020. https://www.youtube.com/watch?v=GNHck9U026o

12 DJ Vlad. "Zab Judah on Floyd Mayweather."

13 "Black Mafia Family Members Sentenced to 30 Years" (press release). US Drug Enforcement Administration. Archived from the original on September 16, 2011. Retrieved February 17, 2020.

14 DJ Vlad. "Zab Judah on Floyd Mayweather."

15 Fries, Jacob. "Judah and Brother Robbed." *New York Times.* July 6, 2001. https://www.nytimes.com/2001/07/06/sports/boxing-notebook-judah-and-brother-robbed.html

16 "Zab Judah Street Fight Miami." YouTube video. March 12, 2020. https://www.youtube.com/watch?v=pd9Pfs8iO3I

17 DJ Vlad. "Zab Judah Tells Crazy Story of 3 Men Trying to Rob Him, Beating 1 Up, Crashing Their Car." VladTV. March 17, 2020. https://www.youtube.com/watch?v=NxAkgJ4Yfp0&t=454s

18 Rafeal, Dan. "Zab Judah Awake in Hospital after Brain Bleed." *ESPN.* June 9, 2019. https://www.espn.com/boxing/story/_/id/26937667/zab-judah-awake-hospital-brain-bleed

19 B-Real. "Zab Judah." *The Smokebox.* March 19, 2020. https://www.youtube.com/watch?v=VQLyBJVflq8

20 "Countdown to Cotto vs. Judah." https://www.youtube.com/watch?v=-uPaOIbrOC4&t=633s

21 "Epic Fight: Oscar De La Hoya vs. Felix Trinidad." YouTube video. March 9, 2018. https://www.youtube.com/watch?v=_bLkW55hYOg

22 Watkins, Greg. "Floyd Mayweather & Zab Judah: Hip-Hop, Boxing, & Beef." *All Hip-Hop.* April 7, 2006. https://allhiphop.com/features/floyd-mayweather-zab-judah-hip-hop-boxing-beef-T8PyWb7Ea02d46Hu7PlWpA

23 Watkins, Greg. "Floyd Mayweather & Zab Judah."

24 Watkins, Greg. "Floyd Mayweather & Zab Judah."

25 Watkins, Greg. "Floyd Mayweather & Zab Judah."

26 Watkins, Greg. "Floyd Mayweather & Zab Judah."

27 "Zab Judah vs. Floyd Mayweather." YouTube video. June 27, 2016. https://www.youtube.com/watch?v=dS3NIo7YT08

28 "Zab Judah vs. Floyd Mayweather."

29 "Zab Judah vs. Floyd Mayweather."

30 Jay-Z. *Decoded.* New York: Spiegel & Grau, 2010, p. 79.

31 (qtd. in) Veran, Cristina. "Breaking It All Down." *The Vibe History of Hip-Hop.* ed. Alan Light. New York: Three Rivers Press, 1999, p. 59.

32 "Eminem: Hotboxin' with Mike Tyson." March 19, 2020. https://www.hotboxinpodcast.com/eminem

33 Banks, Alec. "The Oral History of 'Mama Said Knock You Out.'" *Rock the Bells.* https://www.rockthebells.com/blogs/articles/mama-said-knock-you-out

34 Banks, Alec. "The Oral History."

35 Banks, Alec. "The Oral History."

36 Banks, Alec. "The Oral History."

37 Banks, Alec. "The Oral History."

38 "All Access: Stiverne vs. Wilder." YouTube video. January 5, 2015. https://www
.youtube.com/watch?v=Q-yVrzt0v_Y

39 "All Access: Deontay Wilder—Showtime." YouTube video. June 4, 2015. https://www
.youtube.com/watch?v=EAoSQ7LAhJs&t=323s

40 Forman, Murray. "'Represent': Race, Space, and Place in Rap Music." *That's the Joint:*
The Hip-Hop Studies Reader. Eds. Murray Forman and Mark Anthony Neal. 2nd edition.
New York: Routledge, 2011, p. 247.

41 "Eminem: Hotboxin' with Mike Tyson."

42 "DJ Jazzy Jeff & the Fresh Prince Featuring Mike Tyson and Don King Performing 'I
Think I Can Beat Mike Tyson.'" YouTube video. June 3, 2015. https://www.youtube.com/
watch?v=jam_t-gj7HM

43 "Mike Tyson to Head Record Label." *MTV News.* April 24, 1998. http://www.mtv
.com/news/151712/mike-tyson-to-head-rap-label/

44 "Hotboxin' with Mike Tyson: Record Label." *Hotboxin' with Mike Tyson.* May 31,
2019. https://www.facebook.com/hotboxinpodcast/videos/mike-tyson-record-label/
889991061338598/

45 *Mike Tyson: 2-Disc Knockout Edition.* ESPN Home Entertainment, 2006.

46 Richardson, Pierre. "The Man Behind the Most Intimidating Walk-Out Music of All
Time." *On the A Side.* January 26, 2016. https://ontheaside.com/uncategorized/the-man
-behind-the-most-intimidating-boxing-walk-out-music-of-all-time/

47 Ebert, Roger. "Do The Right Thing: Movie Review." *Roger Ebert.com.* https://www
.rogerebert.com/reviews/great-movie-do-the-right-thing-1989

48 Thomas, Ben Beaumont. "How We Made Public Enemy's Fight the Power." *The*
Guardian. March 7, 2016. https://www.theguardian.com/culture/2016/mar/07/how-we
-made-public-enemy-fight-the-power

49 Thomas, Ben Beaumont. "How We Made Public Enemy's Fight the Power."

50 Thomas, Ben Beaumont. "How We Made Public Enemy's Fight the Power."

51 "Spike Lee Sold Out Mike Tyson to Don King." HBO Sports, 1989. https://www
.youtube.com/watch?v=jx2IGxh8Kt8&t=323s

52 On April 4, 2016, Chuck D was the keynote speaker for the annual hip-hop week
festivities at Siena College. I am the founder and chief organizer of this event. As part
of Chuck D's on-campus duties, the rap icon had dinner with me and my students. As is
often the case when rap legends visit my campus, our conversations often turn to boxing.
These excerpts are from our conversation regarding Mike Tyson and "Welcome to the
Terrordome." I am recalling this conversation to the best of my ability.

53 *One Night in Vegas.* Dir. Reggie Rock Bythewood. ESPN Films, 2011.

54 Smith, Danyel. "Introduction." *Tupac Shakur: By the Editors of Vibe.* New York:
Crown Publishers, Inc, 1997.

55 *Tupac: Resurrection.* Dir. Laura Lazin. MTV Films, 2003.

56 *Tupac: Resurrection.*

57 "Mike Tyson: Power 106 Los Angeles." YouTube video. April 5, 2012. https://www
.youtube.com/watch?v=D5UUePbJROc

58 "2Pac Full Unseen Interview (1992) Speaks on Police Brutality." YouTube video.
January 20, 2018. https://www.youtube.com/watch?v=rRdVJzMhwzg&t=919s

59 "Mike Tyson: Power 106 Los Angeles."

60 Broder, John (September 23, 1992). "Quayle Calls for Pulling Rap Album Tied to Murder Case." *Los Angeles Times*. Retrieved November August 1, 2020.

61 *One Night in Vegas.*

62 "2Pac on *The Arsenio Hall Show* 1994." YouTube video. January 17, 1997. https://www.youtube.com/watch?v=8njCvy5vhW8

63 *One Night in Vegas.*

64 "Mike Tyson: Power 106 Los Angeles."

65 *Tyson*. Dir. James Toback. Sony Pictures, 2009.

66 *Tupac: Resurrection.*

67 Powell, Kevin. "Ready to Live." *Tupac Shakur: By the Editors of Vibe*. New York: Crown Publishers, Inc, 1997, pp. 46–47.

68 Powell, Kevin. "Ready to Live."

69 *Tupac: Resurrection.*

70 Powell, Kevin. "Ready to Live."

71 Powell, Kevin. "Ready to Live."

72 *Tupac: Resurrection.*

73 *Tupac: Resurrection.*

74 *Tupac: Resurrection.*

75 "Mike Tyson: Power 106 Los Angeles."

76 "Tyson: I Was Comfortable in Prison." HLN. June 4, 2013. https://www.youtube.com/watch?v=5w4cZiZpAYw

77 "Dr. Dre—Keep Their Heads Ringin'." YouTube video. September 15, 2013. https://www.youtube.com/watch?v=T82MqeAwAio

78 This song was never officially released but the chorus to the song can clearly be heard when listening to the Showtime Sports broadcast.

79 "Mike Tyson Tells Untold Story of Tupac." YouTube video. June 27, 2020. https://www.youtube.com/watch?v=6KwvyoizRSA

80 "2Pac: Road to Glory." YouTube video. July 17, 2011. https://www.youtube.com/watch?v=J9uSI0MeYNc

81 Once again, Tupac's words of encouragement in his post-fight celebration with Tyson can clearly be heard on the Showtime Sports broadcast. "Mike Tyson and Tupac 1996." YouTube video. October 2, 1995. https://www.youtube.com/watch?v=MLKu_FtCumU

82 "Biggie & Puffy Break Their Silence—'96 Vibe Cover Story, pg. 4." *Vibe*. March 9, 2012. https://www.vibe.com/p/biggie-puffy-break-their-silence-95-vibe-cover-story-pg4

83 "Mike Tyson on His Friendship with Tupac." *ExpediTIously Podcast, with T.I.* April 21, 2020. https://www.youtube.com/watch?v=tCfFEpgXgjo

84 "Tupac Shakur—The Last Interview (1996)." *Vibe*. May 15, 2018. YouTube video. https://www.youtube.com/watch?v=XinRhEPs76c&t=620s

85 "Inside the Mind of Shakur." *Tupac Shakur: By the Editors of Vibe*. New York: Crown Publishers, Inc., p. 97.

86 "Biggie Speaks on 2Pac's Death (1997)." YouTube video. December 2, 2017. https://www.youtube.com/watch?v=uMAmScFw02Q&t=317s

87 *One Night in Vegas.*

88 "2Pac Let's Get It On (Last Song Tupac Recorded)." YouTube video. September 2015. https://www.youtube.com/watch?v=48ZRS9iOUoY

89 "Leon Sat by 2Pac at the Tyson Fight Before He Was Murdered." VladTV. YouTube video. November 5, 2020. https://www.youtube.com/watch?v=zQ0h6vfWZnw

90 "Mike Tyson: Power 106 Los Angeles."

91 Marriott, Rob. "Ready to Die." *Tupac Shakur: By the Editors of Vibe.* New York: Crown Publishers, Inc., p.116.

92 "Mike Tyson on His Friendship with Tupac."

93 "Greg Kading on How He Got Keefe D to Confess Orlando Anderson Shot 2Pac." VladTV. YouTube video. July 6, 2017. https://www.youtube.com/watch?v=E8GUtbYRX4A

94 "Compton Gang Unit's Theory on Orlando Baby Lane Anderson Killing 2Pac." VladTV. YouTube video. June 19, 2017. https://www.youtube.com/watch?v=pecQ9UG6v3U

95 "Compton Gang Unit's Theory."

96 "BG Knocc Out on Close Friendship with Orlando Anderson." VladTV. YouTube video. June 11, 2011. https://www.youtube.com/watch?v=9eC4Sdiy9g8&t=583s

97 *One Night in Vegas.*

98 Orejuela, Fernando. *Rap and Hip Hop Culture.* New York: Oxford University Press, 2015, p. 138.

99 Westhoff, Ben. "Miami Heat: Has the Southern Rap Giant Lost Its Hip-Hop Spark?" *The Guardian.* November 4, 2015. https://www.theguardian.com/music/2015/nov/04/miami-heat-has-the-southern-rap-giant-lost-its-hip-hop-spark

100 Green, Tony. "The Dirty South." *The Vibe History of Hip-Hop.* ed. Alan Light. New York: Three Rivers Press, 1999, p. 267.

101 Green, Tony. "The Dirty South."

102 Green, Tony. "The Dirty South."

103 "Roy Jones Jr.—Beyond the Glory." YouTube video. October 3, 2011. https://www.youtube.com/watch?v=hDjvSn7xNkE&t=1222s

104 "Roy Jones Jr.—Beyond the Glory."

105 "Roy Jones Jr.—Beyond the Glory."

106 "Roy Jones Jr.—Beyond the Glory."

107 "1988 Olympics—Boxing 71 Kg. Final Part 2." YouTube video. June 23, 2012. https://www.youtube.com/watch?v=kTDHleWhxP0

108 "Roy Jones Jr. Reveals His Favorite Rapper of All Time." Fight Hype. YouTube video. April 12, 2016. https://www.youtube.com/watch?v=uKgKpx9hlEM

109 The Associated Press. "With Many Outside Interests, Jones Tries to Keep His Focus." *New York Times.* July 23, 2006. https://www.nytimes.com/2006/07/23/sports/othersports/23royjones.html

110 "Bernard Hopkins vs. Roy Jones Jr." YouTube video. June 2, 2014. https://www.youtube.com/watch?v=uE3t6BBgVpE

111 "Roy Jones Jr. vs. James Toney." YouTube video. April 19, 2003. https://www.youtube.com/watch?v=3vdHJFJeijw

112 "Roy Jones Tells Story about Fighting Mike McCallum to Help Him with Money Troubles." Fight Hub TV. YouTube video. October 28, 2017. https://www.youtube.com/watch?v=fTQwJWxH65k

113 "Roy Jones Jr. vs. Montell Griffin 1." YouTube video. September 26, 2019. https://www.youtube.com/watch?v=W9SfAiRCoWo&t=3575s

114 "Roy Jones Jr. vs. Montell Griffin II." YouTube video. September 29, 2019. https://www.youtube.com/watch?v=iZKR4pLzW7g&t=900s

115 "Roy Jones Jr. vs. Virgil Hill." YouTube video. October 12, 2016. https://www
.youtube.com/watch?v=7uch5bfyUbc

116 Prince, James. *The Art and Science of Respect*. Houston: N-the-Water Publishing,
2018, p. 220

117 Prince, James. *The Art and Science of Respect*, p. 239.

118 Prince, James. *The Art and Science of Respect*, p. 240.

119 "HBO Boxing Archives: Jones—Tarver 1 Preview." YouTube video. February 18,
2009. https://www.youtube.com/watch?v=HvAMPRQ-6nA

120 "Roy Jones Jr. vs. Antonio Tarver." YouTube video. February 7, 2014. https://www
.youtube.com/watch?v=vZaqWz9LbFA&t=12s

121 Prince, James. *The Art and Science of Respect*, p. 240.

122 "Fat Joe: I Begged Roy Jones Not to Knock Me Out After 'Lean Back' Line." VladTV.
YouTube video. September 18, 2018. https://www.youtube.com/watch?v=emHMUcnge_g

123 "Roy Jones Jr. Talks about Confronting Fat Joe." YouTube video. April 2, 2015.
https://www.youtube.com/watch?v=qvaTHk9PgUY&t=2s

124 "2005 01 10 Roy Jones Jr. vs. Antonio Tarver 3." YouTube video. January 31, 2016.
https://www.youtube.com/watch?v=ZTcWVUYetko

125 Hess, Mickey. "The Rap Career." *That's the Joint: The Hip-Hop Studies Reader*. Eds.
Murray Forman and Mark Anthony Neal. New York: Routledge, 2011, p. 634.

126 Prince, James. *The Art and Science of Respect*, p. 220.

127 Prince, James. *The Art and Science of Respect*, p. 224.

128 Prince, James. *The Art and Science of Respect*, p. 227.

129 Rafael, Dan. "Floyd's Toughest Foe a Journeyman?" ESPN. May 1, 2012. https://
www.espn.com/blog/dan-rafael/post/_/id/1076/floyds-toughest-foe-a-journeyman

130 "Mayweather vs. Hatton 24/7, Episode 1." YouTube video. January 22, 2019. https://
www.youtube.com/watch?v=ZMykLiLInFM

131 Smith, Tim. "Stormy Mayweather." *New York Daily News*. April 30, 2007. https://
www.nydailynews.com/sports/more-sports/stormy-mayweather-article-1.207879

132 "Floyd Mayweather Jr.'s Dad Won't Be in Corner of Title Fight."
Mercury News. May 4, 2007. https://www.mercurynews.com/2007/05/04/
floyd-mayweather-jr-s-dad-wont-be-in-corner-of-title-fight/

133 "Mayweather vs. Hatton 24/7, Episode 1."

134 "Floyd Mayweather vs. Gregorio Vargas." YouTube video. December 12, 2017.
https://www.youtube.com/watch?v=wgd-fCF3Ou0

135 Prince, James. *The Art and Science of Respect*, p. 247.

136 Prince, James. *The Art and Science of Respect*, p. 229.

137 "Floyd Mayweather Jr. vs. Diego Corrales." YouTube video. June 27, 2019. https://
www.youtube.com/watch?v=gO1LqJhQ3CM&t=2439s

138 Peter, Josh. "Mayweather Does Crazy Things with Money." *Detroit Free Press*. April
28, 2015. https://www.freep.com/story/sports/2015/04/28/floyd-mayweather-manny
-pacquiao/26511359/

139 "Floyd Mayweather vs. Jose Luis Castillo II." YouTube video. July 1, 2013. https://
www.youtube.com/watch?v=8lgpeXrt26E

140 "Bob Arum—I Paid $600,00 to Settle the Beef Between Floyd Mayweather
and James Prince." YouTube video. January 23, 2016. https://www.youtube.com
/watch?v=g5rYTL6oiP0

141 Prince, James. *The Art and Science of Respect*, p. 246.

142 Caldwell, Brandon. "A Brief History of Houston Rap Executive J. Prince." *Vice*. February 17, 2015. https://www.vice.com/en/article/695wv7/a-brief-history-j-prince-rap-a-lot-drake-birdman-diddy-diss-courtesy-call

143 Smith, Christopher Holmes. "'I Don't Like to Dream About Getting Paid': Representations of Social Mobility and the Emergence of the Hip-Hop Mogul." *That's the Joint: The Hip-Hop Studies Reader*. Eds. Murray Forman and Mark Anthony Neal. New York: Routledge, 2011, p. 672.

144 "James Prince Interview at Power 99." YouTube video. October 1, 2018. https://www.youtube.com/watch?v=yDtLwjVyjQY

145 50 Cent. *From Pieces to Weight*. New York: MTV Books, 2005, p. 165.

146 50 Cent. *From Pieces to Weight*, p. 57.

147 50 Cent. *From Pieces to Weight*, p. 57.

148 Toure. "Is This Rap's Logical Conclusion?" *The Guardian*. March 21, 2003. https://www.theguardian.com/music/2003/mar/28/artsfeatures

149 50 Cent. *From Pieces to Weight*, p. 179.

150 50 Cent. *From Pieces to Weight*, p. 179.

151 50 Cent. *From Pieces to Weight*, p. 189.

152 "Mike Tyson's Epic Post-Fight Rant After First Round TKO of Lou Savarese." YouTube video. November 4, 2010. https://www.youtube.com/watch?v=MMySIkG99g4

153 "50 Cent Talks Beefing & Killing." YouTube video. March 14, 2004. https://www.youtube.com/watch?v=DiI3x-qP8eg

154 "50 Cent Talks to Lil Wayne about Buying Mike Tyson's House." YouTube video. July 8, 2020. https://www.youtube.com/watch?v=kijGEMBrsO8

155 50 Cent Talks to Lil Wayne about Buying Mike Tyson's House."

156 Jackson, Kourtnee. "The Origins of the 50 Cent and Floyd Mayweather Beef." *ShowBiz Cheat Sheet*. June 11, 2020. https://www.cheatsheet.com/entertainment/the-origin-of-50-cent-and-floyd-mayweathers-beef.html/

157 "Floyd Mayweather vs. DeMarcus Corley." YouTube video. September 6, 2019. https://www.youtube.com/watch?v=KPwqssEquj4&t=131s

158 Biographical information for James McNair in this paragraph was cited from the following article: Bagga, Ashley. "P-Reeala's Wiki: Facts to Know about the Philthy Rich Records CEO." *Earn the Necklace*. July 24, 2018. https://www.earnthenecklace.com/p-reala-wiki/

159 "P Reala—Speaks on Running a Record Label [Philthy Rich Records]." CISETV. YouTube video. October 5, 2011. https://www.youtube.com/watch?v=zB-H8YJGtU8

160 "Lou DiBella, Damon Dash Join Forces." *Boxing 24/7*. January 27, 2005. https://www.boxing247.com/weblog/archives/103158

161 Prince, James. *The Art and Science of Respect*, p. 233.

162 "Andre Ward Super-Middleweight Boxer and J. Prince CEO Rap-A-Lot Records." *All Hip-Hop*. YouTube video. May 18, 2009. https://www.youtube.com/watch?v=QaXrvtnIuak

163 Weisman, Aly. "50 Cent Files for Bankruptcy." *Business Insider*. July 13, 2015. https://www.businessinsider.com/50-cent-files-for-bankruptcy-2015-7

164 "De La Hoya/Mayweather 24.7." HBO Sports. YouTube video. June 19, 2020. https://www.youtube.com/watch?v=Ki8p7Svln6c

165 "Mayweather vs. Hatton Full Fight." YouTube video. April 3, 2017. https://www.youtube.com/watch?v=EyIEjWtLRXA

166 Serpeck, Evan. "50 Cent vs. Kanye West." *Rolling Stone*. September 6, 2007. https://www.rollingstone.com/music/music-news/kanye-vs-50-cent-71928/

167 Songalia, Ryan. "Sowing the Seeds." *The Ring*. November 2020, p. 19.

168 Monero, Michael. "A Wild Ride." *The Ring*. November 2020, p. 30.

169 Davies, Garith. "The Superstar." *The Ring*. November 2020, p. 53.

170 "Floyd Mayweather Goes Toe-to-Toe with Brian Kenny on SportsCenter." YouTube video. August 28, 2013. https://www.youtube.com/watch?v=Kxb9AUmSrIA

171 Platon, Adelle. "Rick Ross on 50 Cent: I'm the Biggest L He Ever Took." *Billboard*. January 13, 2016. https://www.billboard.com/articles/columns/hip-hop/6843030/rick-ross-50-cent-rolling-stone

172 Velin, Bob. "All Business: Promoter 50 Cent Passionate about Boxing." *USA Today*. November 12, 2012. https://www.usatoday.com/story/sports/boxing/2012/11/29/50-cent-believes-he-can-bring-young-fans-to-boxing/1736487/

173 "All Access Pt. 1—Mayweather vs. Guerrero." YouTube video. April 26, 2013. https://www.youtube.com/watch?v=AkMOA6rjpu0&t=129s

174 Ball, Valentino. "Floyd Mayweather Jr. Calls Out T.I., 50 Cent, and Nelly." *XXL*. August 21, 2014. https://www.xxlmag.com/floyd-50-cent-responds/

175 McCarson, Kelsey. "Why Nobody Is Winning the Floyd Mayweather–50 Cent Beef." Bleacher Report. August 26, 2014. https://bleacherreport.com/articles/2177037-why-nobody-is-winning-the-floyd-mayweather-50-cent-beef

176 "Floyd Mayweather Struggling to Read a Drop." *The Breakfast Club*. YouTube video. August 22, 2014. https://www.youtube.com/watch?v=we9dMyziICQ

177 BillBoard Staff. "50 Cent's Boxing Promotions Company Files for Bankruptcy." *BillBoard*. May 26, 2015. https://www.billboard.com/articles/news/6576064/50-cents-sms-promotions-bankrupt

178 Smith, Cory. "Floyd Mayweather Involved in Altercation with T.I." Bleacher Report. May 25, 2014. https://bleacherreport.com/articles/2074985-floyd-mayweather-reportedly-involved-in-altercation-with-rapper-ti-in-las-vegas

179 Berry, Peter. "50 Cent and Floyd Mayweather's Instagram Beef Gets Worse." *XXL*. June 22, 2018. https://www.xxlmag.com/50-cent-floyd-mayweather-beef-instagram-snitch/

180 Darville, Jordan. "T.I. Shares Floyd Mayweather Diss." *The Fader*. February 15, 2019. https://www.thefader.com/2019/02/15/ti-floyd-mayweather-diss-fuck-nigga

181 Krause, Rebecca. "When Do We Identify with the Bad Guy?" *Kellogg Insight*. March 2, 2020. https://insight.kellogg.northwestern.edu/article/identify-with-the-villain

182 "All Access: Deontay Wilder—Showtime."

183 Akoypan, Manuk. "Deontay Wilder's Knockout Punches Are as Legendary as His Punches." *Los Angeles Times*. February 20, 2020. https://www.latimes.com/sports/story/2020-02-20/deontay-wilder-legendary-costumes-boxing-skills

184 The Wilder-Fury II play-by-play commentary and post-fight interview excerpts were taken from broadcast replay featured on ESPN+ and Top Rank Boxing.

185 Iole, Kevin. "Deontay Wilder Blames 40-Pound Pre-Fight Costume for Loss." Yahoo! Sports. February 24, 2020. https://www.yahoo.com/now/deontay-wilder-says-40-pound-costume-left-his-legs-dead-in-a-seventhround-tko-loss-to-tyson-fury-215534451.html

186 "Teddy Atlas on Deontay Wilder's New Accusations." *The Fight with Teddy Atlas*. YouTube video. November 5, 2020. https://www.youtube.com/watch?v=aXZh14pnOf8

187 "'Embarrassing!' Stephen A. Smith Blasts Deontay Wilder." YouTube video. February 25, 2020. https://www.youtube.com/watch?v=kldoB0T3FAw

188 Riaz, Adnan. "50 Cent Ignites Deontay Wilder Rivalry Again." SPORTbible. February 25, 2020. https://www.sportbible.com/boxing/news-rivalries-50-cent-ignites -deontay-wilder-rivalry-again-by-brutally-trolling-him-20200225

189 Blake, Cole. "Twitter Reacts to Tyson Fury's Dominant Win Over Deontay Wilder." HotNewHipHop. February 23, 2020. https://www.hotnewhiphop.com/twitter-reacts-to -tyson-furys-dominant-win-over-deontay-wilder-news.104480.html

190 de Paor-Evans, Adam. "Mumble Rap: Cultural Laziness or a True Reflection of Contemporary Times?" The Conversation. September 2, 2017. https://theconversation .com/mumble-rap-cultural-laziness-or-a-true-reflection-of-contemporary-times-85550

191 Quoted in the following source: Bhanot, Ankita. "Mumble Rap: A Genre or a Joke?" *Washington Square News.* September 24, 2018. https://nyunews.com/2018/09/23 /mumble-rap-a-controversial-genre-in-hip-hop/

192 Bhanot, Ankita. "Mumble Rap: A Genre or a Joke?" *Washington Square News.* September 24, 2018. https://nyunews.com/2018/09/23/mumble-rap-a-controversial -genre-in-hip-hop/

193 "Adrien Broner Backyard Boxing—Showtime Boxing." YouTube video. December 5, 2013. https://www.youtube.com/watch?v=mfCGqJ1fN-A

194 "Adrien Broner: Portrait of a Fighter (HBO Boxing)." YouTube video. July 11, 2012. https://www.youtube.com/watch?v=nJ3_fD3zrrQ&t=4s

195 BN Staff. "Long Read: The Man Behind Adrien Broner." *Boxing News.* December 21, 2016. https://www.boxingnewsonline.net/long-read-beyond-adrien-broner-meet-one-of -boxings-best-trainers-mike-stafford/

196 "Adrien Broner: Portrait of a Fighter (HBO Boxing)."

197 Broner's interview was excerpted from the following video: "All Access / Manny Pacquiao vs. Adrien Broner." YouTube video. January 9, 2019. https://www.youtube.com /watch?v=5wuS0m_Jg2Y&t=655s

198 "Adrien Broner Grew Up in 'Treacherous' Cincinnati, Faced 57 Years at 17." VladTV. YouTube video. August 12, 2020. https://www.youtube.com/watch?v=A0mKoYq 5Khw&t=109s

199 "Adrien Broner Reveals Jailhouse Moment." Showtime All Access. YouTube video. January 2, 2019. https://www.youtube.com/watch?v=KxpHbTdLIko

200 Knight, Cameron. "Adrien 'The Problem' Broner Can't Seem to Avoid Problems." *The Cincinnati Enquirer.* April 17, 2017. https://www.cincinnati.com/story /news/2017/04/20/police-boxer-adrien-broner-found-shot-up-suv-arrested-warrant /100685784/

201 "Daniel Ponce de Leon vs. Adrien Broner." YouTube video. May 16, 2012. https://www.youtube.com/watch?v=-Xb_znQoJoY

202 "Adrien Broner vs. Vicente Escobedo Full Fight HD." YouTube video. May 2, 2020. https://www.youtube.com/watch?v=tKSlLyhRqI8

203 "Adrien Broner vs. Perez Post Fight Big Talk." YouTube video. February 25, 2012. https://www.youtube.com/watch?v=qbE1enuimNo

204 "Adrien Broner vs. Antonio DeMarco 2012." YouTube video. July 3, 2015. https://www.youtube.com/watch?v=h-a6XB2OCwc&t=140s

205 "Adrien Broner vs. Paulie Malignaggi Crazy Press Conference." YouTube video. May 4, 2013. https://www.youtube.com/watch?v=lsDFVdQ26tU&t=679s

206 "Full Fight—Paulie Malignaggi vs. Adrien Broner." DAZN Boxing. YouTube video. June 24, 2020. https://www.youtube.com/watch?v=ybcgOtLX9Ac

207 "Adrien Broner on Tension with Floyd Mayweather." VladTV. YouTube video. August 20, 2020. https://www.youtube.com/watch?v=VxhPYsKGuRw

208 "Adrien Broner on Tension with Floyd Mayweather."

209 "All Access: Adrien Broner vs. Marcos Maidana." Showtime Sports. YouTube video. December 7, 2013. https://www.youtube.com/watch?v=Iej1Te5qo0w&t=1207s

210 "Adrien Broner on Getting Knocked Down for the 1st Time by Maidana." VladTV. YouTube video. August 20, 2020. https://www.youtube.com/watch?v=0E_9DK-EFUo&t=216s

211 "Adrien Broner Tells His Life Story (full interview)." VladTV. YouTube video. August 20, 2020. https://www.youtube.com/watch?v=WaWyaJZ-Akk&t=610s

212 Songalia, Ryan. "Fabolous' Adrien Broner Insult the Latest in Long Boxing-Rap Tradition." *The Ring*. January 15, 2014. https://www.ringtv.com/312595-fabolous-adrien-broner-insult-the-latest-in-long-boxing-rap-tradition/

213 "Heated Adrien Broner vs. Shawn Porter—Final Press Conference." Fight Hub TV. YouTube video. June 18, 2015. https://www.youtube.com/watch?v=vkJg008oCOo

214 "Broner vs. Porter Full Fight: June 20, 2015." Premier Boxing Champions. YouTube video. July 1, 2015. https://www.youtube.com/watch?v=RMARLmdFsFg&t=209s

215 "Adrien Broner Tells His Life Story (full interview)."

216 "Adrien Broner on Mayweather Calling Him an Alcoholic, Starting Beef with Floyd." VladTV. YouTube video. May 27, 2016. https://www.youtube.com/watch?v=8ETj-RLGKp8&t=19s

217 "Adrien Broner Calls Out Floyd Mayweather after Victory." YouTube video. April 1, 2016. https://www.youtube.com/watch?v=0r5-r-ldXf8

218 Knight, Cameron. "Adrien 'The Problem' Broner Can't Seem to Avoid Problems."

219 "Adrien Broner 'Slammer (Panda Freestyle)' Floyd Mayweather / TMT Diss." World Star Hip-Hop. YouTube video. May 18, 2016. https://www.youtube.com/watch?v=C_c20ZzqYCw

220 "Adrien Broner vs. Mikey Garcia Post Fight." YouTube video. June 29, 2017. https://www.youtube.com/watch?v=pXXOEpBBFX4

221 "Adrien Broner vs. 6ix9ine Both Trade Words." Fight Hub TV. YouTube video. August 16, 2018. https://www.youtube.com/watch?v=8AwBwdEUclk

222 "Broner Erupts into Tantrum After Fight Ends in Draw with Jessie Vargas." YouTube video. April 22, 2018. https://www.youtube.com/watch?v=oh0bMLmla7w

223 "Pacquiao vs. Broner Post-Fight Interviews." *Showtime Sports*. YouTube video. January 20, 2019. https://www.youtube.com/watch?v=y78DSZhhyM4

224 "Adrien Broner Says He Turned Back into a Street Rapper." We The Culture TV. YouTube video. May 26, 2020. https://www.youtube.com/watch?v=iU02eGPaWho

225 Shaffer, Cory. "Boxer Adrien Broner Thrown in Jail After Judge Holds Him in Contempt of Court." *Cleveland*. November 2, 2020. https://www.cleveland.com/court-justice/2020/11/boxer-adrien-broner-thrown-in-jail-after-judge-holds-him-in-contempt-in-assault-lawsuit-the-jig-is-up-today.html

226 "Mike Tyson and Snoop Dogg Smoke Weed and Talk Business." *Hotboxin' with Mike Tyson*. February 26, 2020. https://www.youtube.com/watch?v=MuqazbZY94M&t=4s

WORKS REFERENCED

Adler, Bill. Personal interview, May 21, 2020.

"Adrien Broner Backyard Boxing—Showtime Boxing." YouTube video. Uploaded by Showtime Sports on December 5, 2013. https://www .youtube.com/watch?v=mfCGqJ1fN-A

"Adrien Broner Continues to Trash Talk to Team Porter at Final Press Conference." YouTube video. Uploaded by Hustle Boss on July 18, 2015. https://www.youtube.com/watch?v=YoY-FeLonh0

"Adrien Broner Erupts into Tantrum After Fight Ends in Draw with Jessie Vargas." YouTube video. Uploaded by Frankie Knuckles on April 22, 2018. https://www.youtube.com/watch?v=oh0bMLmla7w

"Adrien Broner Grew Up in 'Treacherous' Cincinnati, Faced 57 Years at 17." VladTV. YouTube video. August 12, 2020. https://www .youtube.com/watch?v=A0mKoYq5Khw&t=109s

"Adrien Broner: Portrait of a Fighter." YouTube video. Uploaded by HBO Boxing on July 11, 2012. https://www.youtube.com /watch?v=nJ3_fD3zrrQ

"Adrien Broner Reveals Jailhouse Moment." YouTube video. Uploaded by Showtime Sports on January 2, 2019. https://www.youtube.com /watch?v=KxpHbTdLIko

"Adrien Broner Says He Turned Back into a Street Rapper." YouTube video. We The Culture TV. May 26, 2020. https://www.youtube.com /watch?v=iU02eGPaWho

"Adrien Broner 'Slammer (Panda Freestyle)' Floyd Mayweather / TMT Diss." *World Star Hip-Hop*. YouTube video. May 18, 2016. https://www.youtube.com/watch?v=C_c20ZzqYCw

"Adrien Broner vs. Antonio DeMarco 2012." YouTube video. July 3, 2015. Uploaded by Jennifer Taylor on July 3, 2015. https://www .youtube.com/watch?v=h-a6XB2OCwc&t=140s

"Adrien Broner vs. Mikey Garcia Post Fight." YouTube video. Uploaded by Trainer T on June 29, 2017. https://www.youtube.com/watch?v =pXXOEpBBFX4

"Adrien Broner vs. Paulie Malignaggi Crazy Press Conference." YouTube video. Uploaded by Max Boxing on May 4, 2013. https:// www.youtube.com/watch?v=lsDFVdQ26tU&t=679s

"Adrien Broner vs. Perez Post Fight Big Talk." YouTube video. Uploaded by Andre Grant on February 25, 2012. https://www.youtube.com /watch?v=qbE1enuimNo

"Adrien Broner vs. 6ix9ine Both Trade Words Online as 250K Bet Placed on Broner Losing." Fight Hub TV. YouTube video. August 16, 2018. https://www.youtube.com/watch?v=8AwBwdEUclk

"Adrien Broner vs. Vicente Escobedo Full Fight HD." YouTube video. Uploaded by Boxing Modern Classics on May 2, 2020. https://www .youtube.com/watch?v=tKSlLyhRqI8

Akopyan, Manouk. Personal interview, March 17, 2020.

———. "Deontay Wilder's Knockout Punches Are as Legendary as His Punches." *Los Angeles Times*. February 20, 2020. https://www .latimes.com/sports/story/2020-02-20/deontay-wilder-legendary -costumes-boxing-skills

"All Access: Adrien Broner vs. Marcos Maidana." Showtime Sports. YouTube video. Uploaded by Showtime Sports, December 7, 2013. https://www.youtube.com/watch?v=Iej1Te5qo0w&t=1207s

"All Access—Manny Pacquiao vs. Adrien Broner." YouTube video. Uploaded by Fox Sports XM on January 9, 2019. https://www .youtube.com/watch?v=5wuS0m_Jg2Y&t=655s

"All Access Pt. 1—Mayweather vs. Guerrero." YouTube video. Uploaded by Charlie Brown Boxing on April 26, 2013. https://www .youtube.com/watch?v=AkMOA6rjpu0&t=129s

"All Access: Stiverne vs. Wilder." YouTube video. Uploaded by Showtime Sports, January 5, 2015. https://www.youtube.com/watch ?v=Q-yVrzt0v_Y

"Andre Ward Super-Middleweight Boxer and J. Prince CEO Rap-A-Lot Records." *All Hip-Hop*. YouTube video. May 18, 2009. https://www .youtube.com/watch?v=QaXrvtnIuak

Associated Press. "With Many Outside Interests, Jones Tries to Keep His Focus." *New York Times*. July 23, 2006. https://www.nytimes.com /2006/07/23/sports/othersports/23royjones.html

Atlas, Teddy. "Teddy Atlas on Deontay Wilder's New Accusations." *The Fight with Teddy Atlas*. YouTube video. November 5, 2020. https:// www.youtube.com/watch?v=aXZh14pnOf8

Bagga, Ashley. "P-Reeala's Wiki: Facts to Know about the Philthy Rich Records CEO." *Earn the Necklace*. July 24, 2018. https://www .earnthenecklace.com/p-reala-wiki/

Ball, Valentino. "Floyd Mayweather Jr. Calls Out T.I., 50 Cent, and Nelly." *XXL*. August 21, 2014. https://www.xxlmag.com/floyd-50 -cent-responds/

Banks, Alec. "The Oral History of 'Mama Said Knock You Out.'" Rock the Bells. September 2, 2020. https://www.rockthebells.com/blogs /articles/mama-said-knock-you-out-boxing

———. "Some of the Biggest Names in Boxing Reflect on 'Mama Said Knock You Out.'" Rock the Bells. September 2, 2020. https://www .rockthebells.com/blogs/articles/mama-said-knock-you-out-boxing

Ben Folds Five. "Boxing." *Self-titled*. Astralwerks, 1995.

Bentt, Michael. Personal interview, March 15, 2020.

Berger, Phil. "A Boxer's Father Who Won't Let Go." *New York Times*. March 1, 1989. https://www.nytimes.com/1989/03/01/sports/boxing -a-boxer-s-father-who-won-t-let-go.html

"Bernard Hopkins vs. Roy Jones Jr." YouTube video. Uploaded by The Prodigy on June 2, 2014. https://www.youtube.com/watch?v=uE3t6 BBgVpE

Berry, Peter. "50 Cent and Floyd Mayweather's Instagram Beef Gets Worse." *XXL*. June 22, 2018. https://www.xxlmag.com/50-cent -floyd-mayweather-beef-instagram-snitch/

Bhanot, Ankita. "Mumble Rap: A Genre or a Joke?" *Washington Square News*. September 24, 2018. https://nyunews.com/2018/09/23 /mumble-rap-a-controversial-genre-in-hip-hop/

Big Daddy Kane. Personal interview, December 8, 2020.

"Biggie & Puffy Break Their Silence—'96 Vibe Cover Story, pg. 4." *Vibe*. March 9, 2012. https://www.vibe.com/p/biggie-puffy-break -their-silence-95-vibe-cover-story-pg4

"Black Mafia Family Members Sentenced to 30 Years" (press release). *US Drug Enforcement Administration*. Archived from the original on September 16, 2011. https://web.archive.org/web/20110916143544 /http://www.justice.gov/dea/pubs/states/newsrel/2008/detroit091208a .html

Blake, Cole. "Twitter Reacts to Tyson Fury's Dominant Win Over Deontay Wilder." HotNewHipHop. February 23, 2020. https://www.hotnewhiphop.com/twitter-reacts-to-tyson-furys -dominant-win-over-deontay-wilder-news.104480.html

"Bob Arum—I Paid $600,00 to Settle the Beef Between Floyd Mayweather and James Prince." YouTube video. Uploaded by ESPN on January 23, 2016. https://www.youtube.com/watch?v=g5rYTL 6oiP0

B-Real. "Zab Judah." *The Smokebox*. YouTube video. BeRealTV. March 19, 2020. https://www.youtube.com/watch?v=VQLyBJVflq8

Broder, John. "Quayle Calls for Pulling Rap Album Tied to Murder Case." *Los Angeles Times*. September 23, 1992. https://www.latimes .com/archives/la-xpm-1992-09-23-mn-1144-story.html

Bronze Nazareth. Personal interview, May 5, 2020.

Burke, Kareem. Personal interview, April 15, 2021.

Caldwell, Brandon. "A Brief History of Houston Rap Executive J. Prince." *Vice*. February 17, 2015. https://www.vice.com/en/article /695wv7/a-brief-history-j-prince-rap-a-lot-drake-birdman-diddy-diss -courtesy-call

Camacho Jr., Hector. Personal interview, April 11, 2020.

Campbell, Brian. "Mike Tyson vs. Roy Jones Jr. Results, Takeaways: Snoop Dogg Steals the Show." *CBS Boxing*. November 29, 2020. https://www.cbssports.com/boxing/news/mike-tyson-vs-roy-jones -jr-results-takeaways-iron-mike-comes-out-a-winner-as-snoop-dogg -steals-the-show/

Chang, Jeff. *Can't Stop, Won't Stop*. New York: Picard/St. Martin's Press, 2005.

Cintron, Kermit. Personal interview, May 18, 2020.

Corely, Demarcus. Personal interview, March 24, 2020.

Crow, Kelly. "The Patriarch and the Fighting Sons." *New York Times.* June 19, 2000. https://www.nytimes.com/2000/06/19/sports/boxing -the-patriarch-and-the-fighting-sons.html

D Smoke. Personal interview, September 4, 2020.

Darville, Jordan. "T.I. Shares Floyd Mayweather diss." *The Fader.* February 15, 2019. https://www.thefader.com/2019/02/15/ti-floyd -mayweather-diss-fuck-nigga

Davies, Garith. "The Superstar." *The Ring.* November 2020, p. 53.

Deck, Inspectah. Personal interview, March 18, 2020.

de Paor-Evans, Adam. "Mumble Rap: Cultural Laziness or a True Reflection of Contemporary Times?" The Conversation. September 2, 2017. https://theconversation.com/mumble-rap-cultural-laziness -or-a-true-reflection-of-contemporary-times-85550

DiBella, Lou. Personal interview, September 22, 2020.

DJ Vlad. "Adrien Broner on Getting Knocked Down for the 1st Time by Maidana." VladTV. YouTube video. August 20, 2020. https://www .youtube.com/watch?v=0E_9DK-EFUo&t=216s

———. "Adrien Broner on Mayweather Calling Him an Alcoholic, Starting Beef with Floyd." VladTV. YouTube video. May 27, 2016. https://www.youtube.com/watch?v=8ETj-RLGKp8&t=19s

———. "Adrien Broner on Tension with Floyd Mayweather." VladTV. YouTube video. August 20, 2020. https://www.youtube.com/watch ?v=VxhPYsKGuRw

———. "Adrien Broner Tells His Life Story (full interview)." VladTV. YouTube video. August 20, 2020. https://www.youtube.com/watch ?v=WaWyaJZ-Akk&t=610s

———. "Fat Joe: I Begged Roy Jones Not to Knock Me Out After 'Lean Back' Line." VladTV. YouTube video. September 18, 2018. https:// www.youtube.com/watch?v=emHMUcnge_g

———. "Leon Sat by 2Pac at the Tyson Fight Before He Was Murdered." VladTV. YouTube video. November 5, 2020. https:// www.youtube.com/watch?v=zQ0h6vfWZnw

———. "U-God on Mike Tyson Robbing His Mom, Pulling Earrings Out of Her Ears." VladTV. YouTube video. May 16, 2019. https:// www.youtube.com/watch?v=hHCndq3KDCE

———. "Zab Judah on Floyd Mayweather, Mike Tyson, Pernell Whitaker, Big Meech." VladTV. YouTube video. March 20, 2020. https://www.youtube.com/watch?v=GNHck9U026o

———. "Zab Judah Tells Crazy Story of 3 Men Trying to Rob Him, Beating 1 Up, Crashing Their Car." VladTV. YouTube video. March 17, 2020. https://www.youtube.com/watch?v=NxAkgJ4Yfp0& t=454s

Do the Right Thing. Directed by Spike Lee, performances by Spike Lee, Danny Aiello, Ossie Davis, Universal Pictures, 1989.

Dr. Dre. "Let Me Ride." *The Chronic.* Death Row, 1992.

Dropkick Murphys. "The Warrior's Code." *The Warrior's Code.* Hellcat, 2005.

Dylan, Bob. "Hurricane." *Desire.* Columbia Records, 1975.

———. "Who Killed Davey Moore?" *The Bootleg Series, Vol. 6.* Columbia Records, 2004.

Ebert, Roger. "Do The Right Thing: Movie Review." *Roger Ebert.com.* Reposted, May 27, 2001. https://www.rogerebert.com/reviews /great-movie-do-the-right-thing-1989

el-Hakim, Khalid. Personal interview, April 13, 2020.

"'Embarrassing!' Stephen A. Smith Blasts Deontay Wilder." YouTube video. Uploaded by ESPN UK on February 25, 2020. https://www .youtube.com/watch?v=kldoB0T3FAw

Emmanuel C.M. "50 Cent Bets 750K That Floyd Mayweather Jr. Can't Read Very Well." *XXL.* August 21, 2014. https://www.xxlmag.com /50-cent-750k-floyd-mayweather-jr-harry-potter/

50 Cent. *From Pieces to Weight.* New York: MTV Books, 2005.

"50 Cent Gives Details About the Beef Between Him and Mayweather!" YouTube video. Uploaded by Power 106 Los Angeles on November 29, 2012. https://www.youtube.com/watch?v=91Pcx8b9x80

"50 Cent Talks Beefing & Killing." YouTube video. Uploaded by Latifah Watty on March 14, 2004. https://www.youtube.com/watch?v=DiI3x -qP8eg

"50 Cent's Boxing Promotions Company Files for Bankruptcy." *BillBoard.* May 26, 2015. https://www.billboard.com/articles/news /6576064/50-cents-sms-promotions-bankrupt

"50 Cent Talks to Lil Wayne about Buying Mike Tyson's House." YouTube video. Uploaded by Chrome Juice on July 8, 2020. https:// www.youtube.com/watch?v=kijGEMBrsO8

"Floyd Mayweather Goes Toe-to-Toe with Brian Kenny on Sports Center." YouTube video. Uploaded by ESPN on August 28, 2013. https://www.youtube.com/watch?v=Kxb9AUmSrIA

"Floyd Mayweather Jr.'s Dad Won't Be in Corner of Title Fight." *Mercury News*. May 4, 2007. https://www.mercurynews.com/2007 /05/04/floyd-mayweather-jr-s-dad-wont-be-in-corner-of-title-fight/

"Floyd Mayweather's New Rap Song—Yep." YouTube video. Uploaded by moneyfmj on Dec 6, 2007. https://www.youtube.com/watch ?v=qEC12ieb8TI

"Floyd Mayweather Struggling to Read a Drop." *The Breakfast Club*. YouTube video. August 22, 2014. https://www.youtube.com/watch ?v=we9dMyziICQ

Forman, Murray. "Represent': Race, Space, and Place in Rap Music." *That's the Joint: The Hip-Hop Studies Reader*. Eds. Murray Forman and Mark Anthony Neal. 2nd edition. New York: Routledge, 2011, p. 247.

Fries, Jacob. "Judah and Brother Robbed." *New York Times*. July 6, 2001. https://www.nytimes.com/2001/07/06/sports/boxing-notebook -judah-and-brother-robbed.html

Green, Tony. "The Dirty South." *The Vibe History of Hip-Hop*. ed. Alan Light. New York: Three Rivers Press, 1999, p. 267.

Griff, Professor. Personal interview, April 30, 2020.

Griffin, Montell. Personal interview, March 12, 2020.

Gunz, Peter. Personal interview, December 7, 2020.

Hardy, Heather. Personal interview, April 17, 2020.

Hauser, Thomas. "The Evolution of the Ring Walk: Key Moments that Changed Boxing Ring Walks Forever." *Sporting News*. November 14, 2018. https://www.sportingnews.com/us/boxing/news/greatest-boxing -ring-walks-music-evolution/xjbud3xfr2bx18ti7r4g8kzpy

Haylock, Zoe. "Everything We Know About Pop Smoke's Death." *Vulture*. July 9, 2002. https://www.vulture.com/2020/03/pop-smoke -death-what-to-know.html

"HBO Boxing Archives: Jones—Tarver 1 Preview." YouTube video. Uploaded by Chris Metler, February 18, 2009. https://www.youtube .com/watch?v=HvAMPRQ-6nA

Hess, Mickey. "The Rap Career." *That's the Joint: The Hip-Hop Studies Reader*. Eds. Murray Forman and Mark Anthony Neal. New York: Routledge, 2011, p. 634.

Hoffman, Justin. Personal interview, February 28, 2021.

Hopkins, Bernard. Personal interview, April 17, 2020.

Houston, Akil. Personal interview, March 11, 2020.

Iole, Kevin. "Deontay Wilder Blames 40-Pound Pre-Fight Costume for Loss." Yahoo! Sports. February 24, 2020. https://www.yahoo.com /now/deontay-wilder-says-40-pound-costume-left-his-legs-dead-in-a -seventhround-tko-loss-to-tyson-fury-215534451.html

Jackson, Kourtnee. "The Origins of the 50 Cent and Floyd Mayweather Beef." *ShowBiz Cheat Sheet*. June 11, 2020. https://www.cheatsheet .com/entertainment/the-origin-of-50-cent-and-floyd-mayweathers -beef.html/

"James Prince Interview at Power 99." YouTube video. Uploaded by Power 99 Philadelphia on October 1, 2018. https://www.youtube .com/watch?v=yDtLwjVyjQY

Jay-Z. *Decoded*. New York: Spiegel & Grau, 2010, p. 79.

Johnson, Reggie. Personal interview, July 28, 2020.

Judah, Zab. Personal interview, February 19, 2020.

Katz, Mark. *Groove Music: The Art and Culture of the Hip-Hop DJ*. New York: Oxford University Press, 2012, p. 7.

Knight, Cameron. "Adrien 'The Problem' Broner Can't Seem to Avoid Problems." *Cincinnati Enquirer*. April 20, 2017. https://www .cincinnati.com/story/news/2017/04/20/police-boxer-adrien-broner -found-shot-up-suv-arrested-warrant/100685784/

Krause, Rebecca. "When Do We Identify with the Bad Guy?" *Kellogg Insight*. March 2, 2020. https://insight.kellogg.northwestern.edu /article/identify-with-the-villain

Larson, Peter. "How Inglewood's D Smoke Went from Teaching High School to Winning Netflix Hip-Hop Competition." *Los Angeles Daily News*. July 2, 2020. https://www.dailynews.com/2020/07/02 /how-inglewoods-d-smoke-went-from-teaching-school-to-winning-a -netflix-hip-hop-competition/

Lepak, John. Personal interview, February 16, 2020.

LL Cool J, with Karen Hunter. *I Make the Rules*. New York: St. Martin's Paperbacks, 1998.

"Long Read: The Man Behind Adrien Broner." *Boxing News*. December 21, 2016. https://www.boxingnewsonline.net/long-read-beyond -adrien-broner-meet-one-of-boxings-best-trainers-mike-stafford/

"Lou DiBella, Damon Dash Join Forces." *Boxing 24/7.*
January 27, 2005. https://www.boxing247.com/weblog/archives
/103158

Marriot, Rob. "Ready to Die." *Tupac Shakur: By the Editors of Vibe.*
New York: Crown Publishers, Inc, 1997, p. 116.

Martin, Christy. Personal interview, June 12, 2020.

Mathematics. Personal interview, March 13, 2020.

"Mayweather vs. Hatton 24/7, Episode 1." YouTube video. Uploaded by
Benny Szyszka on January 22, 2019. https://www.youtube.com
/watch?v=ZMykLiLInFM

McCarson, Kelsey. "Why Nobody Is Winning the Floyd Mayweather–50
Cent Beef." Bleacher Report. August 26, 2014. https://bleacherreport
.com/articles/2177037-why-nobody-is-winning-the-floyd-mayweather
-50-cent-beef

"Mike Tyson's Epic Post-Fight Rant After First Round TKO
of Lou Savarese." YouTube video. Uploaded by Nathan Noah
on November 4, 2010. https://www.youtube.com/watch?v=
MMySIkG99g4

"Mike Tyson—If You Show UP—Soulja Boy Diss Song." YouTube
video. Uploaded by Mike Tyson on January 12, 2017.
https://www.youtube.com/watch?v=tpLlhh8LL8g

"Mike Tyson Tells Untold Story of Tupac." YouTube. Uploaded by
Tupacalypse Today, June 27, 2020. https://www.youtube.com
/watch?v=6KwvyoizRSA

"Mike Tyson to Head Record Label." *MTV News.* April 24,
1998. http://www.mtv.com/news/151712/mike-tyson-to-head-rap
-label/

Monero, Michael. "A Wild Ride." *The Ring.* November 2020,
p. 30.

Mora, Sergio. "At That Time 'Moment of Truth' by Gangstarr. Overall,
I'm West Coast All the Way, Pac or Quik." January 2, 2020. 8:48
PM. Tweet.

Morrissey. "Boxers." *World of Morrissey.* BMG Rights Management,
1995.

"Muhammad Ali Daughter 'May May' on Being a Rapper (1992)."
YouTube video. Uploaded by Relentless Rick on December 5, 2018.
https://www.youtube.com/watch?v=nafEeS7CWOk

Odiaga, LVR. "50 Cent Shot, Wounded, in New York." *MTV*. May 25, 2000. http://www.mtv.com/news/1428802/50-cent-shot-wounded -in-new-york/

One Night in Vegas. Directed by Reggie Rock Bythewood, performances by Mike Tyson, Tupac Shakur, and Michael Eric Dyson. ESPN Films, 2011.

Orejuela, Fernando. *Rap and Hip Hop Culture*. New York: Oxford University Press, 2015, p. 138.

Oschs, Phil. "Davey Moore." *The Early Years*. Vanguard Records, 2000.

Pabon, Jorge. "Physical Graffiti: The History of Hip-Hop Dance." *Davey D's Hip-Hop Corner*. June 24, 1999. https://www.daveyd .com/historyphysicalgrafittifabel.html

"Pacquiao vs. Broner Post-Fight Interviews." YouTube video. Uploaded by Showtime Sports, January 20, 2019. https://www.youtube.com /watch?v=y78DSZhhyM4

Paz, Vinnie. Personal interview, April 2, 2020.

Peter, Josh. "Floyd Mayweather Does Crazy Things with Money." *Detroit Free Press*. April 28, 2015. https://www.freep.com/story /sports/2015/04/28/floyd-mayweather-manny-pacquiao/26511359/

Pina, Aris. Personal interview, April 20, 2020.

Platon, Adelle. "Rick Ross on 50 Cent: I'm the Biggest L He Ever Took." *Billboard*. January 13, 2016. https://www.billboard.com /articles/columns/hip-hop/6843030/rick-ross-50-cent-rolling-stone

Politi, Steve. "Is Floyd Mayweather a Jersey Guy?" *New Jersey*. May 1, 2015. https://www.nj.com/boxing-news/2015/05/floyd_mayweather _is_a_jersey_g.html

Powell, Kevin. "Ready to Live." *Tupac Shakur: By the Editors of Vibe*. New York: Crown Publishers, Inc, 1997, pp. 46–47.

"P Reala—Speaks on Running a Record Label [Philthy Rich Records]." CISETV. October 5, 2011. https://www.youtube.com /watch?v=zB-H8YJGtU8

Prezzy. "A History of 50 Cent and Mayweather Jr's Love/Hate Relationship." *XXL*. July 30, 2018. https://www.xxlmag.com/50 -cent-floyd-mayweather-jr-beef-timeline/

Prince, James. *The Art and Science of Respect*. Houston: N-the-Water Publishing, 2018.

Public Enemy. "Fight the Power." *Fear of a Black Planet.* Def Jam, 1989.

———. "Public Enemy No. 1." *Yo! Bum Rush the Show.* UMG, 1987.

———. "Welcome to the Terrordome." *Fear of a Black Planet.* Def Jam, 1989.

R.A. the Rugged Man. Personal interview, August 4, 2020.

Rafeal, Dan. "Zab Judah Awake in Hospital after Brain Bleed." *ESPN.* June 9, 2019. https://www.espn.com/boxing/story/_/id/26937667/ zab-judah-awake-hospital-brain-bleed

———. "Floyd's Toughest Foe a Journeyman?" *ESPN.* May 1, 2012. https://www.espn.com/blog/dan-rafael/post/_/id/1076/floyds-toughest -foe-a-journeyman

"Rhythm + Flow—D Smoke." YouTube video. Uploaded by Netflix on February 5, 2020. https://www.youtube.com/watch?v=OBkgrYOy VYA

Riaz, Adnan. "50 Cent Ignites Deontay Wilder Rivalry Again." SPORTbible. February 25, 2020. https://www.sportbible.com /boxing/news-rivalries-50-cent-ignites-deontay-wilder-rivalry-again -by-brutally-trolling-him-20200225

Richardson, Pierre. "The Man Behind the Most Intimidating Walk-Out Music of All Time." *On the A Side.* January 26, 2016. https:// ontheaside.com/uncategorized/the-man-behind-the-most-intimidating -boxing-walk-out-music-of-all-time/

Rodriguez, Ranaldo. "The 5 Worst Musical Careers by Professional Boxers." *Houston Free Press.* May 4, 2012. https://www .houstonpress.com/music/the-5-worst-musical-careers-by-professional -boxers-6777218

Rosenthal, Michael. "10 Songs About Boxers." *The Ring.* October 26, 2020. https://www.ringtv.com/122225-10-songs-about-boxers/

"Roy Jones Jr.—Beyond the Glory." YouTube video. Uploaded by ibhof2, October 3, 2011. https://www.youtube.com/watch?v=hDjv Sn7xNkE&t=1222s

"Roy Jones Jr. Reveals His Favorite Rapper of All Time." Fight Hype. April 12, 2016. https://www.youtube.com/watch?v=uKgKpx9hlEM

"Roy Jones Jr. Talks about Confronting Fat Joe." YouTube video. Uploaded by ESPN, April 2, 2015. https://www.youtube.com /watch?v=qvaTHk9PgUY&t=2s

"Roy Jones Tells Story about Fighting Mike McCallum to Help Him with Money Troubles." Fight Hub TV. October 28, 2017. https://www.youtube.com/watch?v=fTQwJWxH65k

"Roy Jones Jr. vs. James Toney." YouTube video. Uploaded by Boxing Las Vegas on April 19, 2003. https://www.youtube.com/watch?v=3vdHJFJeijw

"Roy Jones Jr. vs. Montell Griffin 1." YouTube video. Uploaded by Jay Skeylow on September 26, 2019. https://www.youtube.com/watch?v=W9SfAiRCoWo&t=3575s

"Roy Jones Jr. vs. Montell Griffin II." YouTube video. Uploaded by Jay Skeylow on September 29, 2019. https://www.youtube.com/watch?v=iZKR4pLzW7g&t=900s

Schaffer, Corey. "Boxer Adrien Broner Thrown in Jail after Judge Holds Him in Contempt in Assault Lawsuit." *Cleveland*. November 2, 2020. https://www.cleveland.com/court-justice/2020/11/boxer-adrien-broner-thrown-in-jail-after-judge-holds-him-in-contempt-in-assault-lawsuit-the-jig-is-up-today.html

Schwarz, Nick. "Floyd Mayweather Has the Final Word on 50 Cent's Reading Challenge." *USA Today*. September 4, 2014. https://ftw.usatoday.com/2014/09/floyd-mayweather-50-cent-reading-challenge-michael-brown

Serrano, Shea. *The Rap Year Book*. New York: Abrams Image, 2015.

Simon & Garfunkel. "The Boxer." *Bridge Over Troubled Water*. Columbia Records, 1970.

Simon, Rachel. "Why Isn't Eminem in Southpaw?" *Bustle*. July 28, 2015. https://www.bustle.com/articles/100329-why-isnt-eminem-in-southpaw-the-rapper-has-a-good-reason-for-staying-out-of-the

Smith, Christopher Holmes. "I Don't Like to Dream About Getting Paid': Representations of Social Mobility and the Emergence of the Hip-Hop Mogul." *That's the Joint: The Hip-Hop Studies Reader*. Eds. Murray Forman and Mark Anthony Neal. New York: Routledge, 2011, p. 672.

Smith, Cory. "Floyd Mayweather Involved in Altercation with T.I." Bleacher Report. May 25, 2014. https://bleacherreport.com/articles/2074985-floyd-mayweather-reportedly-involved-in-altercation-with-rapper-ti-in-las-vegas

Smith, Danyel. "Introduction." *Tupac Shakur: By the Editors of Vibe.* New York: Crown Publishers, Inc, 1997.

Smith, Tim. "Stormy Mayweather." *New York Daily News.* April 30, 2007. https://www.nydailynews.com/sports/more-sports/stormy -mayweather-article-1.207879

Songalia, Ryan. "Fabolous' Adrien Broner Insult the Lasted in Long Boxing-Rap Tradition." *The Ring.* January 15, 2014. https://www .ringtv.com/312595-fabolous-adrien-broner-insult-the-latest-in-long -boxing-rap-tradition/

Springsteen, Bruce. "The Hitter." *Devils & Dust.* Bruce Springsteen, 2005.

Sun Kill Moon. "Duk Koo Kim." *Ghosts of the Great Highway.* Caldo Verde Records, 2003.

Thomas, Ben Beaumont. "How We Made Public Enemy's Fight the Power." *The Guardian.* March 7, 2016. https://www.theguardian .com/culture/2016/mar/07/how-we-made-public-enemy-fight-the -power

The Killers. "Tyson vs. Douglas." *Wonderful Wonderful.* Island Records, 2017.

"3D Launches Debut Album on Roy Jones Jr.'s Label BHE." *CISION PRWeb.* June 22, 2006. https://www.prweb.com/releases/2006/06 /prweb401943.htm

T.I. "Mike Tyson on His Friendship with Tupac." *ExpediTIously Podcast, with T.I.* April 21, 2020. https://www.youtube.com/watch ?v=tCfFEpgXgjo

Toney, James. Personal interview, March 10, 2020.

Toure. "Is This Rap's Logical Conclusion?" *The Guardian.* March 21, 2003. https://www.theguardian.com/music/2003/mar/28 /artsfeatures

"2Pac Full Unseen Interview (1992) Speaks on Police Brutality." YouTube video. Uploaded by Top Flight on January 20, 2018. https://www.youtube.com/watch?v=rRdVJzMhwzg&t=919s

"2Pac on *The Arsenio Hall Show* 1994." YouTube video. Uploaded by Steffen Flindt on January 17, 1997. https://www.youtube.com /watch?v=8njCvy5vhW8

"2Pac: Road to Glory." YouTube video. Uploaded by kmerovich on July 17, 2011. https://www.youtube.com/watch?v=J9uSI0MeYNc

Tupac Resurrection. Directed by Laura Lazin, performances by Tupac Shakur, Suge Knight, and Dr. Dre. MTV Films, 2003.

"Tupac Shakur—The Last Interview (1996)." YouTube video. Uploaded by reelblack on May 15, 2018. https://www.youtube.com/watch?v=XinRhEPs76c&t=620s

Tyson. Directed by James Toback. Performance by Mike Tyson, music by Salaam Remi. Sony Pictures, 2009.

"Tyson: I Was Comfortable in Prison." HLN. June 4, 2013. https://www.youtube.com/watch?v=5w4cZiZpAYw

Tyson, Mike. "Eminem: Hotboxin' with Mike Tyson." *Hot Boxin' with Mike Tyson.* March 19, 2020. https://www.youtube.com/watch?v=vvSySR8RdzY&t=316s

———. "Hotboxin' with Mike Tyson: Record Label." *Hotboxin' with Mike Tyson.* May 31, 2019. https://www.facebook.com/hotboxinpodcast/videos/mike-tyson-record-label/889991061338598/

———. "Mike Tyson and Snoop Dogg Smoke Weed and Talk Business." *Hotboxin' with Mike Tyson.* February 26, 2020. https://www.youtube.com/watch?v=MuqazbZY94M

Tyson: 2-Disc Knockout Edition. Performances by Brian Kenny, Bert Randolph Sugar, and Larry Holmes. ESPN Home Entertainment, 2006.

Velin, Bob. "All Business: Promoter 50 Cent Passionate about Boxing." *USA Today.* November 12, 2012. https://www.usatoday.com/story/sports/boxing/2012/11/29/50-cent-believes-he-can-bring-young-fans-to-boxing/1736487/

Veran, Cristina. "Breaking It All Down." *The Vibe History of Hip-Hop.* ed. Alan Light. New York: Three Rivers Press, 1999, p. 59.

VIBEonline. "Inside the Mind of Shakur." *Tupac Shakur: By the Editors of Vibe.* New York: Crown Publishers, Inc., 2021, p. 97.

Wakelin, Johnny. "(Muhammad Ali) Black Superman." Single. Pye Records, 2002.

Watkins, Greg. "Floyd Mayweather & Zab Judah: Hip-Hop, Boxing, & Beef." *All Hip-Hop.* April 7, 2006. https://allhiphop.com/features/floyd-mayweather-zab-judah-hip-hop-boxing-beef-T8PyWb7Ea02d46Hu7PlWpA

Westhoff, Ben. "Miami Heat: Has the Southern Rap Giant Lost Its Hip-Hop Spark?" *The Guardian*. November 4, 2015. https://www .theguardian.com/music/2015/nov/04/miami-heat-has-the-southern -rap-giant-lost-its-hip-hop-spark

Witherspoon, Tim. Personal interview, March 21, 2020.

Zevon, Warren. "Boom Boom Mancini." *Sentimental Hygiene*. Virgin Records, 1987.

BeatBoxing is set in 10-point Sabon, which was designed by the German-born typographer and designer Jan Tschichold (1902–1974) in the period 1964–1967. It was released jointly by the Linotype, Monotype, and Stempel type foundries in 1967. Copyeditor for this project was Shannon LeMay-Finn. The book was designed by Brad Norr Design, Minneapolis, Minnesota, and typeset by New Best-set Typesetters Ltd.

CPSIA information can be obtained
at www.ICGtesting.com
Printed in the USA
JSHW040845270921
19025JS00002B/2

9 781949 590395